Museum of Anthropology
University of Michigan
Technical Reports
Number 18

RESEARCH REPORTS IN ARCHAEOLOGY
Contribution 13

The Henderson Site Burials:

Glimpses of a Late Prehistoric Population in the Pecos Valley

by

Thomas R. Rocek

John D. Speth

Ann Arbor
1986

Printed in the
United States of America

ISBN 0-915703-08-4

To

Matthew and Karen Henderson

and

Jack and Patricia Patterson

For their efforts to preserve
and bring to light a small but
priceless part of New Mexico's
prehistoric cultural heritage.

ACKNOWLEDGMENTS

First and foremost, we would like to express our deepest appreciation to Matt and Karen Henderson for their permission to excavate the Henderson Site and for their gracious hospitality throughout the course of the project. Their generosity and enthusiasm made our work at the site truly pleasurable.

We would also like to thank the many volunteers who participated in the project at one stage or another. They endured dust, heat, baths up to their elbows in preservatives, and architecture which frequently was less than cooperative. Among the many who participated were Richard Ford, Elsa French, Michelle Hegmon, Andrea Hempel, Lee Horne, Jane Holden Kelley, Dave Killick, Dana Lepofsky, Robert (Bus) Leslie, Bryce Little, Claire McHale, Gretchen Neve, Lisa Oneal, Jeff and Mary Parsons, Christine Peschel, Juan Ramirez, Cathy Rudelich, Priscilla Schuster, Andrea Sinclair, Dave Snow, Gil Stein, Molly Sutphen, Carlos Tabares, Wirt (Chip) Wills, Regge Wiseman, and Lisa Young.

Numerous work-study students over the years helped in the tedious but vital process of washing and labeling the tens of thousands of items recovered in two seasons of field work at the site. These included Julie Fremuth, Debra Holmes, Jennifer Lo, Mindy Martin, Paula Murphy, Laurie Ochsner, Esther Osgood, Dennis Renaud, Allison Stupka, and Tom Suchyta.

We also would like to express our gratitude to Richard I. Ford for his help in the ethnobotanical identifications; to John B. Burch for identifying the freshwater mussels and Artie L. Metcalf for providing us with information on their ecology and Holocene distributional history; to James H. McLean for identifying the marine shells; to Sandy Carlson for determining the species and temporal placement of the brachiopod fossil from Feature 3; to Richard C. Lange for dating the Henderson archaeomagnetic samples and Jeffrey L. Eighmy for recalibrating the results when we discovered we had inadvertently used an obsolete mean local magnetic declination; to David Snow, Carla Sinopoli, Regge Wiseman, Barbara Mills, T. J. Ferguson, and Stephanie Whittlesey for helping to identify and classify the ceramic vessels; to Larry Banks, Michael Jacobs, Michael Collins, Harry Shafer, Robert Leslie, Dee Ann Story, Curtis Tunnell, David Dibble, William Parry, and Bruce Huckell for helping us track down the unusual chert material of the "turkey tail" biface from Feature 36; and to Helga Teiwes for her excellent photographs of bifaces on similar chert in the Arizona State Museum. We also owe many thanks to B. Holly Smith for examining the dental attrition in the skeletal sample, helping in the description and analysis of the wear, and providing helpful suggestions regarding the dental remains. Nathaniel H. Rowe, Jr. very kindly examined and described the dental anomaly on Feature 8, and Sharon L. Brooks provided X rays of the specimen. Stanley M. Garn provided us with helpful references as well as discussion regarding the unusual fused toe phalanges identified on several of the burials. Karen R. Rosenberg not only read through an earlier version of this report and provided numerous helpful suggestions, but also examined the Henderson pelves and provided us with descriptions of parturition scars. Jane Buikstra, Wirt H. Wills, and Milford H. Wolpoff provided assistance above and beyond the call of duty by reading earlier versions of the manuscript and offering many helpful suggestions for improvements. Their efforts are greatly appreciated.

We are very much indebted to Sally Horvath, the Museum's editor, and to David Anderson, for their invaluable help in turning the final manuscript into a publishable document. Similarly, Kay Clahassey's superb drafting, artwork, and photography add immeasurably to the report.

Funding for the project was provided by a grant from the National Science Foundation (BNS-7924768). Supplemental funds were generously provided by the Museum of Anthropology, by the Michigan Memorial-Phoenix Project (No. 616), and by the Horace H. Rackham School of Graduate Studies (No. 387965), all of the University of Michigan. A Rackham predoctoral fellowship also provided support for one of us (T.R.R.) during the preparation of this report.

TABLE OF CONTENTS

ACKNOWLEDGMENTS v

LIST OF TABLES xi

LIST OF FIGURES xv

1. THE HENDERSON SITE 1

Introduction 1

Site Description and Chronology 6

Size and Configuration 7

Grid System 7

Excavation Units 7

Chronology 8

Architecture 14

Non-burial Artifacts 23

Subsistence 33

2. THE HENDERSON SITE BURIALS 41

Introduction 41

Burial Descriptions 41

Methods 41

Feature 1 43

Feature 3 51

Feature 8 66

Feature 9 77

Feature 21 81

Feature 25 89

Feature 29 99

Feature 36 109

Feature 40 128

Feature 41 135

3. DISCUSSION 145

The Henderson Population 145

Mortuary Treatment 145

Skeletal Morphology, Summary, and Comparisons: Crania 148

Skeletal Morphology, Summary, and Comparisons: Postcrania 161

Health and Lifeways 164

Conclusions 166

APPENDIX 1: STAGES OF FUSION OF OSSIFICATION CENTRA 169

APPENDIX 2: DEGREE OF DENTAL ATTRITION 171

APPENDIX 3: DENTAL MEASUREMENTS 175

APPENDIX 4: CRANIO-FACIAL AND MANDIBULAR MEASUREMENTS 179

APPENDIX 5: POSTCRANIAL MEASUREMENTS 183

APPENDIX 6: ESTIMATED STATURE OF HENDERSON POPULATION 187

APPENDIX 7: SELECTED CRANIAL NON-METRIC TRAITS 189

APPENDIX 8: SELECTED DENTAL TRAITS 193

APPENDIX 9: ISOLATED HUMAN SKELETAL ELEMENTS 195

APPENDIX 10: ARTIFACTS FROM FEATURE 3 BURIAL 213

APPENDIX 11: ARTIFACTS FROM FEATURE 8 BURIAL 233

APPENDIX 12: ARTIFACTS FROM FEATURE 25 BURIAL 241

APPENDIX 13: ARTIFACTS FROM FEATURE 29 BURIAL 249

APPENDIX 14: ARTIFACTS FROM FEATURE 36 BURIAL 263

APPENDIX 15: ARTIFACTS FROM FEATURE 40 BURIAL 287

APPENDIX 16: PERISHABLE VEGETAL ARTIFACTS FROM HENDERSON 291

APPENDIX 17: LOT NUMBER SYSTEM 297

REFERENCES CITED 343

LIST OF TABLES

Page

1. Size of Henderson Site 9
2. Location and size of excavation units 10
3. Radiocarbon dates from Henderson Site: Provenience and sample description 15
4. Radiocarbon dates from Henderson Site: Original dates and calibration 18
5. Archaeomagnetic dates from Henderson Site: Provenience and sample description 20
6. Archaeomagnetic dates from Henderson Site: Laboratory data used to compute dates 22
7. Archaeomagnetic dates from Henderson Site: Dates 23
8. Room size and number of floors 24
9. Provenience of burials from Henderson Site 42
10. Selected cranial measurement and index means: Henderson Site and comparisons 151
11. Femoral and humeral measurements from Henderson Site and selected comparative samples 162
12. Fusion of toe elements: Distal and middle phalanges of fifth digit 163
13. Mandibular molar wear stage and wear-plane angle 165

A1. Stages of fusion of ossification centra 170

A2. Degree of dental attrition 172

A3. Dental measurements 176

A4. Cranio-facial and mandibular measurements 180

A5. Postcranial measurements 184

A6. Estimated stature of Henderson population 188

A7. Selected cranial non-metric traits 190

A8.	Selected dental traits	194
A9.	Isolated human skeletal elements	196
A10a.	Pottery bowl found with Feature 3 burial: Metric attributes and description	214
A10b.	Pottery jar found with Feature 3 burial: Metric attributes	215
A10c.	Pottery jar found with Feature 3 burial: Description	216
A10d.	Prayer-stick found with Feature 3 burial	217
A10e.	Disc-shell beads found with Feature 3 burial	218
A10f.	*Olivella* shell beads found with Feature 3 burial	219
A10g.	Disc-shaped bone beads found with Feature 3 burial	221
A10h.	Tubular bone beads found with Feature 3 burial	222
A10i.	Turquoise found with Feature 3 burial	225
A10j.	Minerals and fossil found with Feature 3 burial	228
A10k.	Projectile point found with Feature 3 burial: Metric attributes	231
A10l.	Projectile point found with Feature 3 burial: Description of point and material	232
A11a.	Disc-shell beads found with Feature 8 burial	234
A11b.	*Olivella* shell beads found with Feature 8 burial	235
A11c.	Tubular shell beads found with Feature 8 burial	236
A11d.	*Glycymeris* shell bracelets found with Feature 8 burial	237
A11e.	Turquoise found with Feature 8 burial	239
A12a.	Prayer-stick found with Feature 25 burial	242
A12b.	Disc-shell beads found with Feature 25 burial	243
A12c.	*Olivella* shell beads found with Feature 25 burial	244
A12d.	Turquoise found with Feature 25 burial	247
A12e.	Minerals found with Feature 25 burial	248
A13a.	Mussel shell ornaments found with Feature 29 burial	250
A13b.	Bone artifacts found with Feature 29 burial: Metric attributes	251

A13c. Bone artifacts found with Feature 29 burial: Description and materials . 252

A13d. Minerals found with Feature 29 burial 256

A13e. Projectile point or knife found with Feature 29 burial: Metric attributes 257

A13f. Projectile point or knife found with Feature 29 burial: Description of point and material 258

A13g. Lithics found with Feature 29 burial 259

A14a. Disc-shell beads found with Feature 36 burial 264

A14b. *Olivella* and *Agaronia* shell beads found with Feature 36 burial 265

A14c. Turquoise found with Feature 36 burial 268

A14d. Projectile points and knives found with Feature 36 burial (Cluster 1): Metric attributes 270

A14e. Projectile points and knives found with Feature 36 burial (Cluster 2): Metric attributes 272

A14f. Projectile points and knives found with Feature 36 burial (Cluster 1): Description of points and materials 274

A14g. Projectile points and knives found with Feature 36 burial (Cluster 2): Description of points and materials 281

A15a. Pottery bowl found with Feature 40 burial: Metric attributes and description 288

A15b. Turquoise found with Feature 40 burial 289

A16a. Identification of organic materials found with Henderson burials 292

A16b. Attributes of twined matting found with Henderson burials 295

A17a. Lot number system used at Henderson Site 300

LIST OF FIGURES

	Page
1. Location of Henderson Site (LA-1549) in southeastern New Mexico	1
2. Point where Hondo River breaks into Pecos Valley, showing location of Henderson Site (LA-1549) and Bloom Mound	2
3. Aerial photograph, showing location of Henderson Site and Bloom Mound	3
4. View from Henderson Site looking north-northwest over Hondo Valley ..	4
5. View of Henderson Site from valley floor immediately to south of site ...	5
6. Contour map of Henderson Site (LA-1549), showing major excavation units	8
7. Trench A (East Bar) of Henderson Site, showing excavated rooms, features, and location of radiocarbon samples	11
8. Trench F (Center Bar) of Henderson Site, showing excavated rooms, features, and location of radiocarbon samples	12
9. Excavations in Trench A (East Bar), looking south	26
10. Southern half of Room C-5 (Center Bar), looking west	27
11. Excavations in Trench F (Center Bar), looking west-southwest	28
12. Feature 4 hearth, Room C-2, Center Bar	29
13. Feature 13 hearth, Room E-4, East Bar	30
14. Feature 24 hearth or heating pit, Room E-4, East Bar	31
15. Feature 31 hearth (rock-lined) at top of trash deposit in East Plaza	32
16. Feature 35 hearth or heating pit ("ice cream scoop" shape), Pitroom E-3, East Bar	33
17. Trash deposits at south end of East Plaza (Trench C), looking south	34
18. Fire-cracked rock in trash deposits at south end of East Plaza (Trench C; Grid 508N551E), looking north	35
19. Cross sections of burial pits	44
20. Feature 1 burial	45
21. Plan of Feature 1 burial	46

22. Impression of coarse twined matting found near left humerus of Feature 1 burial 47

23. Impression of coarse twined matting found near left side of Feature 1 skull 48

24. Feature 1 skull (left lateral view) 50

25. Feature 1 skull (frontal view) 51

26. Feature 1, supernumerary tooth, between RP_3 and RP_4 52

27. Feature 3 burial 53

28. Closeup of Feature 3 burial 54

29. Plan of Feature 3 burial 55

30. Lincoln B/R bowl found with Feature 3 burial (top view) 56

31. Design of Lincoln B/R bowl found with Feature 3 burial 57

32. Lincoln B/R bowl found with Feature 3 burial (side view) 57

33. Chupadero B/W jar found with Feature 3 burial (top view) 58

34. Chupadero B/W jar found with Feature 3 burial (side view) 59

35. Design of Chupadero B/W jar found with Feature 3 burial 59

36. Prayer-stick (*Populus*?) found with Feature 3 burial 60

37. Miscellaneous artifacts found with Feature 3 and Feature 29 burials . . . 61

38. *Olivella* and *Agaronia* shell beads found with Feature 3, 8, 25, and 36 burials 62

39. Turquoise found with Feature 3, 8, 25, 36, and 40 burials 63

40. Minerals and fossil found with Feature 3, 25, and 29 burials 64

41. Feature 3 skull (left lateral view) 65

42. Feature 3 skull (frontal view) 66

43. Feature 8 burial 67

44. Plan of Feature 8 burial 68

45. Complete *Glycymeris* shell bracelet (No. 1) found with Feature 8 burial (top view) 70

46. Complete *Glycymeris* shell bracelet (No. 1) found with Feature 8 burial (bottom view) 70

47. Broken *Glycymeris* shell bracelet (No. 2) found with Feature 8 burial (top view) 71

48. Broken *Glycymeris* shell bracelet (No. 2) found with Feature 8 burial (bottom view) 71

49. Complete *Glycymeris* shell bracelet (No. 1) found with Feature 8 burial (profile view of hinge area) 72

50. Broken *Glycymeris* shell bracelet (No. 2) found with Feature 8 burial (profile view of hinge area) 72

51. Tubular shell beads found with Feature 8 burial 73

52. Impression of coiled basketry found on chest (between skull and right knee) of Feature 8 burial 73

53. Fragment of plaited yucca basketry or matting found behind skull of Feature 8 burial 74

54. Feature 8 skull (left lateral view) 75

55. Feature 8 skull (frontal view) 76

56. Feature 8, shallow maxillary incisor sockets, associated with short incisor roots 78

57. Feature 8, pitting on posterior area of parietals 79

58. Fused distal foot phalanges (Features 8, 21, 25, 36, 40) 80

59. Feature 8, sacrum 81

60. Feature 9 burial 82

61. Plan of Feature 9 burial 83

62. Feature 9 skull (left lateral view) 84

63. Feature 9 skull (frontal view) 85

64. Feature 21 burial 86

65. Plan of Feature 21 burial 87

66. Twined grass matting found with Feature 21 burial 88

67. Feature 21 cranium (left lateral view) 89

68. Feature 21 cranium (frontal view) 90

69. Feature 21 mandible (left lateral view) 91

70. Feature 21 mandible (frontal view) 91

71. Feature 25 burial 92

72. Plan of Feature 25 burial 93

73. Closeup of prayer-stick (*Juglans* sp., walnut) found with Feature 25 burial 94

74. Plan of prayer-stick (*Juglans* sp., walnut) found with Feature 25 burial, showing location of associated artifacts 95

75. Feature 25 skull (left lateral view) 98

76. Feature 25 skull (frontal view) 99

77. Feature 25, mandible 100

78. Feature 25 maxillary pathology 101

79. Feature 25, example of possible mild periostitis on medial aspect of distal right tibia 102

80. Feature 29 burial 103

81. Plan of Feature 29 burial 104

82. Closeup of left femur of Feature 29 burial, showing cluster of turtle shell "gaming pieces," lithics, and bone "awls" or "hairpins" 106

83. Plan of artifact clusters found with Feature 29 burial 107

84. Turtle shell "gaming pieces" found with Feature 29 burial 108

85. Flakes and cores found with Feature 29 burial 109

86. Utilized flakes and bifacial tools found with Feature 29 burial 110

87. Bone "awls" or "hairpins" and antelope scapula "knife" found with Feature 29 burial 111

88. Left tibia superior epiphyseal breadth 112

89. Feature 36 burial 113

90. Plan of Feature 36 burial 114

91. Closeup of Point Cluster 1, Feature 36, during excavation 115

92. Closeup of Point Cluster 2, Feature 36, during excavation 116

93. Plan of Point Cluster 1, Feature 36 117

94. Plan of Point Cluster 2, Feature 36 118

95. Projectile points and hafted knives found with Feature 36 burial (Cluster 1, Part 1) 119

96. Projectile points and hafted knives found with Feature 36 burial (Cluster 1, Part 2) 120

97. Projectile points and hafted knives found with Feature 36 burial (Cluster 1, Part 3) 121

98. Projectile points and hafted knives found with Feature 36 burial (Cluster 2, Part 1) 122

99. Projectile points and hafted knives found with Feature 36 burial (Cluster 2, Part 2) 123

100. Banded brown chert bifaces in collections of Arizona State Museum, University of Arizona 124

101. Feature 36 skull (left lateral view) 126

102. Feature 36 skull (frontal view) 127

103. Feature 40 burial 129

104. Plan of Feature 40 burial 130

105. Heshotauthla Polychrome bowl found with Feature 40 burial 131

106. Butterfly (No. 1) on exterior of bowl found with Feature 40 burial 132

107. Butterfly (No. 2) on exterior of bowl found with Feature 40 burial 133

108. Butterfly (No. 3) on exterior of bowl found with Feature 40 burial 133

109. Design of Heshotauthla Polychrome bowl found with Feature 40 burial . . 134

110. Feature 40 skull (left lateral view) 135

111. Feature 40 skull (frontal view) 136

112. Feature 41 burial 137

113. Plan of Feature 41 burial 138

114. Feature 41 skull (left lateral view) 140

115. Feature 41 skull (frontal view) 141

116. Feature 41, fused 6th-7th ribs 143

117. Feature 41, malformed 6th thoracic vertebra 144

118. Mandibular molar wear stage and wear-plane angle of Henderson sample, compared with range of hunter-gatherer and horticulturalist wear-plane regression lines 166

1
THE HENDERSON SITE

Introduction

The Henderson Site (LA-1549) is a small, late prehistoric pueblo near Roswell, in Chaves County, southeastern New Mexico (Fig. 1). The pueblo sits at an elevation of about 1186 m (3890 ft) on the crest of a low northeast-trending limestone ridge at the western margin of the Pecos Valley (Figs. 2, 3).[1] Downtown Roswell is only about 17 km (10.5 mi) northeast of Henderson. To the east of the site, one looks out over the broad, flat alluvial expanses of the Pecos Valley. Barely visible in the distance are the low red bluffs that border the eastern side of the valley.[2]

Fig. 1. Location of Henderson Site (LA-1549) in southeastern New Mexico.

---

[1]The Henderson Site is located approximately at 33°18' N, 104°40' W, in the SW 1/4 of the NW 1/4 of Section 6, T. 12 S., R. 23 E., Hondo Reservoir 7.5 minute quadrangle, topographic series (1949).

[2]The Garnsey Site, a mid-fifteenth century bison kill, is about 32 km (20 mi) due east of Henderson. The kill events at Garnsey took place in a small wash only a few hundred meters east of the bluffs (Speth 1983).

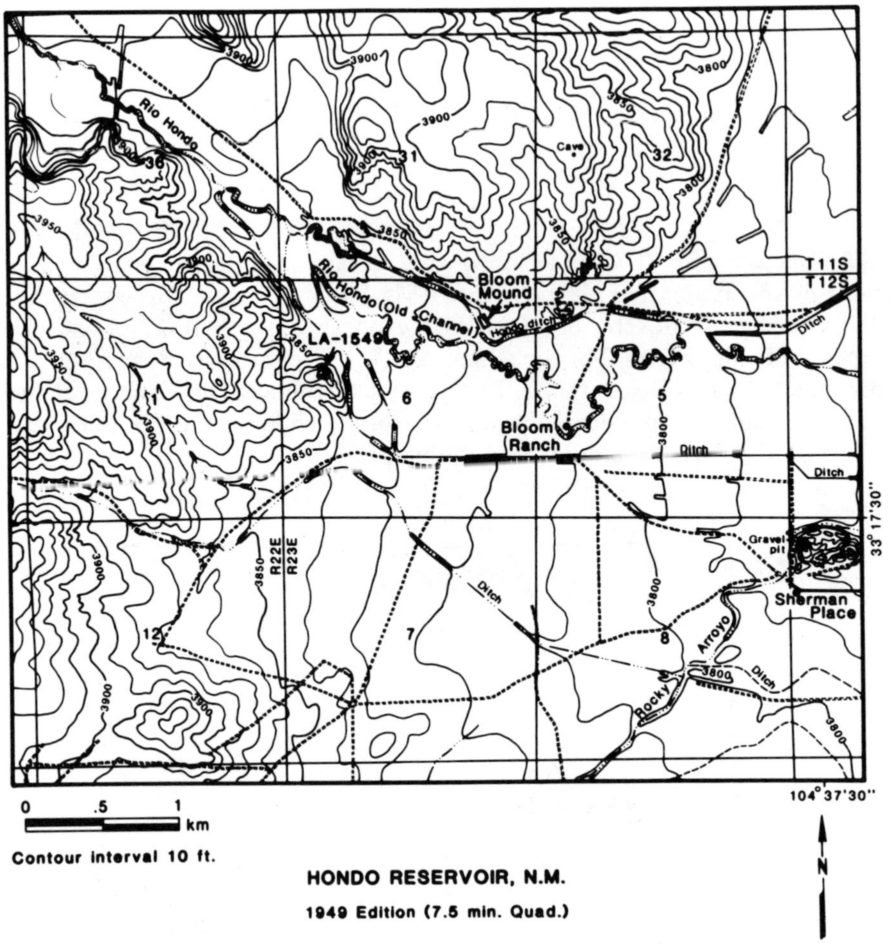

Fig. 2. Point where Hondo River breaks into Pecos Valley, showing location of Henderson Site (LA-1549) and Bloom Mound (adapted from USGS Hondo Reservoir 7.5 Minute Quadrangle, Topographic Series, 1949 Edition).

The Henderson Site also overlooks the Hondo River, one of the largest western tributaries of the Pecos (Fig. 4). The Hondo, which arises in the Sacramento Mountains, cuts its way through a series of limestone ridges as it approaches the Pecos Valley. The Henderson Site sits atop the last or easternmost of these ridges (Fig. 5). The Hondo turns southeast as it cuts through this last ridge, breaking out onto the alluvial flats of the Pecos Valley just north of the site. It then swings northeast through Roswell, turns briefly southeast again for a few kilometers, and empties into the Pecos. Today, as a result of recent lowering of the watertable, and damming and heavy water use upstream, the Hondo is dead, carrying runoff only after severe summer downpours. As recently as the late nineteenth century, however, it was an important, permanent water course (Shinkle 1966:16), and it was undoubtedly important to the prehistoric inhabitants of the Henderson Site.

The thin veneer of soil on the ridge today supports a moderate cover of grama grass (*Bouteloua* sp.), snakeweed (*Gutierrezia sarothrae*), and small scattered shrubs, especially four-wing saltbush (*Atriplex canescens*), mesquite (*Prosopis juliflora*), yucca (*Yucca* spp.), cholla (*Opuntia* spp.), and prickly pear (*Opuntia* spp.). Larger, more dense growths of

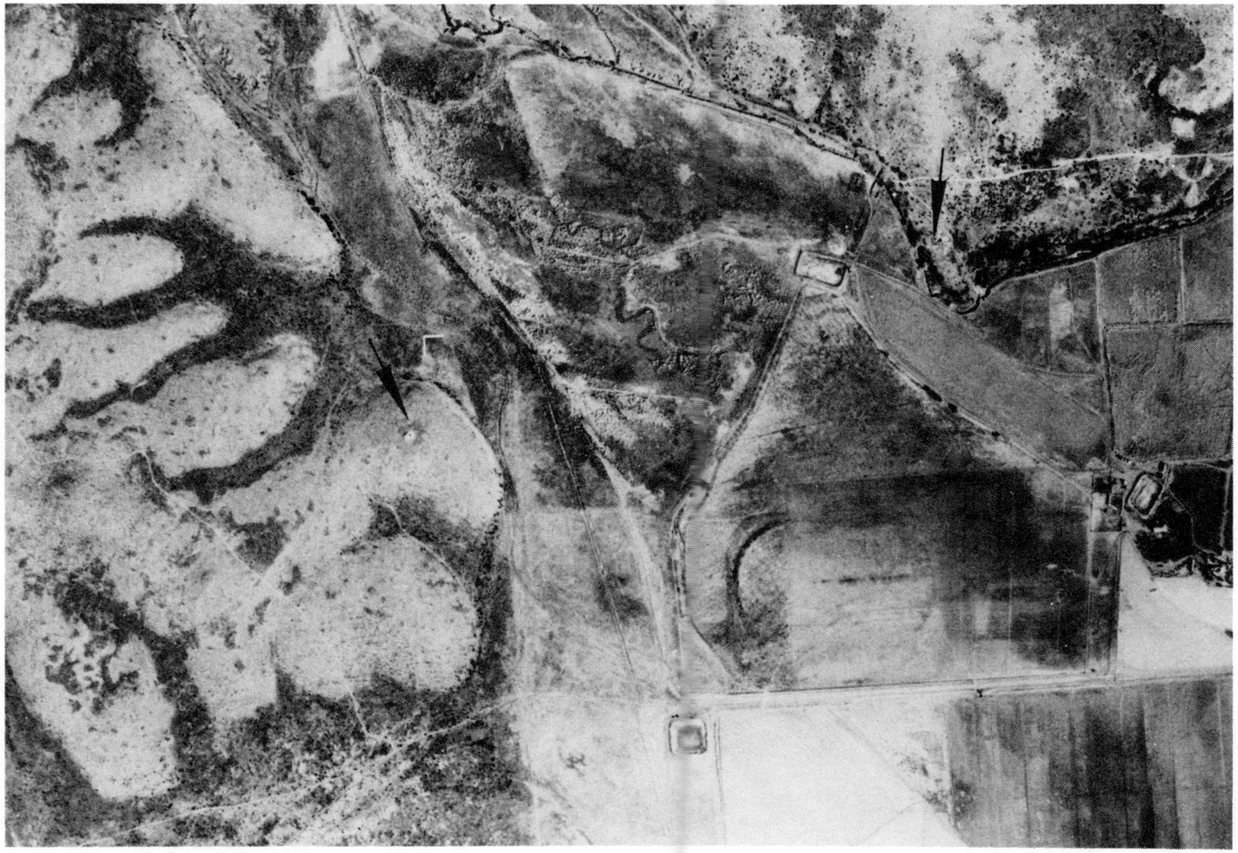

Fig. 3. Aerial photograph, showing location of Henderson Site (left arrow) and Bloom Mound (right arrow). White patch at center of Henderson Site is pothunter's backdirt in Center Bar; East, West, and Main Bars of "E"-shaped site visible as darker zone surrounding Center Bar. Rephotographed from USDA, Agricultural Stabilization and Conservation Service, Photo 35005–177–11L, 1977 (scale ca. 1 in = 0.23 mi).

Fig. 4. View from Henderson Site looking north-northwest over Hondo Valley.

Fig. 5. View of Henderson Site from valley floor immediately to south of site. Center Bar (left arrow); East Bar (right arrow); field vehicle to far left.

cholla occur along the base of the ridge south of the site, and dense stands of sacaton grass grow in swales and along channels on the floor of the Hondo Valley. The only trees visible today from the site are some wild walnuts (*Juglans* sp.), hackberries (*Celtis* sp.), and small cottonwoods (*Populus* sp.) growing in a broken line along the Hondo channel (Fig. 4). There are also a few isolated trees along Rocky Arroyo, a small intermittent tributary of the Hondo to the south of the Henderson Site. Although the area has suffered from overgrazing since the late nineteenth century, the vegetation one sees today is not very different from the treeless, grass-covered landscape noted by the original Government Land Office surveyors in the late 1860s (Government Land Office Survey Plats, Chaves County, New Mexico).

Besides Henderson, there are two other small and more or less contemporary pueblos known in the Roswell area. One of these, Bloom Mound, is located on the opposite side of the Hondo Valley approximately 1.2 km (0.75 mi) east-northeast of Henderson (Figs. 2, 3). This small but important site, which produced at least seven copper bells and a variety of other well-preserved and unusual artifacts, was almost entirely destroyed by local amateurs between the late 1930s and the early 1950s. Most of the materials were lost in a subsequent flood that inundated the Roswell Museum where the artifacts were stored. Fortunately, many of the artifacts were examined and described by Jane Holden Kelley prior to their loss (Kelley 1984). Regrettably, however, the human skeletal materials, which apparently were numerous at Bloom Mound, were lost before they could be examined by a physical anthropologist.

The only other pueblo known in the Roswell area is Rocky Arroyo, a small cluster of rectangular pitroom structures (at least three) located out in the alluvial flats of the Pecos Valley about 6.5 km (4 mi) east of Henderson. This site is on the south side of Rocky Arroyo near its junction with the Hondo. Rocky Arroyo Pueblo has been almost totally destroyed within the last decade by local amateurs using a backhoe. Faunal materials (especially bison, lagomorphs, and at least one macaw), a few artifacts, and a handful of highly fragmentary human skeletal remains (mostly vertebral fragments and phalanges) are all that could be salvaged from the debris on the backdirt spoils of this badly vandalized site. Salvage excavation of fill remaining in one of the vandalized structures was carried out by Regge N. Wiseman of the Museum of New Mexico, yielding an extremely important faunal sample that included hundreds of fish bones (see Wiseman 1985 for a preliminary description of the site, the salvaged pitroom, and the structure's faunal content). When fully analyzed, this material should provide valuable insights into changing subsistence practices and environmental conditions in the Roswell area at approximately the same period of time as the Henderson and Bloom occupations. Given the small size, biased nature, and highly fragmented condition of the Rocky Arroyo human skeletal sample, it has not been included in the present study.

Site Description and Chronology

Two seasons of excavation were conducted at the Henderson Site (1980 and 1981). Analysis of the materials is still far from complete. The present report on the human skeletal materials is the first in a series of reports to be published on the site over the next several years. Only a brief description of the Henderson excavations is presented here. Subsequent reports will deal in greater detail with such topics as methods of excavation, stratigraphy, dating, architecture, artifact descriptions, botanical and zooarchaeological materials, and so forth.

Size and Configuration

The Henderson Site is a single-story "E"-shaped structure, with two small plazas between the bars of the "E" (Fig. 6). The long or "Main" Bar of the "E" is oriented approximately 60° west of true north, with the short bars ("West," "Center," and "East") extending out to the southwest or away from the Hondo. The pueblo, including plazas, covers an area of approximately 2640 m^2. The area occupied by just the room blocks is about 1830 m^2 (see Table 1 for details on the size of the Henderson Site). The area of the structure has been estimated directly from the contour map of the site (Fig. 6). The outer perimeter of the room blocks was arbitrarily assumed to lie at the point where the ground surface first rises noticeably above the surrounding terrain. Since portions of rooms may have collapsed or washed outward, the actual area of the structure is probably somewhat smaller than 1830 m^2. Reducing this figure by 20% produces a more conservative, and perhaps more realistic, estimate of about 1460 m^2. In addition, low piles of small cobbles and gravel (possibly burned) exposed on the surface of the West Bar suggest that this part of the site may in fact consist of one or more roasting features rather than residential structures. There may also be a natural rise in the underlying bedrock in this area of the site. Because the nature of the West Bar remains unclear, excluding it from the area estimate yields an even more conservative value of about 1180 m^2. More precise figures must await large-scale excavations in the future.

Grid System

In our excavations at the Henderson Site, we used a one-meter grid system to record the provenience of artifacts and features. The base datum (Datum A) was placed at a convenient location near the southwest corner of the site. The grid system was then laid out with one axis parallel to the Main Bar of the "E" (approximately N62°W) and the other axis parallel to the shorter arms.

Datum A was arbitrarily assigned a provenience of 500N500E (i.e., 500 m north of, and 500 m east of, an imaginary reference point far to the southwest of the site). This was done to assure that all proveniences would be within the same quadrant, thereby minimizing recording errors that might arise if excavations were going on simultaneously in more than one quadrant. Each one-meter grid unit received its designation from the coordinates of its northeast corner (e.g., Grid Square 500N500E is the one-meter unit immediately southwest of Datum A).

Datum A was also arbitrarily assigned an elevation of 100.00 m. Elevations of artifacts, features, room floors, and the like were shot in with a transit and recorded in meters relative to Datum A. Since Datum A was placed off to the edge of the site, it is somewhat lower than the room blocks; hence, many elevations, except those in the plaza, are above 100.00 m.

Excavation Units

In the two seasons of excavation, we opened up a total of 163 m^2 (73 m^2 in the East Bar, 41 m^2 in the Center Bar, 35 m^2 in the East Plaza, and 14 m^2 in smaller tests at a variety of other locations both on and off the site). Our excavations, therefore, examined approximately 6% of the structure itself and 8% of the East Plaza. We did no work on the West Bar and opened only a single 1-m^2 test unit on the Main Bar (see Table 2 for details on size and location of excavation units; see also Fig. 6).

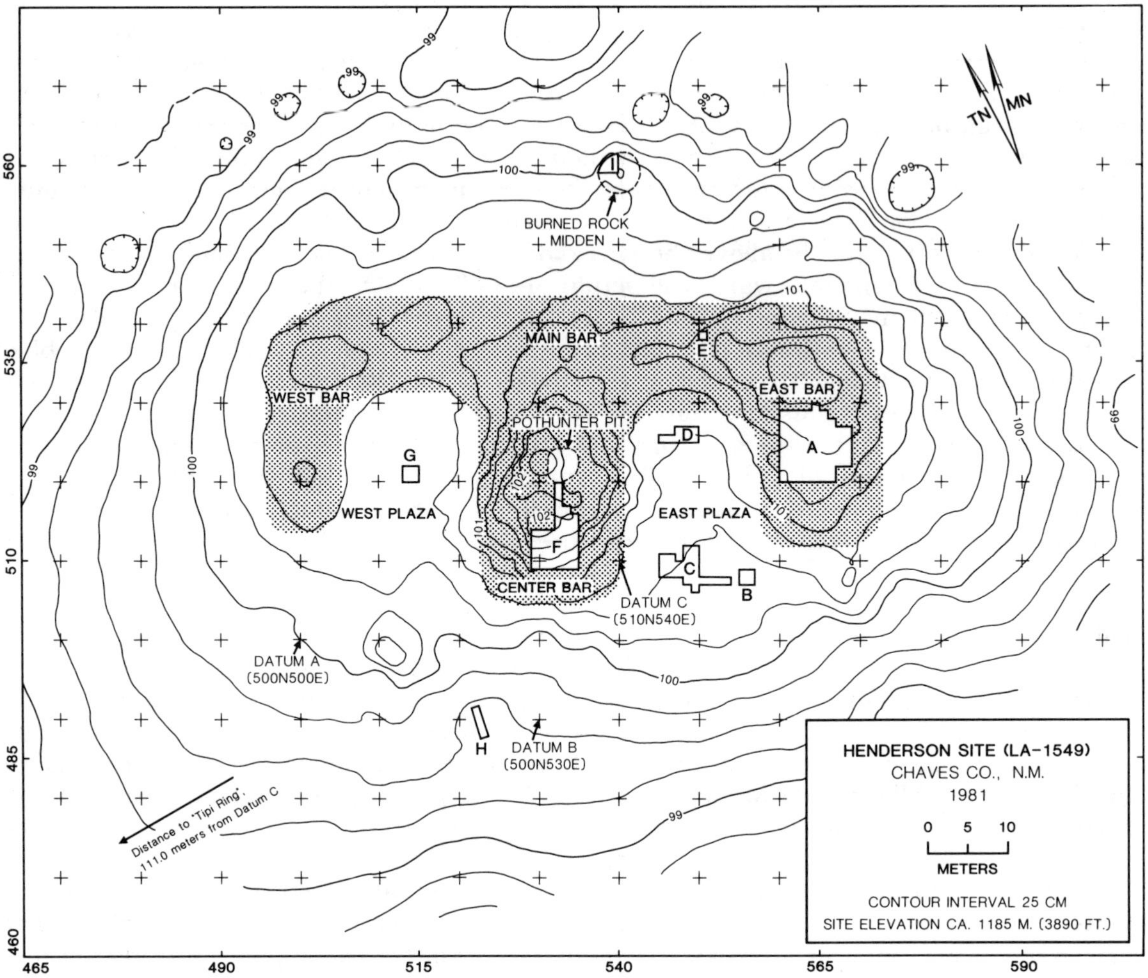

Fig. 6. Contour map of Henderson Site (LA-1549), showing major excavation units (Trenches A-I).

We sampled a total of 11 rooms, including 6 (Rooms C-1 to C-6) in the Center Bar and 5 (Rooms E-1 to E-5) in the East Bar (see Figs. 7, 8 and Table 8 below). All but one of these rooms were above-ground adobe structures. The exception was a nearly square pitroom with rounded corners (Room E-3) in the East Bar which had been partially dug into bedrock (Fig. 9).

Chronology

The dating of the Henderson Site at present is based on its ceramic content, 14 radiocarbon dates, and six archaeomagnetic dates. The ceramics from the site, primarily El Paso Polychrome, Chupadero B/W, and Lincoln B/R, as well as small amounts of Three Rivers R/T, Gila Polychrome, Corona Corrugated, Ramos Polychrome, Heshotauthla

Table 1
Size of Henderson Site (see Fig. 6)

Portion of Site	Area			
	m^2	ft^2	Acres	Hectares
Total Site (Structure and Plaza)	2640	28390	0.65	0.26
Structure Only	1830	19700	0.45	0.18
West Plaza	390	4190	0.10	0.04
East Plaza	420	4500	0.10	0.04
Total Plaza	810	8690	0.20	0.08

Polychrome, Glaze A, and several other non-local types, clearly bracket the occupation between about A.D. 1200/1250 and 1400/1450 (Regge N. Wiseman of the Museum of New Mexico is currently analyzing the site's comparatively large ceramic assemblage).

Archaeomagnetic samples were collected from six hearths and/or heating pits. Ideally, samples should be selected only from features with a high clay content that have been intensely burned, forming a firm, solidly baked substrate. In addition, they should show no evidence of subsequent cracking or slumping. Unfortunately, most of the Henderson features with potential for archaeomagnetic dating had relatively low clay contents and few appear to have been heavily baked. Moreover, the most compact, clayey, and reddened features also tended to contain tiny fissures and cracks. The fissuring and cracking probably stems from shrinkage during firing, and from the fact that most of the features were not deeply buried, exposing them repeatedly to wetting and drying. Multiple samples were collected from each datable feature using 1-in^3 cubes (sampling was done by Wirt H. Wills). The analyses were run in 1982 by Richard C. Lange of the Arizona State Museum through the Paleomagnetism Laboratory in the Department of Geosciences, University of Arizona, Tucson, Arizona. We inadvertently provided the lab with an obsolete mean local magnetic declination of 12.5°, taken directly from a 1949 topographic map. The results, obviously, were unsatisfactory. In 1985, Jeffrey L. Eighmy of the Archaeomagnetic Laboratory at Colorado State University in Fort Collins recalibrated the dates using a more appropriate magnetic declination (11°, 1979–80) and a revised curve for pole positions. These results, summarized in Tables 5–7, are far more satisfactory and agree reasonably well with the ceramic and radiocarbon dates.

The radiocarbon dates, all processed by Beta Analytic in Coral Gables, Florida, were run on wood charcoal and unburned wood samples from hearths, ash lenses, fallen roof members, and upright support beams. All samples, with the exception of Beta-2851, were processed with extra counting time. In preparing samples, care was taken to select fragments of twigs or small branches, or the outer 10–20 rings of larger posts or beams, in order to minimize the spurious effects of dating old wood or the interior of long-lived trees (see discussion in Smiley 1985). In a few cases, such as in the trash deposits in Room C-5 and in the East Plaza, it was necessary to pool samples from arbitrary excavation units.

Table 2
Location and size of excavation units (see Fig. 6)

Trench	Grid Units (Range)	Location	Area (m^2)
A	521–530N561–569E	East Bar	73
B	508–509N556–557E	East Plaza (S. end)	4
C	507–512N546–554E	East Plaza (S. end)	23
D	526–527N546–550E	East Plaza (N. end)	8
E	539N551E	Main Bar	1
F	510–520N530–535E	Center Bar	41
G	521–522N514–515E	West Plaza	4
H	488–492N522–524E	SW. of Center Bar	4
I	560–562N538–540E	Ring Midden	5
A-I	see above	Total Excavated	163
A,E,F	see above	Total in Structure	115
G	see above	Total West Plaza	4
B,C,D	see above	Total East Plaza	35

Clearly, these samples are the least satisfactory. All of the samples, except Beta-2851, were given extended counting time by Beta Analytic to minimize the error factor. While the results presented here provide a reasonable preliminary chronological framework for the site, we are confident that better temporal control for the occupational history of Henderson can be obtained in the future by direct accelerator dating of annuals, especially the numerous corn cobs recovered from the site.

The 14 radiocarbon dates are reported in detail in Tables 3 and 4. We have included the ages calculated using the old Libby half-life (5,570 years), isotopic fractionation values, fractionation-corrected dates using the new half-life (5,730 years), and four different calibration schemes (Ralph et al. 1973 [MASCA]; Damon et al. 1974; Stuiver 1982; Klein et al. 1982). In this way, as dating and calibration procedures are revised and improved, new values can be determined. Similar detailed information is provided in Tables 5–7 for the six archaeomagetic dates, allowing them also to be recalibrated, as necessary, in the future.

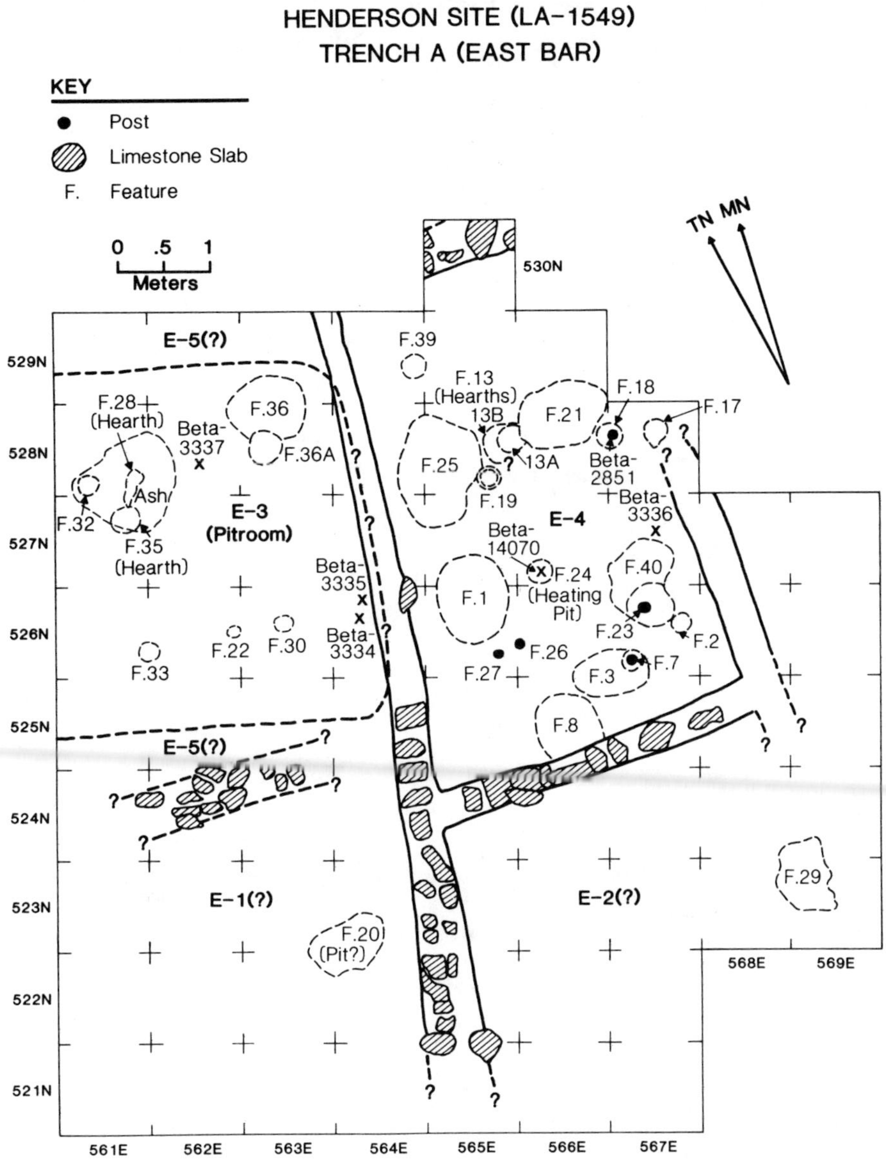

Fig. 7. Trench A (East Bar) of Henderson Site, showing excavated rooms, features, and location of radiocarbon samples.

The radiocarbon and archaeomagnetic dates confirm the general temporal placement of the site suggested by the ceramics, bracketing the occupation between about A.D. 1200/1250 and 1400/1450 (we rely in this discussion particularly on the Stuiver calibration, although the other calibration schemes lead to very similar conclusions). While the temporal resolution at present is far from ideal, the dates appear to fall into two clusters, the first prior to about A.D. 1300, the second in the late 1300s and/or early 1400s. It is premature to conclude that Henderson was abandoned in the mid-1300s until more radiocarbon dates (preferably on annuals) and more archaeomagnetic dates have been run from a much larger number of rooms, but an occupational hiatus is a distinct possibility. In subsequent discussion, we will refer to these clusters of dates as the "early" and "late" phases of oc-

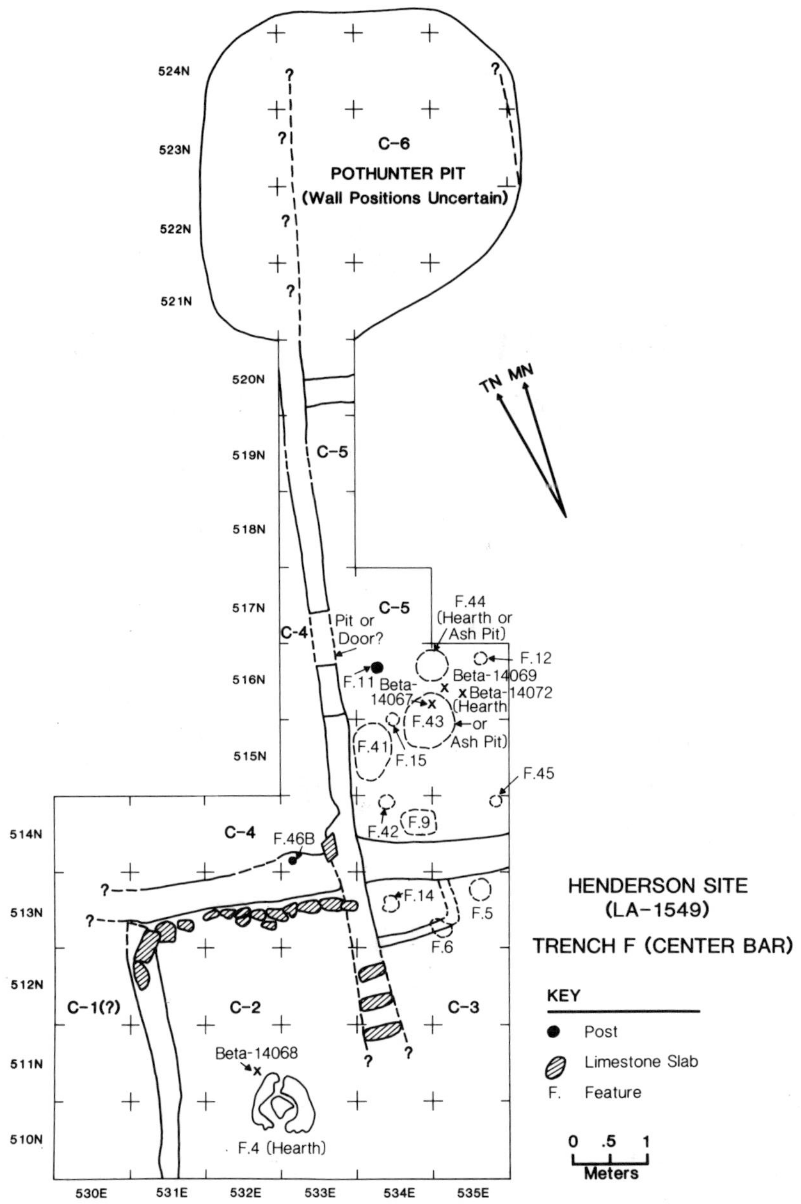

Fig. 8. Trench F (Center Bar) of Henderson Site, showing excavated rooms, features, and location of radiocarbon samples.

cupation; but, we stress the tentativeness of these designations, and underscore the very real possibility that occupation at the site was more or less continuous throughout the fourteenth century.

The basic layout of Henderson probably was established during the early phase of occupation in the 1200s. For example, the average of three radiocarbon dates from Room C-5 in the Center Bar (1 from the hearth or ash pit on the primary floor [Floor 1] and 2 from overlying trash fill) is about A.D. 1290±40 (Stuiver calibration). Similarly, the radiocarbon date from an ash pit or heating pit on the primary floor (Floor 1) of Room E-4 in the East Bar, and three archaeomagnetic dates from two features on the same floor of this structure, bracket its initial occupation between A.D. 1125–1350 and most likely during the 1200s. In addition, two radiocarbon dates (excluding Beta-3334, a partially burned beam fragment, which is clearly too early) and two archaeomagnetic dates from the pitroom (E-3) in the East Bar also point to construction and subsequent reuse of this structure during the 1200s or early 1300s.

The second phase of occupation at the site, in the late 1300s and/or early 1400s, is evidenced by two radiocarbon dates on wooden post or beam fragments associated with trash fill and ephemeral, secondary floors above the main floor in East Bar surface Room E-4, and by an archaeomagnetic date from a hearth (Feat. 4) on what is believed to be the primary floor in Center Bar Room C-2. The single radiocarbon date (Beta-14068) on a very small sample of burned reeds found adjacent to, and stratigraphically slightly above, the hearth in this room produced an anomalously early date (A.D. 980±111; Stuiver calibration) and is rejected. During this second or late phase of occupation, the pitroom in the East Bar appears to have been intentionally sealed and built over with a surface structure (Room E-5).

Four radiocarbon dates have been run on charcoal samples from the bison-filled trash deposits in the East Plaza. Two of these (Beta-8820, Beta-14071) are pooled samples of burned twigs, branches, and larger chunks of charcoal collected from arbitrary, horizontal, 1-m^2 excavation units; the remaining two (Beta-3332, Beta-3333) are samples consisting only of burned twigs and small branches from a rock-lined hearth at the top of the deposit. Three of the four plaza dates are remarkably similar; the fourth (Beta-14071) is somewhat earlier, and may reflect the built-in age effect of dating remnants of burned structural beams dumped into the plaza trash.

The MASCA (Ralph et al. 1973) and Damon et al. (1974) calibrations of the plaza dates can be interpreted in two different ways. On the one hand, they can be used, much like the other dates from the site, to argue for two phases of occupation, one in the late 1200s or early 1300s, the other toward the end of the 1300s. On the other hand, these same data can be used to argue for more or less continuous trash accumulation in the plaza, and hence for some sort of occupation at Henderson throughout the 1300s.

The Stuiver calibrations of these dates are equally ambiguous, in this case because the radiocarbon dates, when calibrated, cross the curve at two different places. Depending on which values we choose, we can argue that the trash deposits date only to the early phase, or only to the late phase, or to both phases, or that activity continued in the plaza, without major interruption, throughout the 1300s. In other words, on the basis only of the radiocarbon evidence, the East Plaza trash, with its remarkable quantities of bison bone, could have accumulated during either or both of the occupational phases identified at the site; and it may actually span the entire fourteenth century, thereby indicating that there was no real hiatus of activity at Henderson. In the near future, we hope to resolve this dilemma by direct accelerator dating of annuals such as corn in the plaza trash. This would eliminate the error introduced by dating samples of charcoal that were pooled from arbitrary excavation levels, and which may have contained wood from recycled beams or from the interior rings of long-lived trees.

In sum, the Henderson Site occupation can be placed with some confidence between about A.D. 1200/1250 and 1400/1450. The dates appear to fall into two clusters, possibly indicating two phases of occupation (the first in the 1200s and early 1300s, the second in the late 1300s and early 1400s), possibly separated by a brief period in the mid-1300s when the site may have been abandoned. At least one nearly square pitroom with rounded corners was incorporated directly into the layout of the surface rooms during the first phase of occupation. This pitroom was no longer in use during the late occupational phase at the site, but there may have been other pitroom structures in use at this time that have not yet been discovered. Tremendous quantities of bison were processed by the Henderson inhabitants in the East Plaza, but the calibrated radiocarbon dates, while internally consistent, are compatible with either or both of the two temporal phases at the site, and in fact could point to more or less continuous activity in the plaza throughout the fourteenth century. There is a striking degree of correspondence between the Henderson chronology and the sequence of occupation documented at Arroyo Hondo, a large, contemporary pueblo near Santa Fe in north-central New Mexico (Rose, Dean, and Robinson 1981; Lang and Harris 1984). Arroyo Hondo, like Henderson, is situated relatively close to the margins of the grasslands, and bison were an important source of food for the community's inhabitants. The village was founded in the late 1200s and grew to its maximum size in the first third of the 1300s. Population then declined precipitously during the mid-1300s. Renewed growth began in the late 1300s, reaching a peak in the first decade of the fifteenth century. Final abandonment of the pueblo occurred by about A.D. 1425. The parallels in the occupational histories of these two communities are extremely interesting, but the extent to which they are real or fortuitous, and the degree to which the similarities reflect common underlying processes, remain uncertain and issues to be explored more fully in the future.

Architecture

As noted earlier, one of the rooms (E-3 in the East Bar) is a nearly square pitroom with rounded corners which had been partially dug into bedrock (see Figs. 7, 9). The remaining structures that we excavated are above-ground rooms built of adobe, often with upright limestone slabs in the base of their walls (see Figs. 7–11). Some of the rooms, especially those on the margins of the pueblo, may have been of wattle and daub construction. At least four and perhaps six or more upright wooden posts (species not yet identified) supported the roof of each structure. Hearths tended to be located along the midline of the rooms, though usually not at their center. Ash pits and/or heating pits were also found along the midline axis, again offset from the center (Figs. 7, 8, 12–16). The hearth (Feat. 4) in Room C-2, an above-ground structure in the Center Bar, had a pronounced adobe collar (see Fig. 12). In contrast, the hearth (Feat. 35) on the floor of the pitroom (Room E-3) in the East Bar was semi-spherical in shape with no trace of a collar (i.e., "ice-cream scoop" shape; see Fig. 16). We found only one possible doorway (connecting Rooms C-4 and C-5; see Figs. 8, 10). This may actually have been a large pit (made prehistorically or by a recent pothunter) that cut into the wall from above after the rooms had been abandoned. Although none of the above-ground rooms was excavated in its entirety, these structures appear to be very large, averaging 5–6 m in length by 2.5–3.5 m in width (see Figs. 7, 8 and Table 8). If all of the rooms in the pueblo are roughly comparable in size, and we use the most conservative estimate (i.e., excluding the West Bar) for the total area of the room blocks (1180 m^2), the entire structure may have about 50 to 70 or more rooms.

The original or primary floors in the rooms generally are well made and plastered; some show multiple replasterings. In two cases (Rooms E-3 and E-4), the primary floor is overlain by at least two secondary occupation surfaces or floors, each separated from the preceding surface by 15 cm to 20 cm of fill (see Table 8). The secondary floors are seldom as well made as the original floors and lack evidence of multiple replasterings. Table 8 lists the number of floors found in each of the tested rooms. The number of secondary floors in several of the rooms is uncertain, because their higher elevation has exposed them to considerable vandalism, weathering, and erosion. It is difficult to determine whether the fill separating floors accumulated during brief periods of room abandonment, or instead was added intentionally during room remodeling to raise the level of the floor. The rela-

Table 3
Radiocarbon dates from Henderson Site:
Provenience and sample description (see Figs. 6–8)

Lab No.[1]	Sample Provenience					Sample Description
	Grid Unit/ Item No.	Feat. No.	Depth (m)	Location	Room No.	
Beta-2851	528N567E/3	18	101.05	East Bar	E-4	Unburned upright roof support beam; outer 20± rings; contemporary with, or postdates, Floor 1.
Beta-3332	512N550E/A	31	100.13–100.00	East Plaza	—	Sample A from rock-lined hearth at top of East Plaza trash deposit (see Fig. 15); pooled burned twigs and small branches; sample split into A (Beta-3332) and B (Beta-3333).
Beta-3333	512N550E/B	31	100.13–100.00	East Plaza	—	Sample B (see Beta-3332)
Beta-3334	526N564E/4	—	100.64	East Bar	E-3 (Pitroom)	Partially burned wood beam fragment lying on Floor 1; close to Beta-3335.
Beta-3335	526N564E/5	—	100.64	East Bar	E-3 (Pitroom)	Large pieces of wood charcoal lying on Floor 1; close to Beta-3334.
Beta-3336	527N567E/11	—	101.06	East Bar	E-4	Horizontal burned wood beam fragment (with remnants of bark); in small pit-like feature (unnumbered) just above Floor 1.

Table 3 (cont.)

Lab. No.[1]	Sample Provenience					Sample Description
	Grid Unit/ Item No.	Feat. No.	Depth (m)	Location	Room No.	
Beta-3337	528N562E/5	—	100.75–100.70	East Bar	E-3 (Pitroom)	Pooled wood charcoal from ash lense on Floor 2; pooled from area ca. 30 cm in diameter; provides age for floor and associated hearth (Feat. 28).
Beta-8320	508N549E/A	—	99.50–99.40	East Plaza	—	Wood charcoal pooled from fill of 1 m^2 unit at base of East Plaza trash deposit (10 cm thick horizon).
Beta-14067	515N534E	43	100.60	Center Bar	C-5	Wood charcoal pooled from shallow, broad, unlined, basin-shaped hearth or ash pit/heating pit on Floor 1; bottom and outer perimeter of feature not sharply defined; feature contained limited amounts of black ash and relatively little charcoal; sample composed of wood specimens of unknown original diameter; sample not adequately field-dried and became slightly moldy.
Beta-14068	511N532E	—	101.15–101.05	Center Bar	C-2	Unidentified burned reeds pooled from area ca. 30 cm in diam. located immediately north of Feature 4 hearth and slightly above Floor 1; sample flagged by lab as very small.

Table 3 (cont.)

Lab No.[1]	Sample Provenience					Sample Description
	Grid Unit/ Item No.	Feat. No.	Depth (m)	Location	Room No.	
Beta-14069	516N535E	—	101.00–100.80	Center Bar	C-5	Burned twigs and small branches (max. diam. ca. 2 cm), pooled from 20-cm thick arbitrary level in 1-m^2 excavation unit; deposit represents stratified trash filling post-dating abandonment of Room C-5; sample from ca. 20–40 cm above Floor 1.
Beta-14070	527N566E	24	101.00	East Bar	E-4	Wood charcoal pooled from thin scatter of black ash and charcoal directly on Floor 1 ringing north edge of Feature 24 ash pit/ heating pit.
Beta-14071	509N549E	—	99.80–99.70	East Plaza	—	Wood charcoal pooled from arbitrary 10-cm thick level of 1-m^2 unit in East Plaza trash deposit; sample primarily twigs and small branches, but also several larger chunks from wood specimens of unknown original diameter; sample not adequately field-dried and became slightly moldy.
Beta-14072	516N535E	—	101.20–101.00	Center Bar	C-5	Burned twigs and small branches (max. diam. ca. 3 cm), pooled from 20-cm thick arbitrary level in 1-m^2 excavation unit; deposit represents stratified trash filling post-dating abandonment of Room C-5; sample from 40-60 cm above Floor 1.

[1]Beta Analytic, Inc., Coral Gables, Florida.

Table 4
Radiocarbon dates from Henderson Site:
Original dates and calibration

Lab. No.[1]	Uncalibrated Age				Calibrated Age (A.D. ±1σ)			
	^{14}C Age[2] (B.P. ±1σ)	^{13}C-Fract. (per mil)	^{14}C Age[3] (B.P. ±1σ)	^{14}C Age[4] (A.D. ±1σ)	Ralph et al. (1973)	Damon et al. (1974)	Stuiver (1982)	Klein et al. (1982)
Beta-2851	460±80	−24.97	460±80	1476±80	1420±90	1458±89	1435±81	1330–1630
Beta-3332	540±30	−24.53	550±30	1384±30	1380±40	1376±48	1335±34; 1410±34	1330–1415
Beta-3333	570±30	−24.67	570±30	1363±30	1363±40	1358±48	1340±34; 1400±34	1320–1410
Beta-3334	980±40	−24.07	1000±40	920±40	980±50	962±51	1010±43	895–1195
Beta-3335	710±30	−25.50	700±30	1229±30	1249±40	1240±42	1285±34	1245–1335
Beta-3336	530±30	−25.22	530±30	1404±30	1390±40	1394±48	1415±34	1335–1420
Beta-3337	730±30	−24.25	740±30	1188±30	1228±40	1203±42	1280±34	1230–1320
Beta-8320	660±40	−26.28	640±40	1291±40	1310±50	1295±50	1305±43; 1380±43	1255–1405
Beta-14067	610±40	−23.72	630±40	1301±40	1311±50	1303±50	1310±43; 1380±43	1260–1405
Beta-14068	1080±110	−25.03	1080±110	838±110	910±120	886±121	980±111	670–1180
Beta-14069	670±40	−20.01	750±40	1178±40	1220±50	1194±50	1270±43	1210–1330
Beta-14070	820±40	−23.29	850±40	1075±40	1090–1140±50	1102±51	1200±43	1045–1260

Table 4 (cont.)

Lab. No.[1]	Uncalibrated Age				Calibrated Age (A.D. $\pm 1\sigma$)			
	^{14}C Age[2] (B.P. $\pm 1\sigma$)	^{13}C-Fract. (per mil)	^{14}C Age[3] (B.P. $\pm 1\sigma$)	^{14}C Age[4] (A.D. $\pm 1\sigma$)	Ralph et al. (1973)	Damon et al. (1974)	Stuiver (1982)	Klein et al. (1982)
Beta-14071	850±40	−23.14	880±40	1044±40	1084±50	1074±51	1160±44; 1180±44	1035–1250
Beta-14072	650±40	−22.70	690±40	1239±40	1259±50	1249±50	1290±43	1240–1350

[1]Beta Analytic, Inc., Coral Gables, Florida.
[2]Old (Libby) half-life (5,570 years); age referenced to year A.D. 1950; not corrected for ^{13}C-fractionation.
[3]Old (Libby) half-life (5,570 years); age referenced to year A.D. 1950; corrected for ^{13}C-fractionation.
[4]New half-life (5,730 years); age referenced to year A.D. 1950; corrected for ^{13}C-fractionation.

Table 5
Archaeomagnetic dates from Henderson Site:
Provenience and sample description (see Figs. 6–8)

Lab. No.	Grid Unit	Feat. No.	Depth (m)	Location	Room No.	Sample Description
HS001	510–511N 532–533E	4	101.05	Center Bar	C-2	Shallow, thinly plastered, basin-shaped hearth with raised adobe collar (Fig. 12); on Floor 1; ca. 80 cm in diam.; collar rises 2.5 cm above floor; pit bottom 2.5 cm below floor; plaster lining gray, 0.5 cm thick, badly cracked by roots; unconsolidated, gravelly substrate; collar orange, friable adobe, cracked by roots; hearth close to modern surface; integrity of samples for dating poor.
HS002	528N565E	13A	101.00	East Bar	E-4	Shallow, thinly plastered, basin-shaped hearth without raised adobe collar (Fig. 13); on Floor 1; 30–35 cm diam.; bottom 5.0 cm below floor; Feat. 13A is remodelling of Feat. 13B; both associated with Floor 1 (different replastering episodes); hearth truncated by Feat. 21 burial pit; plaster lining 0.25 cm thick, cracked by roots; burn extends through lining and 0.25–0.5 cm into gravelly substrate; integrity of samples for dating moderate.
HS003	528N565E	13B	101.00	East Bar	E-4	Shallow, thinly plastered, basin-shaped hearth without raised adobe collar (Fig. 13); on Floor 1; 40 cm diam.; bottom 6.0 cm below floor; Feat. 13B remodelled to form smaller hearth (13A); hearth truncated by Feat. 21 burial pit; plaster lining 0.5 cm thick, over orange adobe substrate; integrity of samples for dating moderate.
HS004	527N566E	24	101.00	East Bar	E-4	Small, shallow plaster-lined hearth or heating pit without raised adobe collar (Fig. 14); circular plan, conical profile; on Floor 1; 25 cm diam.; bottom 7.0 cm below floor; plaster lining orange, gravelly, 2.0 cm thick, badly cracked; integrity of samples for dating moderate.

Table 5 (cont.)

Lab. No.	Grid Unit	Feat. No.	Depth (m)	Location	Room No.	Sample Description
HS005	527–528N 561E	28	100.75	East Bar	E-3	Shallow basin-shaped pit dug into room fill; not plaster lined; without adobe collar; on Floor 2; 60–80 cm diam.; bottom 10 cm below floor; substrate burned; feature filled with loose chunks of burned adobe; overlain and surrounded by circular ash zone; samples poorly consolidated; integrity of samples for dating moderate.
HS006	527N561E	35	100.60	East Bar	E-3	Small, thinly plastered semi-spherical ("ice cream scoop") hearth without raised adobe collar (Fig. 16); on Floor 1; 30 cm diam.; bottom 12 cm below floor; substrate homogeneous, burned, uncracked; integrity of samples for dating good.

Table 6
Archaeomagnetic dates from Henderson Site:
Laboratory data used to compute dates[1]

Lab. No.	(N) No. of Samples[2]	(EXP) Altern. Field used for Demagnetization (Oersteds)	(J) Mean Magnetization (Gauss)	(I) Mean Paleomagnetic Inclin. (°)	(D) Mean Paleomagnetic Declin. (°)	(α-95) Radius of 95% Circle of Confid. about Mean Direction	(K) Precision Parameter	(PLAT) Virtual Geomagnetic Pole Lat. (°)	(PLONG) Virtual Geomagnetic Pole Long. (°)	(DM) Semi-major Axis of 95% Oval of Confidence about Pole Position (°)	(DP) Semi-minor Axis of 95% Oval of Confidence about Pole Position (°)
HS001	6	H150	6.312922E-04	54.31	1.51	4.4	229.81	88.02	294.09	6.23	4.38
HS002	14	H200	1.032401E-04	57.37	346.94	1.3	891.87	78.02	192.90	1.95	1.42
HS003	8	H100	1.432835E-04	56.18	351.25	2.4	540.84	82.06	193.38	3.43	2.47
HS004	12	H050	1.284584E-03	56.75	349.82	2.6	270.36	80.77	194.14	3.84	2.78
HS005	7	H100	1.707963E-04	57.48	355.83	4.9	155.36	84.12	221.38	7.11	5.20
HS006	10	H050	5.164382E-04	58.64	348.86	2.0	560.22	79.18	202.61	3.03	2.25

[1] Table presents laboratory data as reported in June 1982 by Richard C. Lange, Arizona State Museum and Paleomagnetism Laboratory, Department of Geosciences, University of Arizona, Tucson, Arizona (see Irving 1964:52-71; Tarling 1971:75-78). When the samples were submitted to Arizona in 1981, we inadvertently provided the lab with an obsolete magnetic declination of 12.5°, taken from the 1949 Hondo Reservoir 7.5 minute quadrangle map. The samples themselves had been collected in 1980-81. In October 1985, Jeffrey L. Eighmy, Archaeomagnetic Laboratory, Department of Anthropology, Colorado State University, Fort Collins, Colorado very generously recalibrated the dates, using a revised declination of 11° (value for 1979-80) and an updated version of the curve for pole positions. Eighmy's recalculated values for (D), (PLAT), and (PLONG) have been incorporated into this table, and Table 7 below presents the revised results.
[2] Sample size 1 in^3.

Table 7
Archaeomagnetic dates from Henderson Site: Dates[1]

Lab No.	Room No.	Feature No.	$a-95$[2]
HS001	C–2	4	A.D. 680– 730, 900–1025, 1375–1425
HS002	E–4	13A	A.D. 1000–1075, 1125–1300
HS003	E–4	13B	A.D. 925–1025, 1175–1325
HS004	E–4	24	A.D. 925–1075, 1150–1350
HS005	E–3	28	A.D. 925–1025, 1175–1425
HS006	E–3	35	A.D. 1000–1075, 1150–1325

[1]Archaeomagnetic analyses run in 1982 by Richard C. Lange of the Arizona State Museum through the Paleomagnetism Laboratory, Department of Geosciences, University of Arizona, Tucson, Arizona (see Irving 1964:52–71; Tarling 1971:75–78). Results recalibrated in October 1985 by Jeffrey L. Eighmy, Archaeomagnetic Laboratory, Department of Anthropology, Colorado State University, Fort Collins, Colorado using more appropriate mean local magnetic declination and revised curve for pole positions (see Table 6, footnote 1 above).
[2]"...represents the size of a circle centered on the mean direction of a sample within which the true mean direction is likely to fall with 95% confidence" (Eighmy 1980:82).

tively uniform thickness of the fill layers and the scarcity of trash may point to the latter. The floors in each room have been numbered sequentially, with Floor 1 being the oldest or primary floor.

Non-burial Artifacts

The Henderson artifacts, other than those associated directly with burials, are still being studied and only a few general remarks can be made here (see Appendix 17 for artifact labeling procedures). Several hundred complete and fragmentary arrow points were recovered. The vast majority of these are Washita points made of locally available cherts, with side notches located about one-third of the way from the base toward the tip, and the base lightly to strongly concave. Fresnos, many of which may be unfinished Washitas, are also relatively numerous. Only a few points were recovered that can be classified as basally notched Harrells and Garzas, and these for the most part were found in surficial contexts. Their scarcity at Henderson is consistent with an abandonment date for the site sometime prior to about A.D. 1450 (see discussion in Parry and Speth 1984). A few small, corner-notched arrow points were also found.

Aside from points, the large lithic assemblage contains relatively few formal tools. Most common among these are small, thick, crudely flaked ovoid bifaces. Endscrapers are very rare, an interesting aspect of the Henderson assemblage in light of the quantities of bison that are present. Most other items that show signs of use are unstandardized flakes

Table 8
Room size and number of floors (see Figs. 7, 8)

Room No.[1]	Location	Interior Length (m)	Interior Width (m)	Floor No.[2]	Ave. Floor Elevation[3] (m)	Comments
C-1	Center Bar	?	?	?	?	Floor not reached in excavation
C-2	Center Bar	?	2.60	1	101.05–101.10	Floor close to surface, badly eroded; number of replastering episodes not determined; burned roof beam fragments on floor; ephemeral higher floors may have been missed or eroded off.
C-3	Center Bar	?	?	1	100.63–100.67	Number of replastering episodes not determined
C-4	Center Bar	?	?	?	?	Floor not reached in excavation
C-5	Center Bar	5.90	?	1	100.58–100.63	At least 2 replastering episodes, each 1–1.5 cm thick.
C-6	Center Bar	?	2.90?	1	100.55–100.60?	Pothunter's pit destroyed most of Room C-6; wall positions and floor elevation tentative; Floor 1 may have had at least 3 replastering episodes, each 1–1.5 cm thick.
E-1	East Bar	?	?	1	ca. 101.05	Floor close to surface, badly eroded; ephemeral higher floors may have been missed or eroded off.
E-2	East Bar	?	3.65	1	ca. 101.05	Floor close to surface, badly eroded; ephemeral higher floors may have been missed or eroded off.

Table 8 (cont.)

Room No.[1]	Location	Interior Length (m)	Interior Width (m)	Floor No.[2]	Ave. Floor Elevation[3] (m)	Comments
E-3	East Bar	4.00	?	1 2 3?	ca. 100.60 ca. 100.75 ca. 100.90?	Pitroom abandoned after 100.90 m floor and intentionally sealed with sterile adobe; upper surface of seal at 101.05 m served as Floor 1 for Room E-5 which was built over pitroom.
E-4	East Bar	5.40	3.55	1 2 3?	101.00–101.05 101.25–101.30 101.49–101.51?	Floor 1 had 3 replastering episodes, each 1–1.5 cm thick.
E-5	East Bar	?	?	1	ca. 101.05	Ephemeral higher floors may have been missed or may have eroded off; Floor 1 formed by upper surface of sterile adobe used to seal underlying Pitroom E-3.

[1] C, Center Bar; E, East Bar.
[2] Floor 1 is oldest or primary floor in room.
[3] Elevation relative to Datum A (100.00 m).

Fig. 9. Excavations in Trench A (East Bar), looking south. Room E-4 in center foreground with exposed burial features. a, Feature 1 (backfilled); b, Feature 3; c, Feature 8 (backfilled); d, Feature 21; e, Feature 25; f, Feature 40; g, Feature 29. Pitroom E-3 in right foreground; front arrow points to Feature 36 (not visible); rear arrow indicates metate fragment in wall foundation (note adjacent complete metate).

Fig. 10. Southern half of Room C-5 (Center Bar), looking west. Location of Feature 9 indicated by collapsed floor over burial pit (e); Feature 41 (not exposed) beneath photo board. Note limestone slabs in wall foundation; arrow denotes possible door or pit; hearths and/ or ash pits not visible; a-d, possible post holes.

Fig. 11. Excavations in Trench F (Center Bar), looking west-southwest. Room C-5 in center foreground; excavator in Room C-3; Room C-2 in center background (Feat. 4 hearth under plastic).

Fig. 12. Feature 4 hearth, Room C-2, Center Bar. Note adobe collar.

with irregularly retouched or utilized edges. Most of the lithics (tools and debitage) are made of locally available bluish-grey to beige cherts. Only a few pieces of obsidian, Alibates, Tecovas, and probable Edwards Plateau are present in the assemblage.

Intermingled with large quantities of fire-cracked rock and stratified midden deposits in the East Plaza (Trench C; see Figs. 6, 17, 18) were crude, cleaver- and chopper-like tools of limestone, probably used in processing bison (bones from more than 30 individuals were recovered). Most of these tools were subangular to subrounded pieces of limestone with only a few removals to form a cutting edge. Limestone percussion flakes in the deposits attest to the expedient manufacture of these tools as they were needed, as well as to their damage in use.

Fig. 13. Feature 13 hearth (to right of photo board), Room E-4, East Bar. Note sealed collared pit (Feat. 19) directly above board. Location of unexcavated Feature 25 burial pit directly above Feature 19.

Fig. 14. Feature 24 hearth or heating pit, Room E-4, East Bar (trowel points north).

Two-handed manos made of a variety of non-local materials and large, massive trough metates of limestone were common at Henderson (Fig. 9, center right). Fragmentary specimens were often incorporated into the foundations of walls (Fig. 9, arrow at center right).

Only two polished, full-grooved axes (1 complete specimen from the East Bar; 1 broken butt end from the trash deposits in the East Plaza) and no shaft straighteners or smoothers were recovered. Hammerstones of non-local materials were relatively abundant.

Fig. 15. Feature 31 hearth (rock-lined) at top of trash deposit in East Plaza (trowel points north).

A tiny, fired-clay horn fragment, almost certainly of a bison, attests to the presence of ceramic figurines at the site. This unusual item was found (by screening) in the fill between Floors 1 and 2 of Room E-4 in the East Bar. This fill is dated by radiocarbon to the later occupational phase at the site. It is of course possible, however, that the specimen actually dates to the earlier phase and became incorporated within the later deposits as a result of rodent or other disturbance. The horn, 1.8 cm in length by 0.6 cm in diameter at its base, is curved longitudinally and tapers to a sharp point. The clay is brown. It was broken near its base from the figurine, the rest of which unfortunately was not found.

Worked bone artifacts (e.g., awls, spatulas) were uncommon in non-burial contexts. No bison scapula hoes, tibia digging sticks, or other typical Plains bone artifacts were encountered. There were a few large freshwater mussel shells (*Cyrtonaias tampicoensis*) which had serrated, worn edges indicating their use as cutting and/or scraping tools; other valves of the same species provided raw material for fashioning ornaments (see discussion below). Interestingly, with the exception of two pieces of probable mussel shell found with the Feature 29 burial, ornaments made from the valves of freshwater mollusks were not encountered in our sample of burials.

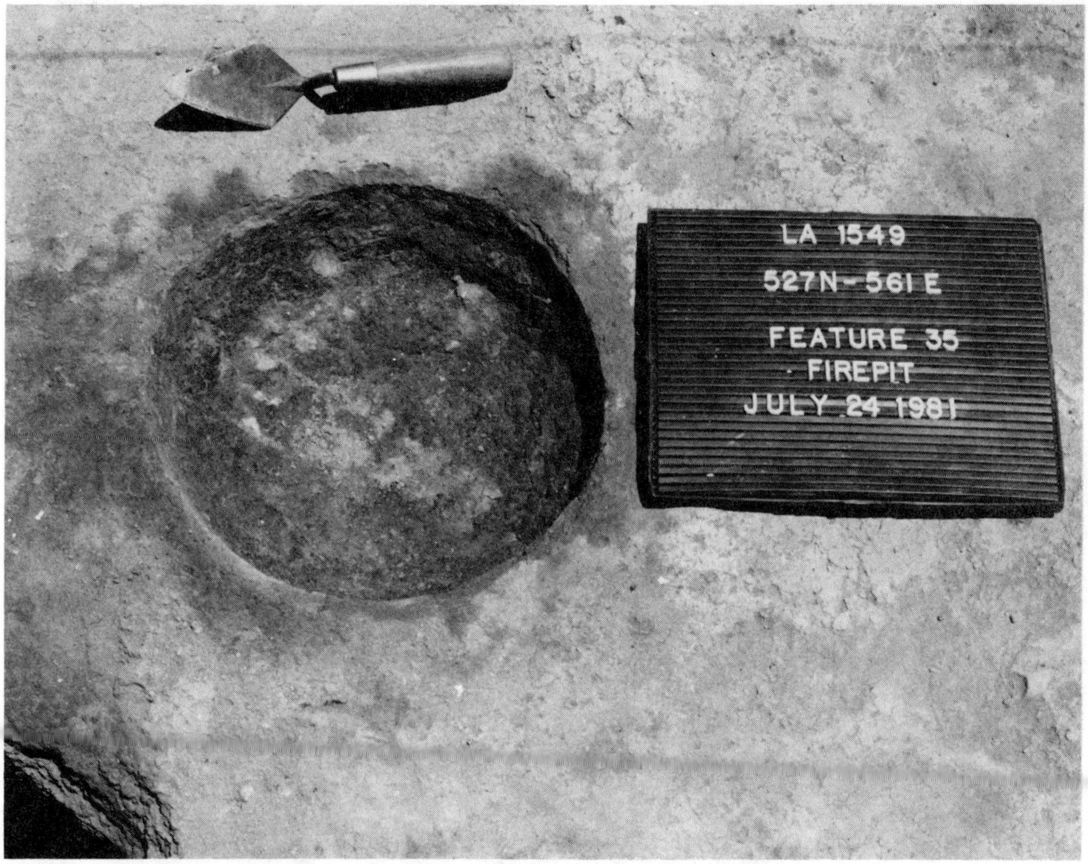

Fig. 16. Feature 35 hearth or heating pit ("ice cream scoop" shape), Pitroom E-3, East Bar (trowel points north).

Scattered throughout the deposits, as well as eroded out on the surface, were isolated turquoise pendants, tiny white disc-shell beads, *Olivella* shell beads, quartz and fluorite crystals, and other items. While these were almost certainly displaced from burials by rodents or other sources of disturbance, they are not included in the detailed analyses of burial accompaniments reported here.

Perhaps the most striking aspect of the Henderson artifact assemblage is the virtual absence of Plains-type artifacts and raw materials, despite the site's proximity to the Plains. With the striking exception of the points and knives with the Feature 36 burial and the abundance of bison bones in the plaza trash, virtually everything else (lithic materials, ceramics, obsidian, turquoise, marine shell, etc.) points to local sources or to sources west of the Pecos.

Subsistence

Excavation during the 1980 season was confined largely to rooms in the Center and East Bars of the "E". In addition to providing data on architecture and room function, we hoped that work in the rooms would yield stratified samples of trash suitable for reconstructing basic patterns of subsistence. However, by the end of the first season it be-

Fig. 17. Trash deposits (partially excavated to bedrock) at south end of East Plaza (Trench C), looking south. Note quantities of fire-cracked rock in profiles and in backdirt pile (left background).

Fig. 18. Fire-cracked rock in trash deposits at south end of East Plaza (Trench C; Grid 508N551E), looking north.

came clear that the rooms we had sampled were unburned and contained relatively little trash; thus, they were unlikely to yield the economic data we were seeking. As a consequence, in 1981 we shifted our focus to the south end of the East Plaza where previous testing had revealed relatively deep midden deposits, filled with fire-cracked rock, animal bone (especially bison), lithic and ceramic artifacts, and other trash (see Figs. 17, 18).

Analysis of the faunal and floral remains recovered by screening from the trash deposits in the East Plaza and from elsewhere on the site is far from complete. In addition, hundreds of large flotation samples were collected during both seasons of excavation, and these too have not been completely processed. Nevertheless, a number of preliminary observations can be made concerning subsistence patterns at the site.

Burned maize cobs are present throughout the deposits, although they never occur in abundance. Their comparatively low frequency is probably more an artifact of poor conditions of preservation (and perhaps the use of cobs as fuel) than a sign that corn was an insignificant part of Henderson diet. A more precise picture of the dietary importance of corn must await inspection of the float samples for burned maize cupules, and perhaps isotopic measurements directly on the human skeletal material. Aside from wood charcoal and a few walnut shell fragments, other macroscopic plant food remains have not been observed (this, of course, is likely to change dramatically once the float samples are analyzed).

The faunal remains are extremely interesting. In terms of numbers of individuals, cottontail rabbits (*Sylvilagus audubonii*) outnumber all other mammals. Jackrabbits (*Lepus californicus*) and black-tailed prairie dogs (*Cynomys ludovicianus*; not all are necessarily food remains, since some skeletal elements may represent intrusive burrowing into the deposits) are next in frequency, and then bison (*Bison bison*). Deer (*Odocoileus* sp.) and antelope (*Antilocapra americana*) are both present but rare (i.e., there are many more individuals of bison than of deer and antelope combined). Rodents other than prairie dogs, even gophers (*Thomomys bottae*), are rare. Visual inspection of the float samples suggests that the scarcity and lack of variety of rodents is real rather than an artifact of using quarter-inch screens. Birds, both aquatic and non-aquatic, are uncommon, and turkeys (*Meleagris gallopavo*) are noteworthy for their absence. There are a few fragments of egg shell, but these may not be identifiable to species.

The bison remains raise some interesting questions. First, bison is abundant at the site, especially in the trash deposits at the south end of the East Plaza (Trench C). These relatively small excavations produced hundreds of bones, mostly intact articular ends of limb elements with attached shaft segments, from more than 30 individuals. Second, bison are far more abundant at the site than deer and antelope combined. Finally, over 70% of the bison are males (based on sexing the proximal femur, humerus, and tibia; the latter is the most common bison element at the site). Even most of the immature bison are males (again based on sexing the proximal tibia; the measurements for most unfused tibias at Henderson consistently fall above those for adult females from Henderson and Garnsey, and for modern comparative specimens—for measurements used, see Speth 1983).

If a predominance of males is a sign that hunting took place primarily during the spring (males are selectively procured at that time of year because they are in better physiological condition than females; see arguments in Speth 1983), then the Henderson Site has produced little or no evidence of a fall or early winter bison hunt. Perhaps bison were unavailable in or near the Pecos Valley at this time of year. This seems unlikely, however, in light of the available historical data for the area. Thus, for example, three of the earliest Spanish expeditions to explore the Pecos Valley—Chamuscado (1581), Espejo (1582), and de Sosa (1590)—observed tracks, dung, and bones between the months of July and December, although they never actually encountered living animals (Hammond and Rey 1966:88–90, 207–209, 259–264). The Mendoza-Lopez expedition, which crossed the Pecos River just south of the New Mexico state line in mid-January 1684, observed numerous bison in and adjacent to the valley (Bolton 1946:328–333). This same expedition recrossed the Pecos somewhat farther south on its return in the latter part of May 1684, again encountering bison throughout the region (Bolton 1946:342). A 1785–1786 Spanish account of attempts to establish peace with the Comanches and enlist their aid to subdue the Mescalero Apaches indicates that bison normally wintered in the Pecos Valley region:

> They next went on to confer about the proposed translation of the war to the neighborhood of the Rio del Norte to which Ecueracapa [Comanche chief] responded that. the nation, being pleased, agreed to it. He was only awaiting the return of those who were going with our expedition to begin the campaigns through that region [Mescalero country] with ardor, assuring that they would be so much more active from October until spring because during this time the buffalo herds on which they subsisted particularly [ranged] from the Rio Pecos to the west. Thus they would have this source nearby to provide themselves with supplies so that he could always have parties combing the enemy country as they had resolved. [Thomas 1932:319–320; brought to our attention by A. H. Schroeder]

A report on a reconnaissance of the Sacramento Mountains in January 1850 by a detachment of the United States Army indicated that the Mescalero Apaches had moved to the Pecos Valley or the country to the north to hunt "where the buffalo ranges at this season of the year" (Steen 1850, cited in Basehart 1974:23, 87). A letter written on November 24, 1875 from Bosque Grande, New Mexico, a point on the Pecos River about 60 km (35 mi) north of Roswell, states that:

> There are a great many buffalo on the Pecos all around Bosque. I went out the other day and killed one and it was very fat. Tell Add and Willie to come down and take a buffalo hunt. Billy Maxwell and some Mexicans are here from Fort Sumner hunting buffalo. [Klasner 1972:142]

Finally, George Causey, an Anglo buffalo hunter on the southern high plains, reputedly observed bison sometime during the winter of 1878 in the sand hill country directly east-southeast of Roswell (Whitlock 1970:10–11).

Thus, while the three earliest Spanish expeditions to explore the Pecos saw no actual herds of bison anywhere along the valley, they did observe their tracks, dung, and skeletal remains, indicating that bison made regular use of the valley. Unfortunately, the precise time of year when animals were present cannot be determined from the accounts. The seventeenth-, eighteenth-, and nineteenth-century Spanish and Anglo accounts make it clear that bison frequented the valley, at times in considerable numbers, from October or November well into spring. It seems unlikely, therefore, that the absence of evidence for a fall or early winter hunt at Henderson can be attributed to the absence of bison in the region at that time of year. This conclusion must be viewed with caution, however, because all of the historical accounts fall within the general time frame of the "Little Ice Age", a period which witnessed major climatic and environmental changes throughout the northern hemisphere (see discussion and references in Speth 1983). It is possible that the fall and winter grazing range of bison during the thirteenth- and fourteenth-century

Henderson occupation differed from the pattern which emerged during the "Little Ice Age." The late nineteenth-century Klasner and Causey accounts also must be viewed with caution, because in these two cases the presence of bison in the Pecos Valley area may reflect an anomalous situation brought about by the slaughter of the southern herd. This tragic event was in full swing in the 1870s, and may have driven innumerable animals off the high plains in search of refuge from the hunters.

The lack of evidence for a fall-early winter hunt at Henderson, of course, could stem from the fact that bison hunting took place far enough from the village that virtually no female postcranial remains were transported back. It is also possible that bison were not hunted at that time of year, because hunting conflicted with other, more important activities. Finally, the Henderson Site may have been abandoned each fall and not reoccupied until late winter or spring. Thus, while presently ambiguous, the bison data raise a number of very intriguing questions about the nature of subsistence patterns and settlement systems in the Pecos Valley during the late prehistoric period, and are a central focus of our ongoing research in the region.

The Henderson Site also produced a relatively large sample of non-mammalian faunal remains, including fish (especially catfish and suckers) and large freshwater mussels. Some of the catfish are quite large, and more than one species is represented. The mussels have been identified by John B. Burch, Curator of Mollusks in the Museum of Zoology at the University of Michigan. According to Burch, all of the identifiable valves and valve fragments are from the same species, *Cyrtonaias tampicoensis*, a form that today is confined to the Rio Grande below Big Bend National Park and to the lowermost reaches of the Pecos River in Texas (Metcalf 1982:50). Based on dated fossil and archaeological occurrences, Metcalf (1982:52) feels that *C. tampicoensis* has been gone from southeastern New Mexico for approximately the last 3,000 years. Its presence in quantity at Henderson therefore is of some interest.

Many of the valves at the site were clearly used as raw material for making ornaments, especially pendants. In addition to the ornaments themselves (which are usually too small to be identified securely to species), many of the valves have rectangular or ovoid pieces missing from them that have clearly been cut out with a sharp instrument. Thus, it is possible that the valves represent raw material that was traded into the Roswell area from sources to the south and southeast. On the other hand, the fact that the valves are relatively numerous in the trash, many with no signs of having been used for making ornaments, and the fact that some of them are burned, point to their use as a food source. If so, it seems more likely that they were collected somewhere in the Roswell area. The same species has recently been discovered at a small, transitory campsite, the Townsend Site, located only a few kilometers north of Roswell (information from the 1984 Annual Report, Research Section, Laboratory of Anthropology, Museum of New Mexico, Santa Fe, p. 14). This site, which like Henderson dates between A.D. 1200–1400, shows no evidence of onsite ornament manufacturing. Thus, it is very likely that *C. tampicoensis* inhabited the Pecos River and/or some of its tributaries in southeastern New Mexico as recently as the fourteenth century A.D.

In sum, the subsistence data from Henderson reflect a mixed economy, based on horticulture, hunting (and presumably gathering), and fishing. Dental data, including wear patterns and caries frequencies, also point toward a combination of horticulture and hunting and gathering, although the indications of the horticultural dietary component are more strongly marked (discussed later in the report). Unfortunately, the exact proportional contribution of each is unknown, and more precise estimates probably will require isotopic studies of the human skeletal material itself. Like the economic base, the settlement system of which Henderson was a part is poorly known at present. Archaeologists dealing with prehistoric puebloan communities in other parts of the Southwest would almost certainly assume that a village the size of Henderson was inhabited year round. While year-round occupation is certainly plausible, the bison data raise the interesting possibility that this may not have been the case. Quite unlike the traditional puebloan model, and more reminiscent of the Plains Village pattern in the Middle Missouri area, Henderson may have been seasonally abandoned by some or all of its inhabitants from sometime after the fall harvest until late winter or early spring, a possibility which remains to be explored more closely using other data from the site (e.g., eruption and wear-stage of deer and antelope dentitions, growth lines in catfish pectoral spines, and so forth).

2
THE HENDERSON SITE BURIALS

Introduction

Although the rooms at Henderson produced very little in the way of economic data, they nevertheless yielded a small but extremely valuable sample of human skeletons, which is the focus of the present report. Every room that we tested below the level of the primary floor yielded at least one burial. The only above-ground room we excavated almost entirely (Room E-4 in the East Bar) produced six burial features (containing 7 individuals), and a local amateur reputedly recovered at least nine individuals in an unknown number of burials from a room in the Center Bar (Room C-6?). These latter individuals, unfortunately, have been lost. It seems clear, therefore, that additional sub-floor sampling in rooms already partially tested, as well as future work in other rooms, will substantially enlarge the sample of burials from Henderson, and permit our very tentative conclusions to be reevaluated on a more reliable and secure basis.

A total of ten burial features (11 individuals) was recovered during the 1980 and 1981 seasons, in addition to a small number of isolated human bones. The locations of the burial pits are shown in Figs. 7–10 and summarized in Table 9. Each burial was assigned a feature number as it was discovered. Since other features, such as post holes and storage pits, were also assigned numbers as they were discovered, the burial numbers are not consecutive.

Much of the human skeletal material was in relatively good condition (intact) but fragile and subject to damage in excavation. Therefore, all burials received preservative treatment in the field. Features 1, 21, 25, 29, 36, 40, and 41 were treated with a diluted solution of a plastic-type floor finish (Benwood's™ One Hour Clear Finish), the skulls of Features 3 and 36 were treated with a dilute solution of Elmers™ Glue, and Features 8 and 9, along with most of Feature 3 and a few elements of Feature 1, were treated with a solution of butyl acetate (Duco™ Cement) in acetone. Subsequently, all burials received treatment and/or reconstruction in the laboratory. A sample of untreated bone (in most cases 1 femur and several ribs) was retained from each individual.

Burial Descriptions

Methods

The present section describes each burial separately. The stratigraphic context, burial position and long axis[3] orientation, an inventory of body parts, and preservation of each feature are discussed. Body orientation and position descriptions are primarily derived from feature maps and photographs and thus may be subject to minor error. In addition, the sex, age, general appearance, and pathologies of each individual are con-

---

[3]The long axis is the visually estimated orientation of the thoracic through lumbar vertebrae.

Table 9
Provenience of burials from Henderson Site (see Figs. 7–10)

Feature No.	Room No.	Location	Grid Units (Range)
1	E-4	East Bar	526–527N565E
3	E-4	East Bar	525–526N566–567E
8	E-4	East Bar	525N566E
9	C-5	Center Bar	514N534–535E
21	E-4	East Bar	528–529N566E
25	E-4	East Bar	527–528N564–565E
29	E-2	East Bar	523–524N568–569E
36	E-3	East Bar	528–529N562–563E
40	E-4	East Bar	526–527N567E
41	C-5	Center Bar	515N533–534E

sidered. Sex was determined for the adults primarily by examination of the pubis following the method of Phenice (1969), with secondary confirmation provided by examination of other elements.

Age was estimated using the pubic symphysis (McKern and Stewart 1957; Gilbert and McKern 1973)[4], endocranial closure (Todd and Lyon 1924; Krogman 1973), epiphyseal fusion (Krogman 1973), sternal and manubrial condition (Stewart 1954), evidence of degenerative change (Ubelaker 1978), and relative degree of dental attrition. Alveolar condition is described according to Turner (1979:626). Dental attrition is described after Smith (1984). Caries were identified by simple visual inspection. All caries or features identified as "possible caries" are no larger than the smallest class of pathology defined by Koritzer (1977). Finally, a series of cranial and postcranial measurements was taken, and various observations were tabulated; these are summarized for all of the burials in Appendices 1–8. These figures should be used only after reference to the

[4]Lack of the Gilbert and McKern comparative casts and lack of experience with this method may have limited its accuracy in this study. Ages derived from epiphyseal fusion data were based on Tables 5 and 6 in Krogman (1973). These ages have *not* been corrected for inter-sexual differences in rates of fusion, but raw fusion data are provided, where relevant, in Appendix 1.

relevant feature condition descriptions. Appendix 9 summarizes the isolated human bone recovered. Burial accompaniments are described briefly in the text for each feature; detailed inventories are provided in Appendices 10–16.

Feature 1

Stratigraphic context. Feature 1 was a bell-shaped pit containing an adult female burial (Figs. 7, 19–21). It was located in Room E-4 in northern Grid 526N565E and extreme southern Grid 527N565E. Part of the outline of the burial pit was recognized at 101.13 m elevation, and may originate from the disturbed 101.25 m surface (Floor 2); the pit is definitely intrusive through the 101.05 m floor (Floor 1). At the 101.13 m level, the feature was 190 cm long (north-northeast by south-southwest) by 160 cm wide, and roughly oval in form. Below this level, the pit edges were vertical (north-northeast wall) to slightly undercut (south-southwest wall), with a maximum north-northeast to south-southwest length of 205 cm at 100.75 m elevation. The feature narrowed into a broad bowl-shaped bottom upon which the burial rested at 100.45 m. The feature was dug into underlying fill of earlier occupations. Its walls were smooth and even but not plastered or finished in any other way. The volume of the pit preserved below the elevation of Floor 1 was about 350 liters.

The pit fill was a friable light brown sand and adobe mixture with sparse small (ca. 1 cm diameter) gravel near the top, turning into a less compacted, gravelly (ca. 2–5 cm diameter, subrounded) dark brown silt at 100.90 m elevation. This dark uncompacted fill surrounded the burial, with concentrations of even darker organic-rich silt loam fill in immediate contact with the skeleton. Small charcoal chunks, non-human bone, and sparse cultural material were present in the fill.

Position and orientation. The burial lay in a horizontal position upon its right side, with the long axis oriented approximately north-northeast (skull) to south-southwest. The occipital of the cranium and the vertebral column followed the contour of the east and northeast face of the pit wall. The face was oriented west, and slightly above the horizontal. The mandible was articulated, with the mouth slightly open. The cervical vertebrae projected south-southeast from the cranial base, and the remainder of the vertebral column curved further south to south-southwest. The right arm was extended nearly parallel to the long axis of the body and slightly in front (west) of it. The right hand extended under the femoral shafts and was folded at approximately 90 degrees so that the digits pointed east-southeast toward the pelvis and the palmar surface faced northeast. The left humerus rested atop the rib cage parallel to the body's axis. The left elbow was flexed at roughly a 90 degree angle with the radius and ulna running east-southeast to west-northwest. The left hand was sharply folded under at the wrist so that the digits pointed southeast back towards the body and their palmar surfaces faced upwards.

The legs were flexed at the hips (left femur approximately 65 degrees, right femur approximately 45 degrees relative to the long axis of the body); the knees were flexed unevenly with the left leg (approximately 15 degrees) tighter than the right (approximately 25 degrees). Thus the knees lay west of the body, with the right knee slightly northeast of the left. The left foot was loosely flexed (approximately 135 degrees relative to the tibia) with the digits pointing south-southwest and the dorsal surface facing upwards; the right foot's digits pointed west-southwest (approximately 100 degrees relative to the tibia) and the plantar surface was exposed.

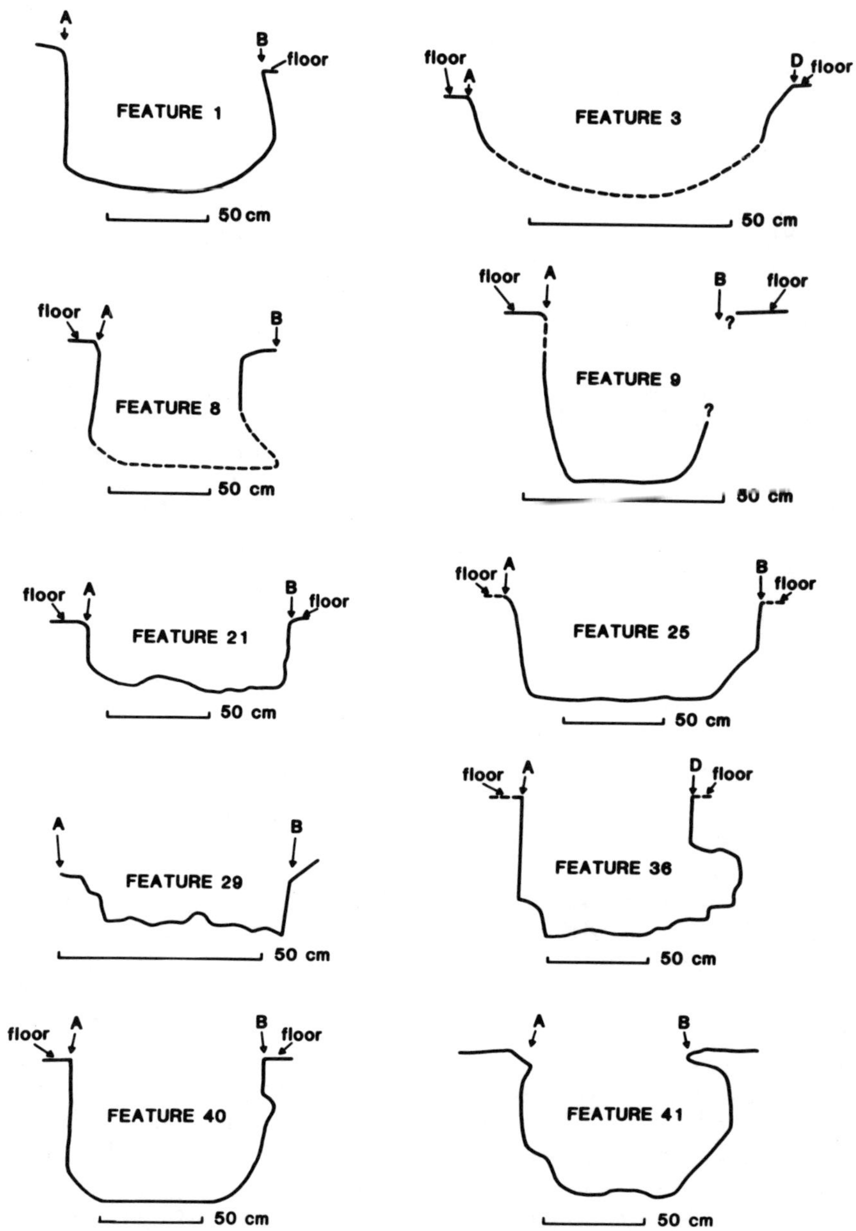

Fig. 19. Cross sections of burial pits (Features 1, 3, 8, 9, 21, 25, 29, 36, 40, 41). See individual feature plans for location of cross sections.

Burial accompaniments. One or more layers of coarse twined matting surrounded the entire burial. In most places, all that remained were impressions in the surrounding sediment; samples of these were salvaged by solidifying pieces of matrix with preservative (see Figs. 22, 23). Near the skull, a few actual warp fragments were recovered, which were identified by Richard I. Ford as grass. No identifiable remains of the weft were preserved. Details of the matting are provided in Appendix 16. Aside from the matting, no other artifact associations were identified.

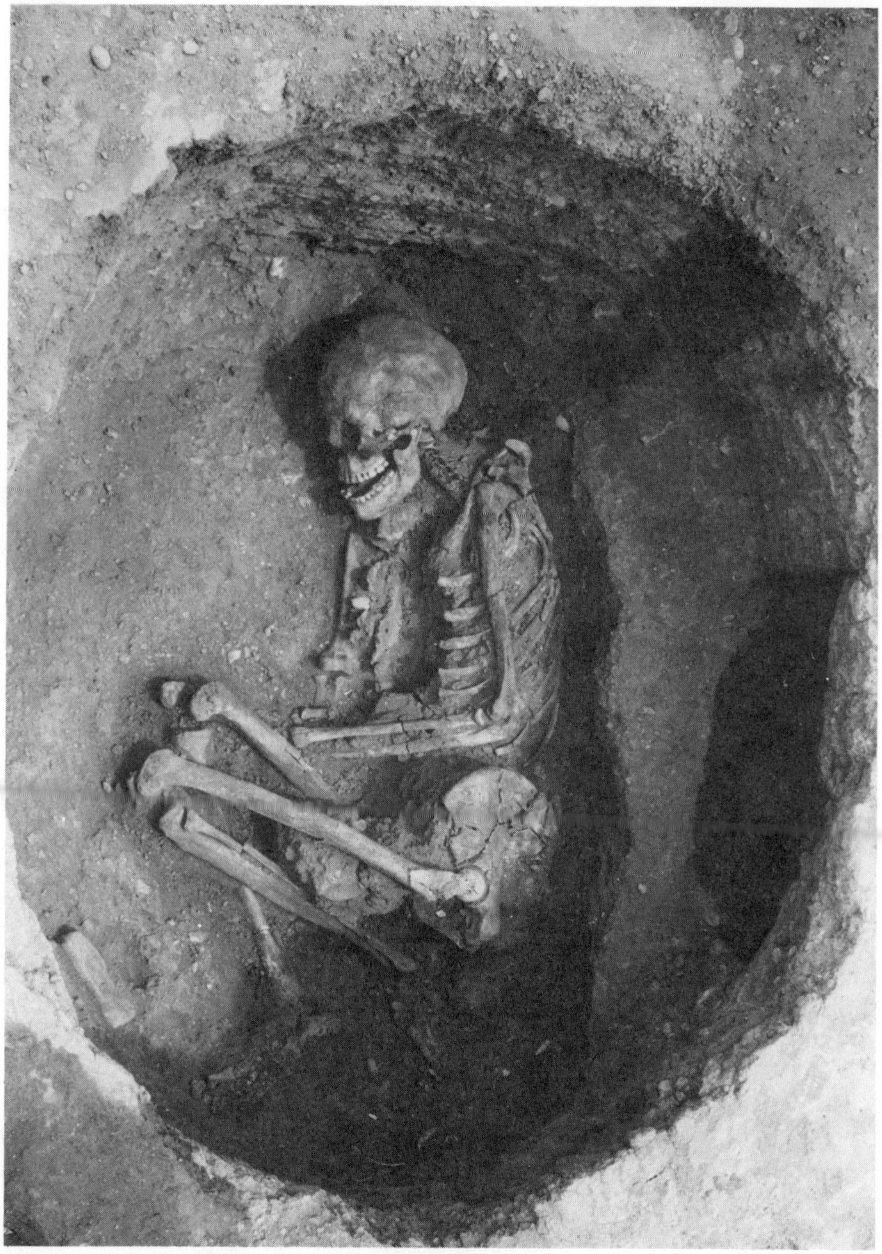

Fig. 20. Feature 1 burial. Note rock between legs.

A subangular, roughly circular limestone rock, approximately 10 cm in diameter and 4 cm in thickness, was located between the legs of the burial, between the midshaft and proximal end of the femora (see Fig. 20). The placement of this rock is analogous to that seen in Feature 40 (see below). However, unlike Feature 40, no fetal remains were found under the rock or elsewhere in the feature (see Appendix 9 for inventory of isolated bones found in feature fill). Since similar limestone rocks were encountered scattered throughout the fill, the rock between the legs may not have been placed there intentionally.

Skeletal inventory and condition. As outlined above, the skeleton in Feature 1 was fully articulated and almost the entire skeleton was recovered: all long bones, the cranium and mandible, both scapulae, both clavicles, both patellae, complete right ribs and

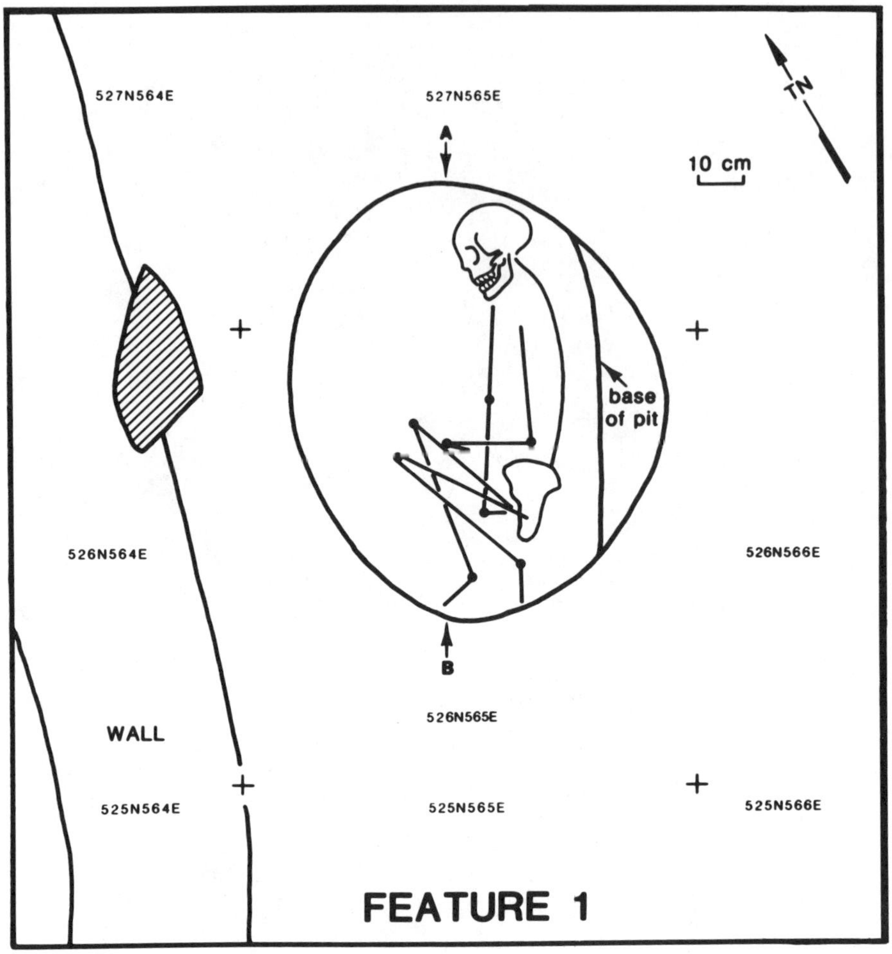

Fig. 21. Plan of Feature 1 burial.

most of each of the left ribs, nearly complete pelvis and sacrum, complete vertebral column (including four coccygeal vertebrae), sternum with xiphoid process, manubrium, hyoid, all carpals except the left triquetral, all metacarpals, all hand phalanges, all tarsals and metatarsals, all foot phalanges (except the right fifth digit second phalanx, the left second through fourth digit terminal phalanges, and the left third and fifth digit second phalanges), and several sesamoids and unidentifiable fragments.

The condition of the burial was less than ideal, however, since many of the bones had numerous cracks along which they broke apart when moved. The application of preservative in the field limited the degree of damage and permitted reconstruction in the laboratory; however, the left innominate, left portion of the sacrum, left femur, and left ribs were particularly affected. These latter elements were in large part reconstructable, but were sufficiently damaged and distorted that even after reconstruction they remained in several large sections which could not be accurately articulated.

Even on those bones where the damage is not so extensive, as on the skull and much of the right half of the skeleton, the effects of crushing can not be ignored. Almost all elements exhibit some small cracks indicative of deformation.

Fig. 22. Impression of coarse twined matting found near left humerus of Feature 1 burial (see Appendix 16, Table A16a, No. 1 for details).

Particularly serious deformation which may be reflected in measurements include:

a) The skull was crushed laterally in such a way that cracks are evident along the frontal from glabella to bregma. The parietals, probably under the same pressure, cracked on both sides of the sagittal suture, while the suture was pushed superiorly into a low keel near bregma. The left zygomatic arch was cracked and pressed slightly inwards. The mandible cracked just to the right of the symphysis (but was restored). Some anterior-posterior pressure may have also been present, since the occipital exhibits small cracks in the nuchal plane, the sphenoid is cracked near its junction with the occipital, and the external aspect of the coronal suture is squeezed apart near bregma.

b) The right femur is crushed at a point roughly two thirds the length along the shaft so that the distal end of the shaft is slightly bent laterally beyond this point. The left femur shaft is broken and unrestored, since the distal end was retained as an untreated bone sample for Feature 1.

c) The left fibula is heavily bowed medially along much of its mid-shaft.

d) The proximal end of the left ulna is badly crushed and twisted medially relative to the shaft.

Fig. 23. Impression of coarse twined matting found near left side of Feature 1 skull (see Appendix 16, Table A16a, No. 2 for details).

e) Both innominates were crushed and measurements on the left are particularly suspect due to obvious deformation.

Sex. The innominates clearly reveal that the individual was a female: a ventral arc is present and the medial aspect of the ischio-pubic ramus has a sharp ridge. The greater sciatic notch is broad, a slight degree of sub-pubic concavity exists, and a slight pre-auricular sulcus is present on the right innominate (the left auricular area is not fully preserved). The remainder of the skeleton is compatible with this identification.

Age. Repeated attempts to apply the Gilbert and McKern (1973) symphyseal aging method yielded inconsistent results with scores ranging from 6 (29.62±4.43 years) to 12 (39±6.09 years). Both of these age ranges are inconsistent with other evidence of the age of the individual (see below). For this reason, little weight is put on the symphyseal aging of Feature 1. Fusion of the xiphoid process to the sternum (as well as complete fusion of all epiphyses) suggests a mature adult. The sternum and manubrium are in stage 4 or 5 of Stewart's (1954) classification (23–35+ years). Endocranial suture closure is difficult to observe in the complete cranium. The sagittal suture is obliterated along its full extent except in the vicinity of bregma. The coronal suture is open near bregma (this is at least partly a function of post-mortem cracking); laterally the suture becomes more closed and is observable only as a very faint line. The internal aspect of the lambdoidal suture is visible as a crack near lambda, fading to a faint narrow line laterally. These features are not fully consistent, but might support an age in the late twenties. Some confusion concerning degree of closure and post-mortem cracking may exist. Cracking at the junction of the sphenoid and occipital obscures the condition of the synchondrosis.

Dental attrition (Appendix 2) suggests a relatively low age, intermediate between those of Features 40 and 41. Thus an age in the early 20s is suggested.

Finally, the lack of any evidence of arthritis anywhere on the skeleton provides evidence that the individual's age was probably not much greater than the mid-twenties. Thus, ignoring the pubic symphyseal condition, a best estimate of around 21 to 27 years is indicated.

General description, cultural and pathological alterations. Feature 1 is relatively robust for a female. The cranium is very high and relatively short (cranial index 77.9, length-height index 79.1, breadth-height index 101.5), with a prominent occiput, parietal, and slight frontal bossing (see Figs. 24, 25). Glabella is moderately prominent and superciliary arches, though small, are present. The frontal is slightly retreating, following a smooth curve along roughly a third of the length of the parietals; posterior to this point the parietals are deformed into a small flattened area immediately adjacent to the sagittal suture. This flattening extends just posterior to lambda, and is approximately 6 cm high by 4 cm wide, forming an angle of 60 degrees relative to the Frankfort Horizontal Plane[5]. This area probably represents culturally induced lambdoidal deformation. Below the flattening the occipital is vertical down to the superior nuchal ridge. This vertical region includes a relatively flat area about 3.0 cm high by 2.5 cm wide located 4 cm below lambda and forming an angle of 95 degrees relative to the Frankfort Horizontal Plane. This might represent a slight degree of culturally induced occipital deformation, though it may be formed by the natural contour of the occipital combined with the lambdoidal deformation. In occipital view, the cranium has a keeled appearance, but this at least in part relates to post-mortem deformation. The muscle markings of the cranium are moderately developed in the nuchal region and on the supramastoid ridge; the mastoids are small.

The mandible has a broad symphyseal region and a prominent mental protuberance. The gonial angles are slightly inverted.

The degree of dental attrition is indicated in Appendix 2. All teeth were present at the time of death. Light alveolar resorption, indicative of mild periodontal disease, is evident on the maxilla. Most of the mandibular molars along with most or all of the maxillary teeth display slight calculus deposits; the RM^1 and RM^2 have medium calculus on the buccal surface and both M_1s and M_2s have medium calculus on the lingual surface (Brothwell 1972:150). A chronic abscess is present at the RI^1, where the root apex is exposed in a 4 mm by 6 mm opening. The labial aspect of the root apex displays a perforation and the root does not extend to the superior end of the tooth socket. No evidence of post-mortem erosion of the alveolus is present. No caries are visible on any of the teeth.

---

[5]This angle was measured by placing the cranium on its right side with the base towards the observer and laying a straight-edge between orbitale and porion (this requires sighting down onto the cranium). A second straight edge was pressed against the flattened area in the sagittal plane. A transparent protractor was then sighted down onto the intersection of the two straight edges, and the angle was read. An angle of less than 90 degrees is inclined anteriorly.

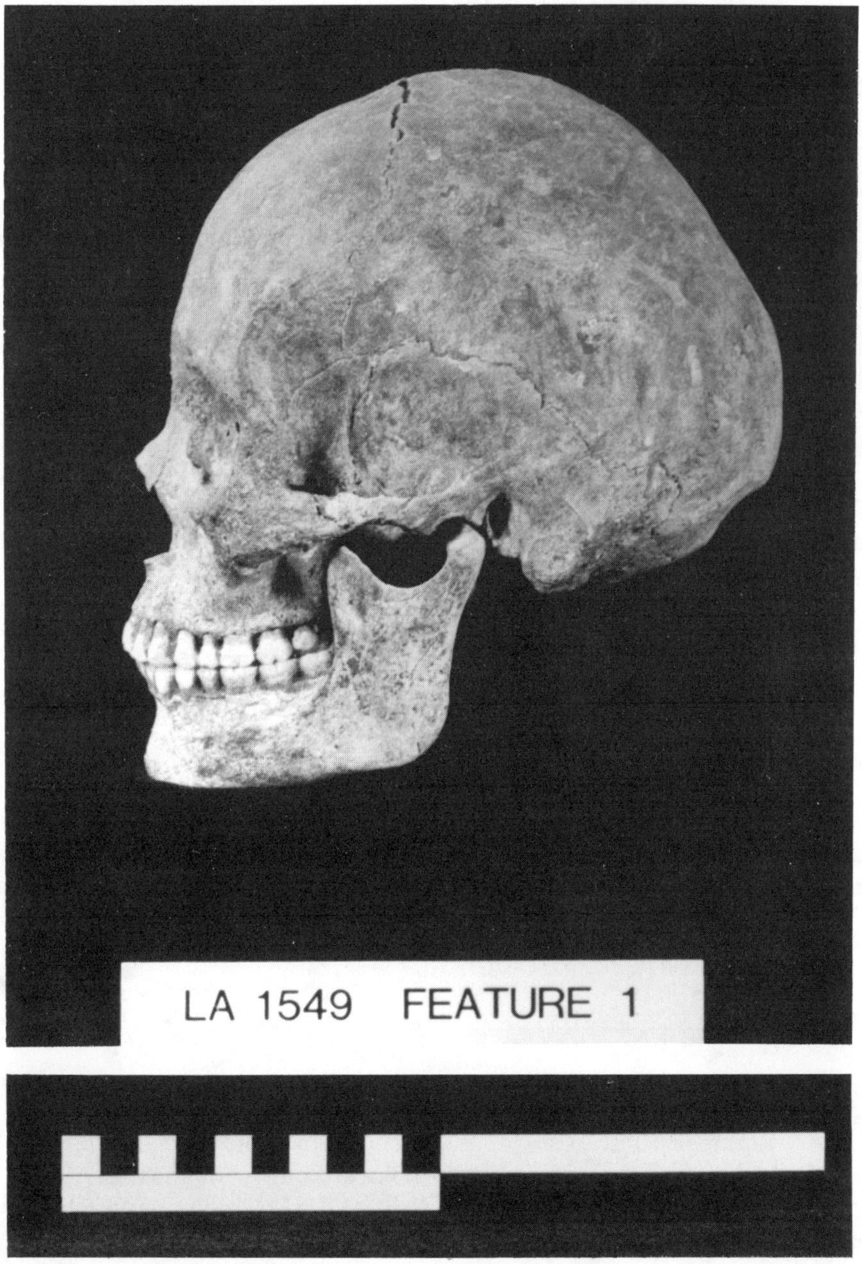

Fig. 24. Feature 1 skull (left lateral view). Same scale applies to Figs. 25, 41, 42, 54, 55, 62, 63, 67, 70, 75, 76, 101, 102, 110, 111, 114, 115.

Three skeletal abnormalities are present. A small extra-sutural bone about 0.9 cm high by 1.7 cm wide is present at the right asterion. A very small (crown diameter ca. 2–3 mm) supernumerary tooth occurs between the mandibular right premolars on their lingual side (see Fig. 26). A small perforation (sternal foramen) is present in the midline of the sternum at approximately its widest point (near the level of the articulation for the fifth rib).

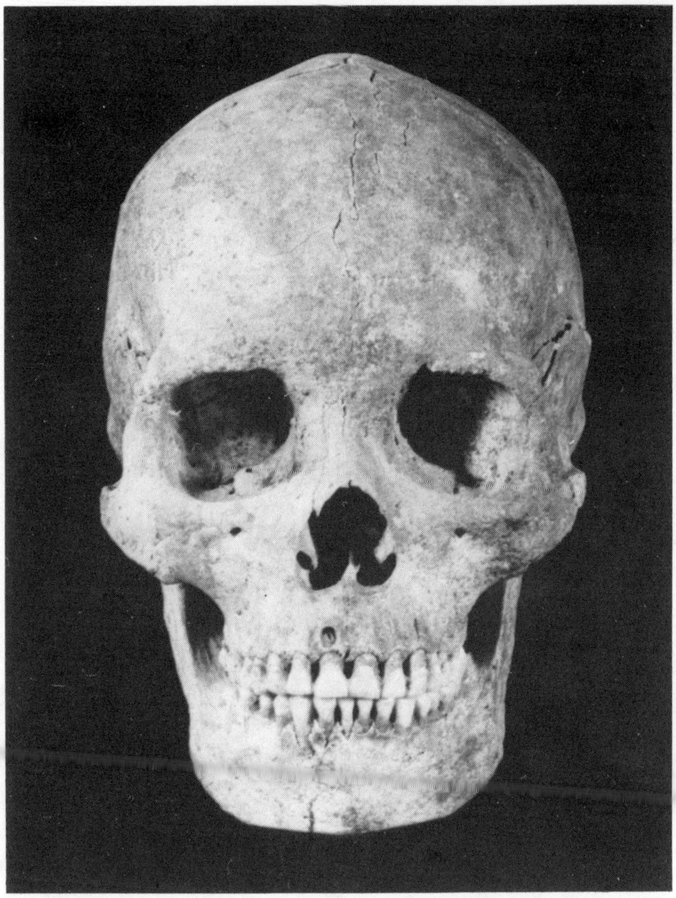

Fig. 25. Feature 1 skull (frontal view). Scale same as in Fig. 24.

One additional postcranial feature should be noted. Slight pitting is present on the dorsal face of both pubes, in the area commonly associated with parturition scars (Suchey et al. 1979). Thus, the individual in Feature 1 probably had borne one or more children.

Feature 3

Stratigraphic context. Feature 3 was a shallow oval pit containing a child burial (Figs. 7, 19, 27–29). It was located in Room E-4 at the intersection of Grids 526N566E, 526N567E, 525N566E, and 525N567E. The feature was initially recognized at the 101.05 m level (Floor 1), where its uncompacted brown fill contrasted sharply with the hard-packed gray floor surface. However, the shallowness of this feature relative to the other burials, the lack of any cap at the Floor 1 level, and the fact that the levels above Floor 1 have a virtually identical composition to the feature fill, suggest that the feature was probably intrusive from a higher level (perhaps the 101.25 m surface, Floor 2) but was not recognized in these upper levels. The pit was thus dug into underlying cultural fill, and had rough, unplastered walls.

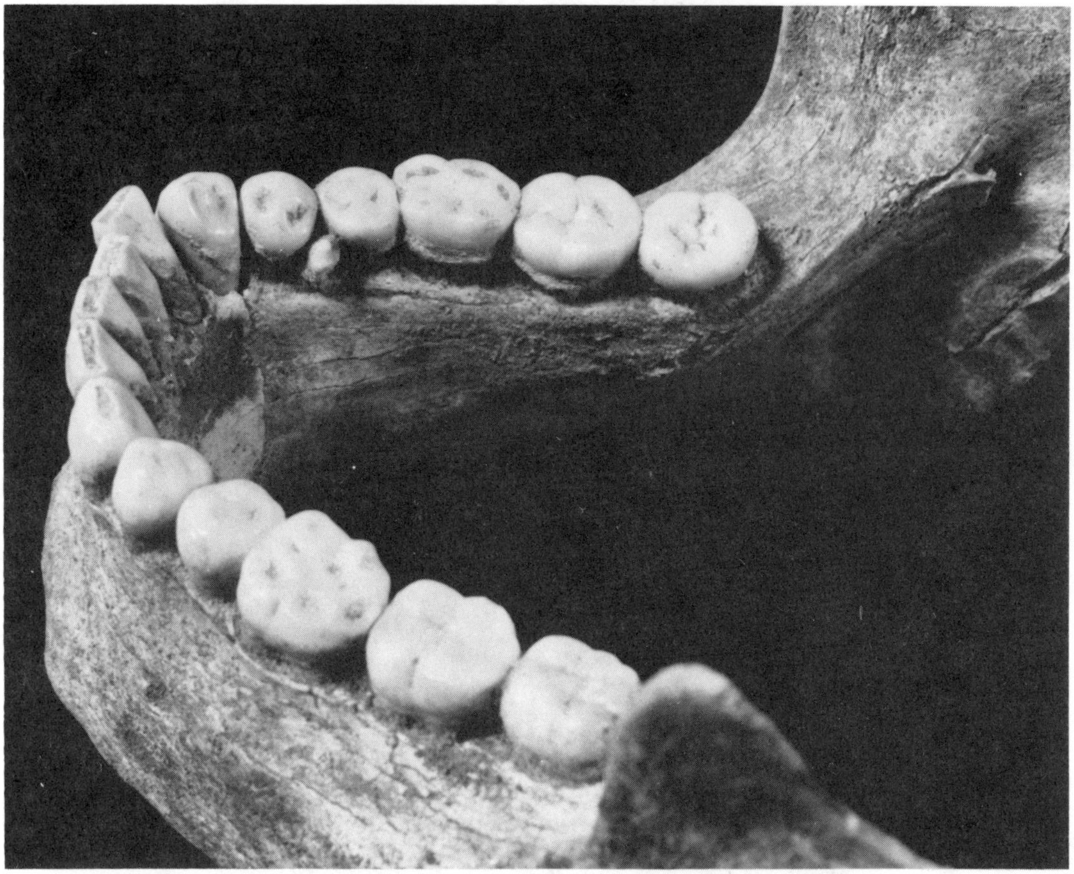

Fig. 26. Feature 1, supernumerary tooth, between RP_3 and RP_4.

At the level of Floor 1, Feature 3 was 79 cm long east-northeast to west-southwest by 48 cm wide. The pit sloped downward steeply to a broad rounded bottom upon which the burial rested at 100.78 m elevation. Thus, the portion of Feature 3 remaining below the level of Floor 1 was 28 cm deep and had a volume of about 77 liters.

A small cylindrical post hole (Feat. 7; 18 cm north-northeast to south-southwest by 16 cm west-northwest to east-southeast, volume 8 liters) was encountered in the northeastern portion of the bottom of Feature 3. Feature 7 contained the remains of a wooden post base (possibly *Populus*; see Appendix 16), which had apparently been broken during the aboriginal excavation of Feature 3. Thus, the post probably antedates the construction of Feature 3.

Both the texture of the Feature 3 fill and the distribution of the skeleton in the pit indicate that a limited amount of rodent disturbance occurred within the feature. A rodent tunnel was visible running into the southern portion of the feature. The distribution of displaced small bone elements (particularly bones of the left hand, the right twelfth rib, and the lumbar vertebral centra) indicates disturbance along the left (north) side of the skeleton from head to foot and disturbance of the lower abdominal region. Both regions of disturbance can be traced towards Feature 7, where bones and associated burial goods were recovered overlying the post fragment. Despite this evidence of disturbance, most of the skeleton is fully articulated and undisturbed.

Fig. 27. Feature 3 burial. Note prayer-stick on chest and nested ceramic vessels on abdomen.

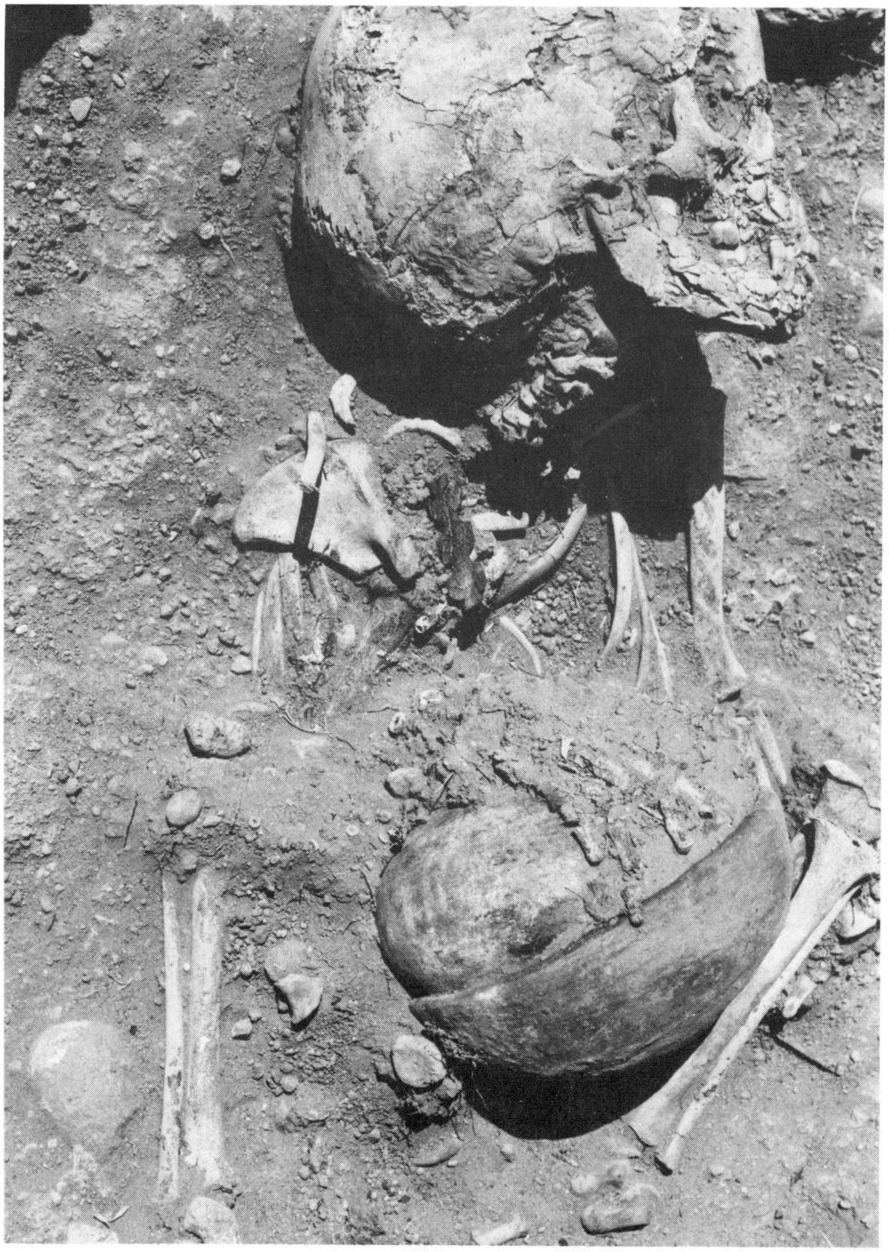

Fig. 28. Closeup of Feature 3 burial. Note prayer-stick on chest and nested ceramic vessels on abdomen.

The pit fill was a homogeneous uncompacted brown sand or silt loam, with occasional gravel of variable size and angularity. No stratification was observed within the pit. The fill contained charcoal and some non-human bone, sherds, and lithics.

Position and orientation. The burial lay in a horizontal position on its back with the long axis oriented west (skull) to east. The cranium with articulated mandible rested on its left side with the face pointing north and slightly above the horizontal. The articulated cervical column stretched down and east-southeast, angling to the east in the thoracic and lumbar region, and running roughly horizontally along the bottom of the pit. The right

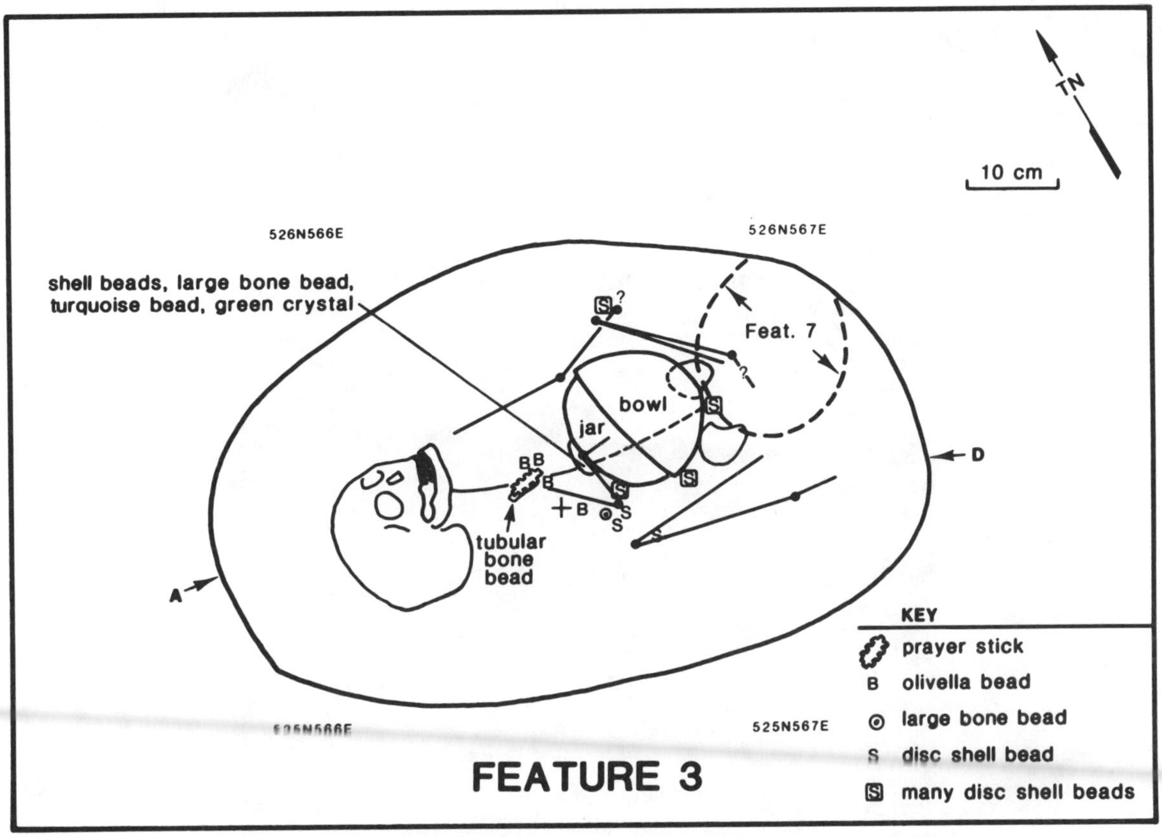

Fig. 29. Plan of Feature 3 burial.

scapula lay dorsal side up on top of the right ribs, and the right humerus extended from the glenoid fossa diverging 30 degrees relative to the long axis of the burial. The arm was flexed, with the radius and ulna running back north and steeply up, so that the distal ends lay over the vertebral column. The radius and ulna were crossed (pronated), so that the hand was oriented dorsal side up with the digits pointing east parallel to the long axis; the digits and metacarpals were spread on top of (and in direct contact with) the jar and bowl described below. The left humerus diverged from the long axis of the burial at an angle of 5 degrees; the elbow made an angle of 155 degrees. The humerus lay ventral side up; the radius and ulna were crossed (pronated) and angled up such that the distal ulna lay north (lateral) of the radius. Thus, the hand probably lay dorsal side up; however, it was disturbed and not recovered in situ.

The pelvis lay with the ilia spread flat below the jar and bowl, with the other pelvic bones in articulation. The right femur was tightly flexed so that it diverged 10 degrees relative to the long axis; the tibia and fibula were also tightly flexed, making an angle of about 15 degrees relative to the femur and diverging to the south (lateral) of the femur. The foot extended dorsal side up straight beyond the distal tibia. The left femur was flexed at 40 degrees relative to the long axis, overlying the left radius and ulna. The knee was tightly flexed, with the tibia and ulna lying directly on top of the femur. The foot was disturbed, but the position of the leg bones and the scatter of foot elements suggest that the foot was twisted medially with the toes pointing south.

Burial accompaniments. Feature 3 had a large number of items associated with it (see Fig. 29). Most prominent was a small Chupadero B/W jar nested inside a small Lincoln B/R bowl, resting on the lower abdomen and between the upper thighs of the burial (Nos. 6a-6b; Figs. 30–35 and Tables A10a-A10c).[6] Both vessels were on their sides, each with its mouth toward the skull. The right hand of the child rested on the surface of the jar, with the wrist more or less above the mouth. The design on the Lincoln B/R bowl is identical to one illustrated by Stewart (1983:53, his Fig. 3b) from the Sierra Blanca region west of Henderson. His specimen, also a bowl, differs only in being substantially larger (22.2 cm in diameter by 10.2 cm in height).

Fig. 30. Lincoln B/R bowl found with Feature 3 burial (top view).

[6]Henceforth in the description of burial accompaniments, each item will be followed, usually in parentheses, by the sequential item number assigned to the object in the field (e.g., No. 1), the number of the text figure that illustrates the item (e.g., Fig. 37a), and the number of the table that provides detailed descriptive data for the item (e.g., Table A10k). A small letter immediately following the text figure number refers to a specific item in a figure that illustrates multiple items. The "A" prefix in a table number indicates that the table is located in one of the appendices, the table number identifies which appendix, and the small letter following the table number identifies the specific table.

Fig. 31. Design of Lincoln B/R bowl found with Feature 3 burial. Scale (cm).

Fig. 32. Lincoln B/R bowl found with Feature 3 burial (side view).

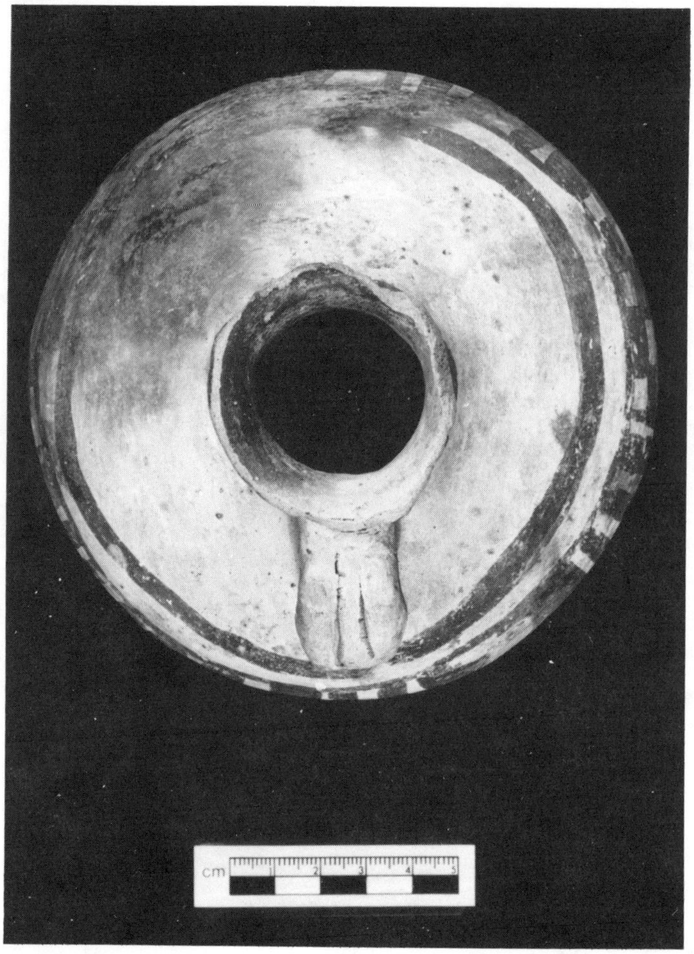

Fig. 33. Chupadero B/W jar found with Feature 3 burial (top view). Note prehistoric damage to rim.

Lying atop the right clavicle and upper chest of the Feature 3 burial was a small plaque or prayer-stick carved from a piece of wood, possibly *Populus* (No. 1; Figs. 27, 28, 36 and Table A10d). The stick was examined by Richard I. Ford of the Laboratory of Ethnobotany at the University of Michigan (see also Appendix 16). Mineralization of the porous structure of the wood, which was responsible for preserving the unusual item, to some extent hampered its identification. The original diameter of the piece of wood from which the plaque was carved was about 5–6 cm. The plaque is flat, and approximately 5.3 cm long by 1.7 cm wide (maximum) by 2.5 mm thick. The distinctive shape of the prayer-stick may represent a stylized corn plant or perhaps a bird feather. The proximal end of the plaque (i.e., the end farthest from the skull) is somewhat irregular and ragged, suggesting that prior to burial it had been broken, perhaps intentionally, from a larger item. The symbolic significance of the item remains unclear.

Several concentrations of beads and other artifacts occurred on the body; these included: (a) 1 tubular bone bead (No. 1; Fig. 37d and Table A10h) and 3, or more likely 4, *Olivella dama* shell beads (Nos. 1–4; Fig. 38a-d; Table A10f) near the prayer-stick, either attached to the stick or worn around the neck (or less likely displaced from the right wrist); (b) 2 large disc-shaped bone beads (Nos. 1–2; Fig. 37b-c and Table A10g), 86 small disc-shell beads (Table A10e), 1 turquoise bead (No. 3; Fig. 39c and Table A10i), and 1 small, bright apple green pebble of fluorite(?) (No. 3; Fig. 40c and Table A10j) around or near the

Fig. 34. Chupadero B/W jar found with Feature 3 burial (side view). Note prehistoric damage to rim.

Fig. 35. Design of Chupadero B/W jar found with Feature 3 burial. Dashed portion of design denotes area obscured by firing cloud. Scale (cm).

right wrist (the green pebble, still embedded in an unidentified grayish-white powdery substance, may have been displaced from the prayer-stick); and (c) a scatter of 58 small disc-shell beads (Table A10e), 2 small turquoise beads (Nos. 1–2; Fig. 39a-b and Table A10i), a miniature obsidian projectile point measuring only 0.81 cm long by 0.66 cm wide (No. 1;

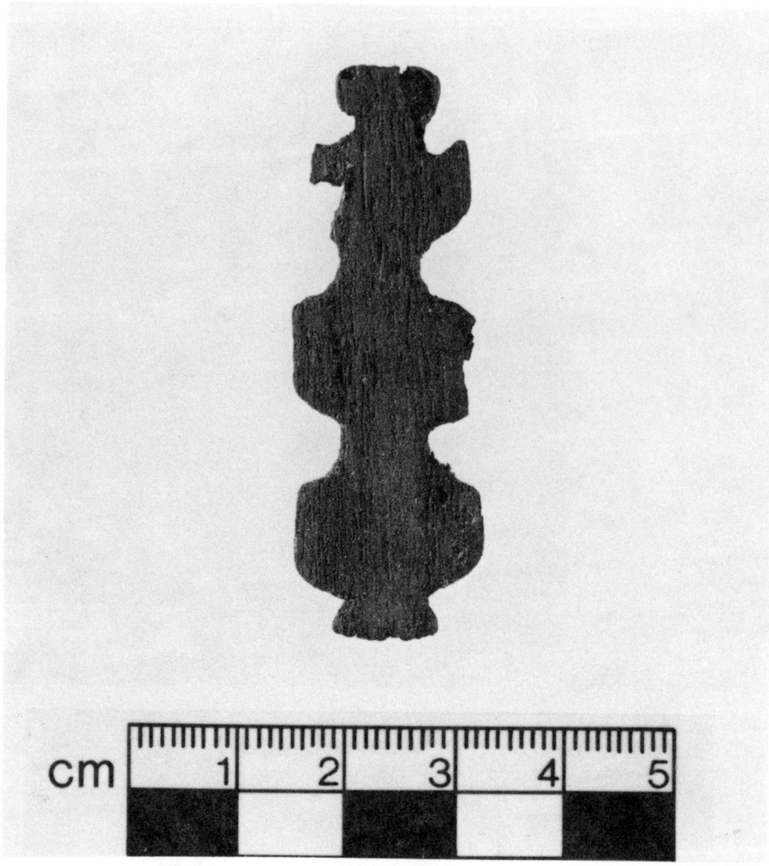

Fig. 36. Prayer-stick (*Populus*?) found with Feature 3 burial.

Fig. 37a and Tables A10k-A10l), a small brachiopod fossil[7] measuring only 0.70 cm in its longest dimension (No. 2; Fig. 40b and Table A10j), and a small clear quartz crystal (No. 1; Fig. 40a and Table A10j) in the Feature 7 post hole (presumably these were originally associated with the left hand or wrist, and were displaced by rodent activity, along with bones of the left hand, wrist, and foot, into the post hole).

Several items were found in the fill within the Chupadero B/W jar. These included 2 moderately large *Olivella* beads tentatively identified as *O. dama* (Nos. 5–6; Fig. 38e-f and Table A10f), each with a single lateral perforation through the shell midway along its longitudinal axis; 2 hollow tubular bone beads (Nos. 2–3; Fig. 37e-f and Table A10h), also with lateral perforations midway along their longitudinal axes, as well as single, deep indentations at both ends of each tube on the face opposite the perforation, and a peculiar small wooden insert or plug (species?) still in place inside one of the tubes (No. 3) directly below the perforation; 2 tiny, unperforated, ovoid turquoise discs (Nos. 4–5; Fig. 39d-e and Table A10i); a small, unworked purple fluorite crystal (No. 4; Fig. 40d and Table A10j); and a single, small, unfused ossification centrum of probable human origin. The turquoise discs had traces of dark black (water-soluble) stains around their perimeter which may have been the remains of mastic. If so, they originally may have been inserts in the

---

[7]We are grateful to Sandy Carlson of the Museum of Paleontology at the University of Michigan for identifying the brachiopod. According to Carlson, the fossil is *Wellerella* cf. *delicatula* (Dunbar & Conrad, 1932), a Lower Permian form known from the Southwestern U.S., Texas, and the mid-continent region.

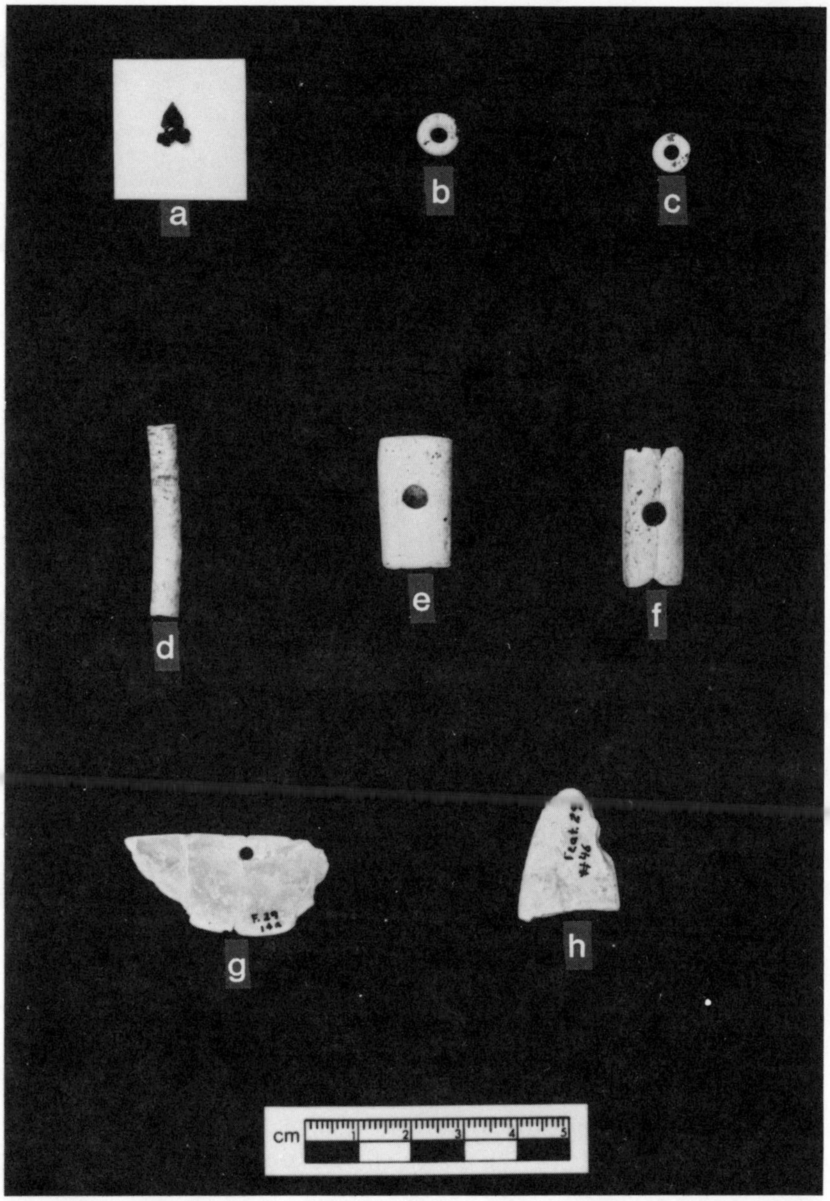

Fig. 37. Miscellaneous artifacts found with Feature 3 and Feature 29 burials. a, Feature 3 (No. 1, miniature obsidian projectile point); b-c, Feature 3 (Nos. 1-2, disc-shaped bone beads); d-f, Feature 3 (Nos. 1–3, tubular bone beads); g-h, Feature 29 (Nos. 14a and 46, mussel shell ornaments). Note that numbers in parentheses in this and subsequent figures are sequential identification numbers assigned to items in the field (see footnote 6).

lateral perforations in the *Olivella* shells or in the tubular bone beads (insertion in the shells is more likely based on the sizes of the discs and the perforations). Their original placement cannot be determined definitively, however, as no traces of mastic were found in any of the perforations. All of these items may have been placed in the jar at the time of burial, but it is more probable that they had slumped or were displaced by rodent activity from the right hand or wrist subsequent to burial.

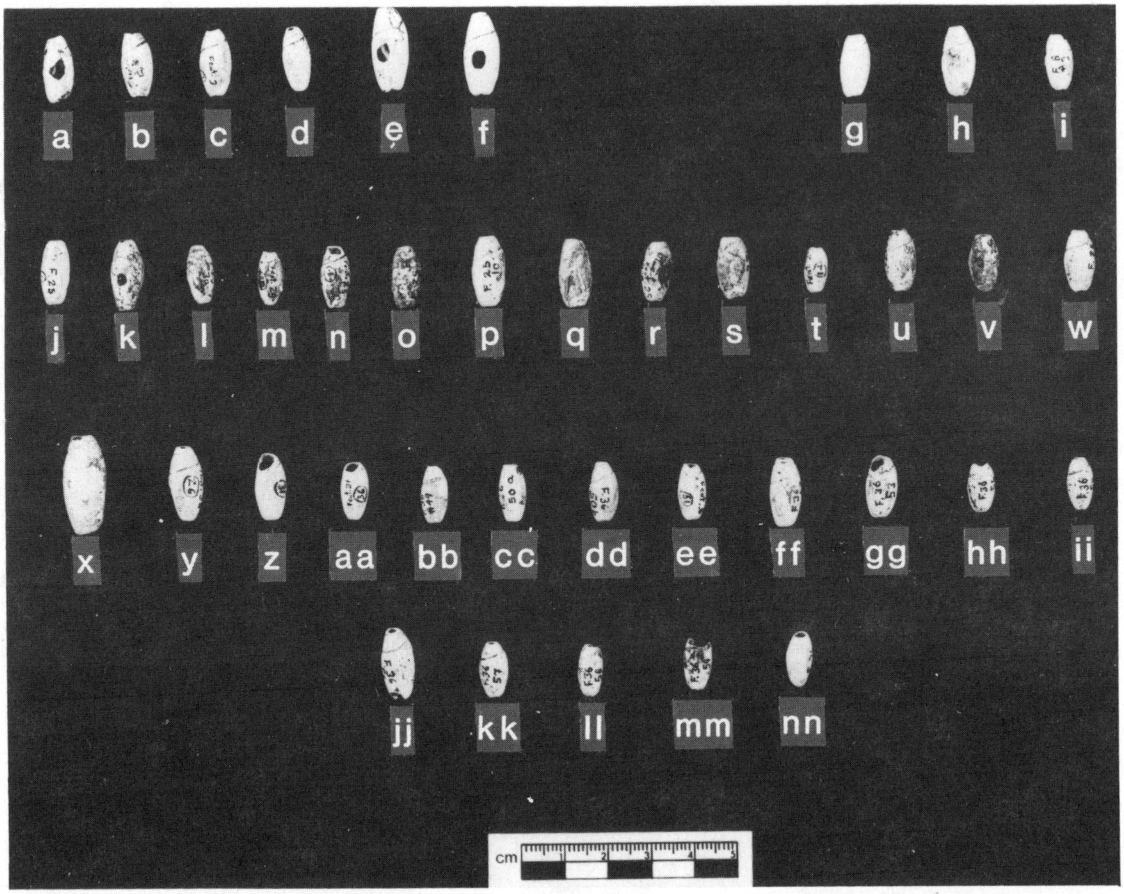

Fig. 38. *Olivella* and *Agaronia* shell beads found with Feature 3, 8, 25, and 36 burials. a-f, Feature 3 (Nos. 1–6); g-i, Feature 8 (Nos. 1–3); j-w, Feature 25 (Nos. 1–2, 3a-3b, 4–5, 10–11, 12a-12b, 14–16, 18); x-nn, Feature 36 (Nos. 1, 26, 31, 36, 49, 50a-50b, 51–60).

The *Olivella* shells from Feature 3 were identified by James H. McLean of the Los Angeles County Museum of Natural History. Based on the relatively large size of the Henderson specimens, McLean believes that they, as well as the other marine shells from the site, derive from sources in the Gulf of California rather than from the Texas coast.

In summary, a single(?) strand of disc-shell beads, with two turquoise beads (and perhaps also the point, brachiopod, and quartz crystal), probably encircled the left wrist; a similar strand of disc-shell beads, with 1 turquoise bead and 2 large disc-shaped bone beads (and perhaps also 2 or 3 *Olivella* beads, 2 tubular bone beads, and 1 or 2 fluorite crystals), encircled the right wrist; and 3 or 4 *Olivella* beads, a tubular bone bead, and perhaps a small green fluorite pebble had been attached to the prayer-stick or perhaps worn around the neck.

Finally, badly decayed traces of fibrous material, identified by Richard I. Ford as warp and weft remnants of twined grass matting (see Appendix 16), were found near the vertebrae, pelvis, and feet. These probably represent some sort of covering that surrounded all or part of the burial but was not preserved. Cordage fragments (z-twist, 2-strand) of unidentifiable vegetal fiber from the same regions of the body may have been part of the matting or may have helped to bind the matting around the burial.

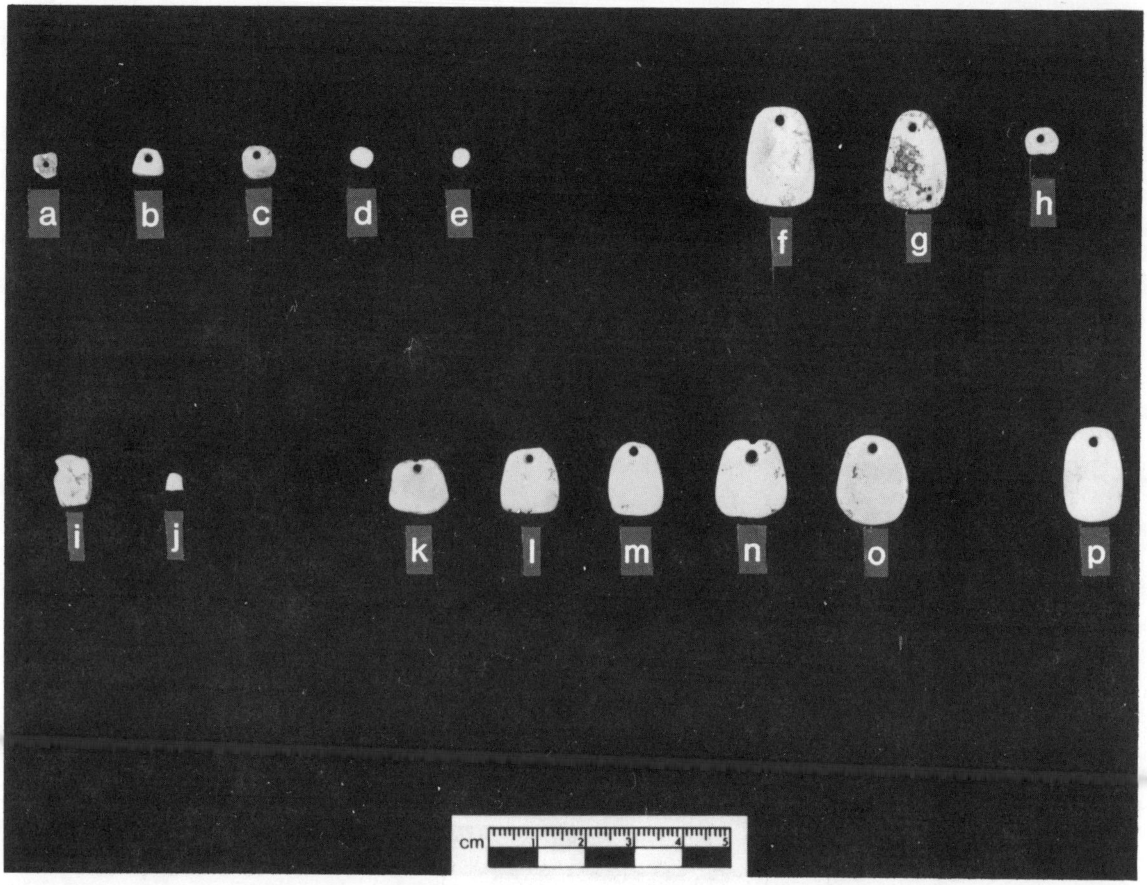

Fig. 39. Turquoise found with Feature 3, 8, 25, 36, and 40 burials. a-e, Feature 3 (Nos. 1–3, beads or pendants; Nos. 4–5, possible inserts); f-h, Feature 8 (Nos. 1–2, earrings; No. 3, bead); i-j, Feature 25 (Nos. 7a-7b, attachments to proximal end of prayerstick); k-o, Feature 36 (Nos. 1–5, pendants); p, Feature 40 (No. 1, pendant).

Skeletal inventory and condition. Aside from the disturbance mentioned in the discussion above, the Feature 3 skeleton was articulated. The material recovered includes all of the long bones with most of their epiphyses, the cranium and mandible, both scapulae, both clavicles, most of each of the ribs, all of the bones of the innominates and much of the sacrum, most of the vertebral column (with the exception of several lumbar centra and one lumbar neural arch), three of the carpals, all of the metacarpals and all but two of the hand phalanges, six of the tarsals, seven of the metatarsals and eleven of the foot phalanges, several probable sternal ossification centra, and several unidentified ossification centra and miscellaneous bone fragments.

The condition of most of the skeleton was moderately good, but several elements were in bad condition.

The skull, being the highest part of the skeleton in the pit, suffered the most deterioration. The right maxilla and mandible are severely fragmented, while much of the rest of the skull, particularly the right side, is cracked and crushed. The face is twisted to the right (clockwise) when seen in superior view (i.e., the left half of the face projects more than the right half) and backwards (inwards) relative to the remainder of the cranium.

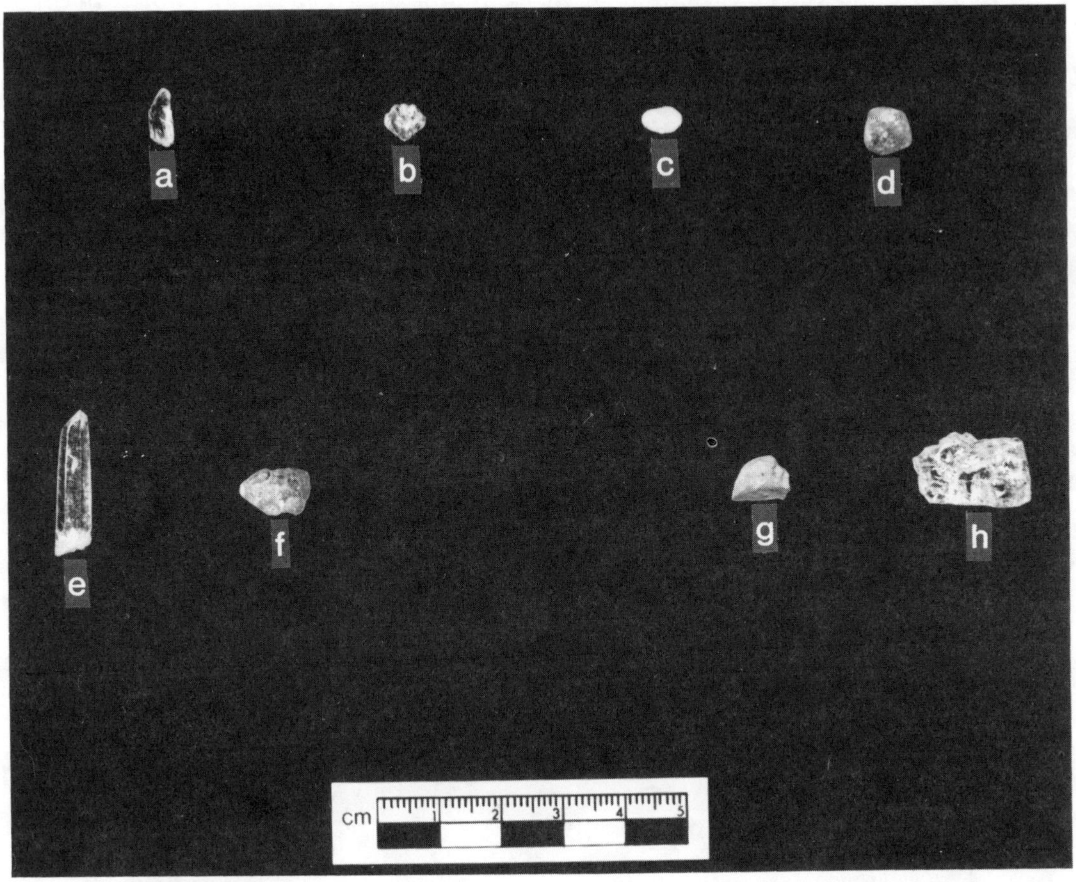

Fig. 40. Minerals and fossil found with Feature 3, 25, and 29 burials. a-d, Feature 3 (No. 1, quartz crystal; No. 2, brachiopod fossil; No. 3, apple green fluorite pebble; No. 4, purple fluorite pebble); e-f, Feature 25 (No. 6, quartz crystal; No. 8, purple fluorite pebble); g-h, Feature 29 (No. 51b, red ocher fragment; No. 61, quartz crystal fragment).

Several of the teeth were displaced from the maxilla and mandible during excavation due to this fragmented condition, and several permanent tooth crowns were exposed by the destruction of the external bone surface of the jaws.

The left femur mid-shaft disintegrated when an attempt was made to remove it in the field.

The sacrum was crushed under the bowl and jar (see above) and the segments are somewhat mixed.

Sex. Sex was not determined for this individual because of its young age.

Age. The skeleton is clearly that of a child, with all ephiphyses unfused and incompletely formed. The metopic suture is closed and obliterated. The deciduous canine roots are all either not easily observable or damaged, but appear to display unclosed apices. Slight dental attrition (Appendix 2) indicates that the deciduous dentition has received some wear. Enough of the outer bone table is broken to show that at least all of the anterior maxillary dentition through M^1 has begun to calcify. Root formation has not begun on any of the permanent maxillary teeth, though the crowns of the I^1s look two-thirds or more complete. Observation of most of the unerupted mandibular permanent teeth is impossible.

Thus, on the basis of the visible tooth eruption, the skeleton is estimated to be that of an individual about 2.5 to 3.5 years old.

General description, cultural and pathological alterations. No gross abnormalities are evident on the skeleton. A single extra-sutural bone about 3 cm high and 4 cm wide is located at lambda. The post-mortem crushing of the cranium rather severely modifies its contours (see Figs. 41, 42). Frontal and parietal bossing are prominent. A flattened area about 4.5 cm high by 3.0 cm wide is present immediately above lambda, making an angle of 55 degrees relative to the Frankfort Horizontal Plane; whether this represents culturally induced lambdoidal deformation or post-mortem deformation is unclear. This area is angled left relative to the midline (i.e., the left side of the occipital is flattened more than the right side). Below this flattening, the occipital extends prominently posteriorly.

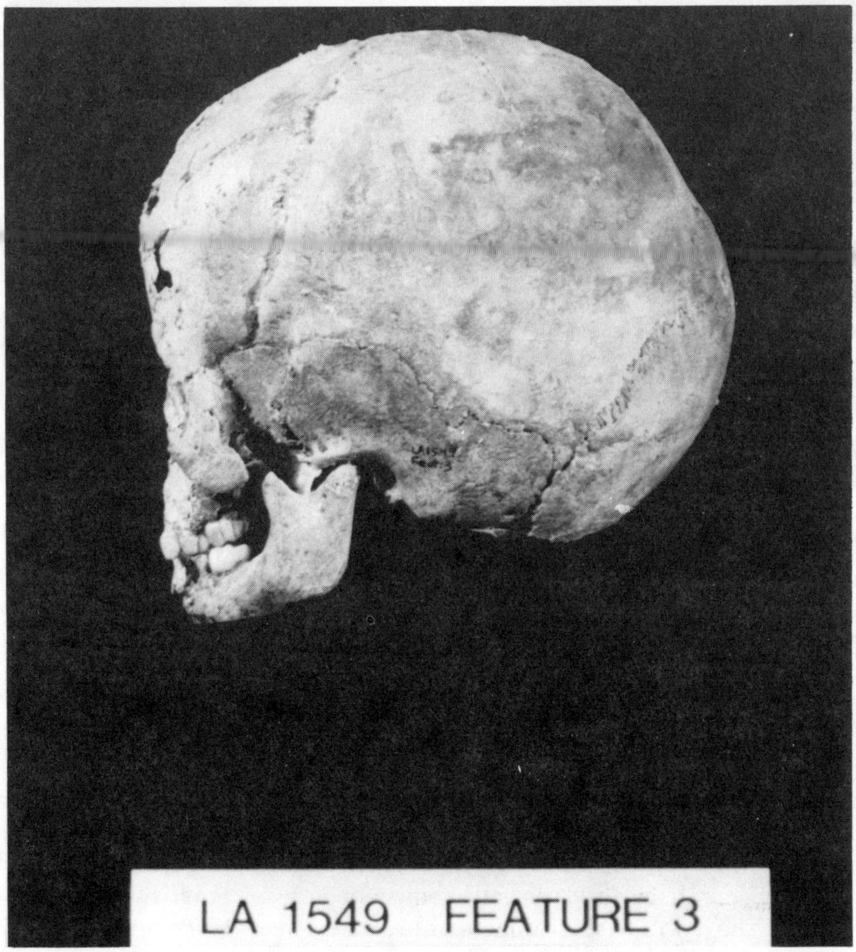

Fig. 41. Feature 3 skull (left lateral view). Scale same as in Fig. 24.

One small possible carious lesion is present on the labial aspect of the left maxillary canine. Appendix 2 summarizes the limited degree of dental attrition.

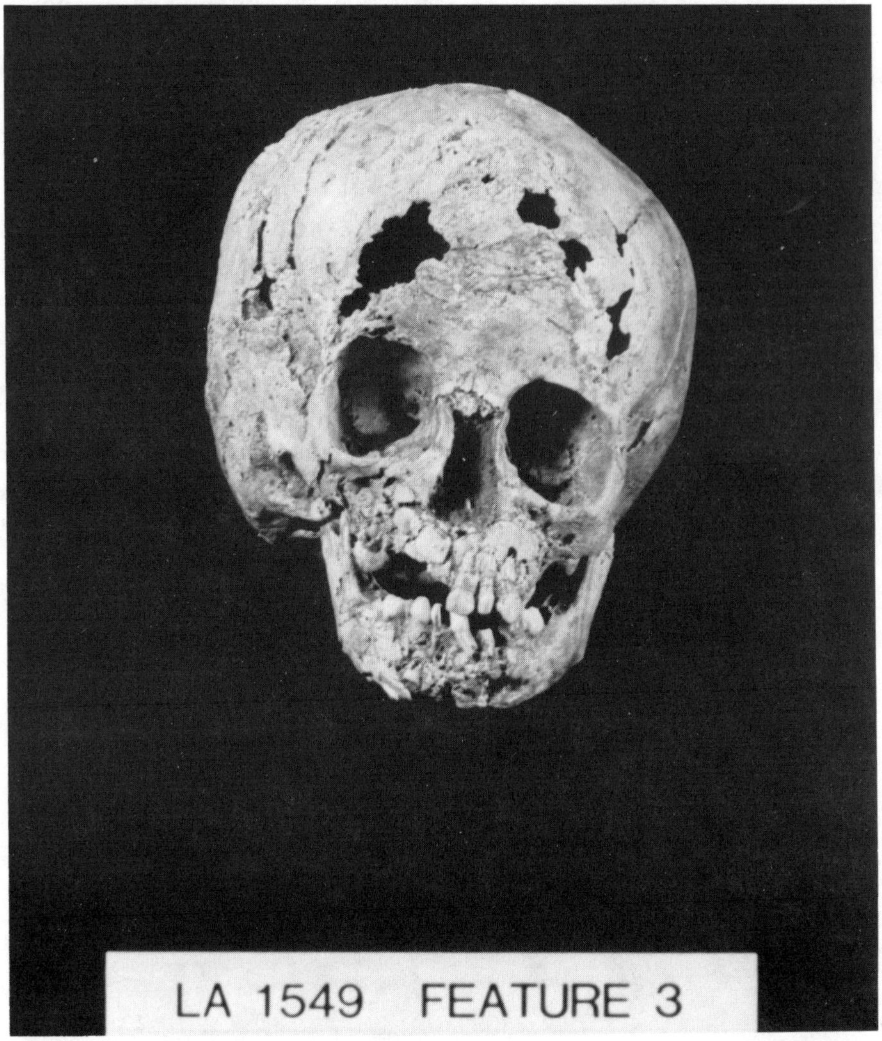

Fig. 42. Feature 3 skull (frontal view). Scale same as in Fig. 24.

A slight degree of shoveling is present on the dI^1s.

Feature 8

Stratigraphic context. Feature 8 was an irregular, rounded pit containing an adult female burial (Figs. 7, 19, 43, 44). It was located in Room E-4 in Grid 525N566E. The Feature 8 pit was sealed below the lowest of the three replasterings of Floor 1 in Square 525N566E, north of (and directly adjacent to) the east-to-west trending wall in that square. Only the two lowest replasterings, one at ca. 100.98 m elevation and one 2 cm deeper, extended over the feature. These plaster layers had slumped in the center of the feature, and had pulled away from the west edge of the pit. The highest replastering noted in the surrounding area at 101.06 m elevation (Floor 1, top replastering) was not present over Feature 8, but was replaced instead by a slightly elevated patch of blocky orange adobe fill.

Fig. 43. Feature 8 burial. Note *Glycymeris* shell bracelets at each elbow and tubular shell beads on left upper arm.

The pit was approximately 67 cm in diameter at the level of Floor 1. The southern edge of the feature abutted the wall but did not cut into it. Overall, the pit was straight sided, though a small undercut area was present in the east end of the pit in the area of the feet and pelvis. The feature edges were rough and uneven and were not prepared or plastered. The maximum pit depth was 61 cm and the bottom was relatively flat and bowl shaped. Total pit volume was about 230 liters.

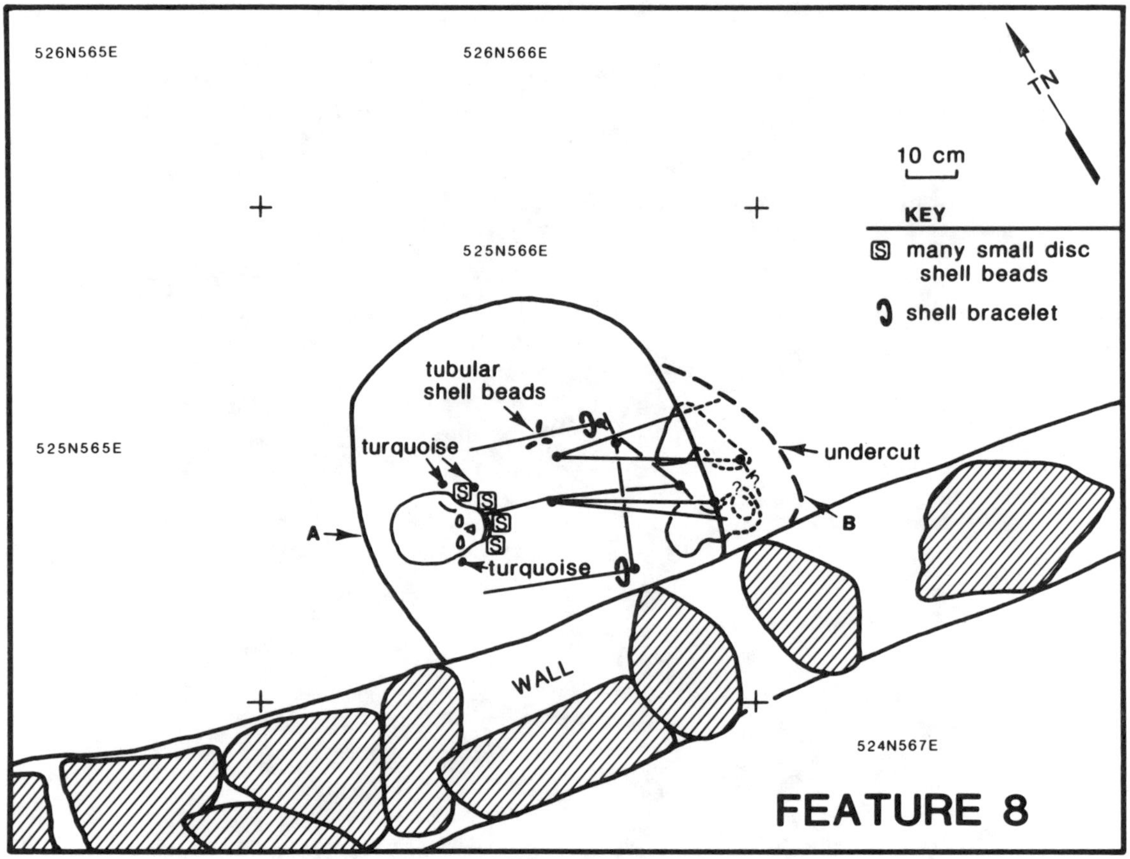

Fig. 44. Plan of Feature 8 burial.

Below the Floor 1 seals, the pit fill was uncompacted, gravelly and brown in color, with no internal stratification. Charcoal, non-human bone, and cultural material was present in the fill. One isolated human hand phalanx, from an individual much younger than the burial in Feature 8, was also present (see Appendix 9).

Position and orientation. The burial lay in a horizontal position on its back, with the long axis oriented west-northwest (skull) to east-southeast. The back of the cranium rested against the west end of the pit so that it was propped up around 45 degrees relative to horizontal. The mandible was articulated with the cranium. The remainder of the axial skeleton lay on the bottom of the pit. The humeri lay nearly parallel with the long axis, diverging slightly (5 to 10 degrees) away from it distally. The arms were flexed inwards so that the left hand lay over the left lower abdomen; the left elbow made an angle of around 135 and the right elbow around 90 degrees. Both hands lay with the palmar surfaces facing downwards.

The bones of the legs lay tightly flexed on top of the axial skeleton and on top of the arm bones. The original degree of flexure could not be determined with certainty since all of the bones simply lay directly on top of each other. The right tibia had fallen over onto its medial surface. The femora converged towards the west-northwest (distal ends), making angles of around 15 and 10 degrees (left and right respectively) relative to the long axis of the skeleton. The lower legs were parallel to each other and made an angle of around 10 degrees with respect to (south of) the long axis. The bones of the feet had all slumped post-mortem. The position in which the bones were found suggests that the feet were close together, with the toes elevated and leaning medially far enough so that they crossed.

Burial accompaniments. Feature 8 was the most abundantly furnished of the female burials recovered. Two matching shell bracelets were present around the lower arms (distal humeri) of the burial, one on each arm (Nos. 1–2; Figs. 45–50 and Table A11d). Both shells were identified by James H. McLean of the Los Angeles County Museum of Natural History as *Glycymeris gigantea* (Reeve, 1843). According to McLean, both derive from sources in the Gulf of California; no species of this genus in the Gulf of Mexico approaches the size of the Henderson specimens. The specimen on the left arm had been broken in two prior to burial and had been repaired, as indicated by biconical holes drilled adjacent to the breaks (a total of 4 holes, 1 on each side of the 2 breaks). The broken specimen originally may have been painted with oblique, parallel stripes or bands on the exterior surface of the shell opposite the hinge area. The color(s) of these stripes can no longer be determined. It is also possible, though less likely, that the parallel bands are the stain left behind by a binding or wrapping which has since decayed.

The left arm also had a string of 3 tubular shell beads around it, higher up (more proximal) on the humerus (Nos. 1–3; Fig. 51 and Table A11c). Two of the beads (Nos. 1–2; Fig. 51a-b) are relatively thin-walled and have been identified tentatively by McLean as uncoiled tips of the vermetid gastropod *Tripsycha tripsycha* (Pilsbry & Lowe, 1932). The third tubular bead (No. 3; Fig. 51c) is much thicker than the others and has a lamellar internal structure. These features, according to McLean, suggest that the specimen probably was carved from a very large bivalve. Unfortunately, the species could not be determined, and hence the source of the shell is unknown. This bead has been decorated by incising two parallel grooves around the perimeter at each end.

Two matching turquoise ornaments (Nos. 1–2; Fig. 39f-g and Table A11e), probably earrings, were recovered adjacent to the skull, just below the level of the gonial region of the mandible, one on each side. A total of 3570 small disc-shell beads, representing 5 or more likely 6 strands, encircled the neck (Table A11a). The necklace also contained a single small, irregular turquoise bead (No. 3; Fig. 39h and Table A11e) and 3 *Olivella dama* (Wood, 1828) beads (Nos. 1–3; Fig. 38g-i and Table A11b). These shell beads, like the others, were identified by James H. McLean. Finally, impressions of coiled basketry were found in the sediment matrix at several locations on the upper torso between the knees and the skull (Fig. 52). While the coil diameters vary somewhat (see Appendix 16), it is likely that only one basket is involved. This item originally was placed directly on the chest of the burial. In addition, traces of very poorly preserved plaited yucca basketry or matting were recovered from the back of the cranium (Fig. 53; see also Appendix 16). This may have been restricted to the area of the head, but traces of decayed fibrous material elsewhere on the skeleton raise the possibility that the entire body originally may have been wrapped in plaited matting.

Skeletal inventory and condition. Aside from the few cases of slumping noted in the previous section, the Feature 8 skeleton was articulated and extremely well preserved. Almost the entire skeleton was recovered: all long bones, the cranium and mandible, nearly complete scapulae, both clavicles, both patellae, all ribs, complete pelvis and sacrum, complete vertebral column (including four coccygeal vertebrae), sternum with xiphoid process and manubrium, hyoid, all carpals except the left pisiform, all metacarpals, all phalanges (hand and foot), all tarsals, all metatarsals, and several sesamoids and unidentified fragments.

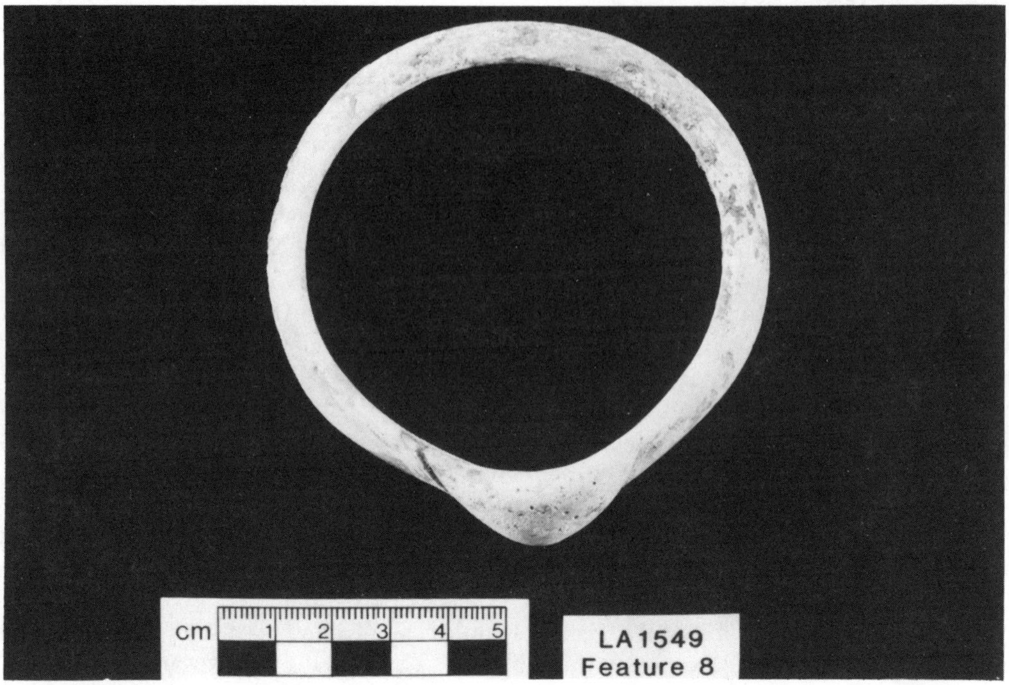

Fig. 45. Complete *Glycymeris* shell bracelet (No. 1) found with Feature 8 burial (top view).

Fig. 46. Complete *Glycymeris* shell bracelet (No. 1) found with Feature 8 burial (bottom view).

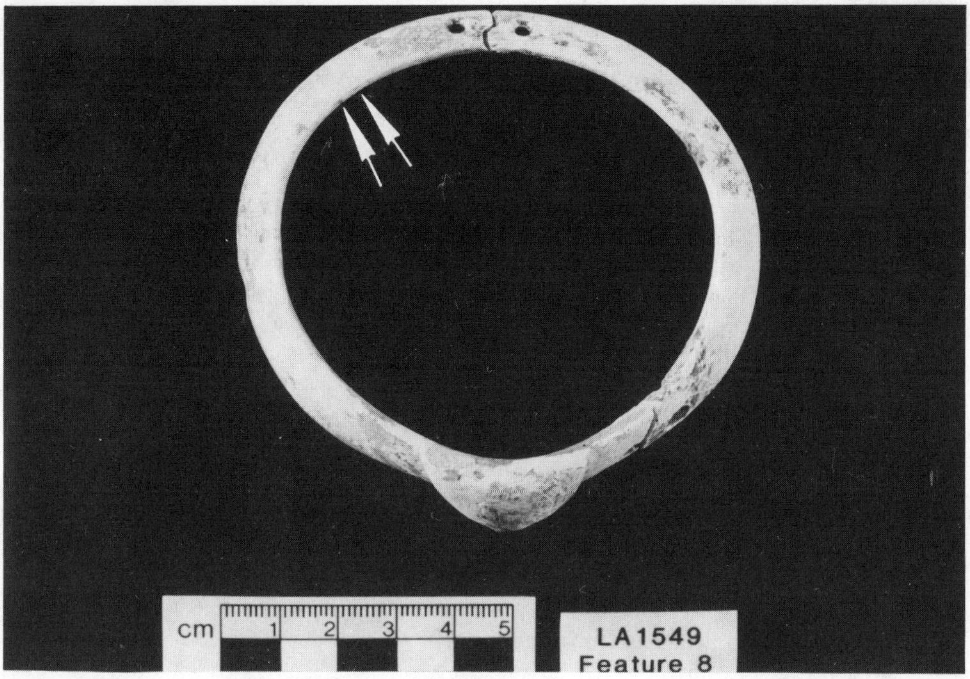

Fig. 47. Broken *Glycymeris* shell bracelet (No. 2) found with Feature 8 burial (top view). Note paired repair holes adjacent to breaks. Arrows denote location of oblique painted bands or stains from former wrapping.

Fig. 48. Broken *Glycymeris* shell bracelet (No. 2) found with Feature 8 burial (bottom view).

Fig. 49. Complete *Glycymeris* shell bracelet (No. 1) found with Feature 8 burial (profile view of hinge area).

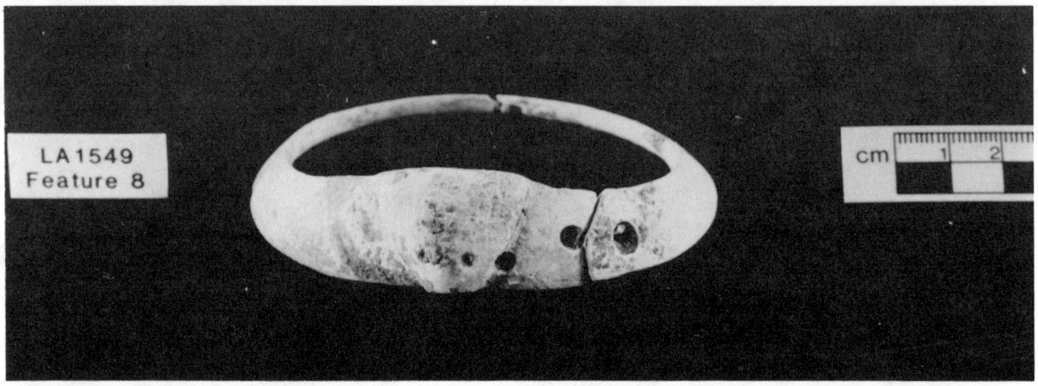

Fig. 50. Broken *Glycymeris* shell bracelet (No. 2) found with Feature 8 burial (profile view of hinge area).

The condition of the skeleton was excellent. Though the bones were fragile and of light weight (presumably due to post-mortem deterioration), only the scapulae and sternum suffered serious breakage.

The cranium exhibits some cracking; the sagittal and coronal sutures cracked open around bregma, the upper portion of the frontal cracked along the sagittal plane, and several smaller cracks occurred on the parietal and frontal. The distal right nasal and a small part of the left zygomatic process were broken off and not recovered. In general, however, this damage does not appear to reflect major post-mortem deformation, but rather cracks due to drying of the bone.

Sex. The innominates clearly reveal that the individual was female. Though erosion of the ventral aspect of the pubis obscures the form of the ischio-pubic ramus and the site of the ventral arc, the sub-pubic angle and the greater sciatic notch are broad, and a slight pre-auricular sulcus is present. The innominates overall are markedly gracile.

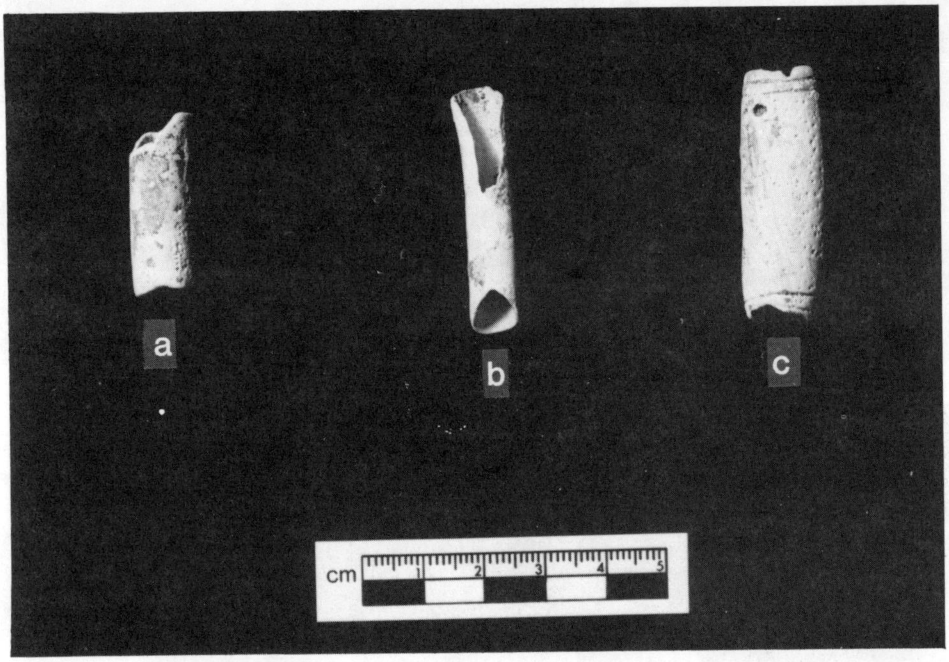

Fig. 51. Tubular shell beads found with Feature 8 burial. a-b, *Tripsycha tripsycha* (Nos. 1–2, made from uncoiled tips of vermetid gastropod); c, unidentified bivalve (No. 3, carved from extremely thick valve).

Fig. 52. Impression of coiled basketry found on chest (between skull and right knee) of Feature 8 burial (see Appendix 16, Table A16a, No. 16 for details).

Fig. 53. Fragment of plaited yucca basketry or matting found behind skull of Feature 8 burial (see Appendix 16, Table A16a, No. 24 for details).

The cranium is consistent with the identification of this individual as female. The mastoids and foramen magnum are small, the superior orbital borders are sharp, the malars are gracile, frontal and parietal bossing is evident, and all muscle marking is poorly developed. The gracile nature of the remainder of the skeleton agrees with this identification.

Age. Gilbert and McKern's (1973) symphyseal aging method yields a score of 0 (right) to 1 (left), indicating an age of 16.00 ± 2.82 to 19.80 ± 2.76 years. The fusion stages of the postcranial skeleton (see Appendix 1) indicate ages of ca. 17.5–20.5 or ca. 20 years (Krogman 1973:Tables 5 and 6 respectively). The sternum is in stage 2 (19–20? years) following Stewart's (1954) classification. Complete closure but incomplete obliteration of the spheno-occipital synchondrosis suggests an age of around 20 years. Observation of endocranial suture development is limited on the complete cranium. No endocranial suture obliteration is visible except in the posterior third of the sagittal suture. The lambdoidal suture is not obliterated along its length as far as it is observable (a surface incrustation obscures it along part of its length in one side of the skull), though it is not wide open. The anterior third of the sagittal and most of the coronal suture are wide open. An age in the late teens or early 20s could be supported by these data.

Dental eruption stage is inconclusive but suggests an age in the late teens or early 20s. RM_3 is fully erupted but not visibly worn; the crowns of the other three third molars are erupted only slightly beyond the level of the alveolus. A crack in the mandible's internal surface reveals that the apex of the RM_3 distal root is unclosed. As indicated in Appendix 2, the Feature 8 permanent dentition is the least worn of all of the burials. In particular, it is worn less than Feature 40 whose postcranial skeleton suggests a similar age (ca. 20 years or slightly younger). Thus, Feature 8 is unlikely to be much over 20 years old and is most probably slightly younger.

No evidence of arthritis is visible anywhere on the skeleton. The total evidence supports an age estimate around 17 to 20 years.

General description, cultural and pathological alterations. The cranium of Feature 8 is gracile and exhibits prominent parietal and frontal bossing (see Figs. 54, 55). The frontal is slightly retreating. Glabella and superciliary arches are not prominent.

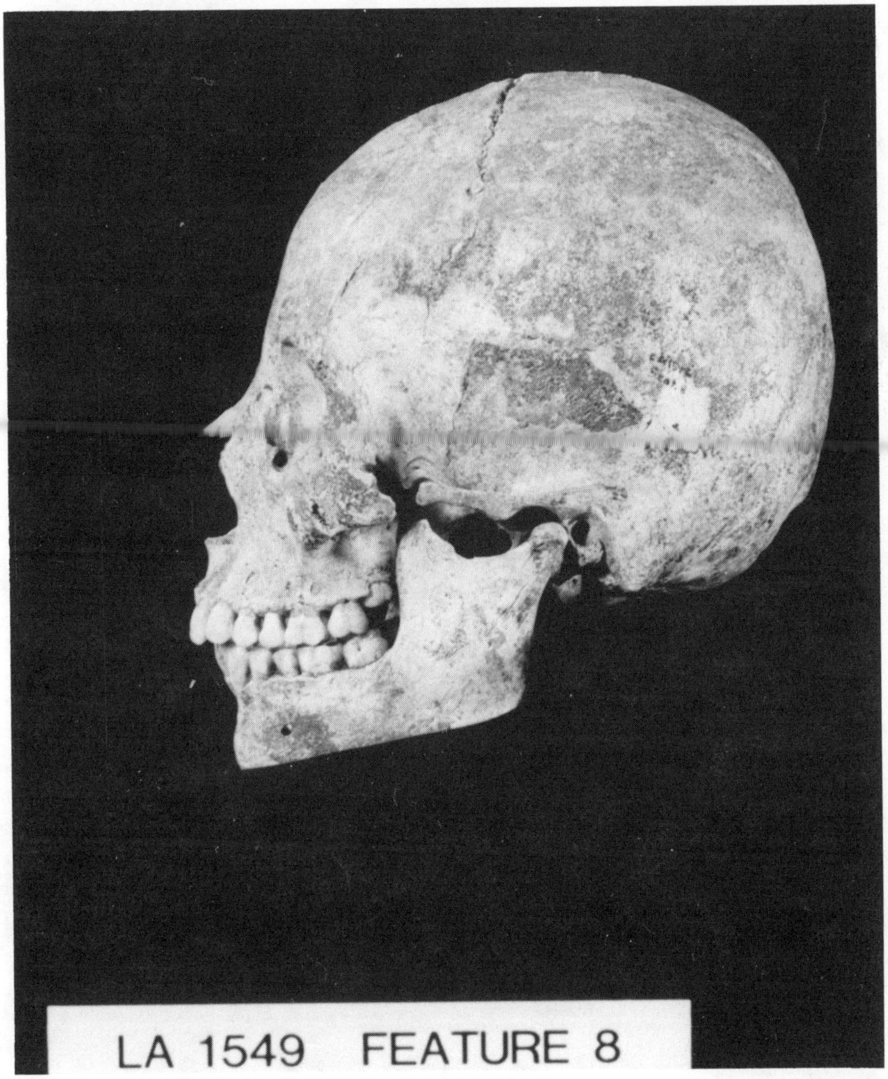

Fig. 54. Feature 8 skull (left lateral view). Scale same as in Fig. 24. Extreme linearity of lower mandible border result of specimen settling in photo cloth.

The cranium is very high, short, and wide (cranial index 87.1, length-height index 87.1, breadth-height index 100.0), but its form is influenced by the deformation described below. The cranium shows occipital deformation of 95 degrees relative to the Frankfort

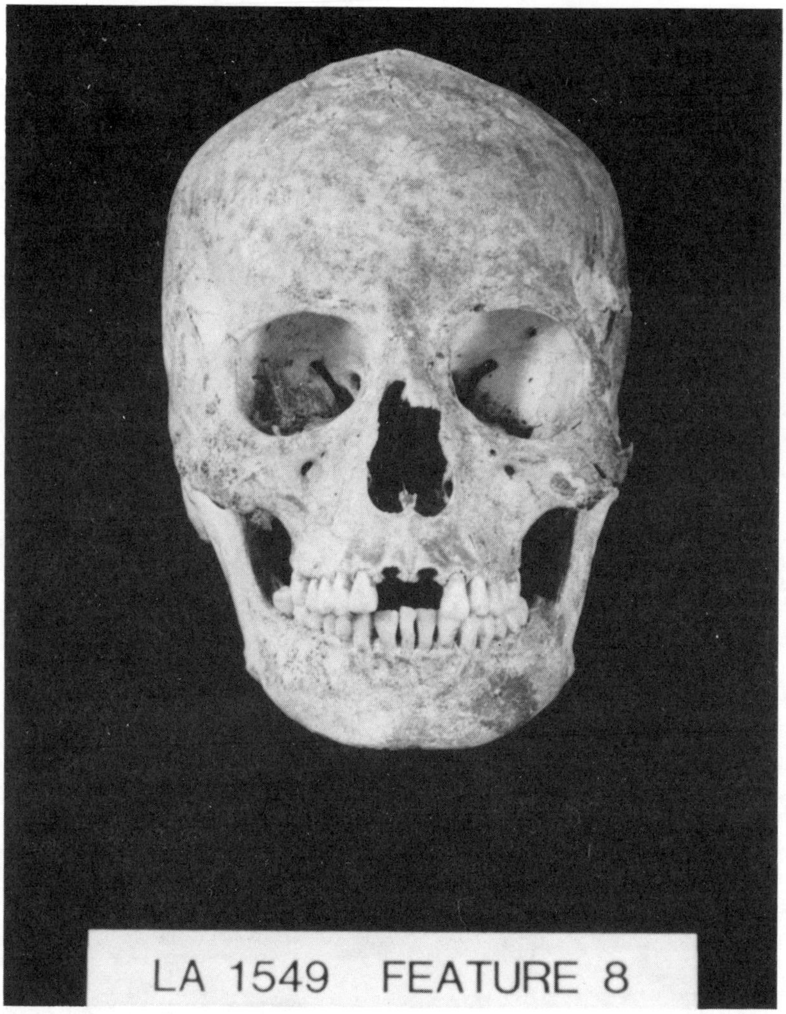

Fig. 55. Feature 8 skull (frontal view). Scale same as in Fig. 24.

Horizontal Plane. This deformation is visible as a symmetrical general flattening of the squamous portion of the occiput, though a truly flat area is absent (the contour remains rounded). This deformation affects the overall form of a significant portion of the cranium and represents moderate culturally induced vertical occipital deformation. In the vicinity of lambda on the posterior parietals and the superior occipital, an area approximately 5.0 cm long by 5.5 cm wide exhibits a more pronounced flatness, at an angle of 60 degrees relative to the Frankfort Horizontal Plane. This latter flattening is a localized effect which may also represent a cultural modification of the cranial form (slight lambdoidal deformation); alternatively, the lambdoidal flattening may be a secondary consequence of the occipital deformation.

Muscle markings are not pronounced anywhere on the cranium or on the mandible. The mandible exhibits a prominent mental protuberance. The gonial angles are slightly everted.

The slight degree of dental attrition is indicated in Appendix 2. All teeth were present at the time of death. Little or no alveolar resorption is visible, and no calculus deposits are present. Caries are present on both M_2s in deep buccal grooves. RM_3 is rotated 90 degrees counterclockwise.

Observation of the I^1 roots was possible because these teeth were lost post-mortem. The teeth have extremely short roots; RI^1 is roughly 5 mm long from apex to the cervical line in the labial aspect, and LI^1 is similar (the LI^1's root is broken and cannot be readily measured). The corresponding incisor sockets are of similar short length, and their internal surfaces are unusually porous (Fig. 56).

Dr. Nathaniel H. Rowe, Jr. examined the incisors visually and radiographically, and states that the form of the roots and sockets indicate a developmental anomaly rather than a traumatic injury or secondary resorption (personal communication). However, no specific cause for the condition could be determined.

Three additional abnormalities or pathologies are present. On the medial posterior portion of both parietals are small areas of pitting possibly characteristic of porotic hyperostosis (Fig. 57). However, these pits are few in number, so that if porotic hyperostosis is in fact responsible for them, it is a very mild case. There may also be some secondary deposition of compact bone over the pits.

The two other pathologies involve abnormalities of bone fusion. On the left foot the two distal phalanges of the fifth digit are fused (Fig. 58). In the vertebral column, the first sacral section remains unfused to the remainder of the sacrum (Fig. 59). The section is fully lumbar vertebra-like in form, with not only well-formed inferior articular facets, but with small transverse processes and no costal elements. Though the second, third, and fourth sacral sections show indications of recent fusion, fusion of the first section is clearly delayed beyond the norm and the section is incompletely formed. (Alternatively, this pattern may be interpreted as a 4-segment sacrum and an extra lumbar vertebra [Reed 1967:32].)

Both humeri exhibit perforation of the olecranon fossae. Finally, one piece of negative evidence is worthy of mention: no dorsal modification of either pubis is evident (Suchey et al. 1979), suggesting possibly that the Feature 8 individual had not borne any children.

Feature 9

Stratigraphic context. Feature 9 was a rounded subrectangular pit containing an infant burial (Figs. 8, 19, 60, 61). It was sealed by the 100.60 m floor level (Floor 1) in Room C-5 in Grid 514N534E and extreme western Grid 514N535E. Possibly two distinct plasterings of Floor 1 cap the feature. The feature abutted a west-northwest to east-northeast trending wall to its south, but did not undercut it. As in the case of Feature 41 (see below), the placement of the feature indicates that it was probably contemporary with the use of the floor. The pit was roughly 35 cm to 40 cm on a side at floor level, with rounded corners. The position of the east-southeast end of the pit was not exactly determined. The sides of the pit were oriented west-northwest to east-southeast and north-northeast to south-southwest. The pit edges curved in to a flat (25 cm wide) base at 100.21 m elevation, giving a total depth of 40 cm. The burial itself was lying about 5 cm above the bottom of the pit. The pit was dug into underlying gravelly sterile fill; its walls were not plastered or finished in any other way. The pit fill was uncompacted, homogeneous, and brown, with sparse gravel. Charcoal, animal bone, and cultural material were present.

No stratigraphy was observed in the pit fill below the multiple floor caps. Despite evident rodent tunnels, disturbance of the skeleton was minimal.

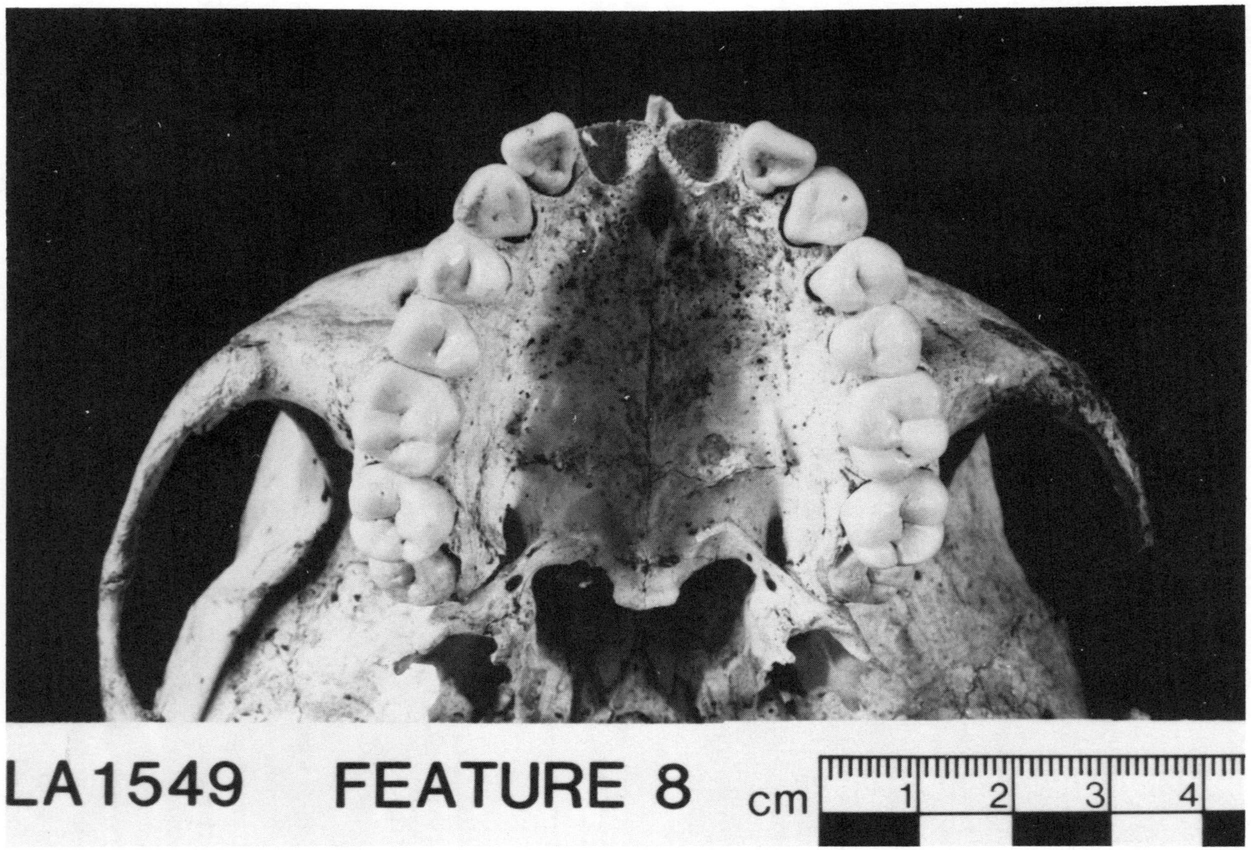

Fig. 56. Feature 8, shallow maxillary incisor sockets, associated with short incisor roots.

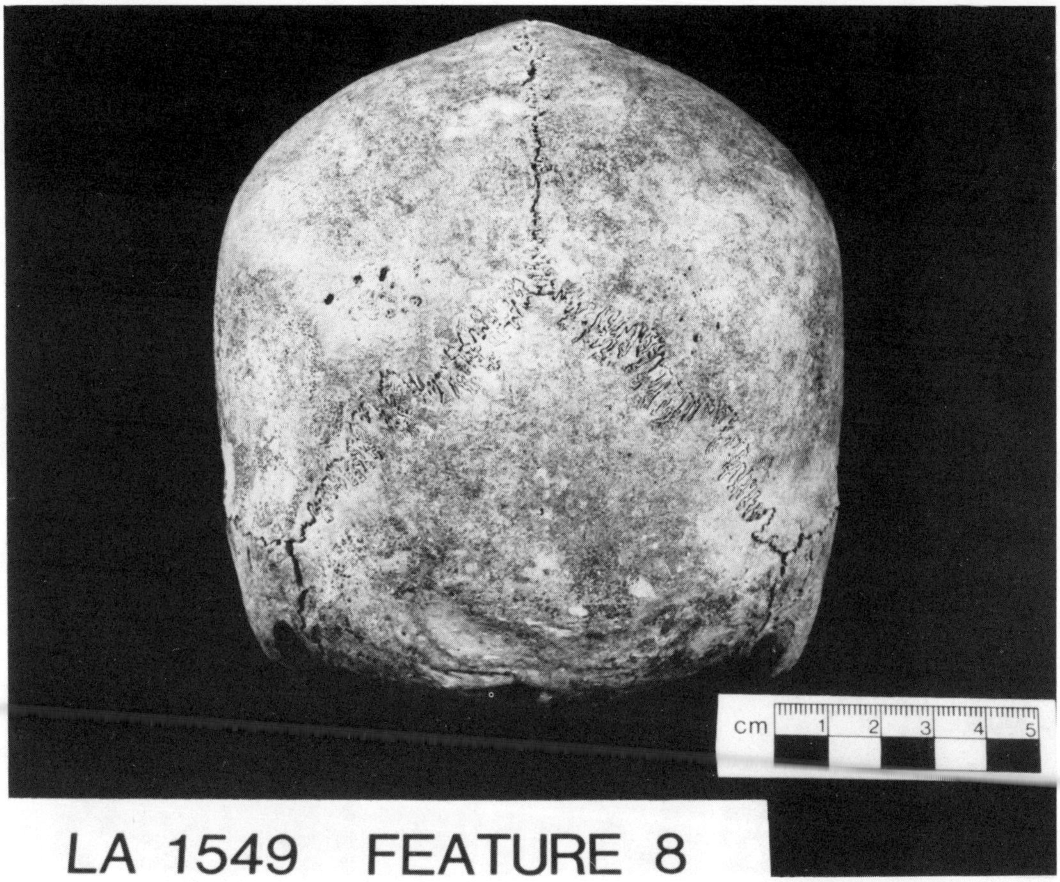

Fig. 57. Feature 8, pitting on posterior area of parietals.

Position and orientation. The skeleton lay horizontally, fully articulated on its right side with the skull to the west-northwest. The skull lay on its right side, with the face pointing above the horizontal and south-southeast. The back was arched from the neck to the pelvis with the concave surface to the south. The thoracic vertebrae were oriented west to east and the lumbars west-northwest to east-southeast; thus the long axis was oriented west-northwest to east-southeast. The left humerus lay on top of the rib cage and angled east 20 degrees relative to the long axis. The left elbow was loosely flexed at around 45 degrees and the left hand extended south-southeast from the forearm. The right humerus lay below and in front of (south of) the rib cage, diverging at approximately 5 degrees from the long axis. The right forearm extended straight beyond the humerus (elbow 180 degrees), with the hand palmar side up below the proximal right femur. The left femur made an angle of about 35 degrees relative to the long axis, with the knee (flexed at 105 degrees) lying approximately over the right elbow. The left foot made a 90 degree angle relative to the leg, with the toes pointing west-southwest. The right femur was more loosely flexed, at about 55 degrees relative to the long axis, while the right knee (which lay below the left distal tibia) was tightly flexed at 30 degrees.

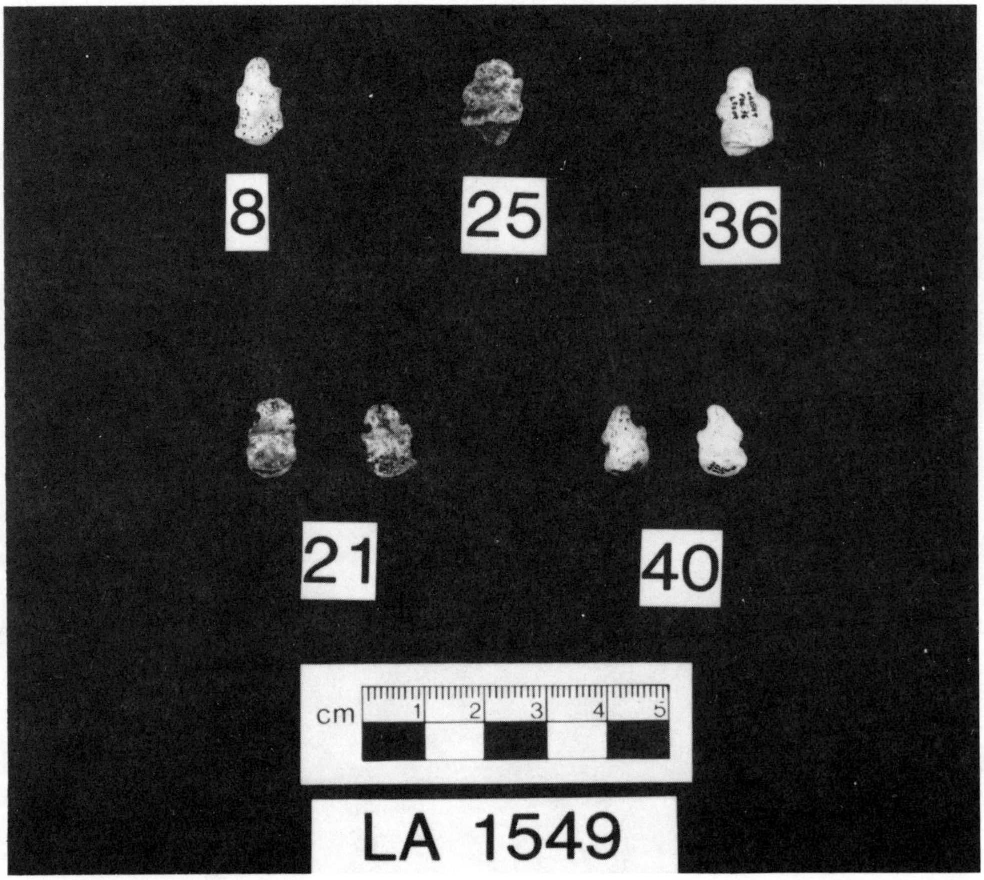

Fig. 58. Fused distal foot phalanges (Features 8, 21, 25, 36, 40).

Burial accompaniments. No definite mortuary associations were recovered, nor was there any evidence of organic material such as the mat wrapping seen on other burials. One bifacial knife or point fragment was located in the fill overlying the left tibia; its relation to the burial is uncertain (see Fig. 61 for location; specimen not tabulated in appendices or illustrated).

Skeletal inventory and condition. The entire skeleton was recovered in excellent condition with the exception of several foot and hand phalanges, carpals and tarsals, and perhaps various ossification centra at early stages of formation. The only portion of the skeleton exhibiting significant post-mortem damage is the skull, which was slightly crushed so that the cranium behind the coronal suture is deformed to the left posteriorly.

Sex. Sex was not determined for this individual because of its young age.

Age. The burial is clearly that of a very young infant. The frontal and mastoid fontanels are open, as is the metopic suture, and none of the teeth are erupted.

Root formation has started on the dI^1s, calcification is complete on one-third to one-half of the occlusal surfaces of M1s, the complete occlusal surfaces of all of the deciduous molars are calcified and the sphenoid fontanel is closed or very nearly closed. The degree of closure of the posterior fontanel is impossible to judge because of post-mortem crushing.

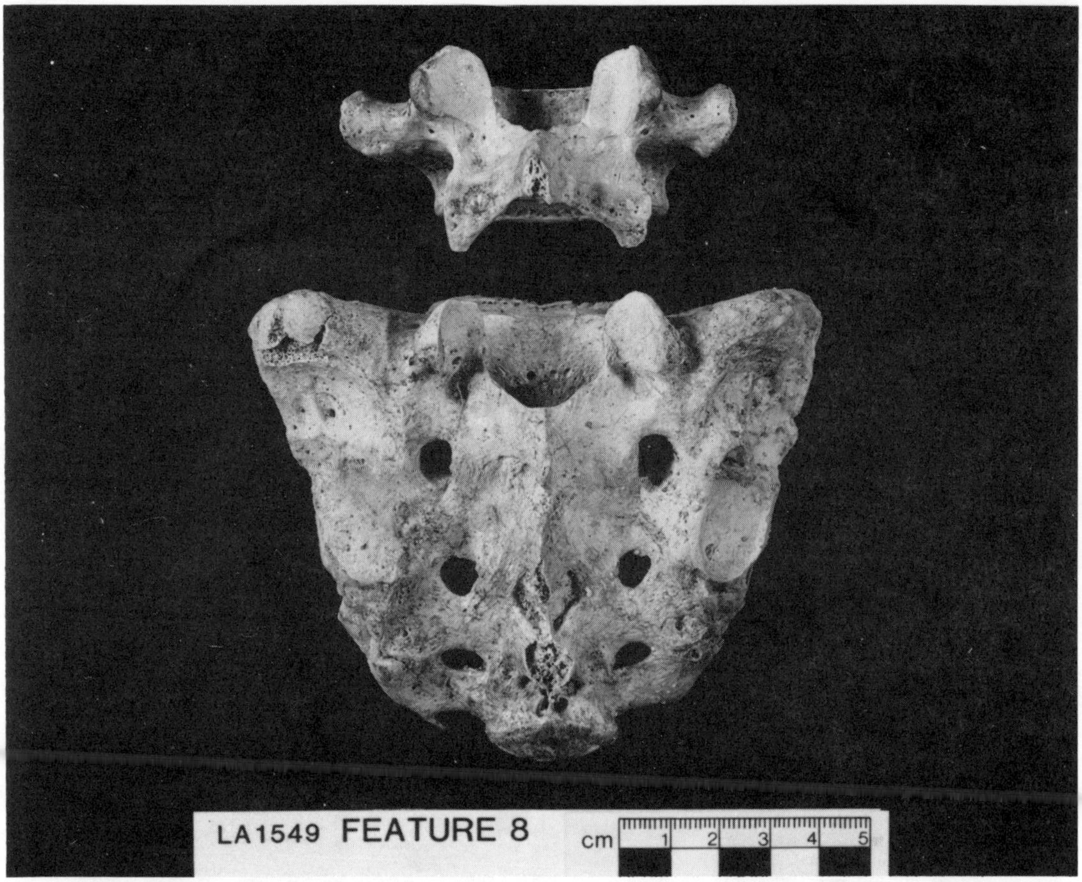

Fig. 59. Feature 8, sacrum. Note lumbar-like form of first sacral segment.

Thus, the individual is not a new-born infant. On the other hand, no teeth are in occlusion, the dM_2 crown is clearly not completely calcified (the completeness of other tooth crowns is less easy to observe in their crypts), and root formation on dI^1 is at an early stage.

Thus, the individual is certainly less than a year old, and an age of 3 to 6 months may be suggested as a best estimate.

General description, cultural and pathological alterations. Given the young age of the individual, few useful observations may be made (see Figs. 62, 63). No obvious gross pathology exists. No deformation that is definitely not attributable to post-mortem crushing is evident. One extra-sutural bone is present at lambda, measuring 1.9 cm wide by 0.8 cm high. A slight degree of shoveling is visible on the dI^1s.

Feature 21

Stratigraphic context. Feature 21 was an irregular oval pit containing an elderly adult female burial (Figs. 7, 19, 64, 65). It was intrusive through the 101.06 m floor level (Floor 1) in Room E-4 in northern Grid 528N566E and extreme southern Grid 529N566E. No evidence of a seal capping the pit at the level of the primary floor was encountered. Moreover, the burial pit truncated part of Feature 13, the principal Floor 1 hearth in the room. These facts both indicate that the burial feature originated from one of the second-

Fig. 60. Feature 9 burial. Skull removed for stabilization and restoration prior to photography.

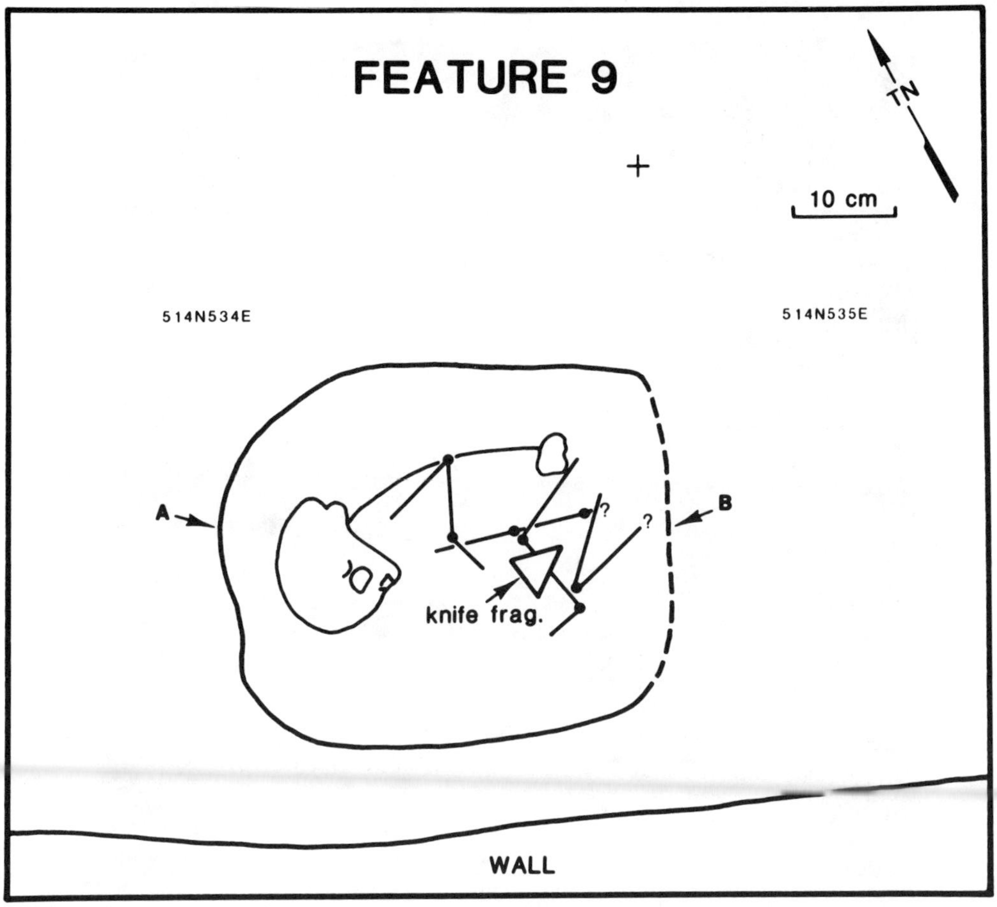

Fig. 61. Plan of Feature 9 burial.

ary floors or occupation surfaces within the structure. The pit was about 1 m long (east to west) and 62 cm wide, with a maximum depth of 34 cm at 100.64 m elevation. The pit walls were steep (nearly vertical), and formed sharp angles with a relatively flat north-northwest sloping floor. The feature was dug into underlying fill of earlier occupations; its walls were not plastered or finished in any other way. The feature exhibited no internal stratigraphy.

Position and orientation. The skeleton was fully articulated, lying on its right side, with the skull to the west-southwest. The cranium was propped up on two rocks that were embedded (probably naturally) near the base of the pit wall. The face was pointing to the south-southeast and leaning at around a 40 degree angle (relative to the vertical) to the west-southwest. The mandible was articulated. The long axis of the burial was oriented west to east with the vertebral column following the northwest and north curved edges of the pit. The left humerus lay on top of the rib cage diverging 20 degrees (north) from the long axis. The left forearm was flexed about 80 degrees relative to the humerus, running south under the left femoral mid-shaft. The left hand extended straight beyond the arm, palmar side up, below the left femur and tibia. The right humerus extended south-southeast at an angle of about 50 degrees relative to the long axis directly under the chin, with the elbow near the southwest edge of the pit. The radius and ulna were tightly flexed back under the chin (nearly parallel to the humerus), and the hand was bent at a right angle to the east-northeast, with the palmar side facing south.

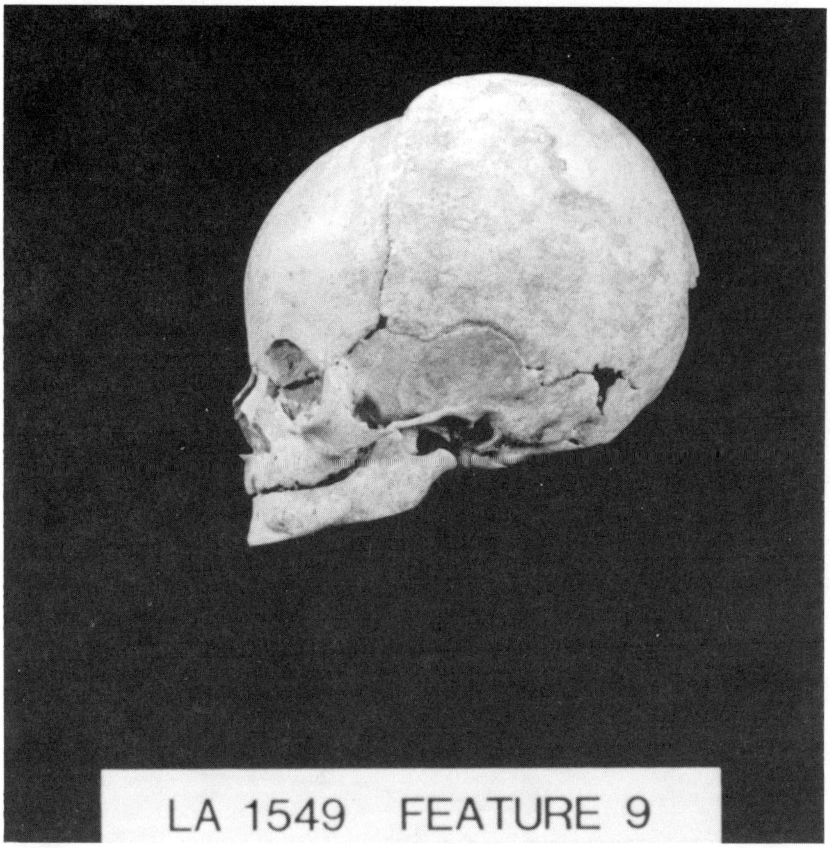

Fig. 62. Feature 9 skull (left lateral view). Scale same as in Fig. 24. Extreme linearity of lower mandible border result of specimen settling in photo cloth.

The lower vertebral column curved further to the east-southeast, so that the pelvis was oriented approximately northwest to southeast. The left femur angled back to the west-southwest at 30 degrees relative to the long axis (but about 60 degrees relative to the lower back/pelvis orientation). Thus, the left knee lay east-southeast of the skull, just northeast of the tightly flexed right elbow. The tibia was tightly flexed at 15 degrees relative to the femur. The left foot was flexed at roughly 90 degrees relative to the tibia, with the toes rising to the south-southeast where they touched the southeast pit wall. The right leg was flexed in a similar manner to the left, lying below the latter and slightly farther to the west-northwest (the right heel lay immediately under the left tibia).

Burial accompaniments. A wrap of twined matting was present around the entire body (see Appendix 16). The warp was made of grass; the weft, and possibly also a binding to hold the mat in place around the body, was cordage (z-twist, 2-strand) of unidentified vegetal fiber. No other artifact associations were identified.

Skeletal inventory and condition. Feature 21 is the most badly crushed of the burials recovered. Essentially the entire skeleton is present: cranium and mandible, the hyoid body with one of its greater horns, at least a portion of each vertebra and the first coccygeal vertebra, fragmentary ribs, both scapulae (fragmentary), sternum and manubrium, both clavicles, the pelvis, most of each of the long bones (see below), the

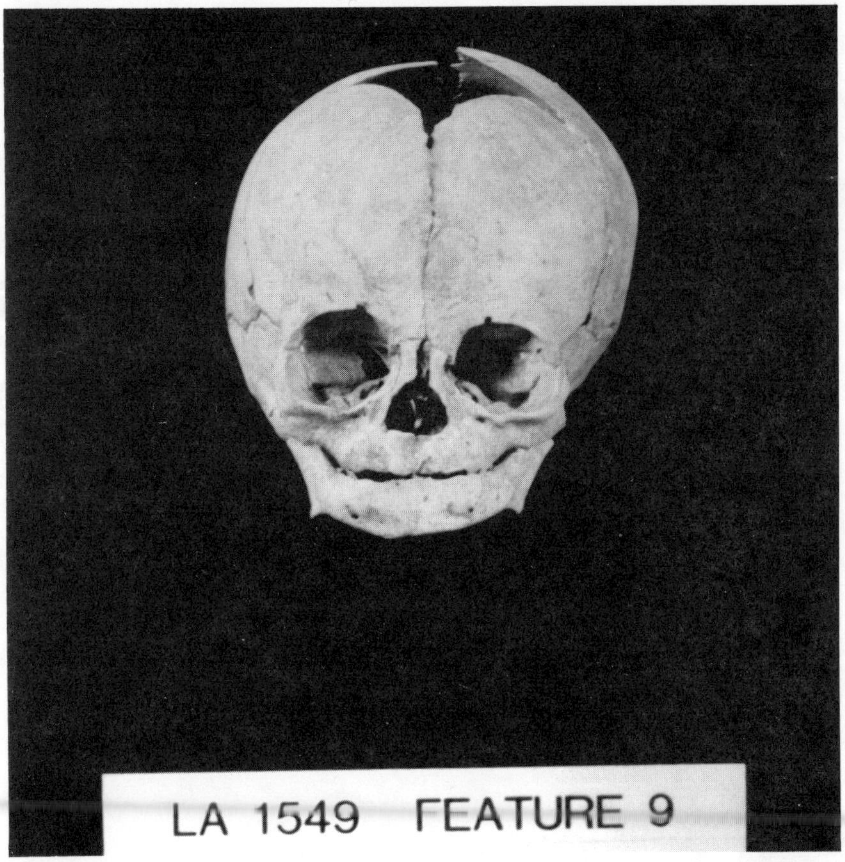

Fig. 63. Feature 9 skull (frontal view). Scale same as in Fig. 24. Conformation of lower mandible border accentuated slightly by settling of specimen in photo cloth.

patellae, all foot and hand bones (with the exception of one hand phalanx), several sesamoids, and numerous miscellaneous fragments. However, the majority of the skeletal elements suffered some degree of crushing and destruction. Particularly notable deformation includes:

a) The entire skull is partially crushed downward in the position in which it lay (i.e., the left parietal and temporal squama as well as the left portion of the frontal and the left malar are broken and crushed inwards, while the corresponding right elements are similarly damaged. The skull, in general, is not measurable. The least damage occurred to the maxilla, mandible, and occipital areas.

b) The left femur, with the exception of the proximal end, is fragmentary.

c) The right distal femur is crushed.

d) The right tibia is too crushed and fragmentary for measurement.

e) The left tibia proximal end is crushed and fragmentary.

f) The right humerus proximal end is crushed and the distal end is fragmentary.

g) The left humerus distal end is fragmentary.

Fig. 64. Feature 21 burial.

Sex. The innominates clearly indicate that the individual is a female: a ventral arc is present bilaterally, sub-pubic concavity exists, the medial aspect of the ischio-pubic ramus has a moderately sharp ridge, the sub-pubic angle is broad, the greater sciatic notch is broad, and a slight pre-auricular sulcus is present. The remainder of the skeleton is relatively robust for a female.

Age. The advanced stage of tooth wear (see below) and the prevalence of minor arthritis indicate that the individual is of advanced age. Application of the Gilbert and McKern (1973) symphyseal aging method yields scores of 12 (39.00±6.09 years) for the right pubis and 11 (36.90±4.94 years) for the left. The form of the sternum and manubrium is in stage 5 (35+ years) of Stewart's (1954) classification. Appendix 2 indicates that dental attrition is not only in advance of all of the other burials, but is considerably greater than the next most worn dentition (Feat. 25, aged 26 to 30 years). Thus, the age is probably considerably greater than 30. The overall appearance of the skeleton indicates a best estimate of 40 or more years of age.

General description, cultural and pathological alterations. Given the crushing of the Feature 21 skull, only limited observations may be made regarding its form (see Figs. 67–70). The cranium is relatively robust, of medium length, with prominent muscle markings (this latter is undoubtedly partly a function of advanced age). The mastoid

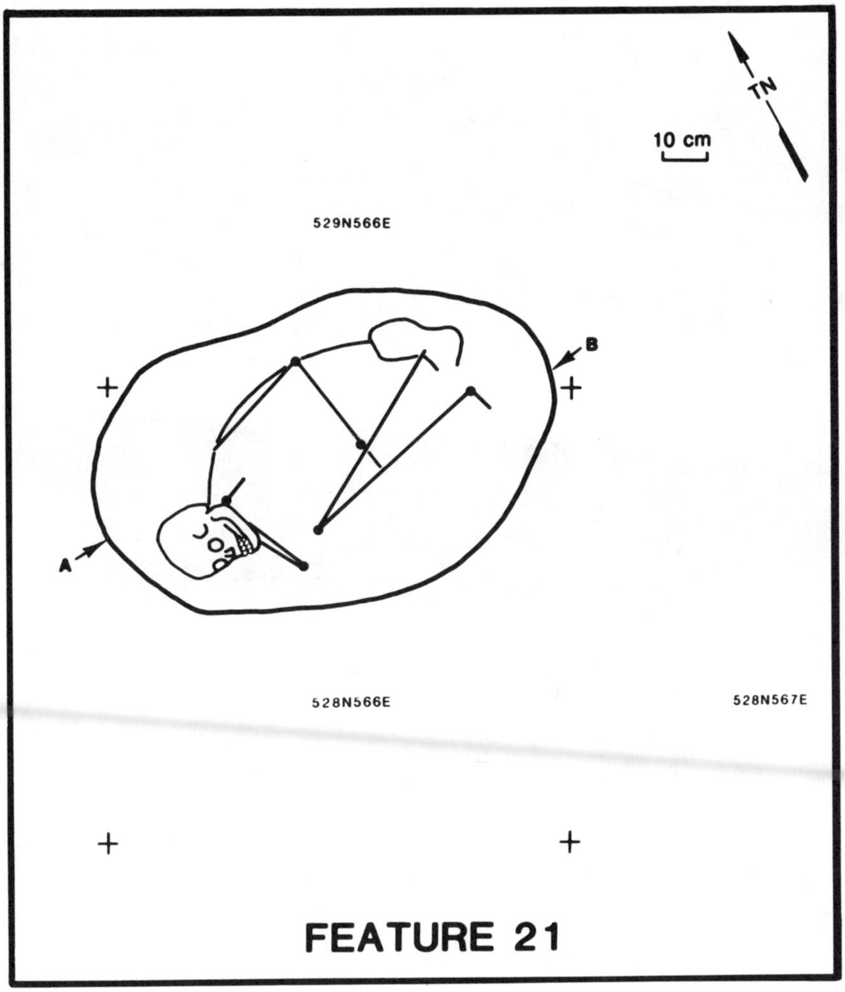

Fig. 65. Plan of Feature 21 burial.

processes and occipital condyles are small, however. The superior orbital margins are blunt, and glabella is moderately prominent. The form of the remainder of the cranium is difficult to describe as a result of the crushing.

A small flattened area about 4.5 cm high by 4.0 cm wide and forming an angle of 60 degrees relative to the Frankfort Horizontal Plane is present extending superiorly from lambda. This area possibly represents culturally induced lambdoidal deformation. Below lambda, the occipital curves in slightly to a prominent nuchal crest, with a small depression just superior to inion. Overall, the appearance of the cranium most closely resembles that of Feature 1, being lambdoidally deformed, relatively robust for a female, and probably relatively high in form.

A small extra-sutural bone ca. 1.5 cm high by 2 cm wide is present at lambda.

The mandible has a broad symphyseal region and a prominent mental protuberance. The gonial angle is slightly inverted (observable only on the right side; the left is broken).

Fig. 66. Twined grass matting found with Feature 21 burial (see Appendix 16, Table A16a, No. 26 for details).

Appendix 2 summarizes the condition of the teeth. RM_1 or RM_2 were lost antemortem as were LM_2, LM^1, LM^2, LM^3, LP^4, RM^1, RM^2, and possibly one of the superior incisors. However, a large number of teeth were present at death considering the advanced stages of wear. Alveolar resorption indicative of periodontal disease is evident on the mandible, but is hard to distinguish from post-mortem erosion of the alveolus. No definite caries or abscesses are visible on the teeth that are present. RP_3, RP_4, and LP_3 display light to medium calculus formation lingually, while RM^3 has a thin layer of calculus over much of its neck and crown.

Several minor skeletal abnormalities are present. The middle and distal phalanges of the fifth toe are fused on both feet (see Fig. 58 above). No additional abnormalities accompany this fusion. In addition, the middle hand phalanx on the left fifth digit has a slight longitudinal split in its distal articular facet and the phalanx itself is shorter and broader than the corresponding right one. Another (unidentified) left hand middle phalanx has an irregular roughened distal articular facet. No corresponding features are visible on the right hand, nor are there corresponding abnormalities visible on other left hand elements. On the left foot, the first digit metatarsal has a small articular facet on the lateral surface on the proximal end; this articulates with a less distinctive raised surface on the medial second metatarsal shaft. No such feature is present on the right foot.

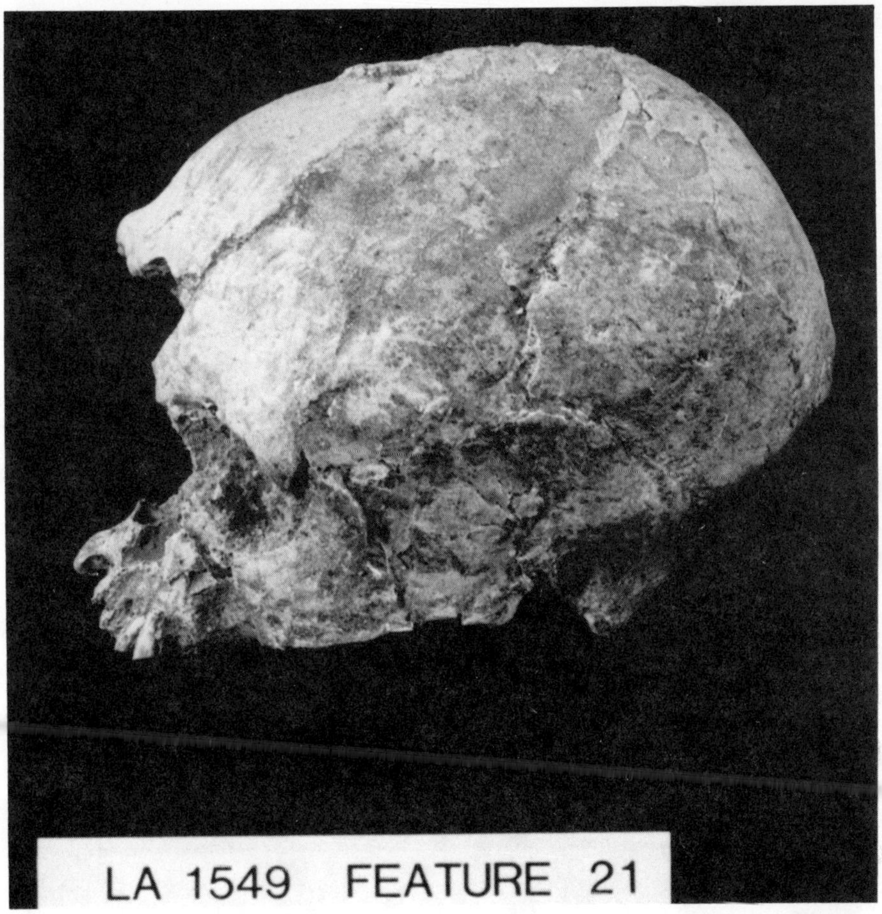

Fig. 67. Feature 21 cranium (left lateral view). Scale same as in Fig. 24. Note extreme crushing.

Slight arthritis is present on articular facets throughout much of the skeleton, particularly on limbs, extremities (particularly the feet), and vertebrae. Most prominent is the vertebral arthritis. Considerable osteophytic growth is present on the lumbar vertebral bodies and to a lesser extent throughout much of the vertebral column. Degeneration (eburnation and pitting) of articular facets is also evident, particularly in the mid to lower cervical vertebrae and the upper thoracics. Elsewhere, the arthritis mainly takes the form of sharply defined or raised edges of articular surfaces.

Finally, one additional postcranial feature is present. Both pubes exhibit slight dorsal pitting in the area commonly associated with parturition scars (Suchey et al. 1979). Thus, the individual in Feature 21 probably had borne one or more children.

Feature 25

Stratigraphic context. Feature 25 was identified as a long oval pit containing an adult male burial, cutting through the 101.06 m floor (Floor 1) in Room E-4 between Grids 528N564E, 528N565E, and northern 527N564E and 527N565E (Figs. 7, 19, 71, 72). Although no seal was identified capping the feature at the floor level, the pit was not recognized above the floor level. Thus, the feature may be contemporaneous with Floor 1, or it

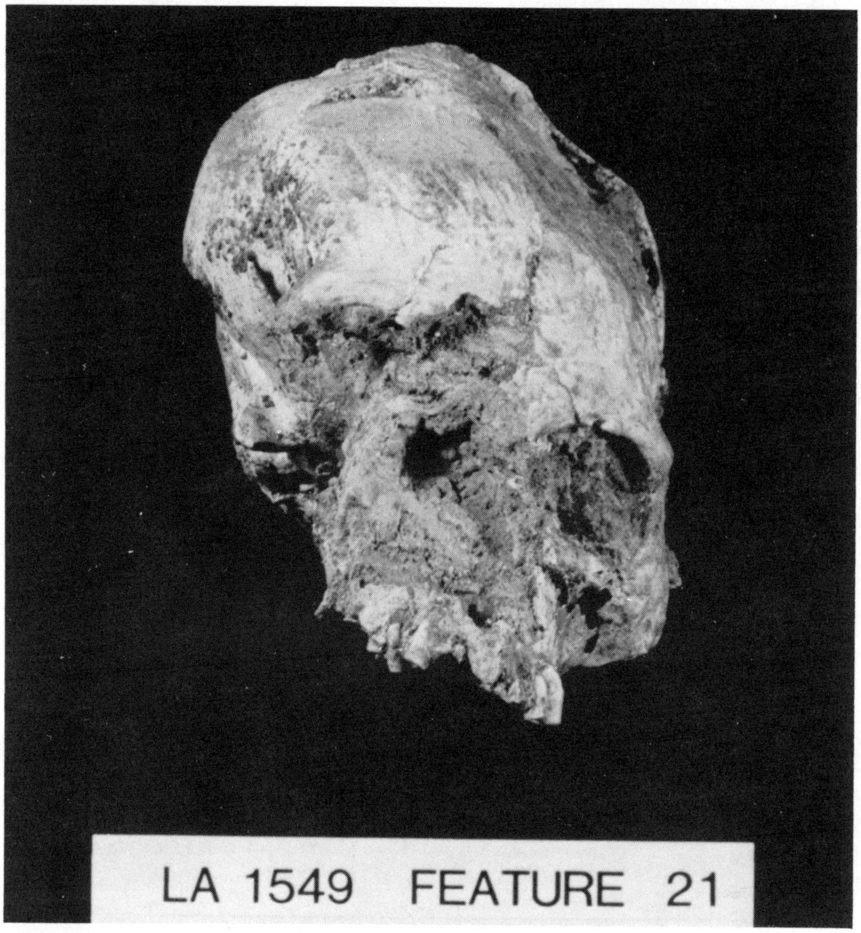

Fig. 68. Feature 21 cranium (frontal view). Scale same as in Fig. 24. Note extreme crushing.

may post-date it. The absence of a seal makes the latter more likely. The pit was oriented with its long axis (128 cm) north-northeast to south-southwest, and was 80 cm wide (east-southeast to west-northwest). It lay immediately to the west-northwest of a possible post hole, Feature 19. The pit walls were steep, forming a rather abrupt but rounded junction with a flat bottom at 100.47 m. Maximum pit depth was 51 cm. Small "shelves" interrupted the walls' smooth profiles at the east-northeast and south-southwest ends of the feature at 100.83 and 100.70 m, respectively. The southwestern "shelf" may be a product of rodent disturbance. The south-southwestern pit wall was nearly vertical only down to 100.75 m, below which it sloped at nearly a 45 degree angle to the north-northeast. The feature was dug into underlying fill of earlier occupations; its walls were even but not plastered or finished in any other way.

The fill was uncompacted and brown, with many subrounded large pebbles (ca. 5 cm in diameter). Large pieces of charcoal were abundant, while non-human bone and cultural material (lithics, sherds) were present in small quantities.

Position and orientation. The skeleton lay fully articulated on its right side, with the skull on the north-northeast end of the pit. The superior surface of the cranium pointed northwest and the skull lay almost face down on the right half of the face; this position may have resulted from the head slumping forward (face down) from a west-

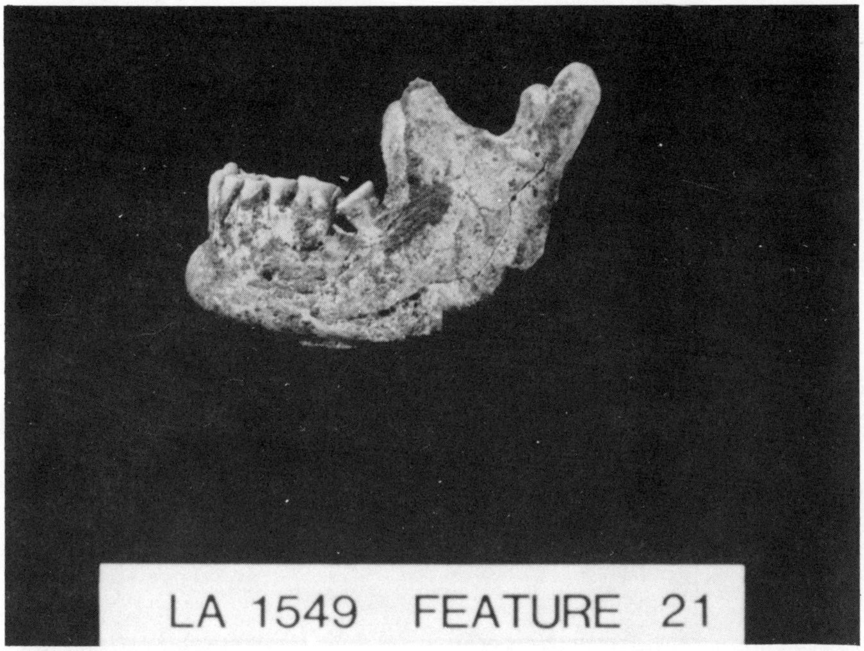

Fig. 69. Feature 21 mandible (left lateral view). Scale same as in Fig. 24.

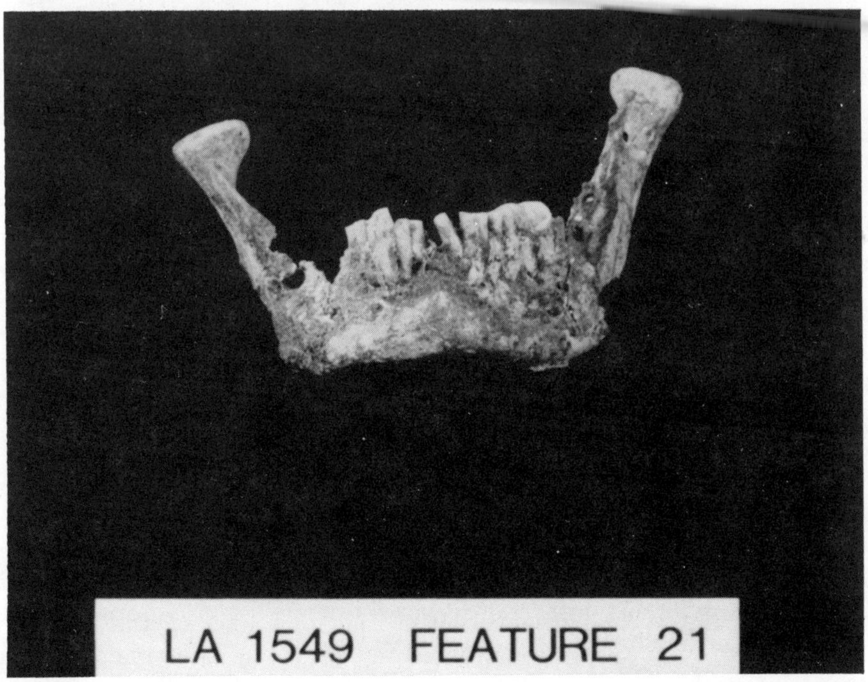

Fig. 70. Feature 21 mandible (frontal view). Scale same as in Fig. 24.

Fig. 71. Feature 25 burial (trowel points north).

northwestward orientation of the face. The neck and upper thoracic vertebrae curved sharply south so that the overall orientation of the long axis of the burial was north-northeast to south-southwest. The left humerus lay on top of the rib cage, running south so that it formed an angle of 30 degrees with the long axis and the elbow lay above the vertebral column. The left elbow was flexed at 90 degrees, and the forearm angled down below the left femur. The left hand lay between the legs, palmar side facing up and southeast, with the digits bent sharply back towards the skull. The right humerus made an angle of about 40 degrees relative to the long axis so that the elbow lay below and behind (southeast of) the vertebral column; and the forearm, flexed at around 80 degrees at the elbow, ran below the ribs to the west. The right hand was extended straight beyond the arm below the right leg, palmar side down, with the digits partially flexed. The lower

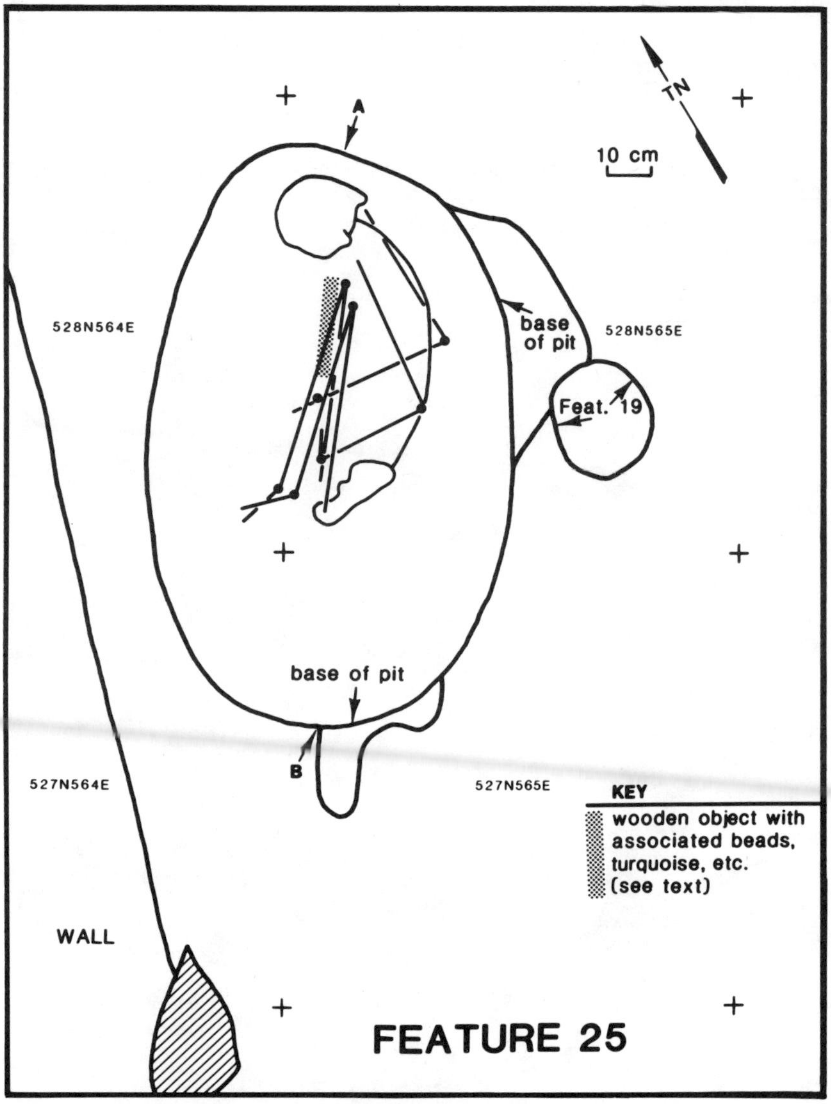

Fig. 72. Plan of Feature 25 burial.

vertebral column twisted so that the pelvis lay nearly horizontally. Both legs were tightly flexed, with the femora lying roughly parallel to the long axis and with the knees tightly flexed at around 5 degrees so that the knees lay just south of the skull and the heels just west-northwest of the proximal femora. The left leg was oriented in a horizontal plane, with the femur east-southeast of the tibia. The left foot made an angle of about 120 degrees relative to the tibia with the digits pointed west-northwest and the volar face down. The right leg was oriented nearly vertically, with the tibia above (as well as northwest of) the femur. The right foot lay with the digits pointed west-southwest and the volar surface down. The skeleton was flexed sufficiently and placed far enough to the north-northeast that it did not extend into the sloping south-southwest end of the pit.

Burial accompaniments. The major artifact associated with this feature was a wooden prayer-stick (No. 1; Figs. 73, 74 and Table A12a) of walnut (*Juglans* sp.). It was made from a two-year-old sprout or new limb from which the bark had been removed and the surfaces squared off or flattened. This reconstruction of its shape is tentative, as the wood was badly decayed and only fragments could be salvaged. The stick was approximately 2 cm wide at its distal end (end closest to the skull), 3.5 cm wide at its proximal end, perhaps 1.5 cm thick, and about 23 cm in length.

Fig. 73. Closeup of prayer-stick (*Juglans* sp., walnut) found with Feature 25 burial (trowel points north).

The upper or distal half of the prayer-stick was covered with 14 (possibly 15) *Olivella* shell beads (Nos. 1–2, 3a-3b, 4–5, 10–11, 12a-12b, 13–16, 18?; Fig. 38j-w and Table A12c; shell bead No. 13 not preserved). All were identified by James H. McLean of the Los Angeles County Museum of Natural History as *O. dama* (Wood, 1828), and based on

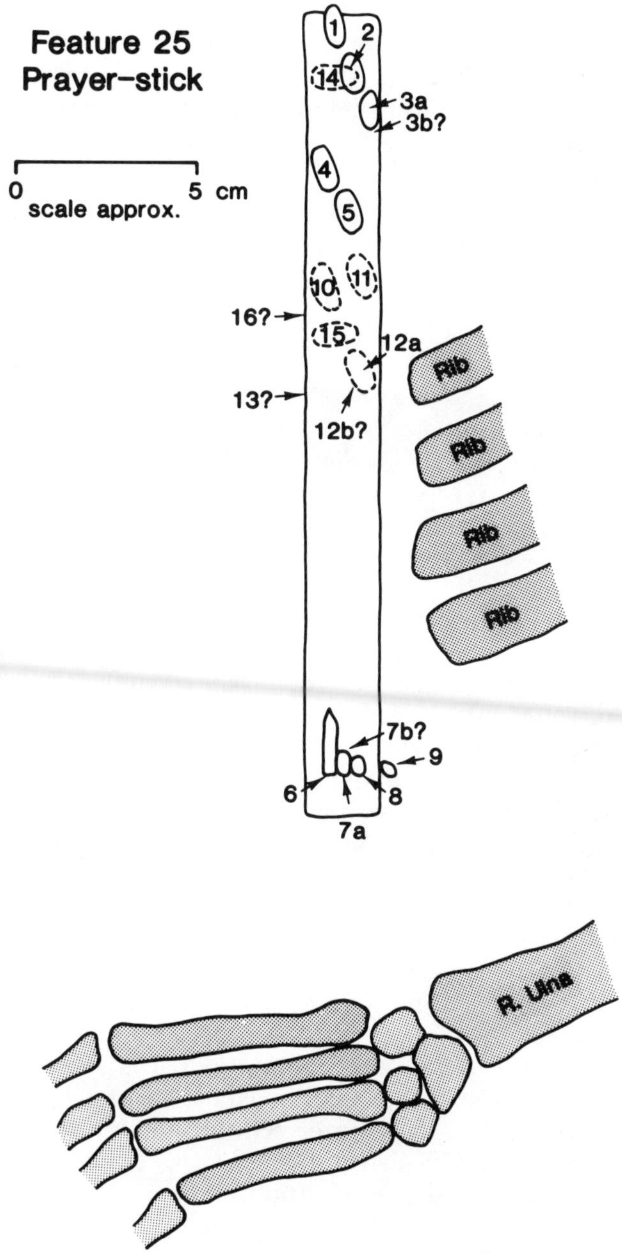

Fig. 74. Plan of prayer-stick (*Juglans* sp., walnut) found with Feature 25 burial, showing location of associated artifacts. Location of items with question marks approximate.

their relatively large size they probably were derived from sources in the Gulf of California rather than from the Texas coast. According to McLean, all appear to be beachworn, although much (or all) of the surface deterioration may be the result of poor preservation conditions.

Several items were attached to the lower or proximal end of the stick, including a small clear quartz crystal (No. 6; Fig. 40e and Table A12e; its termination oriented toward the distal end of the stick), 1 large and 1 tiny piece of turquoise (both unperforated;

Nos. 7a-7b; Fig. 39i-j and Table A12d), a small, rounded, waterworn(?) pebble of purple fluorite (No. 8; Fig. 40f and Table A12e), and perhaps a pea-sized piece of organic material (not preserved or identified). The *Olivella* beads appear to have been strung on a single strand which was wrapped in spiral fashion around the distal half of the stick. The method of attaching the unperforated items to the lower end of the prayer-stick is unclear. No traces of mastic were detectable in the field; however, the extremely poor state of preservation of the stick made detection of mastic virtually impossible. No evidence of coloring, if originally present, was preserved.

The stick was located in front of (west of) the chest, just north of the right hand, running along the chest towards the skull (see Fig. 72). The stick originally may have been placed on the chest of the individual much like the prayer-stick with Feature 3, or it may have been in the right hand (this is less likely); in either case, it had slumped from its original position.

Aside from the *Olivella* beads and other items definitely associated with this object, 3 small disc-shell beads (Table A12b) and 1 *Olivella* bead (No. 18; Fig. 38w and Table A12c) were found in the vicinity of the prayer-stick and originally were probably attached to it. Surrounding the entire burial were the remains of twined grass matting, very similar to the matting around Feature 21 (see Appendix 16).

Skeletal inventory and condition. Feature 25 is well preserved and largely complete. The following elements are present: cranium and mandible, both scapulae and clavicles, all vertebrae, hyoid and fragments of ossified thyroid cartilage, sternum, manubrium, both innominates and sacrum (along with one whole and fragments of several coccygeal vertebrae), all ribs, both humeri, both radii, both ulnae, all carpals except the right triquetral, all metacarpals, all hand phalanges, 1 hand sesamoid, both femora, both tibiae, both fibulae, all tarsals, all metatarsals, all left foot phalanges, all right foot proximal phalanges and 2 right foot middle phalanges, and 2 left foot sesamoids.

Most elements were in good condition, major exceptions being the right femur (broken in several places but not restored since it has been saved as an untreated sample), and the left humerus (shaft warped and the distal end partly crushed). Small cracks are visible on the cranium, but no major post-mortem deformation appears to have occurred.

Sex. The innominates clearly reveal that the individual is a male: no ventral arc is present, no sub-pubic concavity exists, the medial aspect of the ischio-pubic ramus is rounded, the sub-pubic angle is narrow, the greater sciatic notch is narrow, and little to no pre-auricular sulcus is present. The large size and ruggedness of both the innominates and the skull and other postcrania confirm the identification.

Age. Application of the McKern and Stewart (1957) symphyseal aging method yields a score of 11 for the right pubis (29.18±3.33 years) and 10 or 11 for the left (26.05±1.87 years; 29.18±3.33 years), so that an estimate around 28 years is suggested. The sternum and manubrium are in stage 4 to 5 in Stewart's (1954) classification (23–35+ years). Examination of the internal aspect of the cranial sutures shows fusion along the entire observable portion of the sagittal and coronal sutures; portions of the coronal suture remain visible. Thus, an age of around 30 years or more is supported. Dental attrition (Appendix 2) indicates an age considerably greater than Feature 41 but much less than Feature 21; an age in the late twenties or early thirties is supported by this degree of wear. The pattern of attrition is abnormal, however (see below), and thus not directly comparable to the pattern seen on the other burials. Arthritis (see below) similarly suggests a considerably greater age than Feature 1 but less than Feature 21. Overall, a best estimate of age is around 26 to 30 years.

General description, cultural and pathological alterations. The cranium is robust, with well-developed muscle markings (see Figs. 75, 76). It is short and high (cranial index 78.7, length-height index 78.2, breadth-height index 99.3), though these figures may reflect artificial modification (see below). In posterior view, the cranium has a keeled appearance, and some parietal bossing is evident. The supraorbital arches and glabella are prominent. Superior to the arches, the frontal is retreating, dipping in a supraorbital groove, and then continuing in a smooth contour to the parietals which are arched in their anterior half in the keeled form described above. The posterior halves of the parietals are not keeled, but form a relatively flat surface (the flattened area is around 4.0 cm high by 2.0 cm wide, inclined at ca. 55 degrees relative to the Frankfort Horizontal Plane) immediately superior to lambda. Below lambda, just above the superior nuchal line, is a second flat area 3.0 cm high by 3.5 cm wide, forming an angle of 100 degrees relative to the Frankfort Horizontal Plane. Either of these areas may in part represent the effects of slight culturally induced occipital deformation. As indicated above, the nuchal muscle markings are strongly developed as are the large mastoids, prominent temporal lines, and supramastoid ridge.

The mandible has a broad symphyseal region and a prominent mental eminence. The gonial angles are slightly everted.

Several partially obliterated extra-sutural bones are present near lambda, including a large one (2.8 cm high by 4.0 cm wide) just inferior to lambda with two additional bones adjacent to it (ca. 1.5 cm high by 2.3 cm wide on the right; 1.8 cm high by 1.9 cm wide on the left). Another extra-sutural bone, 1.0 cm in diameter, is present along the right lambdoidal suture about 6 cm from lambda, and several other possible extra-sutural bones along the lambdoidal suture are obscured by fusion.

As already mentioned in connection with the age estimate, dental attrition on Feature 25 is in part pathological. Appendix 2 summarizes the degree of wear. All teeth were present at the time of death, though several serious pathologies were present. Wear on all M1s was extreme relative to that on the other teeth, with nearly complete loss of the enamel on the buccal sides of the M_1s and complete loss of the enamel coupled with exposure of the pulp cavity on the lingual sides of the M^1s. Wear on the P^4s and M^2s displays similar anomalously lingually slanted wear, though to a much lesser degree, with only moderate dentin exposure in each case (see Figs. 77, 78).

The exposure of the pulp cavities on the M^1s is accompanied by abscesses, with buccal drainage and root exposure on the right, and slight buccal drainage combined with extensive lingual root exposure on the left; the lingual involvement on the left also exhibits a deep cloaca extending superiorly into the left alveolus (Fig. 77). Additional dental pathology includes an abscess and buccal root exposure on LM_1, two small occlusal caries on RM_3, a small possible occlusal carious lesion on LM_3, slight calculus on most teeth (particularly on the posterior dentition), and light to moderate alveolar resorption (Fig. 78).

Aside from dental pathology, several other abnormalities or pathologies are present on the skeleton. Arthritis is present in several locations on the lower vertebrae, particularly in the form of slight osteophytic development on the bodies of the last thoracic, and second, fourth and fifth lumbar vertebrae as well as on the superior sacral surface. Slight arthritis is also present on the left demi-facet of the last thoracic vertebra, matched by slight arthritis on the twelfth rib articular surface. Most articular facets have well-marked sharp edges.

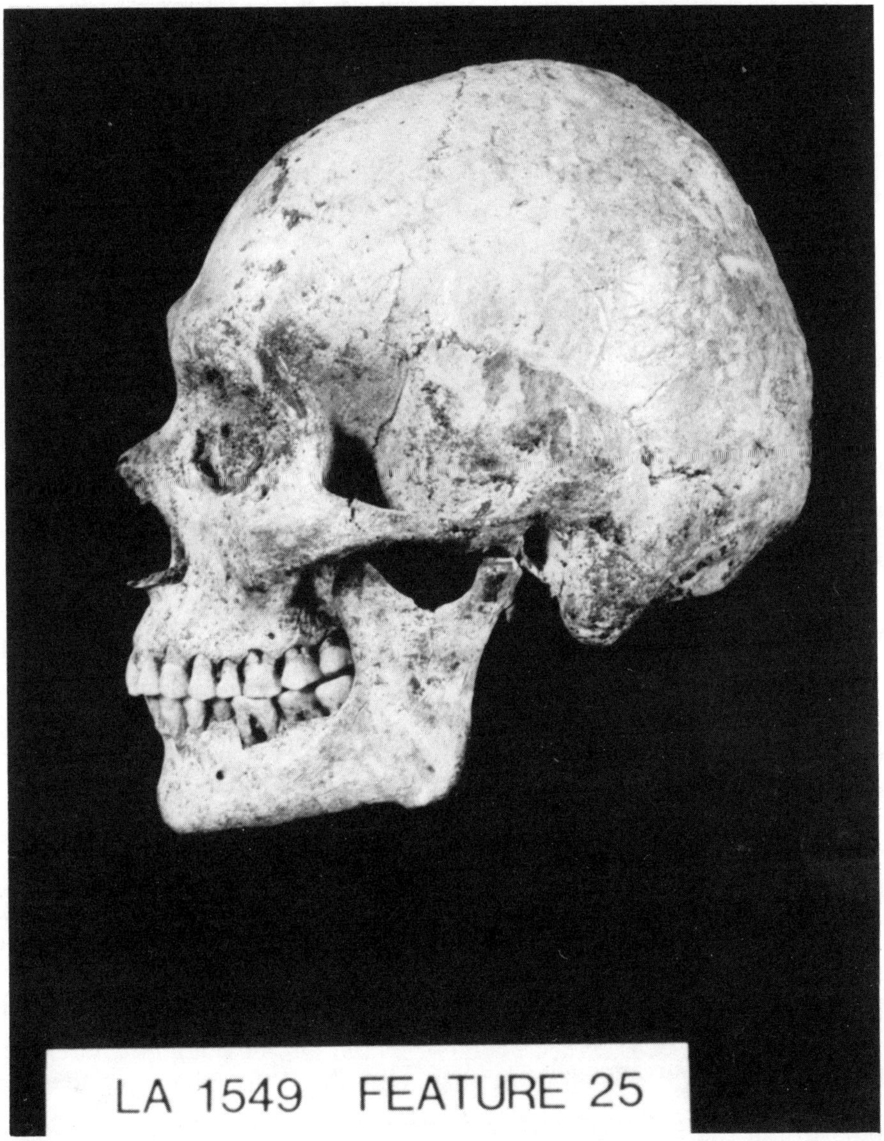

Fig. 75. Feature 25 skull (left lateral view). Scale same as in Fig. 24.

The left twelfth thoracic and left first lumbar transverse processes are asymmetrically large relative to their right counterparts. A similar asymmetry is present in the fifth cervical superior through first thoracic superior articular facets, where these (and all intervening) facets are slightly larger on the left than on the right. No vertebral arthritis is evident accompanying this minor asymmetry. The first coccygeal vertebra is fused to the sacrum.

On the left foot, the fifth digit middle and distal phalanges are fused, and the proximal articular facet exhibits osteophytic development matched by osteophytic growth and eburnation on the distal articular surface on the proximal fifth phalanx (see Fig. 58 above). The corresponding distal and middle phalanges were not recovered on the right foot; the right proximal fifth phalanx is not arthritic.

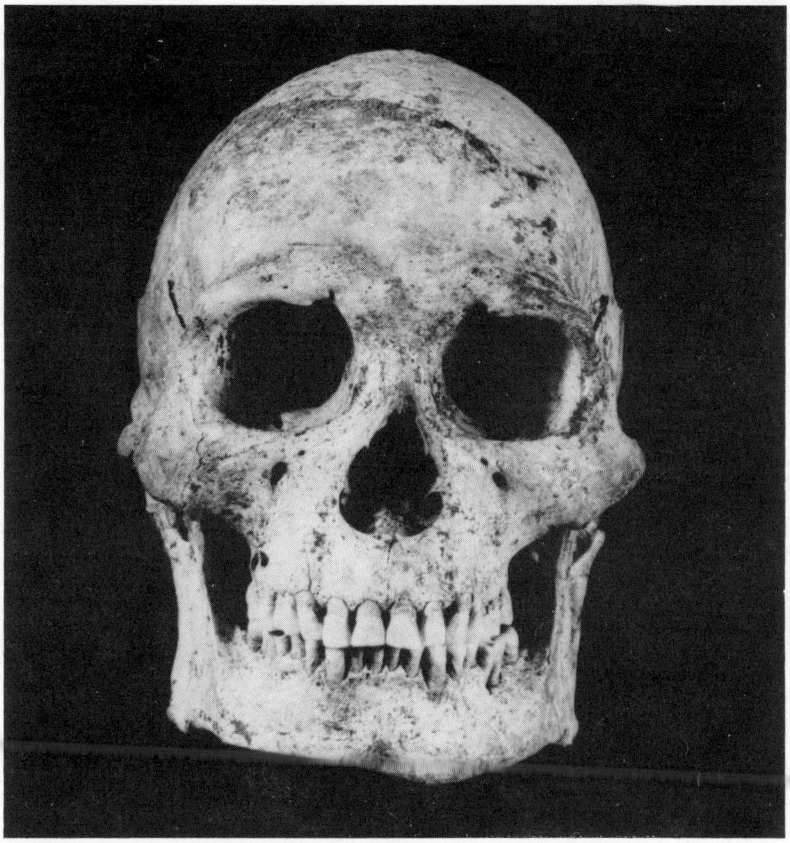

Fig. 76. Feature 25 skull (frontal view). Scale same as in Fig. 24. Asymmetry of lower mandible border result of specimen settling in photo cloth.

Possible slight periostitis is visible on both femora and tibiae. On the right tibia it is present particularly on the lateral face of the proximal end of the shaft, but also occurs at the distal end and to a slight degree near mid-shaft (Fig. 79). The right tibia has patches at the distal end of the shaft (all sides except anteriorly), at a few points near mid-shaft, and posteriorly and laterally at the proximal end. On the right femur it is present on the proximal and distal ends of the shaft both anteriorly and posteriorly, and occurs posteriorly on the rest of the shaft. On the left femur it is present posteriorly along much of the shaft. The possible periostitis is evidenced by a slightly roughened vermiculate appearance of the bone.

Feature 29

Stratigraphic context. Feature 29 was a shallow pit in the eroded remnants of Room E-2(?) containing part of an adult male burial. The pit cuts through the badly eroded surface of Floor 1 (elevation 101.06 m), and possibly originated from a floor or surface higher than this level (Figs. 7, 19, 80, 81). It was located on bedrock directly adjacent to the estimated position of the east wall of the room, in the northwest corner of Grid 523N569E and corners of the three adjacent grids. No cap to the feature was recognized at any level. The approximate shape of the feature, outlined at an elevation of 101.00 m, was roughly rectangular, with rounded corners, and with the outline broken by numerous

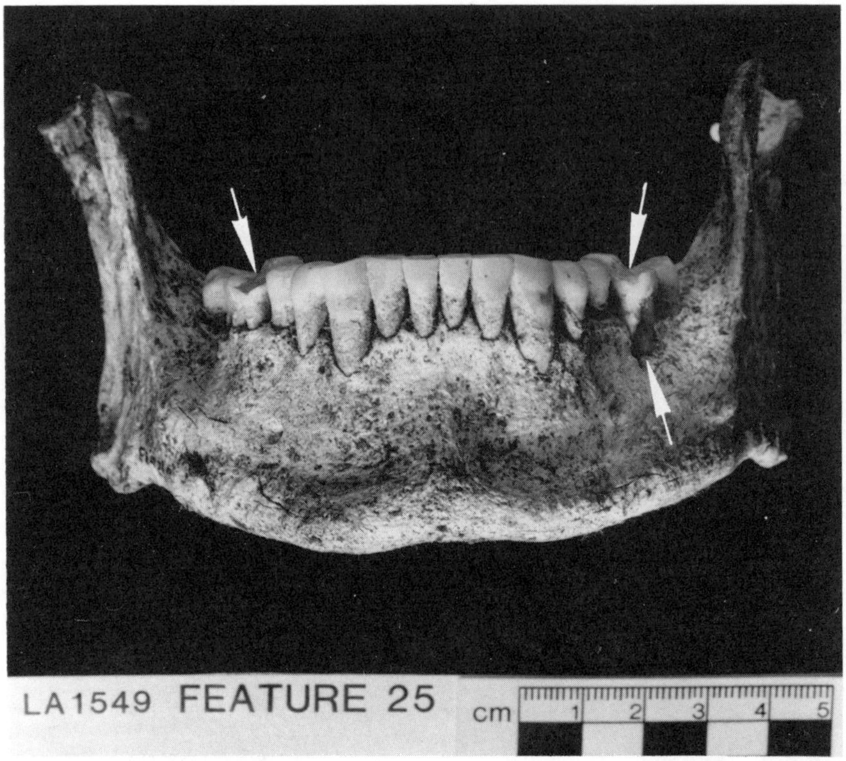

Fig. 77. Feature 25, mandible. Note extreme angled wear and abscessed roots of M_1s (arrows).

limestone blocks protruding into the pit from the underlying bedrock. At this level the long axis of the pit was 77 cm north-south by 57 cm east-west. The pit walls were steep and irregular in form, not plastered or finished in any other way. The pit bottom was approximately flat, dipped slightly to the north, and was composed of blocky irregular limestone bedrock. The deepest point of the pit, near its north end, was at 100.82 m, or about 24 cm below the Floor 1 elevation.

The pit fill was uncompacted, gravelly, and brown-gray in color. No internal pit stratigraphy was evident.

Position and orientation. Since the skeleton was incomplete and partly disarticulated, exact description of the position and orientation is impossible. Both legs and the left foot were essentially intact. The articulated portions of the legs indicate that the skeleton lay on its left side, with the knees tightly flexed at around 10 degrees. The right leg lay on top of the left, with the right tibia mid-shaft lying on top of the left ankle. The right tibia made an angle of about 30 degrees with the left tibia. The left foot was largely articulated, with the metatarsals making an angle of 150 degrees relative to the tibia; the foot lay on its lateral side. The right foot was disturbed beyond the calcaneus, and thus its orientation is uncertain.

The left femoral shaft was oriented southwest to northeast; the right ran west-southwest to east-northeast. Beyond the proximal femora, the skeleton was disarticulated and fragmentary. Near the proximal ends of the femoral shafts were portions of the sacrum and lower thoracic and lumbar vertebrae. Elsewhere in the pit fill a few additional fragments of ribs, vertebrae, and other elements were located. Just west of the distal end

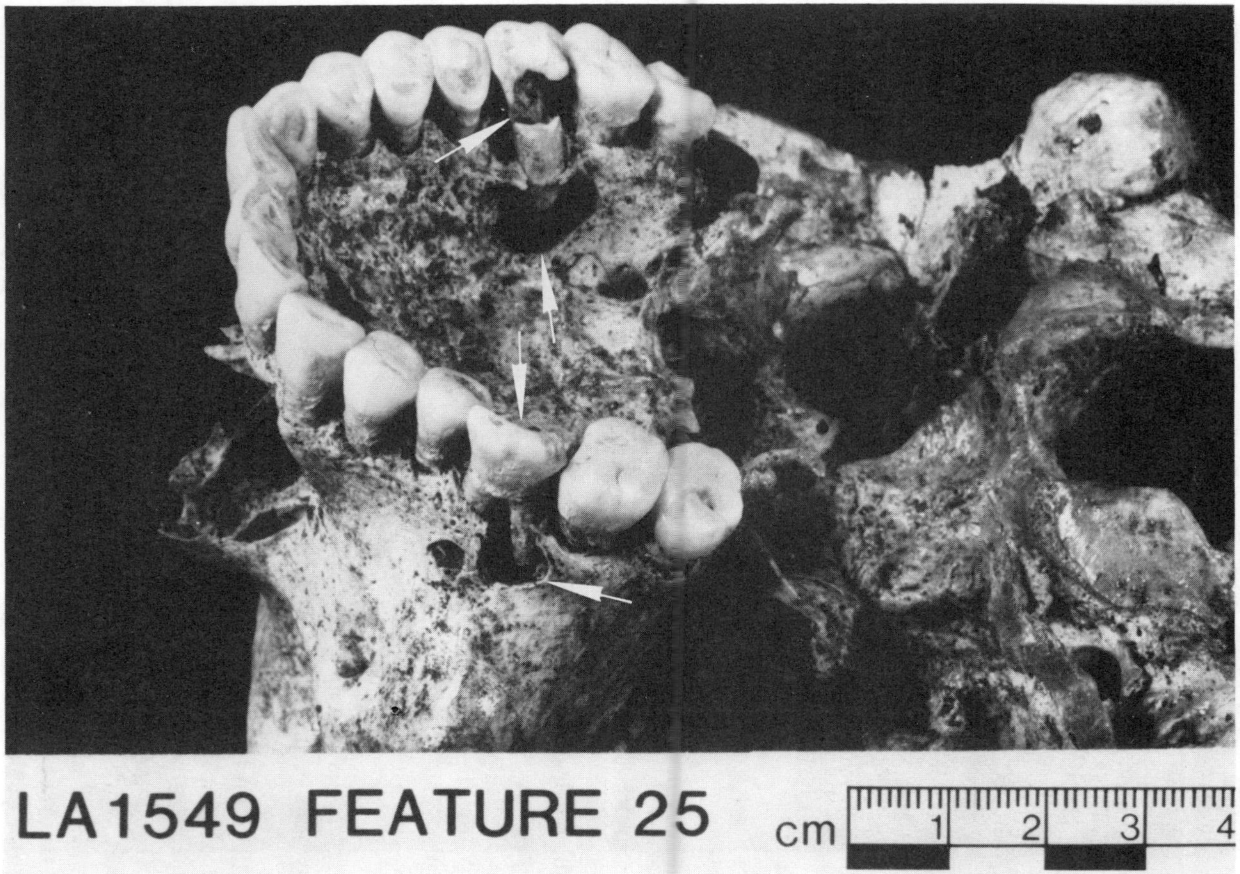

Fig. 78. Feature 25, maxillary pathology. Note extreme wear of both M^1s, and abscesses at apices of roots (arrows).

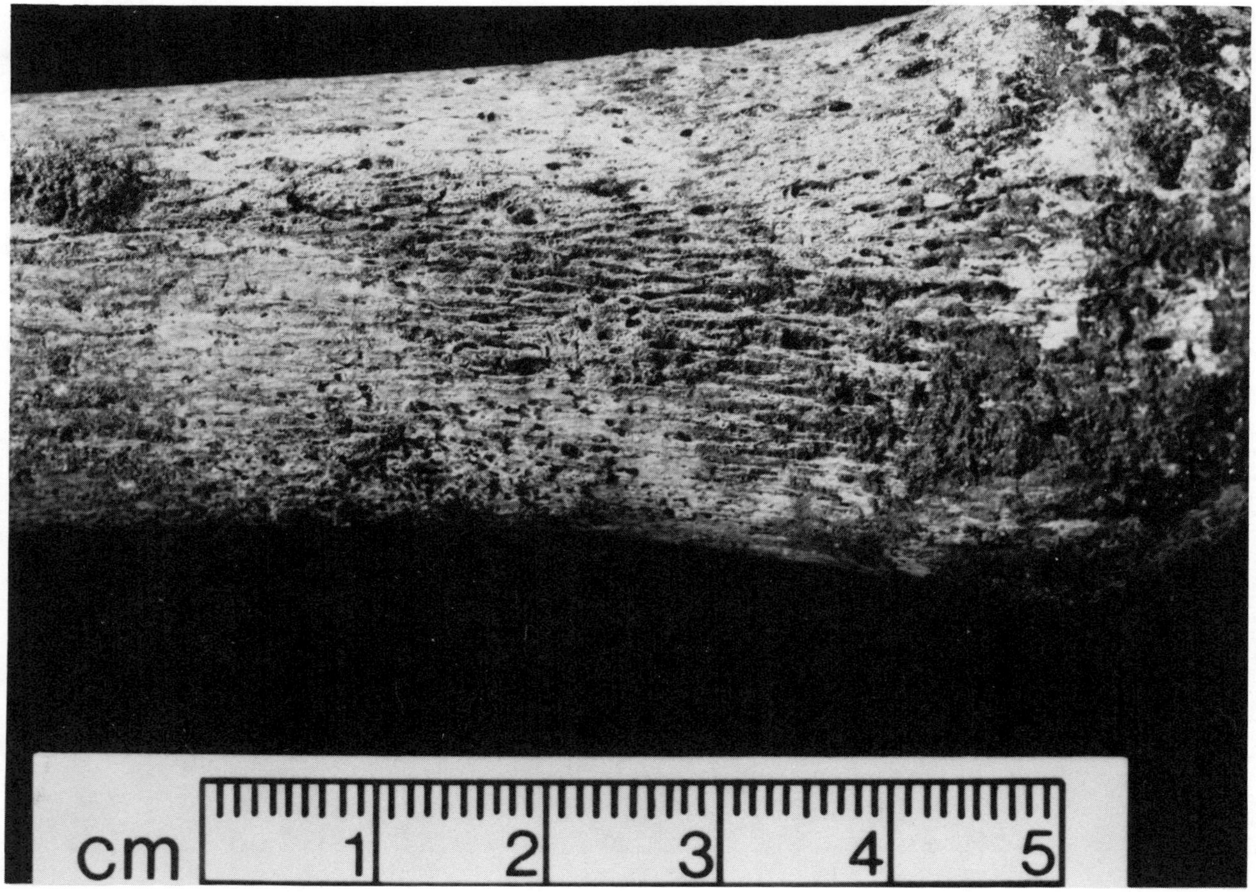

Fig. 79. Feature 25, example of possible mild periostitis on medial aspect of distal right tibia.

Fig. 80. Feature 29 burial. Photo taken after removal of right femur.

of the left femur, the articulated or nearly articulated left elbow (proximal radius and ulna and distal humerus) was oriented with the radius/ulna running roughly parallel to the left femur; about 20 cm to the west-southwest lay the proximal right ulna (oriented roughly parallel to the left).

The overall arrangement of the preserved portions of the burial suggests an original orientation of the long axis of the skeleton prior to disturbance approximately parallel to the long axis of the pit, with the skull (missing) to the north or northeast. The body probably lay on its left side. The knees were tightly flexed, and the arms lay south of the probable position of the skull. The burial was severely disturbed, and much of the upper skeleton had been destroyed, probably by erosion. The placement of the articulated portions corresponds to the position expected in a disturbed articulated burial rather than a secondary burial. The shallowness of the deposits in this portion of the site (about 30 cm above the top of the pit) may have permitted exposure of part of the burial, and rodent disturbance is evident in the condition of the bones and of associated bone artifacts (see below).

Burial accompaniments. Feature 29 was sufficiently disturbed that it is difficult to identify precisely the original context of all of the associated artifacts (see Figs. 82, 83). Adjacent to the two femora and to their north (i.e., tucked between the knees and the probable location of the torso) were two clusters of objects. One of these clusters, located about a third of the way up the left femur from the left knee (and near the fragmentary right elbow), contained a large number of items, including 10 turtle shell "gaming pieces,"

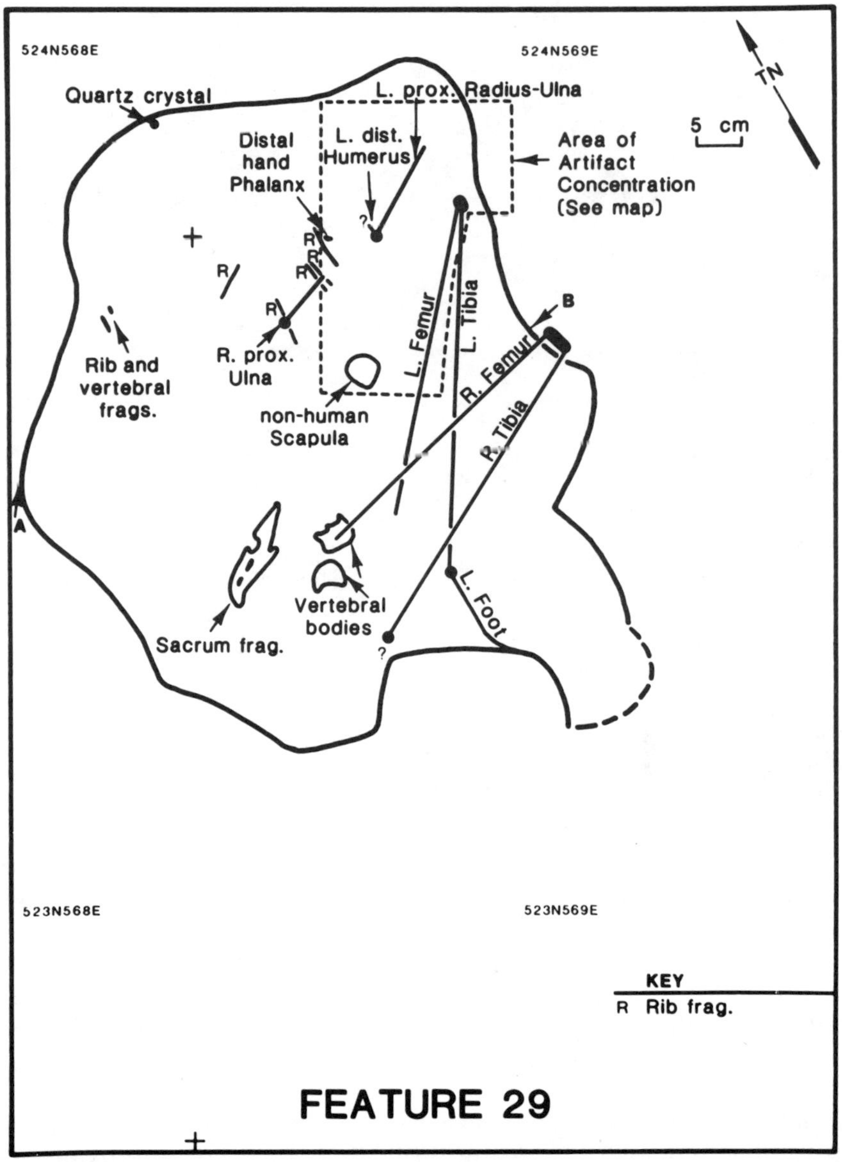

Fig. 81. Plan of Feature 29 burial (see Fig. 83 for detailed map of artifact concentration adjacent to femur).

8 of which are sub-rectangular to ovoid and 2 of which are circular with small perforations penetrating half way through the disc (Nos. 13b, 15–16, 22–28; Fig. 84 and Tables A13b-A13c); 10 flakes (Nos. 18–19, 21, 29, 32–35, 48b, 51a; Fig. 85a-g, Fig. 86a-c and Table A13g), only 3 of which show signs of utilization (Nos. 21, 48b, and 51a; No. 51a is made of a material that may be Alibates); 2 relatively crude, thick, bifaces, one complete (No. 31; Fig. 86d; Table A13g), the other fragmentary (No. 48c; Fig. 86f and Table A13g); a fragment of a large, thin, ovate bifacial knife (No. 36; Fig 86e and Table A13g); a small, broken knife, made of Alibates, with a small, rounded haft-element resembling an eastern Late Archaic "turkey tail" (No. 45; Fig. 86g and Tables A13e-A13f); 3 possible crude core fragments (Nos. 20, 30, 48a; Fig. 85h-j and Table A13g); 1 tiny fragment of red ocher (No. 51b; Fig. 40g and Table A13d); and 2 worked freshwater(?) mussel shell fragments (Nos. 14a, 46; Fig. 37g-h and Table A13a), probably cut from the valves of *Cyrtonaias*

tampicoensis (Lea, 1838).[8] Placed over part of the cluster was a fragmentary, worked antelope scapula (No. 13a and 17, restored; Fig. 87h and Table A13b). One worn and nicked edge suggests the scapula may have been used as a knife or scraping-shredding tool. Traces of red ocher were found on the scapula and on 2 of the flakes (Nos. 18–19). All of the lithics, with the exception of 1 item definitely made on Alibates (No. 45) and 1 item made on a material that may be Alibates (No. 51a), were made on locally derived bluish-gray to gray to tan cherts. Nodules of this material were readily available to the Henderson inhabitants, and could be found weathering out of the limestone ridges west of the site. Approximately 45 cm to the north of the main concentration of grave offerings was a single blocky fragment of clear quartz (No. 61; Fig. 40h and Table A13d). This specimen, found in direct contact with the bedrock walls of the pit but well above the level of the other artifacts, may have been displaced subsequent to burial from its original position. On the other hand, it may be an isolated offering in the grave or perhaps even a spurious item in the pit fill.

The second cluster, located closer to the left knee, contained 8 fragments representing 5 or perhaps 6 or more worked bone "awls" or "hairpins" (Nos. 39–44, 47, 49; Fig. 87a-g and Tables A13b-A13c). All showed severe signs of rodent gnawing and weathering, and were only partially restorable. They were clustered in a parallel arrangement, aligned in about the same orientation as that estimated for the long axis of the burial. The function of these items is unknown.

No evidence of a mat or other covering was identified around the burial, although given its shallow depth the likelihood of preservation would be low.

Skeletal inventory and condition. As noted above, Feature 29 is incomplete, with much of the upper part of the body from the skull to the pelvis missing. Elements present are the distal left humerus, partial left and right radii and ulnae, one distal hand phalanx, several rib fragments, one partial lower thoracic vertebral body, one lumbar(?) vertebral body, several vertebral (and perhaps sacral) processes and articular facets, one partial sacrum, two femora (missing their proximal ends), two patellae, two tibiae, two fibulae, two calcanii and tali, all of the tarsals and metatarsals of the left foot, and two proximal left foot phalanges.

Many elements are broken or fragmentary. Of the long bones, both proximal femora are missing and the anterior face of the extreme distal end of the right femur is broken; the right tibia is essentially intact though the proximal shaft is partially cracked; the left tibia shaft is more shattered and part of the distal end is missing, and the left distal fibula is missing. The left radius is missing the mid-shaft, both ulnae are missing their distal ends. Several elements, particularly the proximal end of the broken left femoral shaft and the anterior shaft of the left tibia, exhibit rodent gnawing.

Sex. Though no diagnostic elements were preserved, the overall robustness of the material suggests that the individual was a male. As shown in Figure 88, measurement supports this interpretation. The left tibial superior epiphyseal breadth was selected because it provides good separation between the sexes (İşcan and Miller-Shaivitz 1984), and

---

[8]These worked mussel shell fragments were too small to be identified. However, numerous identifiable valves, many with cuts where ornament blanks had been removed, were found in room fill and plaza trash at Henderson. All of the identifiable specimens proved to be *C. tampicoensis*; it is quite likely, therefore, that the ornaments from Feature 29 are of the same species. We are grateful to John B. Burch, Curator of Mollusks, Museum of Zoology, University of Michigan, for identifying the site's freshwater mussels.

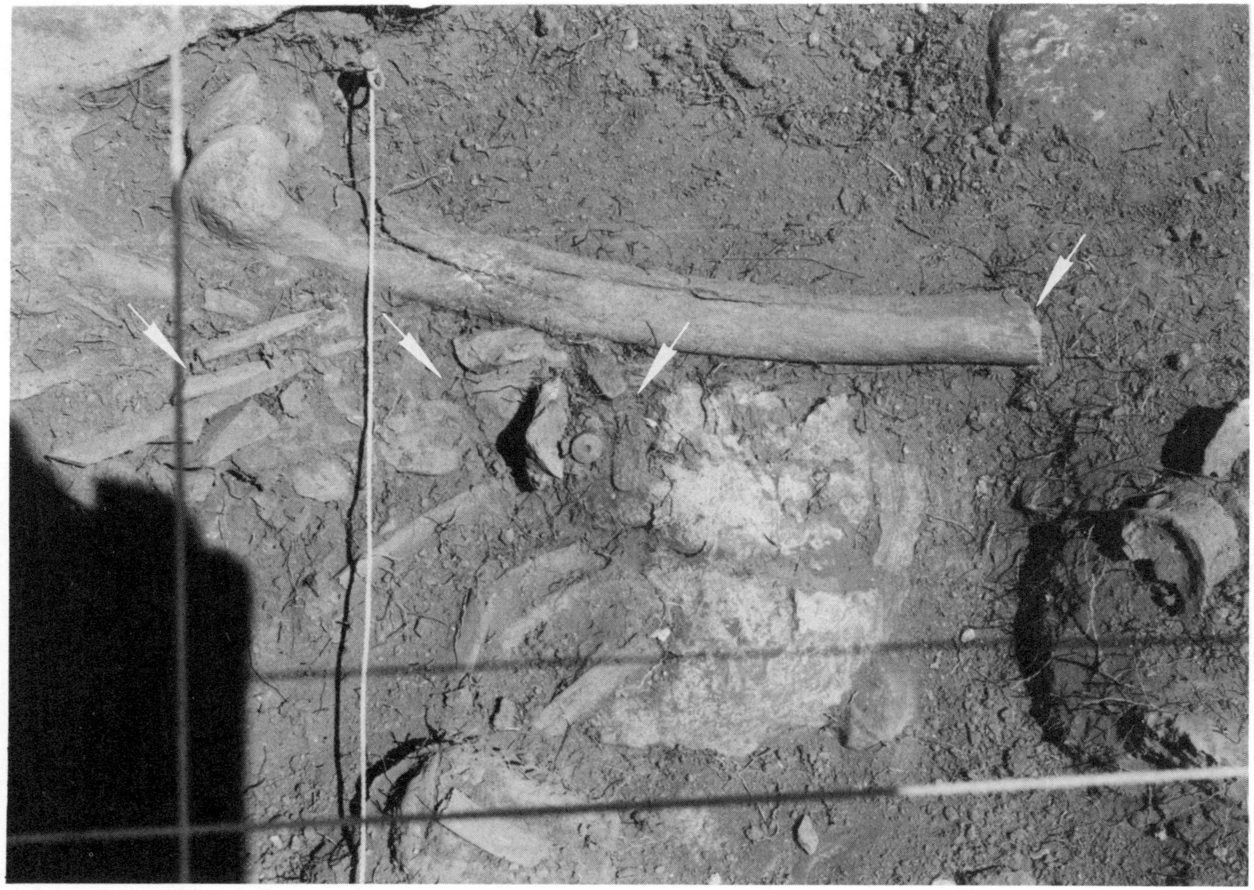

Fig. 82. Closeup of left femur of Feature 29 burial, showing cluster of turtle shell "gaming pieces" (center right arrow), lithics (center left arrow), and bone "awls" or "hairpins" (extreme left arrow). End of femur gnawed by rodents (extreme right arrow). White zone to right of "gaming pieces" is bedrock.

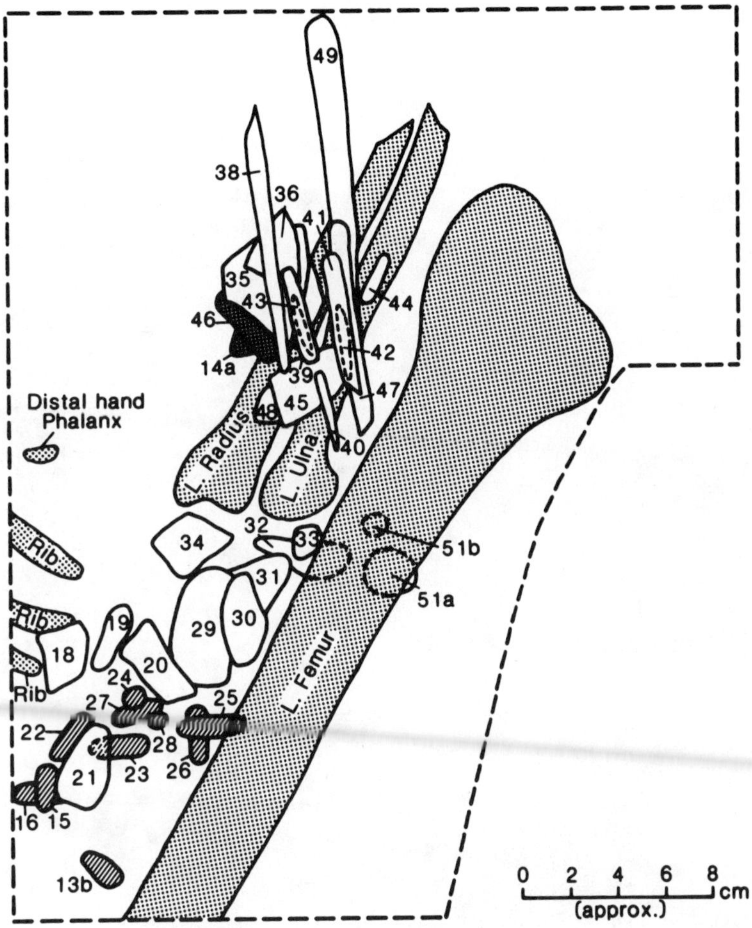

FEATURE 29

Fig. 83. Plan of artifact clusters found with Feature 29 burial (see Figs. 80–82). Turtle shell "gaming pieces" (Nos. 13b, 15–16, 22–28; oblique hatching). Shell ornaments (Nos. 14a, 46; dark stippling). Red ocher fragment (No. 51b). Remaining items are lithics (Nos. 18–21, 29–36, 48a-c, 51a) and bone "awls" or "hairpins" (Nos. 39–44, 47, 49). Antelope scapula "knife" (Nos. 13a, 17; not shown) overlay lithics and "gaming pieces," extending from No. 34 to No. 21. Artifacts not drawn precisely to scale.

because of the number of these elements measurable in the Henderson Site burials for comparison. Similar results are produced by distal femoral measurements, though the sample size is smaller. Thus, Feature 29 may be identified with moderate certainty as a male.

Age. As described below, the widespread occurrence of slight arthritis on essentially all articular surfaces of Feature 29 suggests a relatively advanced age. Arthritis in most cases is comparable to that observed in analogous positions on Feature 21 though slightly less advanced. Arthritis development is in excess of that visible on Feature 25. Thus, an age in excess of 35 years is probable, though of course this is based on very limited data.

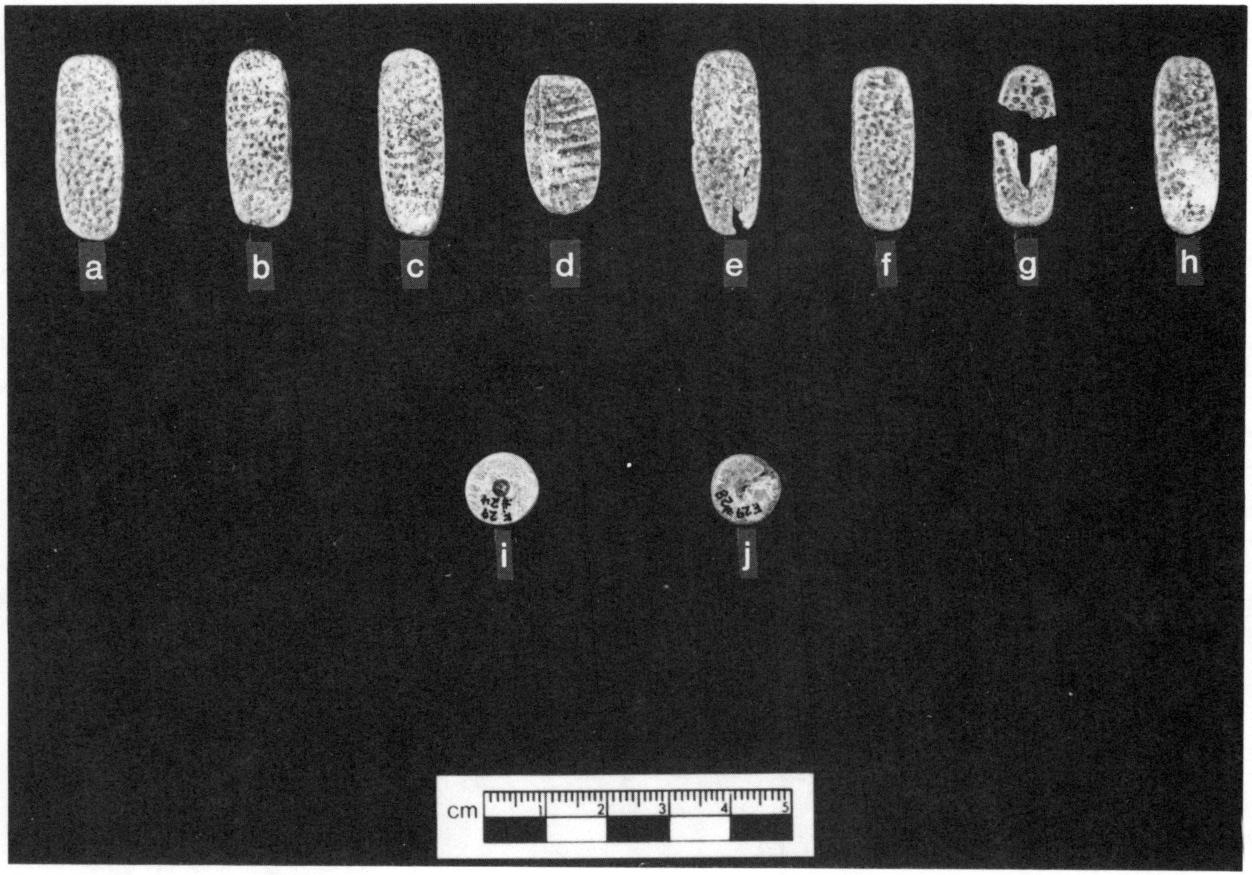

Fig. 84. Turtle shell "gaming pieces" found with Feature 29 burial. a-h, quasi-rectangular, unperforated specimens (Nos. 13b, 15–16, 22–23, 25–27); i-j, circular, semi-perforated specimens (Nos. 24 and 28). No. 24, which may be bone rather than turtle shell, has 2 mutually perpendicular sets of cutmarks or incisions on face opposite perforation.

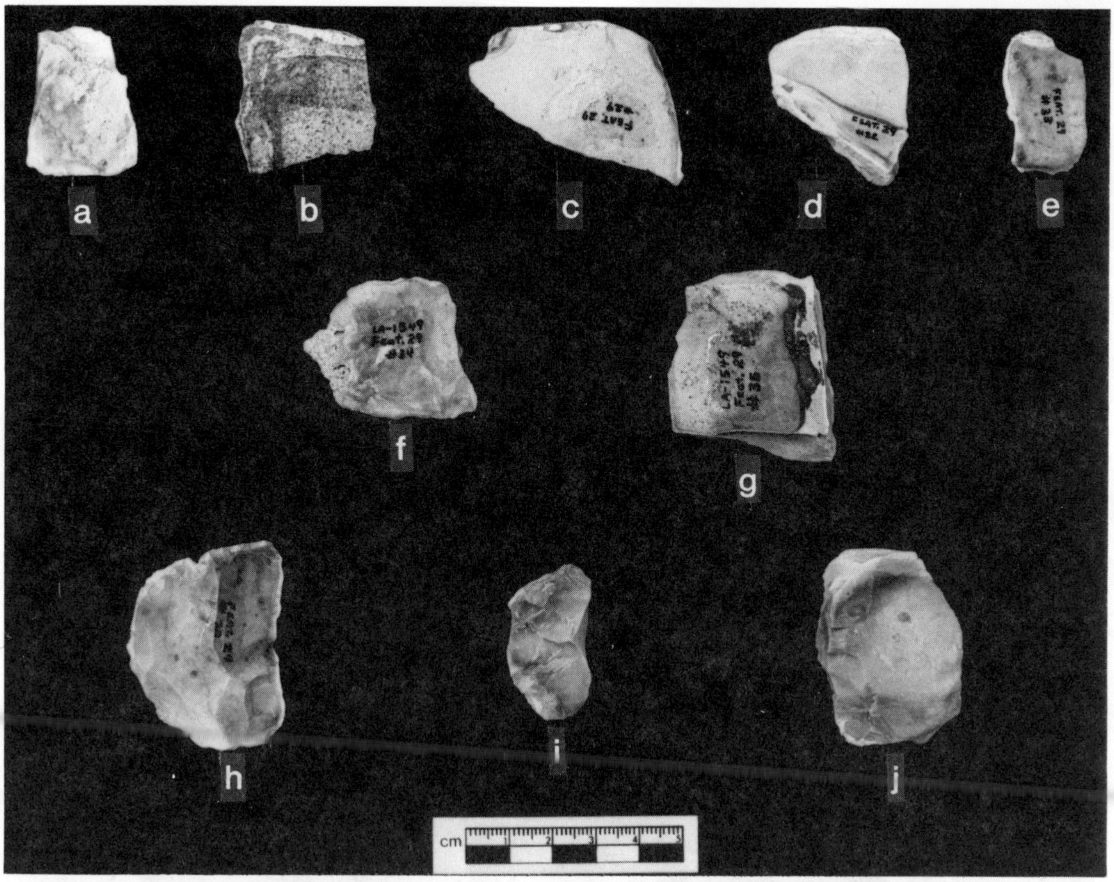

Fig. 85. Flakes and cores found with Feature 29 burial. a-g, unutilized flakes (Nos. 18–19, 29, 32–35); h-j, possible cores or core fragments (Nos. 20, 30, 48a).

General description, cultural and pathological alterations. As indicated above, Feature 29 is clearly an older individual with well-developed markings and ubiquitous arthritis. Arthritis takes the form of slight to moderate osteophytic development on the preserved lumbar vertebral body, and sharply defined edges or sharp raised rims on essentially all articular facets on most elements. No other pathologies are evident.

Feature 36

Stratigraphic context. Feature 36 was an approximately round pit, containing an adult male burial, with a smaller and shallower circular pit (Feat. 36A, a possible post hole) abutting and overlapping with it on its southwestern margin (Figs. 7, 19, 89, 90). The burial is located in the northwest corner of Grid 528N563E, southwest 529N563E, northeast 528N562E, and extreme southeast 529N562E, near the northeast corner of the deep pitroom in the East Bar (Room E-3). The Feature 36 pit was sealed under the 100.60 m floor (Floor 1), and thus is contemporary with or shortly predates the floor; the relation of Feature 36A to 36 is unclear. The Feature 36 pit was 85 cm (west-northwest to east-southeast) by 75 cm (excluding Feat. 36A) at just below the floor level. The walls of the pit were essentially vertical, except in the east-southeast end of the pit where a 25 cm undercut extended from 100.30 m elevation to the pit base. The feature was dug

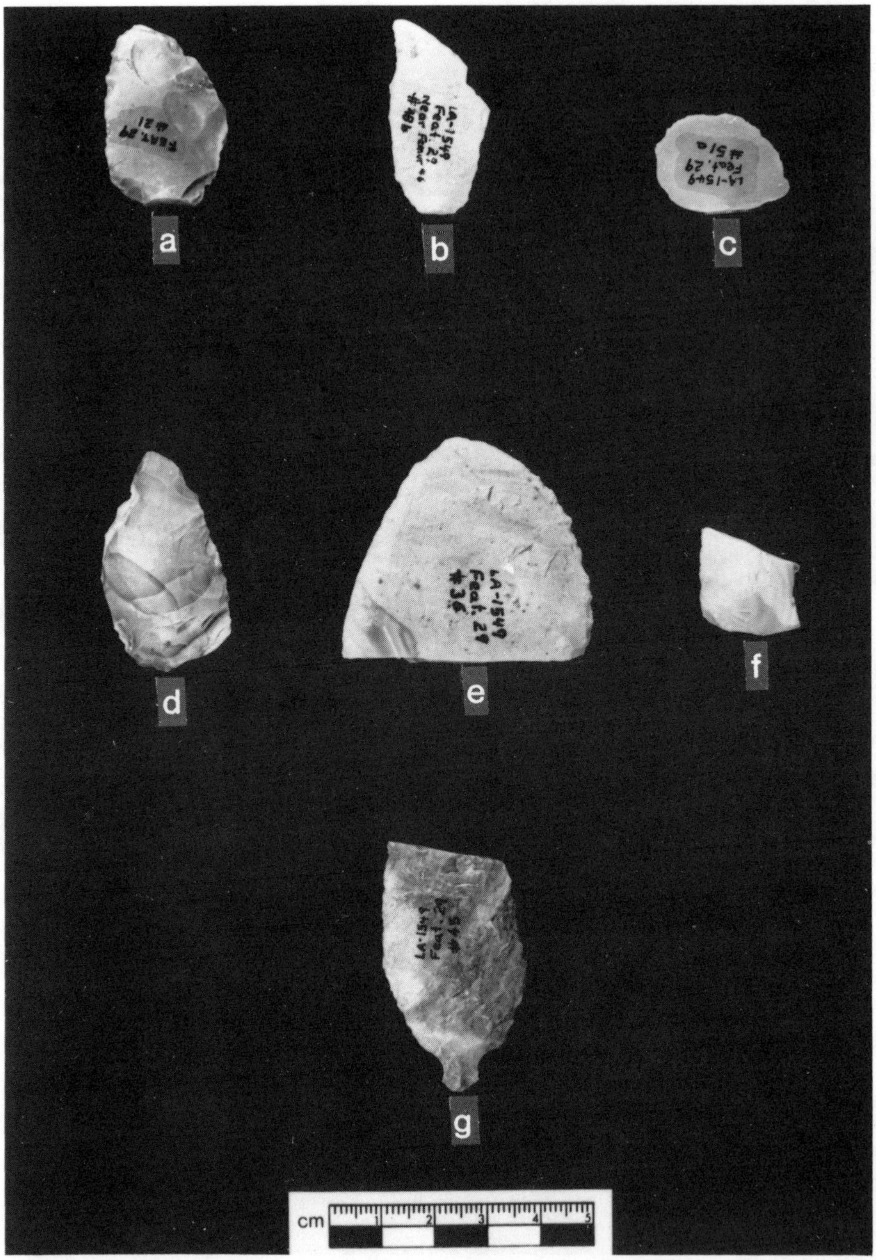

Fig. 86. Utilized flakes and bifacial tools found with Feature 29 burial. a-c, utilized flakes (Nos. 21, 48b; No. 51a, Alibates-like material); d-g, bifacial tools (No. 31, pointed ovate biface; No. 36, large bifacial knife fragment; No. 48c, ovate? biface fragment; No. 45, Alibates point or hafted knife with "turkey tail" haft-element).

through fill down to bedrock; its walls were not plastered or finished in any other way. The pit base was irregular limestone bedrock, dipping slightly west-northwestward, with a maximum depth of 69 cm at an elevation of 99.87 m.

The pit fill was unconsolidated, displayed no internal stratigraphy, and contained numerous small, subrounded pebbles (ca. 3 cm diameter).

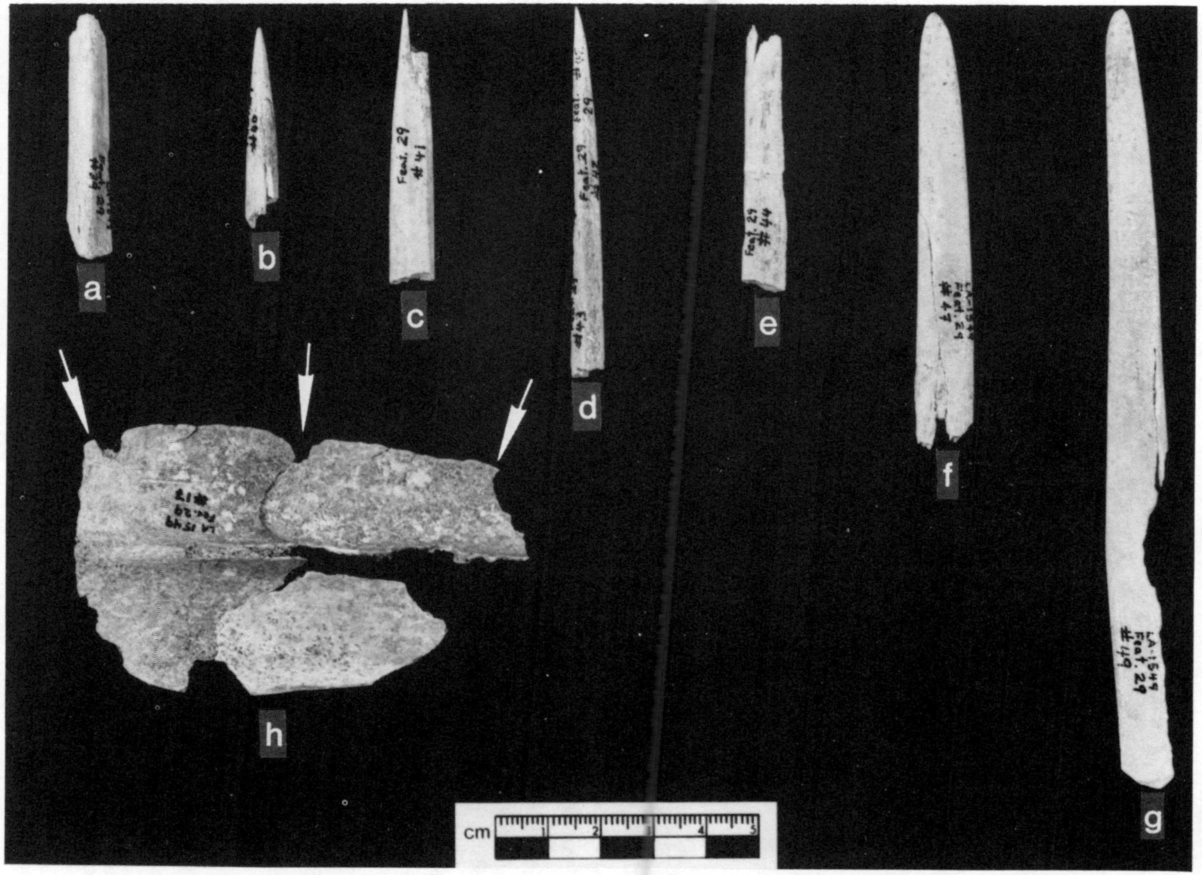

Fig. 87. Bone "awls" or "hairpins" and antelope scapula "knife" found with Feature 29 burial. a-g, "awls" or "hairpins" (Nos. 39–41, 42 and 43 conjoined, 44, 47, and 49); h, scapula "knife" (arrows indicate utilized and nicked working edge).

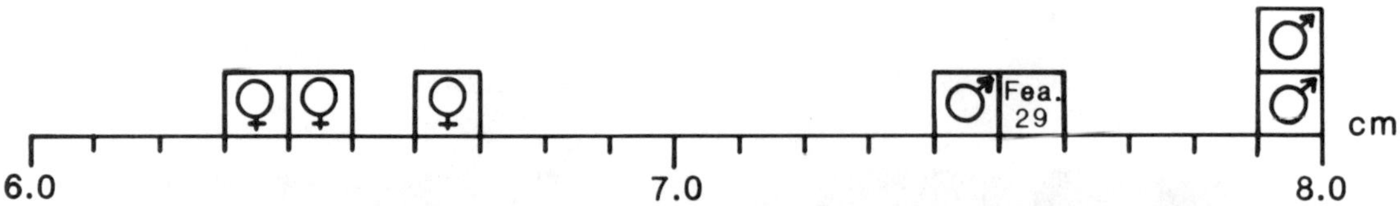

Fig. 88. Left tibia superior epiphyseal breadth.

Position and orientation. The skeleton was fully articulated, lying on its back and left side, with the skull to the east-southeast. The cranium lay on the left temporal, slightly propped up on bedrock inside the under-cut at the east-southeast end of the pit described above. The face pointed south-southwest and slightly above the horizontal. The mandible was articulated, with the mouth slightly open. The long axis of the burial was oriented east-southeast to west-northwest. The proximal right humerus lay just northeast (behind) the rib cage, and angled in (south) about 5 degrees relative to the long axis; thus the right elbow lay over the lower rib cage north of the lower thoracic vertebrae. The elbow was loosely flexed at about 75 degrees, with the forearm passing south over the vertebral column and with the right wrist near the lower left rib cage. The right hand made an angle of about 110 degrees in relation to the arm, lying west-northwest of (and above) the left shoulder, with the palmar surface facing south and the digits approximately to the west. The hand overlay part of a cache of projectile points (Cluster 1, see below). The left humerus ran directly parallel with the long axis (west-northwest), and the left radius and ulna were doubled back (tightly flexed) directly over the humerus. The left hand was palmar side down, and made an angle of around 140 degrees relative to the arm, with the digits pointing toward the skull. The lower vertebrae were progressively further rotated to the degree that the pelvis lay essentially horizontally with the right ilium on the northeast and the left ilium on the southwest. The right femur overlay the pelvis, running to the south-southeast at around 40 degrees relative to the long axis. The right knee was tightly flexed, at around 10 degrees. The left femur lay flexed at an angle of around 20 degrees relative to the long axis with the knee about 10 cm southeast (and below) the right knee. The left leg was tightly flexed so that the tibia ran nearly parallel to the femur. Both feet rested against the west-northwest pit wall, with the digits to the northwest and higher than the heels.

Burial accompaniments. Feature 36 had a total of 43 projectile points and/or hafted knives associated with it (see Figs. 89–99 and Tables A14d-A14g). Twenty-eight of them were in a single cluster (Cluster 1) located on the left ribs next to the left proximal humerus and distal ulna (i.e., extending down the arm from the shoulder) and under the right hand; 14 others were clustered on the lower left abdomen (Cluster 2) in the vicinity of the lumbar vertebrae. One additional point (No. 25), probably displaced from Cluster 2, was located near the left leg between the femur and fibula. A tiny, unworked obsidian flake (No. 21; not tabulated in Appendix 14 or illustrated), only 0.73 cm in length and weighing only 0.11 g, was found directly beneath Cluster 1; this specimen is probably an accidental inclusion from the fill of the burial pit rather than an intentional association with the burial or point cluster.

Fig. 89. Feature 36 burial. Note Point Cluster 1 to right of chest and Point No. 18 (prior to exposure of Point Cluster 2) on lumbar region.

The undisturbed points in each cluster tended to lie roughly parallel to each other. Many of the points in Cluster 1 pointed south (a few north, and a few scattered), away from the body and diverging slightly eastward of the right lower arm orientation. Many of the points in Cluster 2 pointed northwest, towards the lower back, nearly parallel with the femora. The pattern was such as might be produced by laying a bundle of parallel hafted projectiles from the left shoulder to the lower abdomen under the right hand, with 28 of the points aligned towards the shoulder and 15 of them pointing towards the abdomen. No evidence of the shafts was recovered, however. Moreover, the tremendous range of point sizes (weighing from 0.10 g to 58.22 g) makes it more likely that the points were unhafted

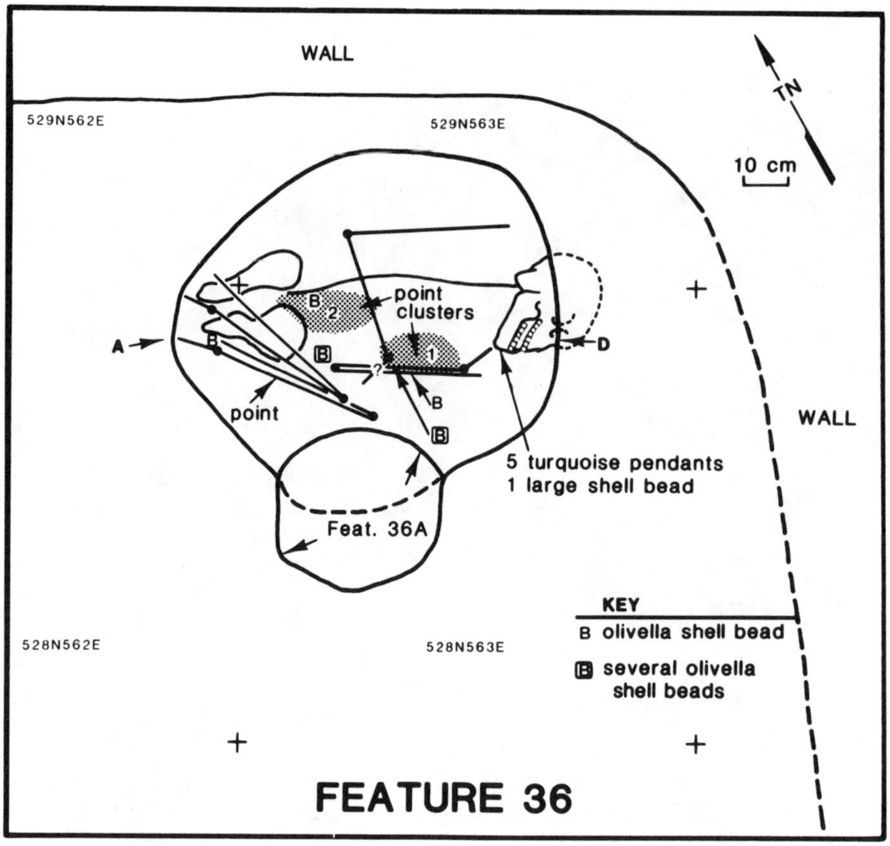

Fig. 90. Plan of Feature 36 burial.

and instead were placed in some sort of perishable container(s) which has since decayed. Very fragmentary traces of coiled basketry (not illustrated), with wooden rods and yucca coils, were identified by Richard I. Ford in the vicinity of Cluster 2, as well as in the gap between the clusters (see Fig. 92 and Appendix 16). The rods were aligned more or less parallel to the orientation of the points in Cluster 2. It therefore seems highly probable that the points near the abdomen were placed on the body in some sort of basket. Cluster 1 may also have been interred in a basket, possibly even in the same one, although differences in the alignment of the two clusters, and the distance separating them, make a single container unlikely. Most of the points in both clusters were coated with red ocher.

The cache is distinctive both in the range of point types it contains and in the materials on which the points are made (see Figs. 95–99 and Tables A14d-A14g). Of the several hundred points and point fragments found throughout the site in non-burial contexts, most are small, side-notched Washitas, the ubiquitous hallmark of the late prehistoric period in the region. Less numerous, but also well represented at the site are small, concave-base triangles or Fresnos. The majority of the Washita and Fresno points are made on materials which were probably available locally as cobbles in the Pecos Valley, or as nodules eroding out of limestone ridges bordering the valley to the west. Very few of the points are made on materials that are demonstrably of Plains origin.

In striking contrast, the points and knives in the Feature 36 cache represent a bewildering array of types, including many probable Archaic varieties. Moreover, many are made on materials from well-known sources in Texas, most notably Alibates, Edwards

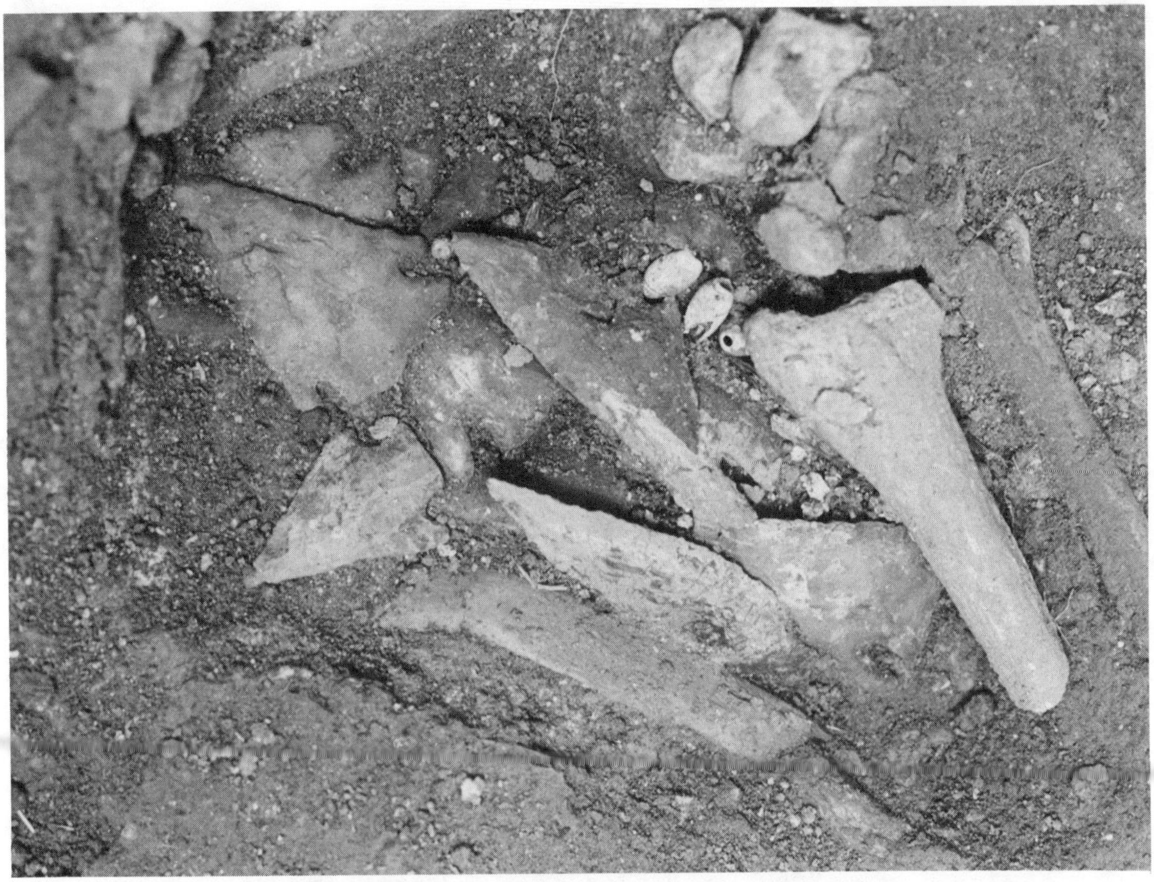

Fig. 91. Closeup of Point Cluster 1, Feature 36, during excavation. Note *Olivella* shell beads.

Plateau, and perhaps Tecovas. We have not made a rigorous attempt to assign points in the cache to specific types because of their unusual context (i.e., as burial offerings in a thirteenth-century New Mexican grave).[9] Nevertheless, the resemblances of many of the specimens to familiar Plains types is striking and worth noting (cf. Bell 1958, 1960; Suhm and Jelks 1962). For example, among the probable Archaic forms, No. 37 (Fig. 98g) may be a Bulverde point, perhaps made on Edwards Plateau chert; Nos. 3, 6, 8, 9, and 18 (Fig. 95c,e,g-h and Fig. 98a, respectively) are either Castrovilles or Marshalls, all fashioned on Edwards; and Nos. 10, 34, and 46 (Fig. 95i, Fig. 98e, and Fig. 97f, respectively) are Shumlas, the latter two of which are also probably made on Edwards.

Particularly curious is No. 41 (Fig. 99b) which, except for its unusual banded, chocolate-brown material, is strikingly similar to Late Archaic "turkey tails" in eastern North America. We have been unable to discover a source for the distinctive material on which No. 41 is made. However, there are three large bifaces in the collections of the Arizona State Museum at the University of Arizona which, while lacking the "turkey tail" haft-element, are almost certainly made on the same material. Two of the specimens are

---

[9]Assistance in identifying point types and materials was provided by Dee Ann Story, Curtis Tunnell, David S. Dibble, Larry D. Banks, Harry J. Shafer, Michael Collins, and Robert H. Leslie.

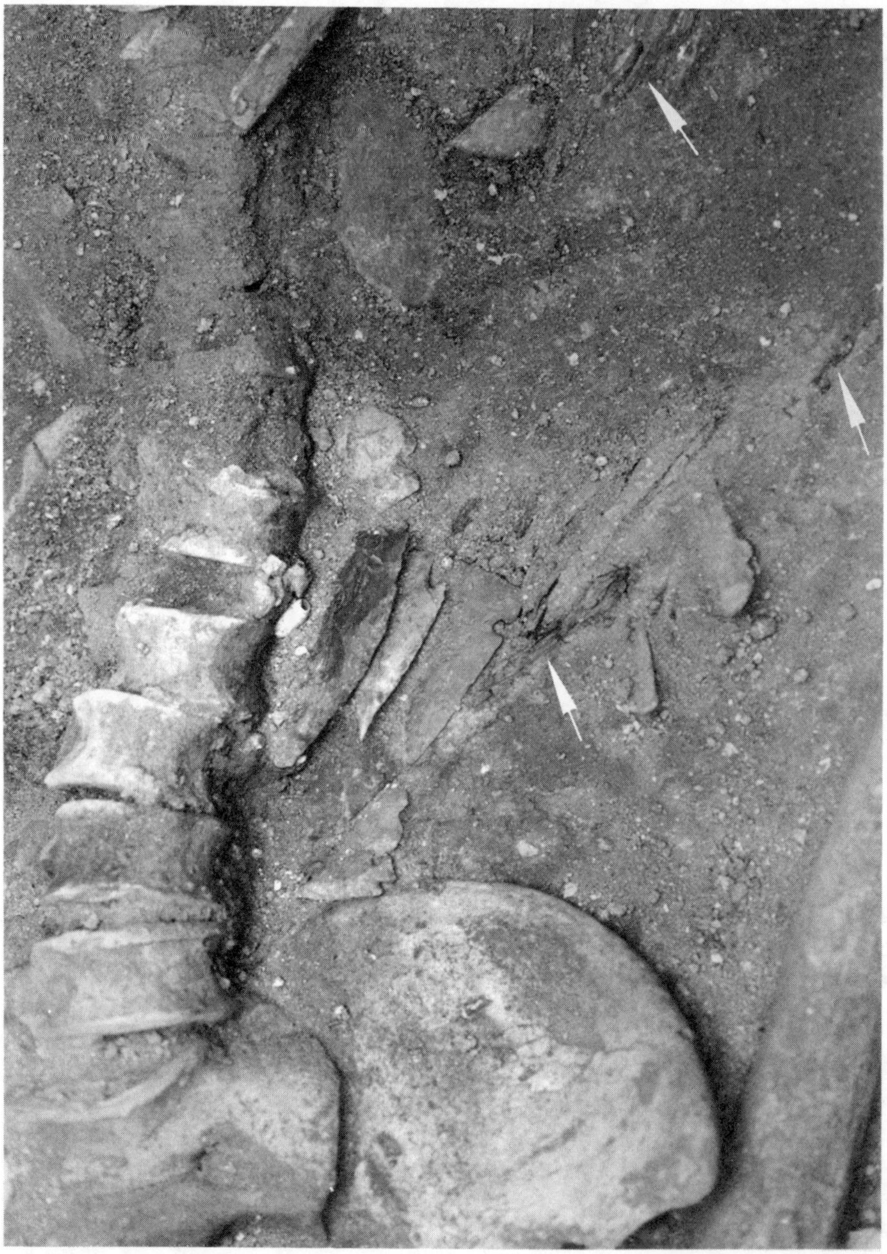

Fig. 92. Closeup of Point Cluster 2, Feature 36, during excavation. Note *Olivella* shell bead adjacent to lumbar and fragmentary wooden rods from yucca coiled basket at right edge of cluster and extending toward upper right corner of photograph (arrows).

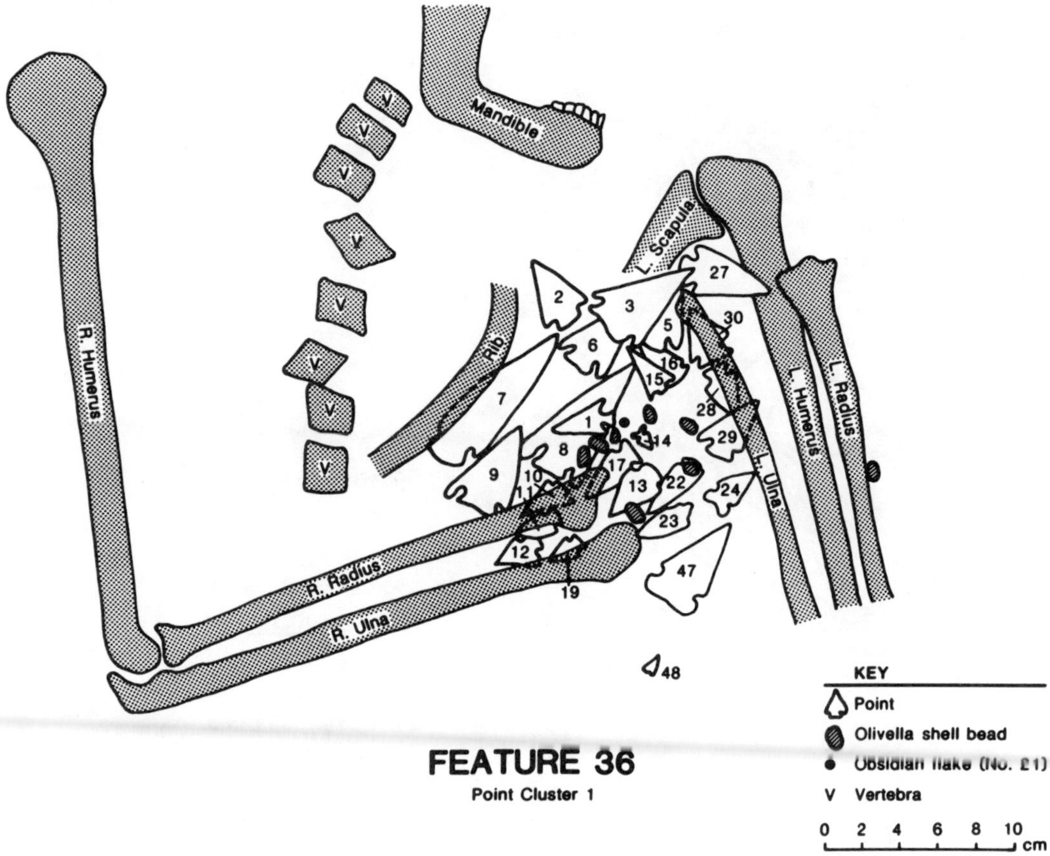

Fig. 93. Plan of Point Cluster 1, Feature 36. Point No. 20 (not shown) below Nos. 15–16, with same orientation as No. 22. Point No. 46 (not shown) below No. 17, with same orientation as No. 27. Cluster included 8 *Olivella* beads (No. 26, adjacent to left radius; Nos. 52–58, numbered clockwise from far left, in midst of point cluster) and 169 small disc-shell beads (not shown). Bones of right wrist and hand (not shown) overlay cluster. Points not drawn to scale.

absolutely identical (at least visually) in both color and texture (ASM catalog numbers GP-12253 and A-30500); the third displays the same banding but is somewhat lighter and more yellowish-brown in color (A-30678). These specimens are illustrated in Fig. 100.[10]

One of the dark brown specimens (GP-12253) is from a burial (No. 5) at the Q Ranch Pueblo (AZ P:13:13), a 200-room masonry structure on Ellison Creek west of Canyon Creek in east-central Arizona. The biface, along with 5 ceramic vessels and 10 small triangular points, was obtained by the Gila Pueblo Foundation in 1930 and donated to the ASM in 1950. The ceramics (1 Gila Red jar, 1 Gila Red pitcher, 3 Pinto-Gila B/R

---

[10]William J. Parry brought the Arizona specimens to our attention. G. Michael Jacobs of the Arizona State Museum generously assisted us in gaining access to whatever information existed concerning the provenience and dating of the bifaces and he also provided us with excellent photographs. The photographs (ASM Negatives 63472 and 63473) were taken by Helga Teiwes of the Arizona State Museum.

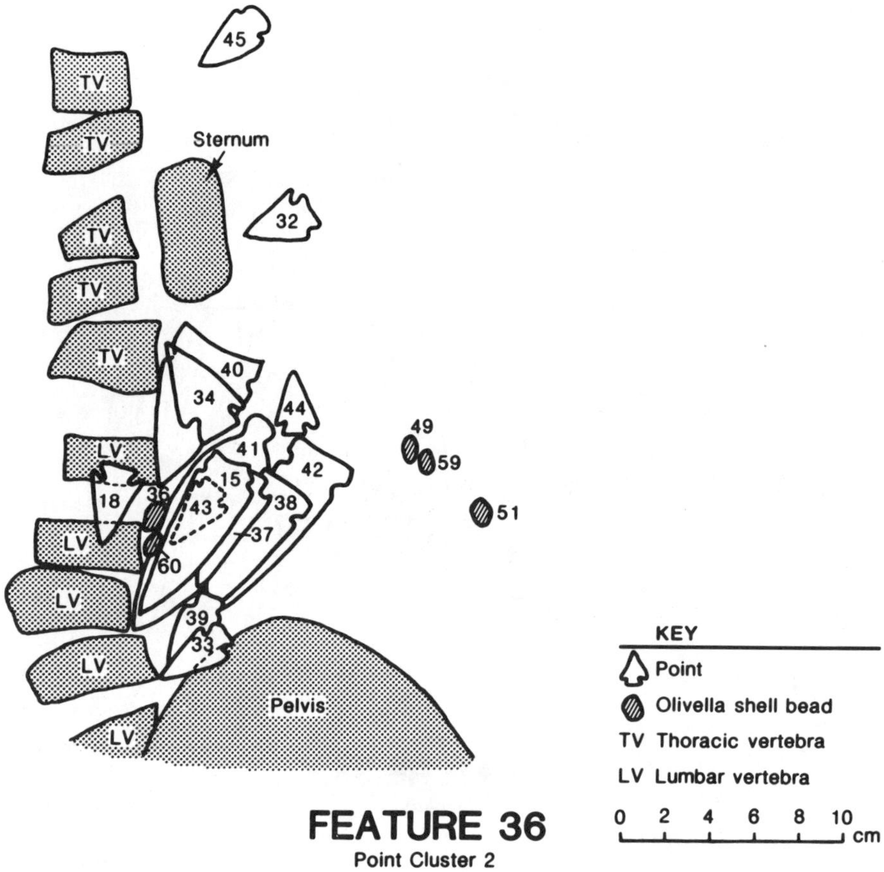

Fig. 94. Plan of Point Cluster 2, Feature 36. Point No. 25 (not shown) on mid-shaft of left fibula. Point superposition in cluster (lowest to highest) is: (40,43,44), 42, 39, 38, (37,33), 15. Cluster included 8 *Olivella* beads (No. 31 [not shown], near point No. 25 at mid-shaft of left fibula; Nos. 50a-50b [not shown], near proximal left femur; Nos. 36, 49, 51, 59–60 directly in point cluster). Points not drawn to scale.

bowls) and architecture suggest a date for the site in the first half of the fourteenth century (G. Michael Jacobs, personal communication). The biface measures 17.2 cm long by 5.7 cm wide by 1.1 cm thick.

The other dark brown biface (A-30500) was collected in the early 1930s from the Gipe Site (AZ N:16:6), a ca. 40-room, basalt boulder pueblo on the east side of Black Mesa on the Agua Fria River near Perry Tank Canyon in central Arizona. This specimen, donated to the ASM in 1965, measures 28.1 cm long by 5.4 cm wide by 1.2 cm thick. The site location and ceramic assemblage suggest occupation of the site during the Tuzigoot Phase of the Verde Valley/Southern Sinagua sequence, or ca. A.D. 1300–1425 (G. Michael Jacobs, personal communication).

The third, lighter colored biface (A-30678) reputedly comes from the Safford area in southeastern Arizona (AZ CC:2:– – –). This specimen, donated to the ASM in 1965, is believed to have been found in the late 1930s. Its chronological placement is unknown (G. Michael Jacobs, personal communication). The biface measures 20.3 cm long by 6.9 cm wide by 0.9 cm thick.

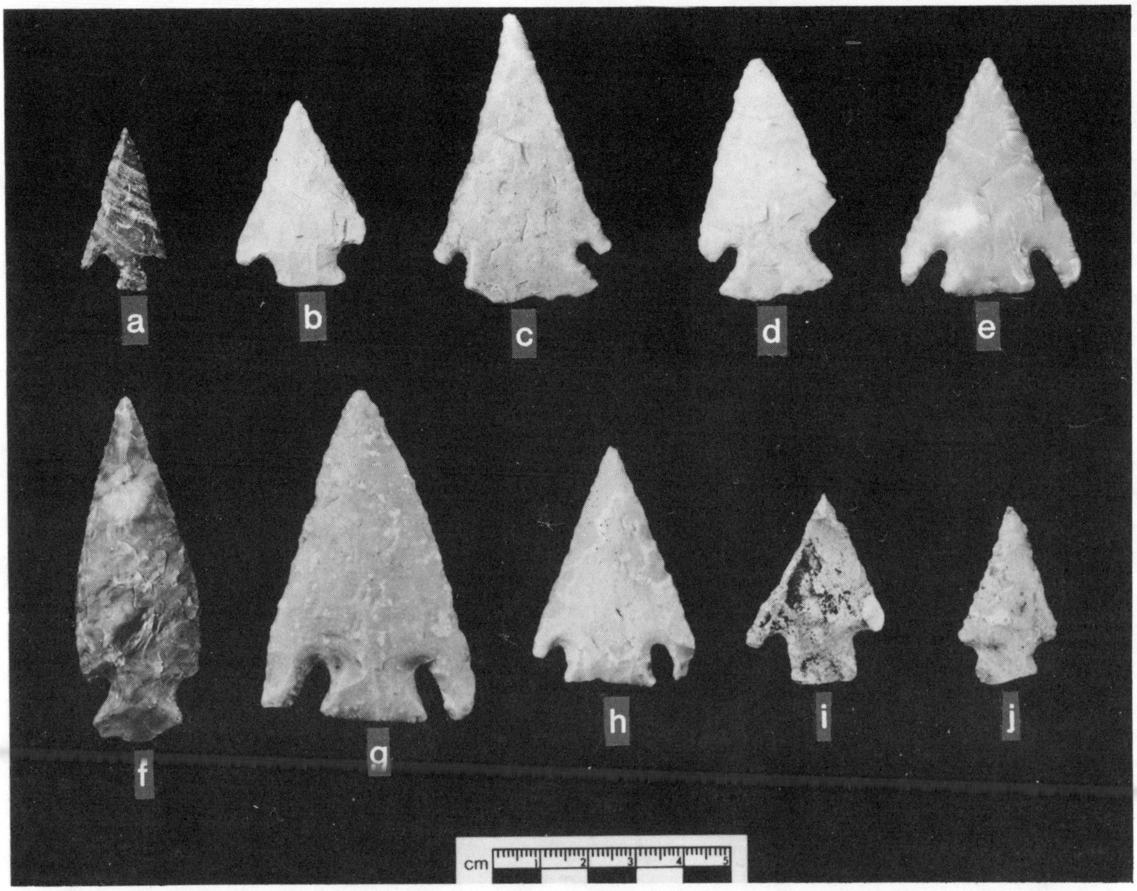

Fig. 95. Projectile points and hafted knives found with Feature 36 burial (Cluster 1, Part 1). a-j, Nos. 1–3, 5–11.

A fourth biface (82–43–53), possibly of similar material (seen by us only on a 35 mm color slide), was recovered in the 1970s from Gila Pueblo (AZ V:9:52) on Pinal Creek near Globe, Arizona (G. Michael Jacobs, personal communication). The material of this biface has thin, wavy, dark brown bands, separated by broad, dull, grayish-white bands. While the pattern of banding is virtually identical to that of the other specimens, the color clearly is not. However, according to Jacobs (personal communication), the biface may have been burned, thereby altering its original texture and color. The site, a cobble and adobe structure with more than 100 rooms, is the type site for the Gila Phase and dates between about A.D. 1300–1400. The specimen, which measures 19.4 cm long by 5.1 cm wide by 1.5 cm thick, is long and leaf-shaped, with one end pointed and the other end nearly straight or only slightly convex. Precise details on the context in which the biface was found are not available.

The three bifaces in the ASM collections with general provenience information appear to date around or after A.D. 1300, a temporal placement not too different from that of the Henderson specimen. Moreover, the one Arizona specimen for which contextual information is known came from a relatively elaborate burial, as did the Henderson biface. Finally, like No. 41, the Arizona bifaces are large, thin, and distinctively flaked by well-controlled percussion. The principal difference between the Henderson specimen and the Arizona bifaces is the "turkey tail" haft-element on the former. No source for the material

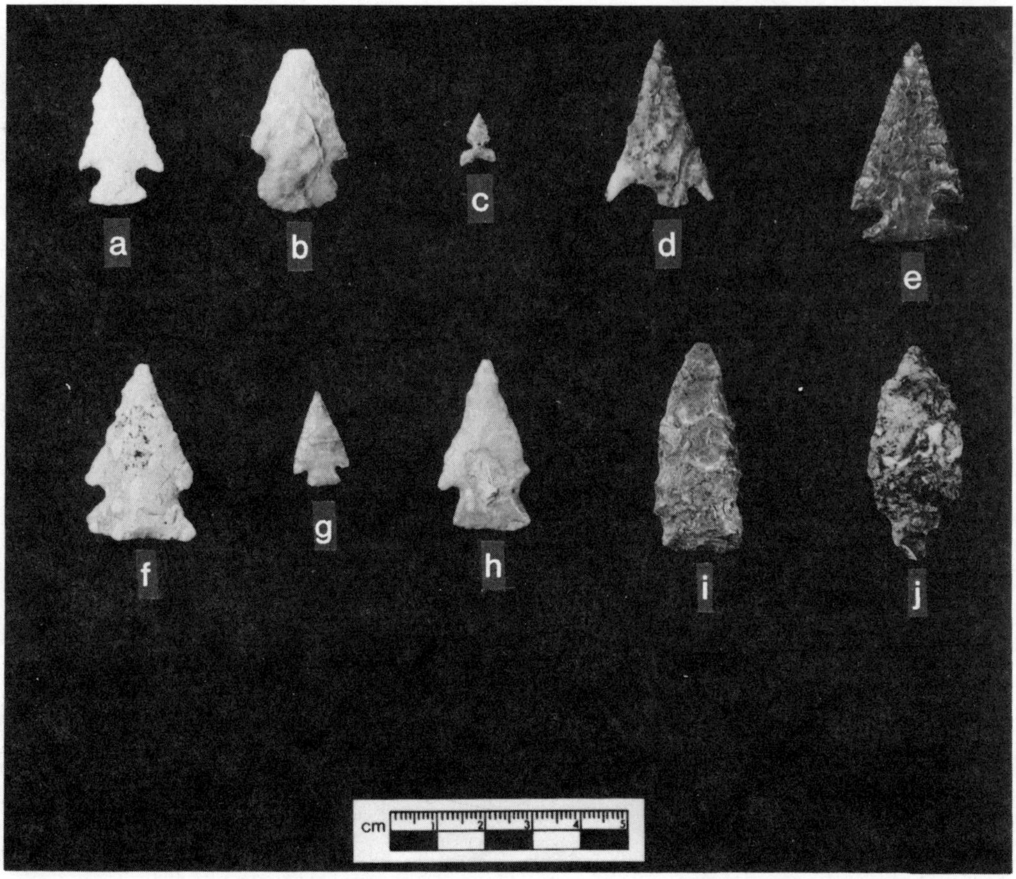

Fig. 96. Projectile points and hafted knives found with Feature 36 burial (Cluster 1, Part 2). a-j, Nos. 12–17, 19–20, 22–23.

has ever been located in Arizona, and debitage is rare or nonexistent (Bruce Huckell, personal communication). While there is a remote possibility that the material is an extremely unusual variant of Alibates (Larry Banks, personal communication), a source somewhere in central Arizona seems more likely.

Among the more recent point types found with the Feature 36 burial are Nos. 12, 19, and 33 (probable Scallorns; Fig. 96a,g and Fig. 98d, respectively), one of which may be made on Edwards Plateau chert; and No. 14 (Fig. 96c), made on Alibates, which is clearly a late prehistoric variety, though probably distinct from the Washita.

Finally, No. 35 (Fig. 98f) and possibly No. 42 (Fig. 99c) are reworked beveled knives, both fashioned on Texas materials (Edwards Plateau and Alibates, respectively).

Many of the other specimens from the cache probably are also Archaic dart points, but they are not as easily assigned to type. Likewise, the materials of many are of unknown origin, and could be either local or derived from more distant sources such as the Guadalupe Mountains, the Lower Pecos, or Trans-Pecos Texas.

The diversity of types and their long temporal span suggest the points are a collection acquired by exchange or through personal forays on to the Plains. The points clearly were not fashioned expressly for burial. Most show signs of heavy use (e.g., edge abra-

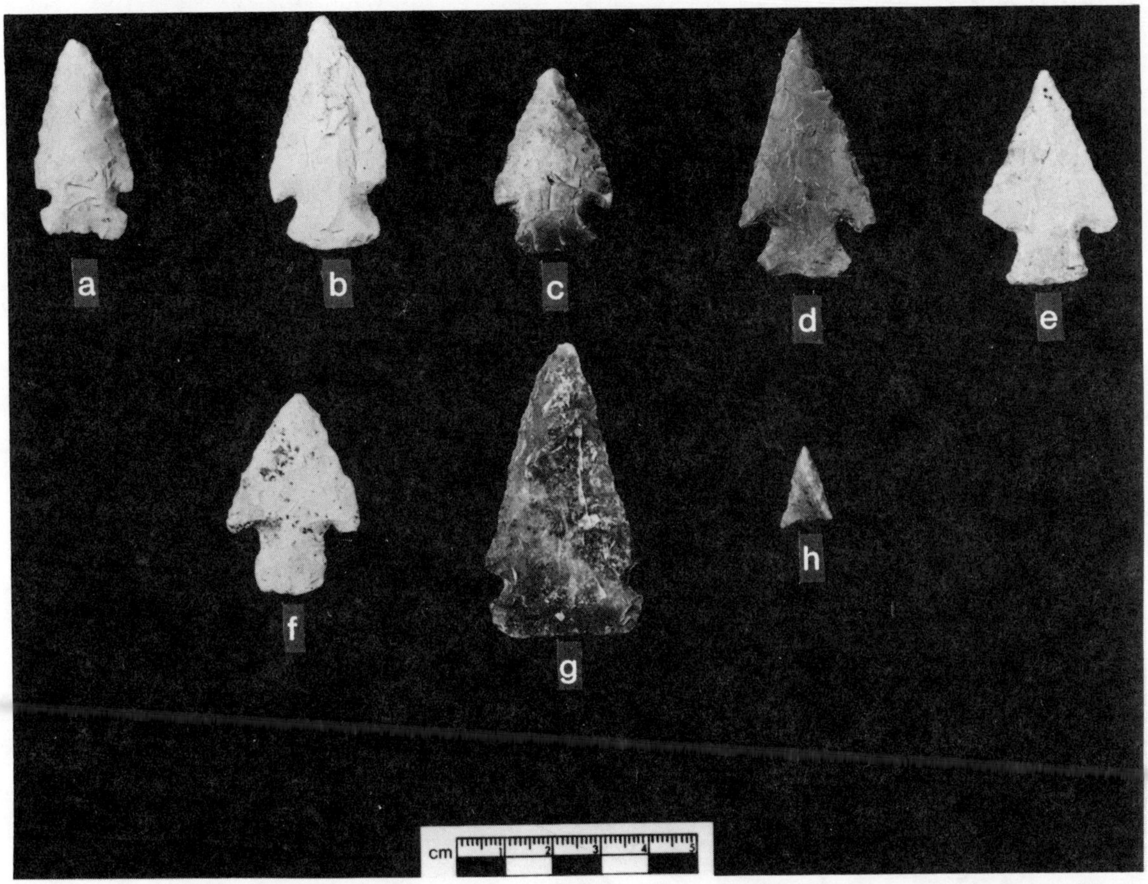

Fig. 97. Projectile points and hafted knives found with Feature 36 burial (Cluster 1, Part 3). a-h, Nos. 24, 27–30, 46–48.

sion, tip and tang damage), and several are heavily patinated or stained with manganese as though they had been exposed on the surface for extended periods before being collected. Several were reworked after the patina had formed. The symbolic significance of the cache is unknown, but it represents one of the few tangible evidences at Henderson of interaction with the Plains.

Along with the points, a concentration of 169 small disc-shell beads (Table A14a) and 7 *Olivella dama* (Wood, 1828) shell beads (Nos. 52–58; Fig. 38ff-ll and Table A14b) was located near the right wrist, either worn around the wrist, or associated with point Cluster 1 (see Fig. 90 and especially Fig. 93 for precise location of *Olivella* beads; disc-shell beads not shown in figures). Two *O. dama* beads (Nos. 36, 60; Fig. 38aa,nn) were located near the lower left abdomen, directly amid the points of Cluster 2, and three additional beads of the same species (Nos. 49, 51, 59; Fig. 38bb,ee,mm) were found near the base of the feature pit a few centimeters south of point Cluster 2 (see Figs. 90 and 94). Isolated *O. dama* beads occurred by the left mid-arm (No. 26; Fig. 38y), left proximal femur (Nos. 50a and 50b; Fig. 38cc-dd), and near the middle of the left leg (No. 31; Fig. 38z). It is likely that much of the scattering of the beads resulted from slumping off of the chest or abdomen, probably from locations near the projectile point clusters and/or from one or both wrists. The *Olivella* shell identifications were made by James H. McLean of the Los Angeles County Museum of Natural History. He noted that the *O. dama* specimens from Henderson are relatively large, suggesting a source (or sources) somewhere in the Gulf of

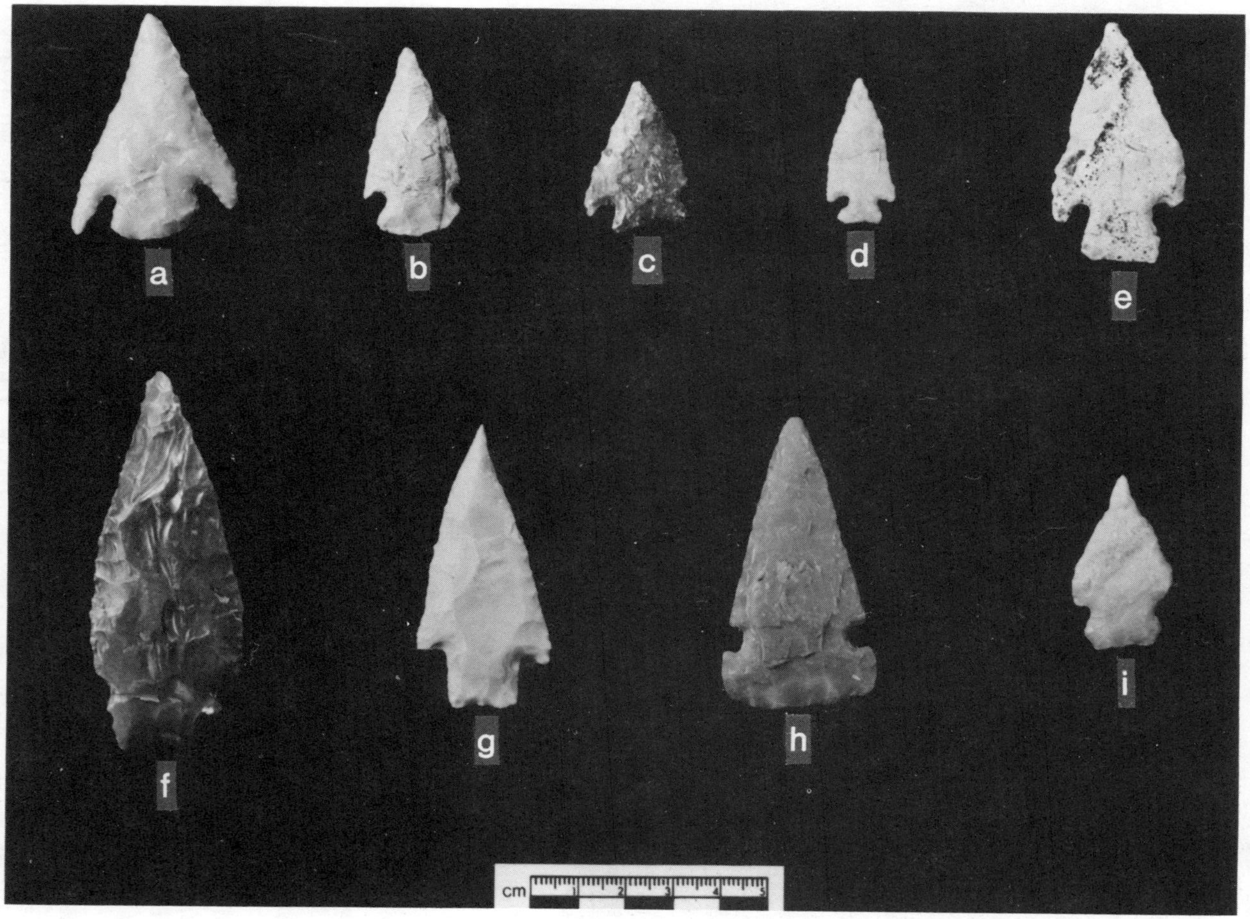

Fig. 98. Projectile points and hafted knives found with Feature 36 burial (Cluster 2, Part 1). a-i, Nos. 18, 25, 32–35, 37–39.

Fig. 99. Projectile points and hafted knives found with Feature 36 burial (Cluster 2, Part 2). a-f, Nos. 40–45.

California. According to McLean, they are too large to have come from the Texas coast. McLean felt that all of the Henderson *Olivella* appear to be beachworn, although some (or all) of the surface deterioration may be the result of poor preservation.

A set of 5 turquoise pendants (Nos. 1–5; Fig. 39k-o and Table A14c) and an unusually large *Olivella*-like shell bead (No. 1; Fig. 38x and Table A14b) were located under the chin, apparently the remains of a necklace. The pendants were found stacked against each other (much like playing cards), the holes for suspending them oriented up toward the chin, and their flat surfaces perpendicular to the chest. The shell bead had been displaced slightly, making it impossible to determine how it was positioned on the necklace relative to the turquoise pendants. This bead, also identified by McLean, is *Agaronia testacea* (Lamarck, 1811); and, like the *O. dama* beads associated with Feature 36 and other features, he attributes the source of bead No. 1 to the Gulf of California rather than to the Texas coast. No disc-shell beads were found with the necklace.

Finally, as noted above, fragmentary traces of coiled basketry, with wooden rods and yucca coils, were found in the abdominal region of the skeleton, underlying both of the arms and the projectile points of Cluster 2. The points from this cluster probably originally had been inside the basket when it was placed on the body. Small traces of decayed organic material near the fingers of the right hand may be additional evidence of basketry,

Fig. 100. Banded brown chert bifaces in collections of Arizona State Museum, University of Arizona. Helga Teiwes, photographer (Neg. 63473). a, GP-12253; b, A-30678; c, A-30500.

perhaps remains of a container for the points of Cluster 1. As noted earlier, both clusters may actually have been placed in a single large or elongated container. We found no evidence that the body had originally been wrapped in matting.

Skeletal inventory and condition. Feature 36 is relatively poorly preserved, though most of the skeleton was recovered. The following elements are present: cranium and mandible, both scapulae (right is fragmentary), both clavicles, portions of most vertebrae, hyoid, sternum, manubrium, both innominates (fragmentary) and sacrum, several coccygeal vertebrae, portions of most ribs, both humeri, both radii (left is incomplete), both ulnae (left is incomplete), all carpals, all metacarpals (some incomplete), all hand phalanges, both femora (right is fragmentary), both tibiae, both fibulae (right is incomplete), all tarsals except the right navicular, all metatarsals except the left fifth, all left foot phalanges, four proximal, two middle and three distal right foot phalanges, two foot sesamoids, and numerous fragments. Most of the elements not identified (particularly vertebrae) are probably represented in part by fragments.

Aside from the incomplete and fragmentary elements mentioned above, the major damage to the skeleton is crushing of the cranium. The frontal and parietals are broken and fragmentary, but in large part restorable to their pre-crushed form. The occipital and temporal bones as well as the bones of the face are severely crushed. The left maxilla is crushed inwards (so that the left tooth row is displaced medially), and the temporals and occipital are crushed and warped so that they do not articulate with the parietals and frontal.

Sex. Though most of the pubes are missing, the innominates indicate that the individual is a male. The sub-pubic angle is narrow, the sub-pubic area is convex, the greater sciatic notch is moderately narrow, and little or no pre-auricular sulcus is present. In addition, the skeleton is the largest of all recovered, both in stature and in the size of articular surfaces (e.g., the femoral heads), so that the identification of male sex is certain.

Age. Since the pubic symphyses were not recovered, the McKern and Stewart (1957) method could not be applied. The individual is an adult, with all epiphyses except for the proximal clavicular epiphyses fused; the latter is in the process of fusion on the left and the relevant area is hidden by post-mortem destruction on the right. This suggests an age of around 20 years or more. Though post-mortem cracking of the cranium obscures observation of endocranial sutural closure, the coronal, sagittal, and lambdoidal sutures all appear to be unfused internally, suggestive of an age no more than a few years over 20. The form of the sternum and manubrium corresponds to Stewart's (1954) stage 3, suggesting an age of around 20 to 23 years. Arthritis is limited (see below) though articular surfaces and muscle markings are well defined.

As indicated in Appendix 2, the Feature 36 dentition is not heavily worn, most closely resembling the wear on Feature 40. However the postcranial skeleton of Feature 36 is in advance of Feature 40, with all long-bone fusion complete and obliterated. Thus, the individual is probably around 20 years old or older, but not much older. Overall, a best estimate of age is probably around 19–22 years.

General description, cultural and pathological alterations. The postcranial skeleton is the most robust of the collection from the Henderson Site, with large bones, large articular surfaces, and prominent muscle markings. The cranium is large, but (perhaps because of the individual's age) muscle markings and other male characteristics are only moderately heavily pronounced (see Figs. 101, 102). The mastoids are large and the supramastoid crests moderate. Glabella and the superciliary arches are moderately prominent. Superior to glabella, the frontal dips in a slight supraorbital groove, and is retreating. The posterior parietals form a slightly flattened area around 3.5 cm in diameter just superior to lambda; this probably represents the unmodified cranial shape. No extra-sutural bones are present. The nuchal area is smooth with poorly developed muscle markings. The cranium is too fragmentary for reliable measurement (see Appendix 4), but approximate values of indices include cranial index between 69.2 and 79.4, length-height index 66.7–69.2, and breadth-height index 89.7–100.0. The cranium most closely resembles Feature 41 in its long narrow form, though it is larger than Feature 41 and perhaps relatively somewhat lower.

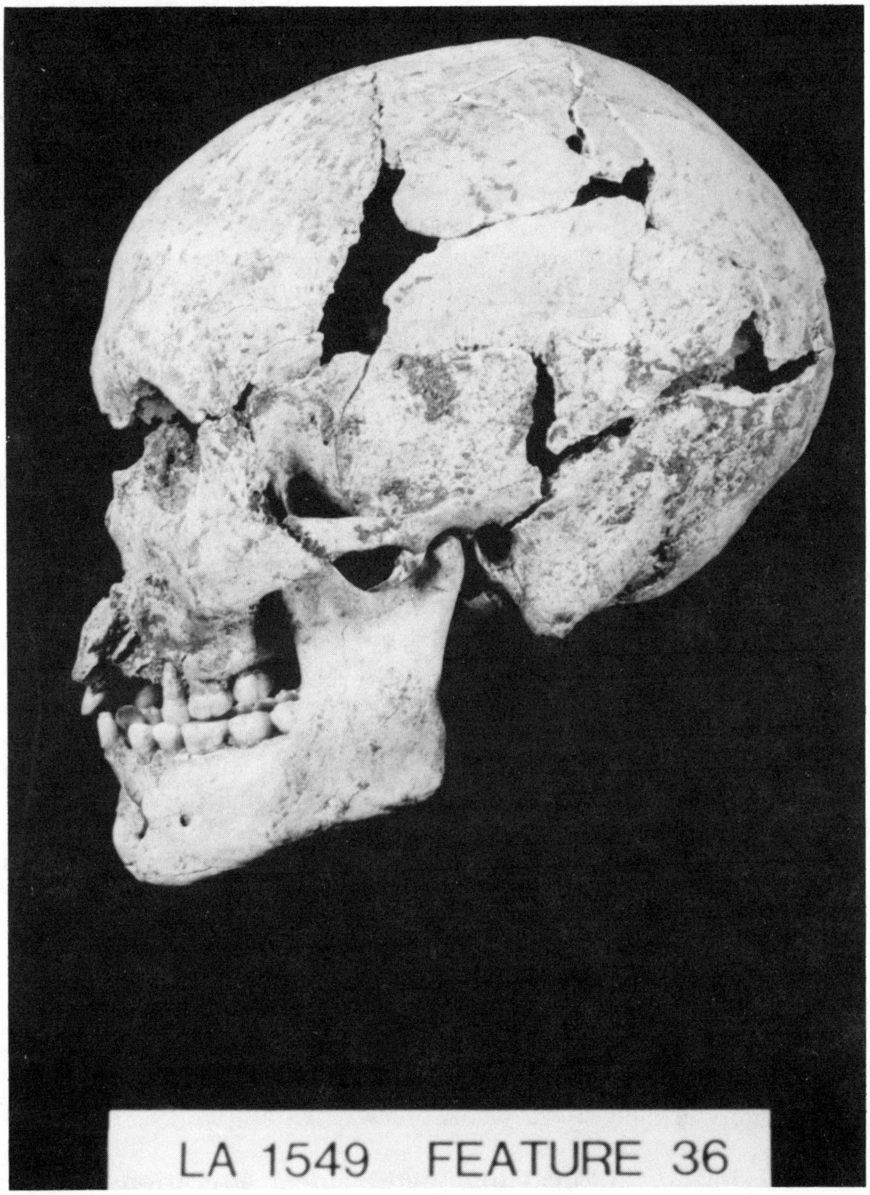

Fig. 101. Feature 36 skull (left lateral view). Scale same as in Fig. 24.

The mandible has a broad symphyseal region and a prominent mental eminence. The gonial angles are straight, neither inverted nor everted.

As Appendix 2 shows, dental attrition is slight. All teeth were present at the time of death. Small occlusal caries are present on RM^3 and RM_2 and a possible carious lesion is present in a deep buccal groove on LM_3. Little or no calculus formation or alveolar resorption is present. A small extra cusp is located distally on LM_3 at approximately the location of the tuberculum sextum.

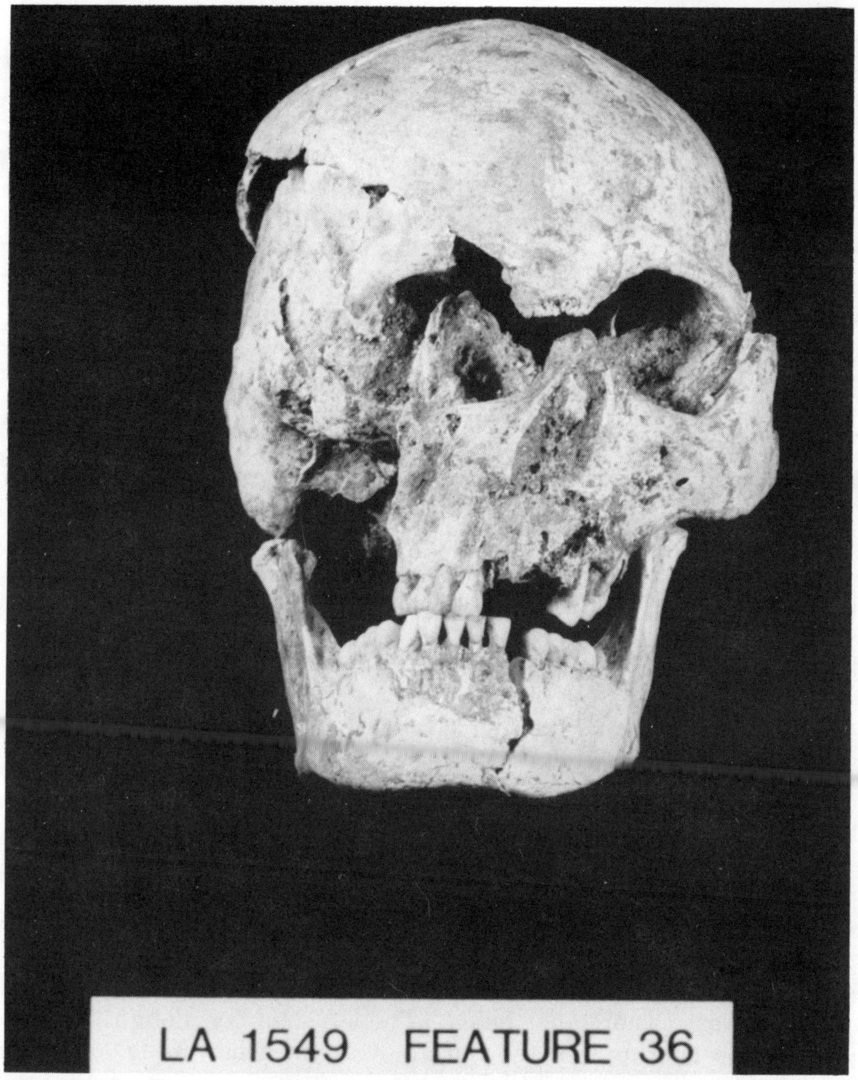

Fig. 102. Feature 36 skull (frontal view). Scale same as in Fig. 24. Note extreme crushing.

The only degenerative reaction noted on the skeleton is very slight osteophytic development on the fifth lumbar vertebral centrum. As noted above, the postcranial skeleton exhibits well-developed muscle markings and articular facets have well-defined edges, but no other arthritic development is evident.

One postcranial abnormality is present. On the left foot the fifth digit middle and distal phalanges are fused; corresponding elements of the right foot were not recovered (see Fig. 58 above).

Feature 40

Stratigraphic context. Feature 40 was a roughly oval to bean-shaped pit containing an adult female burial (Figs. 7, 19, 103, 104). It was located in Room E-4 in northwest Grid 526N567E and southwest Grid 527N567E. Although the pit was not recognized above the level of the primary floor (Floor 1), the absence of a seal over the feature at floor level suggests that it may have been intrusive from one of the secondary floors in the structure. On the other hand, a large post-hole pit (Feat. 23), still containing the base of a post, appears to have been dug into the fill of Feature 40, with the bottom of the post resting about 30 cm above the base of the burial pit. The plastered surface of Floor 1 appeared to extend over the post hole up to the edges of the post itself. This would suggest that Feature 40 originated at the level of the primary floor and was not intrusive from above it. Unfortunately, with the data at hand, the precise stratigraphic placement of this feature remains unclear.

The Feature 40 pit (including the south-southwest end which was formed by Feature 23) was 95 cm long north-south, and 71 cm wide, with the constriction in the east-southeast wall of the pit (marking the junction of Features 40 and 23) located about 40 cm north of the south-southwest end. The pit walls were steep, with irregular eastern and western profiles, curving at 100.50 m elevation inward to join a flat floor at 100.33 m (maximum depth). This feature was dug into underlying fill; its walls were not plastered or finished in any other way. Overall maximum pit depth was 73 cm.

The pit fill consisted of an unconsolidated brown fill with a few cobbles (ca. 5–8 cm), abundant charcoal, and sparse sherds, non-human bone, and lithics.

Position and orientation. Feature 40 contained two individuals, a young adult female and a fetus. The description below refers to the adult. The skeleton was fully articulated, lying on its back and right side, with the skull to the south-southwest. The skull was propped up on limestone pebbles in the fill so that it faced north and slightly above the horizontal, with a slight tilt (in the coronal plane) to the right (east). The neck was bent so that the rest of the vertebral column lay more nearly horizontally, with the long axis oriented south-southwest to north-northeast. The left arm lay along the northwest edge of the pit parallel to the long axis of the burial, with the elbow fully extended (at ca. 180 degrees). The hand extended straight beyond the arm to the north-northeast, and the palmar surface faced east (towards the legs). The right arm was similarly extended along the southeast side of the pit, with the humerus diverging slightly from the long axis (at around 20 degrees) and the elbow extended. The palmar surface of the hand faced towards the legs (west or northwest). The lower vertebrae and pelvis lay at an angle tilted partly to the right (east-southeast). The left leg crossed over the base of the sacrum, making an angle of around 90 degrees with the long axis. The knee was tightly flexed at around 15 degrees, with the heel north of the sacrum. The right femur was angled southeast, making an angle of around 35 degrees relative to the long axis, and the knee was tightly flexed back nearly parallel to the femur (with the heel north-northeast of the right ilium).

The fetus was disturbed, with most of the elements located among or below the adult individual's feet (hence just north-northeast of the pelvic inlet); other elements were scattered in the lumbar and pelvic region and some were with the adult's left hand. Whether this represents post-mortem displacement of an unborn fetus or placement of a prematurely born infant into the grave is not certain.

Burial accompaniments. A large Heshotauthla Polychrome bowl (No. 1; Figs. 105–109 and Table A15a) was inverted over the head of the adult skeleton in the feature (see also Figs. 103, 104). The bowl was complete but had broken in place subse-

Fig. 103. Feature 40 burial. Note placement of rocks over fetus between left femur and tibia, and Heshotauthla Polychrome bowl inverted over head.

quent to burial. There is no evidence that the bowl had been "killed". The interior decoration consists of parallel lines, zigzags, and other geometric elements in black glaze paint; execution of the design is sloppy, with uneven lines that often stop short of, or overshoot, their intended point of termination. The paint shows no signs of dribbling or running, however. On the exterior are three stylized butterflies (or possibly bats or water insects?) in black paint (Nos. 1–3; see Figs. 106–108), one of which has white dots in the wings (No. 1; Fig. 106). In addition, a turquoise pendant (No. 1; Fig. 39p and Table A15b) was located on the upper right ribs, overlying the right scapula (perhaps an earring or more likely a pendant worn around the neck). No other artifactual material was recovered. No mat wrapping, such as was found on most of the other burials, was evident.

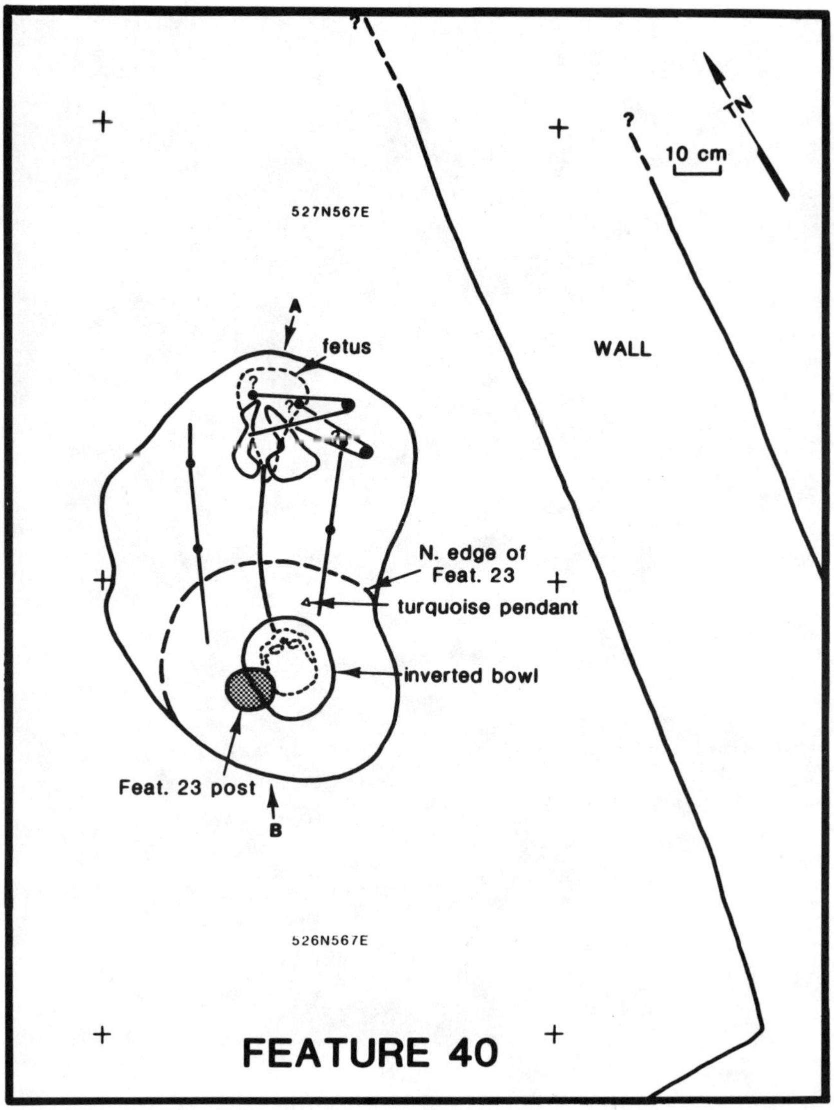

Fig. 104. Plan of Feature 40 burial.

A pair of roughly circular limestone rocks, each ca. 10 cm in diameter and 4 cm to 5 cm in thickness, were located between the left heel and the base of the sacrum, directly over the area from which much of the fetus was recovered. This rock placement resembles that observed in Feature 1 (although in this case no fetus was found).

Skeletal inventory and condition. The Feature 40 adult female is well preserved and largely complete. The following elements are preserved: cranium and mandible, complete vertebral column (some elements incomplete), both clavicles, sternum and manubrium, both scapulae, both humeri, both ulnae, both radii, all carpals, all metacarpals, all hand phalanges except three distal, some rib fragments, complete sacrum and innominates, two coccygeal elements, both femora, both patellae, both tibiae, both fibulae (right is incomplete), all tarsals, all metatarsals, all foot phalanges, and one sesamoid.

Fig. 105. Heshotauthla Polychrome bowl found with Feature 40 burial.

The fetus is also relatively well preserved, though not all elements were recovered. The following elements are preserved: both frontals, right(?) parietal, left parietal fragments, right temporal squama, both temporal petrous portions, left malar, part of the occipital basilar portion, sphenoid fragments, both mandibular halves, both clavicles, a portion of the right scapula, sixteen vertebral centra, twenty vertebral arches, several rib fragments, right humerus, both radii (left is incomplete), both ulnae (right[?] is incomplete), at least one sacral segment, both ilia, both ischia, both femora, both tibiae, possible fibular fragments, several phalanges and metapodials, and numerous unidentified fragments or small ossification centra.

All bones recovered from both individuals are in good condition, though some of the fetal cranial material is warped.

Fig. 106. Butterfly (No. 1) on exterior of bowl found with Feature 40 burial. Note white dots in wings.

Sex. The innominates clearly indicate that the adult individual is a female: sub-pubic concavity is marked, ventral arcs are present bilaterally (although only partially formed), the sub-pubic angle is broad, the greater sciatic notch is broad and a pre-auricular sulcus is present. The medial aspect of the pubis is of intermediate form. The identification of sex is confirmed by the gracility of the entire skeleton and, of course, by the presence of the fetus.

Sex of the fetus is unknown.

Age. Application of the Gilbert and McKern (1973) symphyseal aging method yields scores of zero (16.00 ± 2.82). As Appendix 1 shows, fusion stages of the postcranial skeleton are comparable but slightly more advanced than Feature 8, indicating an age of ca. 18–21 or ca. 20 years (Krogman 1973:Tables 5 and 6, respectively). The sternum is in stage 2 (19–20 years?) following Stewart's (1954) method. Complete closure but incomplete obliteration of the spheno-occipital synchondrosis suggests an age of around 20 years. Observation of the endocranial suture development is limited on the complete cranium. The coronal suture appears partially obliterated laterally, as does the lambdoidal suture. The central coronal and the entire sagittal sutures are unfused. An age in the early 20s is suggested by these data. Dental eruption data are inconclusive but suggest an age in the late teens or early 20s. LM^3 is unerupted, RM^3 is lost post-mortem, and thus was probably erupted, LM_3 is erupted but not in occlusion, and RM_3 is nearly fully erupted and exhibits possible traces of wear.

As indicated in Appendix 2, the dentition of Feature 40 has wear comparable to or slightly greater than Feature 36 and less than Feature 1. Thus an age of slightly over 20 years is suggested. However, the level of postcranial development supports an age very near 20. An overall best estimate of 17 to 23 years may be suggested.

The age of the fetus is assessed on the basis of a femur length measurement of 48.1 mm for the right (more complete) femur without epiphyses. This implies an age of between six and seven fetal months (Bass 1971:171). The small size and early stage of development of the remainder of the skeleton conforms to an age in the fetal range.

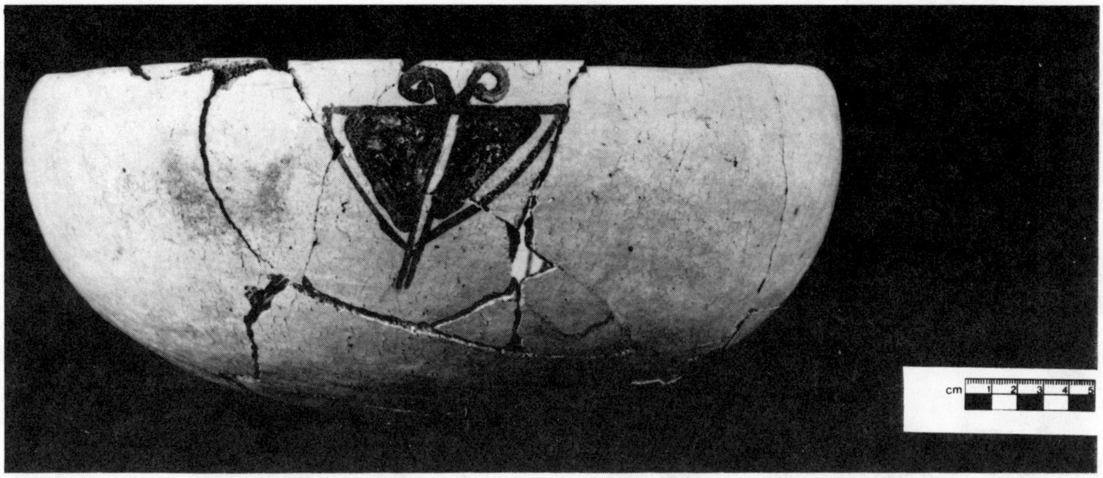

Fig. 107. Butterfly (No. 2) on exterior of bowl found with Feature 40 burial.

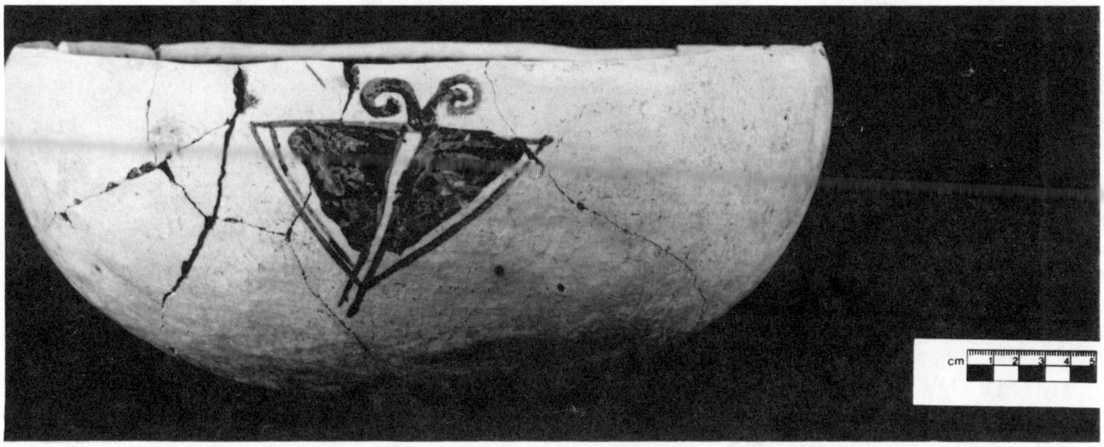

Fig. 108. Butterfly (No. 3) on exterior of bowl found with Feature 40 burial.

General description, cultural and pathological alterations. The cranium, like the rest of the adult skeleton, is gracile and bears poorly developed muscle markings (see Figs. 110, 111). The cranium is very wide and relatively short and high (cranial index 83.9, length-height index 78.0, breadth-height index 92.9), though this probably reflects in part artificial cranial deformation (see below). Parietal and frontal bossing are evident. The superciliary arches and glabella are not prominent. The moderately retreating curve of the frontals continues smoothly to the anterior parietals, but is broken by a flattened area around 3.0 cm high by 4.0 cm wide located 1.5 cm anterior to lambda. The flattened area forms an angle of 45 degrees relative to the Frankfort Horizontal Plane. One and a half centimeters below lambda, a flattened area about 3.0 cm high by 3.5 cm wide forms an angle of 85 degrees relative to the Frankfort Horizontal Plane. These flattened areas probably represent culturally induced deformation, although the lambdoidal flattening is probably at least in part a secondary consequence of occipital deformation and parietal bossing. The remainder of the occipital continues in a relatively smooth curve with little

Fig. 109. Design of Heshotauthla Polychrome bowl found with Feature 40 burial. Figure is schematic to illustrate nature of design; it should not be used to determine exact size or proportion of specific design elements.

development of the nuchal muscle markings. The mastoids are small, zygomatics gracile, and supramastoid crest moderately developed. In occipital view the cranium has a slightly keeled appearance.

The mandible has a broad symphyseal region and a prominent mental eminence. The gonial angles are straight.

Two extra-sutural bones are present near the superior end of the occipital-temporal suture, one on each side. The right one is approximately 1.7 cm high by 0.9 cm wide; the left is 1.9 cm high by 1.0 cm wide.

Dental health is good and, as Appendix 2 shows, attrition is limited. All teeth were present at the time of death, though three were lost post-mortem. No caries are present, calculus formation is slight (limited to discontinuous areas on a few molars and premolars), and little or no alveolar resorption is evident. A minor dental anomaly is present in the form of an extra cusp located disto-lingually (adjacent to the entoconid) on LM_3.

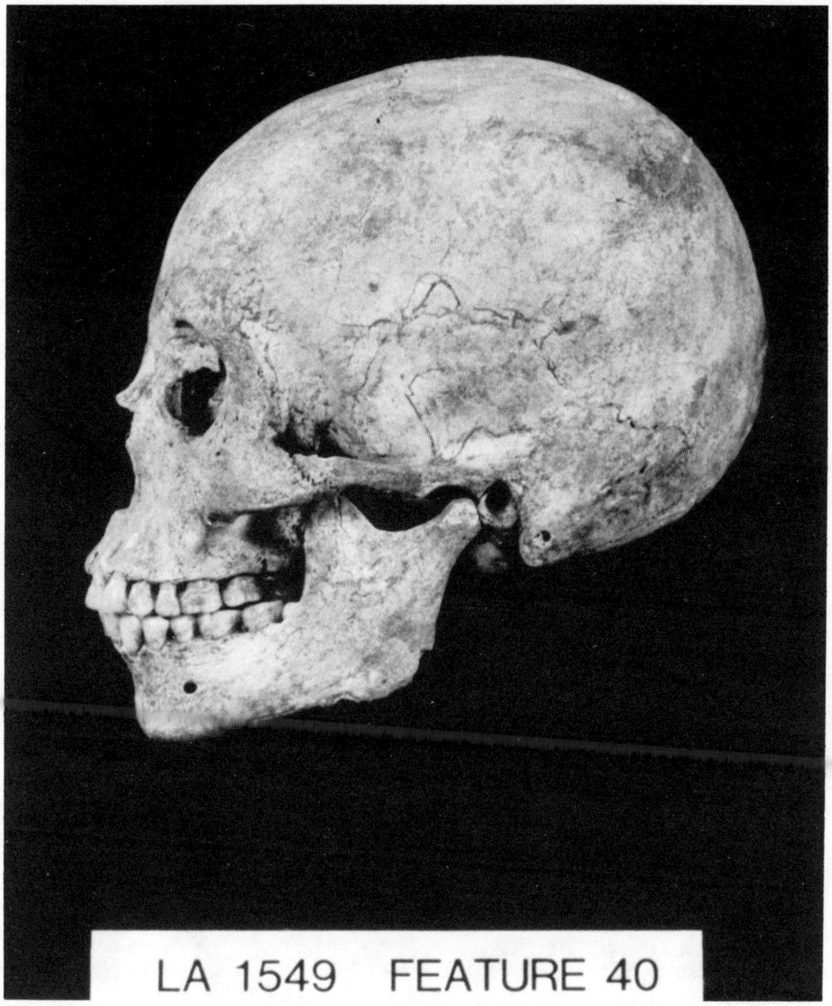

Fig. 110. Feature 40 skull (left lateral view). Scale same as in Fig. 24.

Aside from dental form, several other minor anomalies are present. On the cranium, the jugular foramina are highly asymmetric, with the right measuring slightly more than twice as large as the left. Postcranial anomaly is limited to fusion of the distal and middle phalanges of the fifth digits of both feet (see Fig. 58 above). No arthritis is present. Both humeri have perforated olecranon fossae. The first sacral segment is unfused; however, unlike in the case of Feature 8, the segment is fully sacral in form.

Finally, it is worth noting that, despite the presence of the fetus, no modification of the dorsal face of the pubis is evident (Suchey et al. 1979), suggesting that the individual in Feature 40 never successfully bore a child.

Feature 41

Stratigraphic context. Feature 41 was an irregular elongated pit containing an adult male burial sealed below the 100.60 m level (Floor 1). It was located in Center Bar Room C-5 in western Grid 515N534E and extreme eastern Grid 515N533E (see Figs. 8,

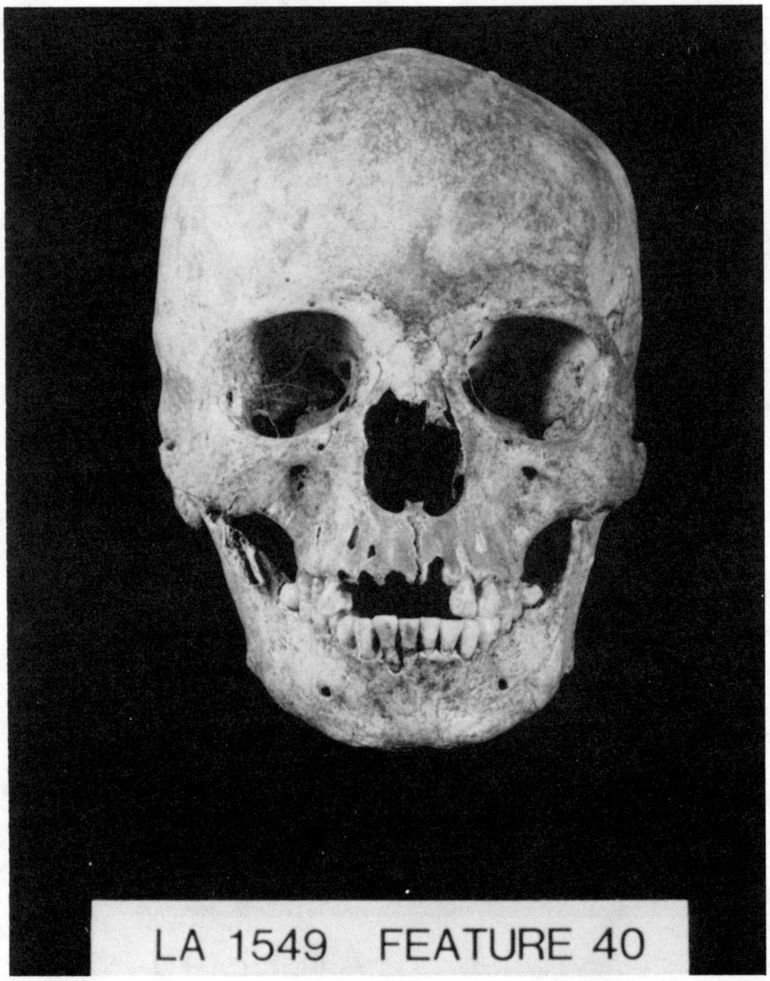

Fig. 111. Feature 40 skull (frontal view). Scale same as in Fig. 24.

19, 112, 113). The pit slightly undercut a north-northeast to south-southwest trending wall (associated with Floor 1) to its west-northwest, but its placement adjacent to the wall (similar to Features 8, 9, and 36) suggests that the burial was positioned in relation to the wall and was thus contemporary with the wall and floor. The long axis of the pit was oriented north-northeast to south-southwest, with a length at the floor level of 78 cm and a width of 50 cm. Below the floor level, the pit was undercut, with a maximum length of 1.05 m at 100.30 m elevation. The walls sloped inward below 100.15 m to a broad basin-shaped base at a maximum depth of 99.85 m. Total pit depth was 75 cm. The feature was dug into underlying fill; its walls were not plastered or finished in any other way.

The pit fill exhibited no stratification. It consisted of an orange clayey matrix mixed with rounded limestone cobbles and sparse charcoal, with a soft organic-rich area immediately adjacent to the skeleton. Non-human bone and cultural material were very limited in quantity. The overall configuration of the pit fill did not suggest major disturbance, though displacement of various skeletal elements (see below) indicates that some minor disturbance did take place.

Fig. 112. Feature 41 burial.

Position and orientation. The skeleton was fully articulated (except for minor disturbance described below), lying on its back, with the skull at the south-southwest end of the pit. The skull was propped against the southwest end of the pit so that it tilted left (north) at about 50 degrees relative to the horizontal with the face pointing slightly above the horizontal to the north-northwest. The neck curved down to the rest of the vertebral column which angled inferiorly slightly to the left. The long axis orientation of the feature was south-southwest to north-northeast. The left humerus paralleled the long axis, and the left elbow was loosely flexed at about 120 degrees. The left hand lay palmar side down over the superior sacral region. The right humerus diverged slightly from the long

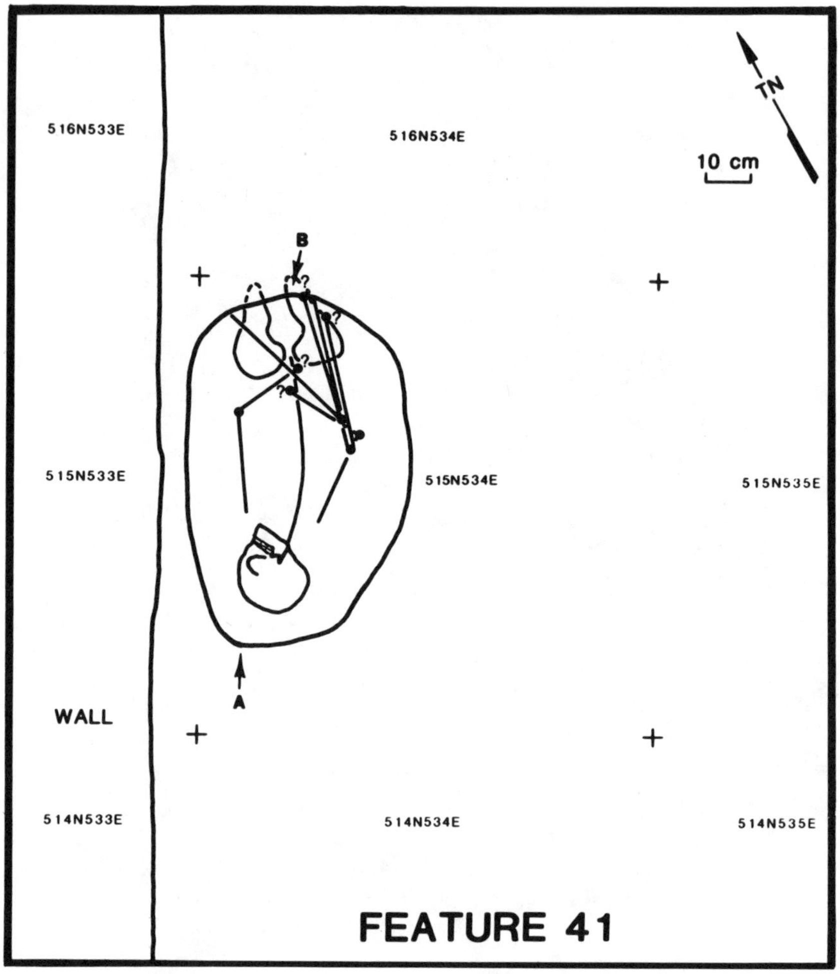

Fig. 113. Plan of Feature 41 burial.

axis (at about 25 degrees) to the northeast. The elbow was loosely flexed at 80 degrees, with the right hand lying palmar side down over the lumbar region just southwest of the left hand. The left femur ran south-southeast across the sacrum, making an angle of 40 degrees relative to the long axis. The left knee was flexed at around 30 degrees. The right femur ran south-southwest at about 20 degrees relative to the long axis with the knee tightly flexed so that the tibia ran nearly parallel to the femur. Thus, the right knee lay just south and below the left knee, over the distal left humerus. The feet lay northeast of the pelvis, with the left foot north of the right.

Despite the overall articulated condition of the burial, many smaller bones were displaced. These included the sternum (under the skull), many hand and foot elements, particularly from the right side (scattered in several clusters in the fill), and several ribs and miscellaneous other elements. This disturbance probably represents rodent activity.

Burial accompaniments. Fragments of fibrous matting occurred around the skeleton, although the nature of the matting or the exact extent to which it covered the body could not be determined. No other artifact associations were identified.

Skeletal inventory and condition. Feature 41 is extremely well preserved and largely complete; only small skeletal elements are missing. The following elements are present: cranium and mandible, complete vertebral column, hyoid body and one greater horn, sternum and manubrium, both clavicles, both scapulae, both humeri, both radii, both ulnae, all carpals, all metacarpals, all hand phalanges except two middle phalanges, all ribs, sacrum, both innominates, three coccygeal vertebrae, both femora, both patellae, both tibiae, both fibulae, left calcaneus and talus, all right tarsals except the first cuneiform, all right metatarsals, six proximal, seven middle, and seven distal foot phalanges.

The condition of all bones is good, though some cracking has occurred.

Sex. The innominates indicate that the individual is male: no ventral arc is present, the sub-pubic angle is narrow, no sub-pubic concavity exists, the medial aspect of the ischio-pubic ramus is rounded and the greater sciatic notch is narrow. The robustness of the rest of the skeleton confirms the identification. However, a pre-auricular sulcus is present on the left innominate.

Age. Application of the McKern and Stewart (1957) symphyseal aging method yields a score of 7 for the right pubis (22.42±.99 years) and 8 for the left (24.14±1.93), so an age around 23 years is suggested. No arthritis is present on the vertebrae or on major joint surfaces; this is compatible with an age in the mid-twenties or less. All sutures visible internally are unfused or incompletely obliterated. Thus an age around 23 years or younger is supported. The form of the sternum and manubrium conforms to Stewart's (1954) stage 3 (20–23 years). The spheno-occipital synchondrosis is fused but not completely obliterated. This implies an age of around 20 years.

Appendix 2 indicates that the Feature 41 dentition is slightly more worn than that of Feature 1 and significantly less than that of Feature 25. This implies an age in the early to mid-twenties. Overall, a best estimate of 21 to 24 years of age may be suggested.

General description, cultural and pathological alterations. The cranium is long and narrow (cranial index 70.8, cranial length-height index 71.4, cranial breadth-height index 100.8; see Figs. 114, 115). The cranium is robust with moderately heavy muscle markings. Glabella and the supraorbital arches are prominent. Superior to the arches the frontal has a supraorbital groove and is retreating. Parietal bossing is not pronounced, and the curve of the parietals continues relatively continuously onto the occiput. A relatively flat area with indistinct boundaries occurs around lambda making an angle of about 55 degrees relative to the Frankfort Horizontal Plane; this most likely represents the unmodified contour of the cranium rather than culturally induced alteration. The mastoid processes and supramastoid crests are large. No extra-sutural bones are present.

The mandible has a broad symphyseal region and a prominent mental eminence. The gonial angles are slightly inverted.

As shown in Appendix 2, dental attrition is slight to moderate. All teeth were present at the time of death, though RM^3 was lost post-mortem. A small carious lesion is present in a groove in the occlusal surface of LM_3. Small possible caries are also present in an occlusal groove on RM_3, in a groove on the bucco-distal surface of LM_3, and in an occlusal groove of RM^2. Little or no alveolar resorption is evident. Slight calculus formation occurs sporadically throughout the dentition. The only dental abnormality noted is a 90 degree counterclockwise rotation of LM_3.

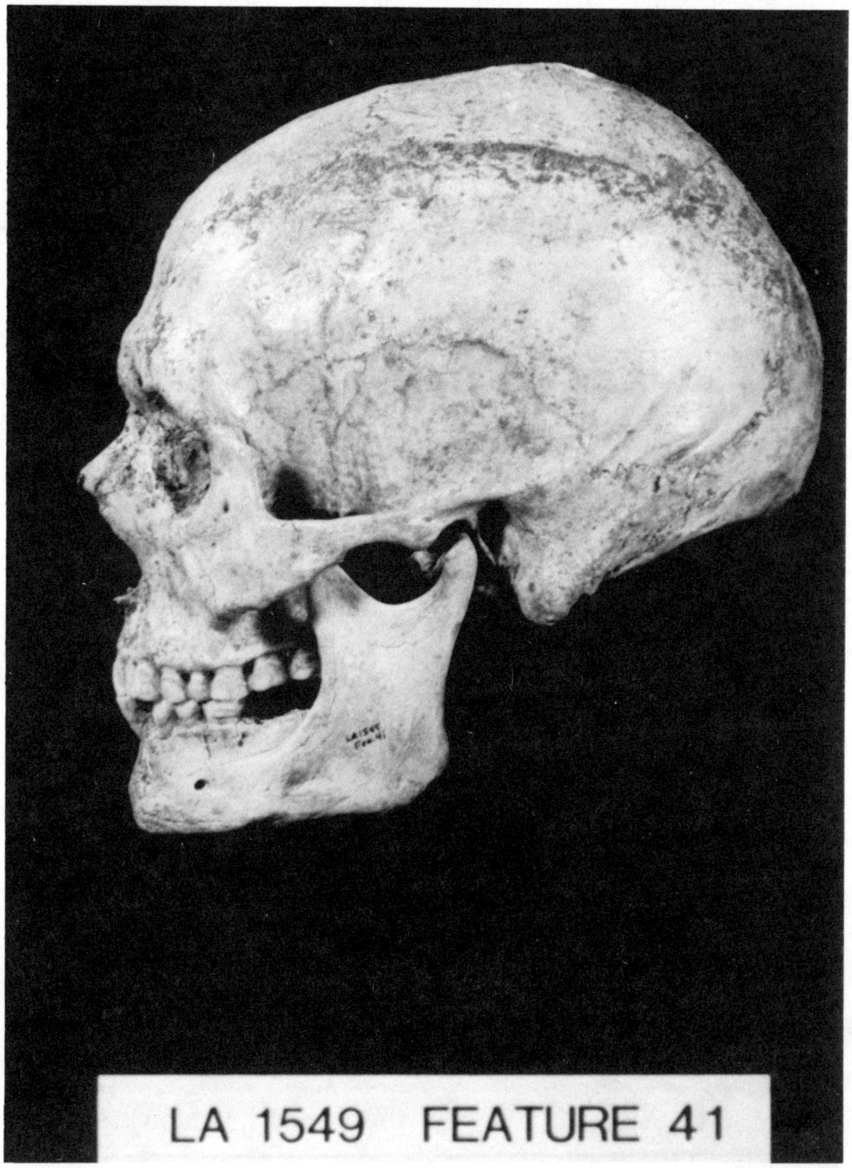

Fig. 114. Feature 41 skull (left lateral view). Scale same as in Fig. 24.

Fig. 115. Feature 41 skull (frontal view). Scale same as in Fig. 24. Asymmetry of lower mandible border result of specimen settling in photo cloth.

The postcranial skeleton displays one notable set of abnormalities. The sixth and seventh ribs are fused to each other at their articular ends; this occurs bilaterally (Fig. 116). The corresponding vertebra, the sixth thoracic, exhibits incomplete development of its centrum (Fig. 117). The centrum is completely absent anteriorly, with partial centrum development laterally (on both sides posteriorly). The anterior and medial edges of the partial centrum portions taper to a narrow edge anteriorly and posteriorly, and a small gap completely separates the two portions of the centrum from each other. The sixth thoracic vertebra has demi-facets on its partial centrum, but lacks facets on its transverse processes, corresponding to a lack of facets on the tubercles of the sixth ribs. The fifth and seventh thoracic vertebral centra are slightly deformed to partially fill the gap in the sixth thoracic centrum.

No arthritic reaction or evidence of trauma is evident around the fused ribs and malformed vertebrae. Thus, the appearance of the abnormality and its bilateral nature suggest a congenital origin.

Elsewhere on the skeleton, only one case of arthritis is present. The proximal end of one of the middle foot phalanges displays osteophytic development. The form and color of this phalanx is different from the rest of the Feature 41 skeleton, and may represent an intrusive element from a different burial (like most of the Feat. 41 phalanges, this foot phalanx was not in articulated position). The remainder of the skeleton bears well-defined articular surfaces but no arthritis.

Additional postcranial features include the presence of a small perforation of the sternum (sternal foramen) slightly left of the midline near the articulation for the fifth rib, and the presence on the left humerus of a slight perforation of the olecranon fossa. The first coccygeal vertebra is fused to the sacrum.

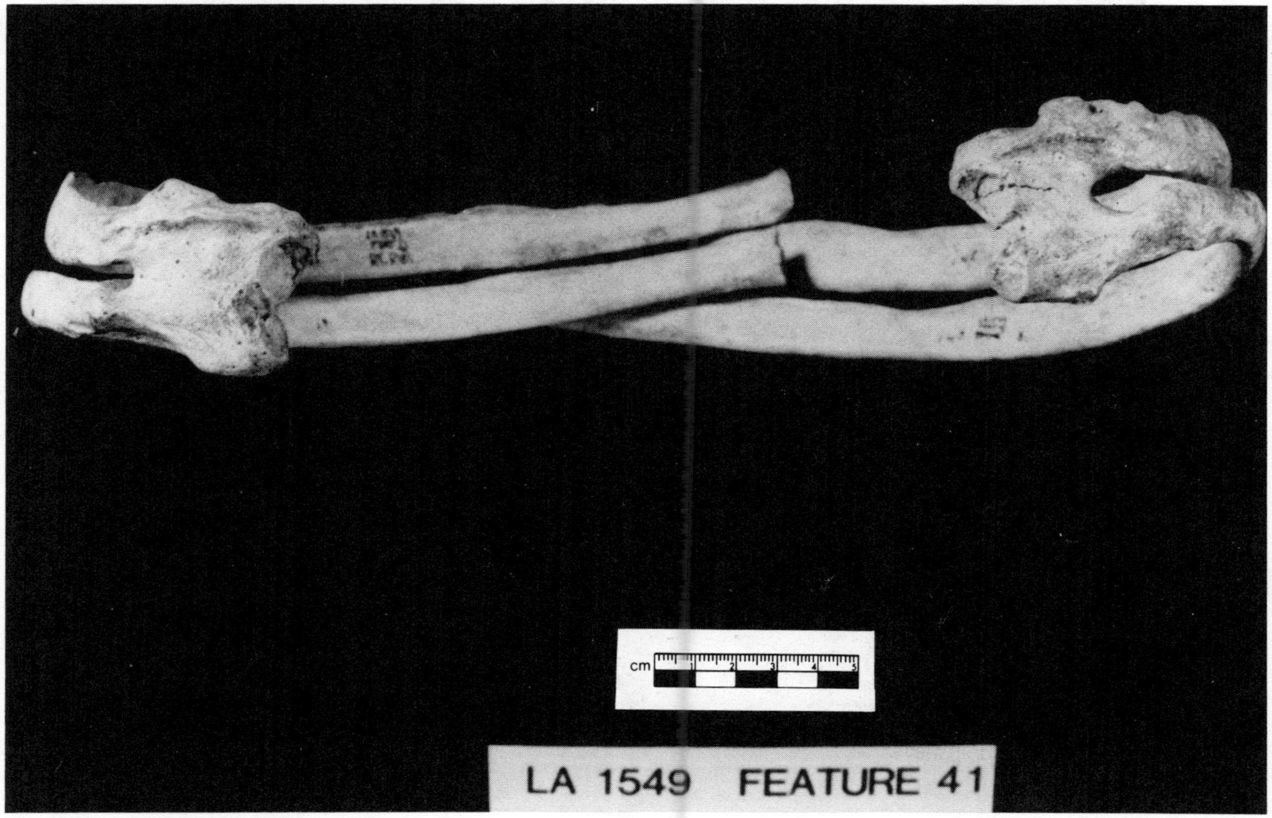

Fig. 116. Feature 41, fused 6th-7th ribs (see Fig. 117 for corresponding malformed thoracic vertebrae).

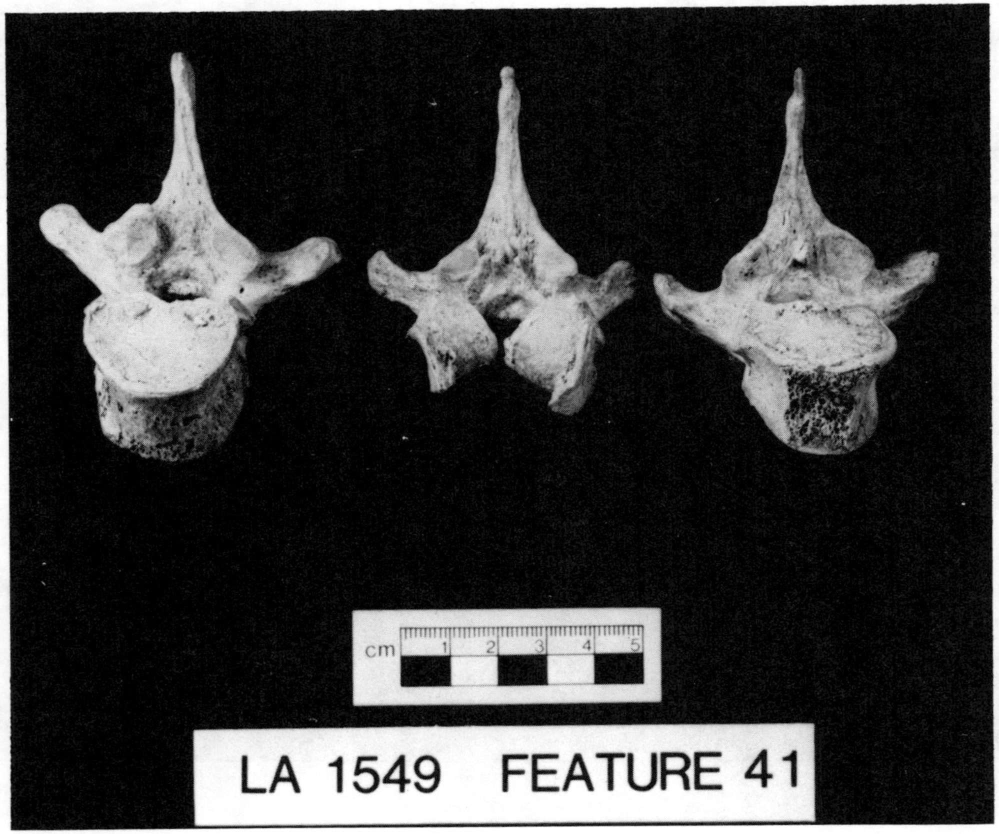

Fig. 117. Feature 41, malformed 6th thoracic vertebra (see Fig. 116 for corresponding fused 6th-7th ribs); 5th thoracic vertebra on right, 7th on left.

3
DISCUSSION

The Henderson Population

Appendices 1–8 provide data on a variety of measurements and observations on the Henderson burial sample. Isolated human skeletal elements are summarized in Appendix 9. The present section is a summary and discussion of some of the salient aspects of the mortuary treatment at the Henderson Site, and of the human skeletal material recovered. The small sample upon which discussion is based should be kept in mind.

A total of 10 distinct burial features were identified at the site, incorporating the remains of 11 individuals (1 fetus, 2 infants, and 8 adults). In general, the burials were well preserved, although the bone appeared partially demineralized in some of the features and exhibited numerous small cracks in several; thus, the majority of each skeleton was treated with preservative. Three of the skeletons (Features 21, 29, and 36) suffered considerable non-reconstructable damage, particularly to the postcrania. Portions of the Feature 21 and 36 skeletons were crushed and fragmented. Feature 29 appears to have been disturbed (probably by surface exposure resulting from shallow burial and/or subsequent erosion), and a large portion of the skeleton was missing. Features 1 and 3 also suffered some significant damage, but this was mostly localized crushing and fragmentation. On the other hand, Features 8, 9, 25, 40, 41, and much of Features 1 and 3 were reconstructable. Given the condition of the Feature 9 infant and the condition of the fetus in Feature 40, little bias of the mortuary sample due to taphonomic processes is suspected.

A total of 4 females, 4 males, two infants, and one fetus were recovered. The sample is too small to permit evaluation of demographic characteristics. Clearly the sex ratio is not skewed. Most of the individuals are relatively young. Only Features 21 and 29 have been identified as exceeding 30 years of age.

Mortuary Treatment

All of the burials recovered from Henderson were in pits below the primary floor of the room. The pits were roughly oval or nearly round in most cases, with steep sides (the Feature 3 pit walls were not steep, but this may be because the higher, steeper part of the pit was not identified). In many cases, a limited amount of undercutting of the pit walls occurred in one or two places to accommodate portions of the body that did not fit the rest of the pit outline; most of the pits are not bell shaped in overall profile, however.

Despite the location of burials below primary room floors (i.e., below Floor 1), it is clear that not all of the burials were directly associated with this floor. Several pits originated at secondary floors or occupation surfaces overlying the primary floor and cut down through it from above. The presence of replastering layers over several of the burials, both adult and infant, suggests that rooms were not invariably abandoned, at least not for extended periods, after an individual was interred in the structure.

No burials were found in the extensive midden deposits excavated in the East Plaza. A single burial, Feature 29, was located at shallow depth in an area where no walls remained intact. However, extrapolation of intact wall segments suggests that it too was located within a room and below the primary floor. Feature 29 was located in an area where bedrock was near the present ground surface, and the burial became partially exposed by erosion some time after burial, resulting in destruction of a large part of the skeleton.

Six of the 10 burials were located below the primary floor of a single large room (Room E-4, see Fig. 9 above) in the East Bar of the pueblo. These burials (Features 1, 3, 8, 21, 25, and 40) originated from at least two different levels. Feature 1, Feature 21, probably Feature 3, and perhaps Feature 25 are intruded through Floor 1 from higher levels. They probably date, therefore, to the late phase of occupation at Henderson, sometime in the late 1300s or early 1400s. Feature 8 was clearly sealed by Floor 1, and Feature 40 may also have been. These burials, therefore, probably date to the early occupational phase at the site, sometime in the 1200s or early 1300s. The Feature 8 pit, sealed beneath the earliest plastering layer of the primary floor, may have been the first burial in this room.

It should be noted that the apparent concentration of burials in a single room may in part be an artifact of incomplete sub-floor testing in the other excavated rooms. Thus, future work may reveal a more uniform distribution of sub-floor burials.

Feature 29 was below the primary floor in the badly eroded remnants of Room E-2. While no absolute dates have been obtained from this room, architectural evidence, particularly the continuity and apparent absence of bonding of the west wall of Rooms E-2 and E-4, suggest that these two structures were built at the same time (i.e., during the early phase of occupation in the 1200s). Since no evidence of a seal over the Feature 29 pit was observed at the level of the primary floor, the burial probably intruded from a secondary floor which has since been stripped off by erosion. This implies that Feature 29 probably dates to the late phase of occupation, and is more or less contemporary with Features 1, 3, 21, and 25 in Room E-4. It should be noted, however, that the severe erosion in Room E-2 may have obliterated any trace of a seal. Thus, the temporal placement of Feature 29 must be regarded as very tentative.

Feature 36 was sealed below Floor 1 in the north end of the pitroom (Room E-3), immediately to the west of Room E-4 which contained the six burials described above. Based on the radiocarbon and archaeomagnetic dates, this burial belongs to the early phase of occupation, and probably is more or less contemporary with Feature 8, and perhaps Feature 40, in the adjoining room. The two remaining burials recovered during the 1980 and 1981 seasons, Features 9 and 41, were sealed below the primary floor (Floor 1) in Room C-5 (see Fig. 10 above), located in the Center Bar about 30 m west-southwest of Room E-4. A local amateur is reputed to have recovered 9 other burials, most or all below primary floor level, from an adjacent room (C-6?) in the Center Bar prior to the beginning of controlled excavations in 1980. Unfortunately, provenience information (and the skeletal material itself) was not preserved.

In sum, a tentative temporal ordering for the Henderson burials may be suggested. Features 8, 9, and 41, and perhaps also 40, probably all belong to the early phase of occupation at the site, placing them during the 1200s or early 1300s. Features 1, 3, and 21, and perhaps 25 and 29, appear to have been buried during the late phase, dating them to the latter part of the 1300s or early 1400s. If the temporal placement of burials outlined here is correct, there appears to be a tendency for the early phase pits in a room to be dug close to, or directly abutting, the walls, while late phase burials are interred farther from the walls, perhaps to avoid disturbing earlier bodies. This pattern is clearly shown by minimum distances measured from cranium (forehead) to nearest wall. The early phase burials (Features 8, 9, 36, and 41) are 25 cm, 21 cm, 38 cm, and 18 cm, respectively, from a wall. In contrast, the late phase burials (Features 1, 3, 21, and 25) are 70 cm, 70 cm, 105 cm, and 60 cm, respectively, from a wall (Feat. 29 could not be included in these comparisons). Feature 40 is the only possible anomaly, being tentatively assigned to the early phase but lying 72 cm from the nearest wall. If this spacing pattern is real and not just an artifact of small sample sizes, Feature 40 may in fact belong to the late phase.

Features 3, 36, and 40 are each associated with post holes. The post holes, however, do not appear to be contemporary with the burials: the Feature 3 burial is later than the post in Feature 7 and truncates it; Feature 40 appears to predate the post in Feature 23; and the relationship of Feature 36 and the Feature 36A post hole is unknown. Thus, the overlap of burials and posts probably represents simple reuse of floor space, and perhaps a tendency to dig new features into the softer fill left in old existing features. Feature 25 was also located near a post hole (Feat. 19) but the two features did not overlap.

Most of the burials were placed on their right sides or on their backs, with legs flexed (the knees usually flexed tightly, the hips more variable). Only one burial (Feat. 29) apparently was placed on its left side; and another, Feature 36 in the East Bar pitroom (E-3), lay on its back and left side. The long-axis orientation of the bodies tended to fall into two broad groups. One of these groups, with orientations varying from west-northwest/east-southeast to west-southwest/east-northeast, included 5 individuals. Four of these (2 females and 2 infants) had their heads at the western end of the pit; the other individual (male) had his head at the eastern end. The other group, also including 5 individuals, was oriented north-northeast/south-southwest. Three of these individuals (2 males and 1 female) had their heads at the northern end of the pit. The other two (1 male and 1 female) had their heads at the southern end. No clear association of burial orientation with age, sex, spatial placement, or stratigraphic level is evident. The two clusters of orientations correspond roughly to burial pits layed out parallel with the walls of the rooms.

Four of the burials, an infant, two adult males, and an adult female (Features 9, 29, 36, and 40, respectively), lacked evidence of some form of mat wrapping around the body. It is not clear whether the absence of matting in these features reflects poor preservation conditions or differences in burial treatment. After decay of the body, the fill in most of the burial pits compressed, creating partially hollow sinks into which moisture could collect seasonally. The presence of patches of finely laminated water-laid silt and clay on the floor of several of the pits, and sometimes directly on the bones, clearly testifies to the activity of water. Repeated wetting and drying probably contributed significantly to the loss of organics such as matting, and was a major factor in demineralizing many of the bones. Curiously, however, these same water-laid sediments sometimes preserved impressions of the matting, making it possible in a few cases to reconstruct both the nature of the covering and its placement around the body. Since no mat impressions were recovered in Features 9, 29, 36, or 40, these individuals may have been buried without a wrapping. We cannot exclude the possibility, however, that matting was originally present but decayed leaving no detectable trace. In the cases where actual fragments of matting or mat impressions were present (Features 1, 3, 8?, 21, 25, 41), they occurred at several points along the length of the skeleton, indicating that originally the entire body had been covered or wrapped. In most cases, the matting was twined (see Appendix 16). Where the mat materials could actually be identified, the warp and weft were grass (Features 1, 3, 21, 25). A single instance of plaited yucca matting (or possibly basketry) was encountered (Feat. 8). This material was found under the skull, and could be the remains of a small basket or head covering, or remnants of matting that once enclosed the entire body. Traces of cordage (z-twist, 2-strand, unidentified vegetal fiber) were found with two of the burials (Features 3 and 21). The cordage may have been woven into the matting itself, or instead may be remnants of binding that helped hold the wrapping around the body.

It is uncertain whether the mat wrapping (and cordage?) is sufficient to account for the flexing of the legs observed on the burials or whether some additional binding is indicated. Most of the extreme flexing of the legs in the sample is seen on burials placed on their backs, where the legs had collapsed in such a way as to pile the elements on top of each other; thus, the original degree of flexure could not be determined.

Aside from the mats, six of the burials, including three lacking evidence of mats, were definitely associated with other artifacts. These included pottery vessels (Features 3 and 40); coiled basketry (Features 8 and 36); a variety of beads, pendants, and other personal ornaments (Features 3, 8, possibly 25 [see below], 36, and 40); flakes, bifaces, knives, scrapers, and projectile points (Features 29 and 36); and bone "awls" or "hairpins," turtle shell "gaming pieces," and shell items (Feat. 29). In addition, Feature 3 contained a carved plaque or prayer-stick made from a piece of wood, probably *Populus*, a miniature obsidian projectile point, a tiny brachiopod fossil, fluorite crystals, and several other items, in addition to the two ceramic vessels and numerous beads. Finally, Feature 25 contained a wooden prayer-stick (walnut) to which were attached a cluster of beads, two pieces of turquoise, two crystals, one of quartz and the other of fluorite, and possibly a pea-sized organic item that unfortunately had decayed and could no longer be identified. A few additional beads recovered out of context in Feature 25 were probably associated with this item, but may have been personal ornaments.

A set of non-artifactual associations which may have cultural significance is the presence of disc-shaped (unworked) rocks between the legs of two of the female burials (Features 1 and 40). In the former case, the rock may be fortuitous; in the latter case, the rock was positioned over an associated fetus. The two other female burials, Features 8 and 21, did not have rocks evident in this position.

A consideration of the context of the associations reveals a pattern, albeit a tentative one, which is wholly consistent with mortuary practices of relatively egalitarian sociopolitical systems elsewhere in the Southwest. The youngest individual (Feat. 9, less than about 6 months old) and the oldest individual (Feat. 21, 40+ years old) did not have definite associated mortuary goods (Feat. 21 did have a mat wrapping, however). Thus, some degree of age classification in burial status might be suggested, with the very old and very young outside the social categories associated with grave goods. However, one of the more elaborate burials, Feature 3, was a child of less than 4 years. The two burials of known sex with the largest quantity of burial associations, Features 29 and 36, are both male. Feature 25, with a prayer-stick, is also male. However, Feature 41, a male, lacks any association, aside from matting, and Feature 8, a female, has a large number of beads of various sorts (including a necklace with at least five or six strands of small disc-shell beads), as well as *Glycymeris* shell bracelets, turquoise earrings, and a coiled basket on her chest. Clearly, a larger sample is needed for a more reliable and informative analysis of the distribution of burial goods.

Skeletal Morphology, Summary, and Comparisons: Crania[11]

The Henderson crania (see Figs. 24, 25, 41, 42, 54, 55, 62, 63, 67–70, 75, 76, 101, 102, 110, 111, 114, 115 above) are of moderately small size (cranial module 14.9, male; 14.4, female). Muscle attachments are not heavily developed on most of the specimens, although this may in part reflect the relatively young age of the individuals. The two older

---

[11]The bases of morphological comparisons are indicated in the text that follows with references to standard osteometric indices, or particular comparative populations.

male crania (Features 25 and 41) do exhibit heavier muscular development than the others at the site. The crania are high relative to their breadth (breadth-height index 100.02, male; 96.45, female)[12] and the females are also very high relative to their length (length-height index 82.5). However, these dimensions, particularly in the females, are affected by artificial deformation. The males are relatively long headed and of only moderate height relative to their length (length-height index 74.8; cranial index 74.8). The female cranial index (85.5) reflects the degree of deformation. Overall, differences in deformation are confounded with inter-sex differences in form; however, the female crania do appear proportionately shorter and broader than the male ones, even when deformation is taken into account (assuming deformation comparable to the Pecos Pueblo sample; see Hooton 1930:40–44). The cranial bases of both sexes are not flattened, and have moderately prominent condyles.

All of the crania, particularly the females, have moderately retreating frontals. Most of the crania exhibit some lambdoidal flattening which is probably, at least in part, natural (not due to deformation). In addition, one of the females (Feat. 1) exhibits probable slight culturally induced lambdoidal deformation, two exhibit probable slight occipital deformation (Features 8 and 40), and in fact all of the females may be slightly deformed (see individual feature descriptions[13]). The child, Feature 3, also shows possible lambdoidal deformation. None of the crania show extreme deformation, however. Of the males, only Feature 25 is possibly slightly deformed occipitally. Parietal bossing is present on both sexes (most marked on the deformed females) and a trace of sagittal keeling is indicated on some of the specimens when seen in occipital view.

The male crania have moderately prominent glabellar eminences and two of the three (Features 25 and 41) have moderate superciliary arch development. All of the Henderson crania have tall (superio-inferiorly) zygoma with considerable lateral, and moderate anterior, projection. The males are also notably chamaeconch (orbital index 81.5) and chamaerrhine (nasal index 53.6). The females have a less broad mid-face, with an orbital index in the mesoconch range (86.2) and a mesorrhine nasal index (51.2). The upper facial index is in the euryene range (48.5) and at the broad end of the mesene range (50.3) for the males and females respectively. Postorbital constriction is marked in both sexes. Females are slightly prognathous, while males are mesognathous (gnathic index 93.8, males; 101.8, females).

The Henderson mandibles are of moderate to broad bicondylar breadth, but overall are rather gracile, with low symphyseal height (Appendix 4). With a single exception (Feat. 25), little or no gonial eversion is present, and slight inversion occurs.

Sexual dimorphism in cranial form and metrics is marked. The different overall cranial form described above, a large difference in mastoid process size, glabellar prominence, superciliary arch development (Feat. 36 exhibits these characteristics to a lesser extent), and overall muscularity distinguish the sexes. The males exhibit slight nasion depression; in females, nasion is not depressed.

---

[12]In this and subsequent discussion, measurements identified as "affected by post-mortem crushing," in Appendix 4 are not included.

[13]Deformation was identified by simple visual inspection. Differences in deformation observed between males and females may in part be confounded with inter-sex differences in cranial form.

The value of any comparison of the Henderson crania with other populations is severely limited by the small size of the Henderson sample, limited publication elsewhere in the region of detailed metric data, variability between authors in measurement definitions (in some cases unspecified), and a paucity of described comparative skeletal material from the area immediately around the Henderson Site. The young age of the females in the Henderson sample must also be considered.

As a rough basis for comparison, metric data on samples of crania from the following populations were examined: various southeastern New Mexican skeletal samples (several sites in the Guadalupe Mountains, an unnamed site in the Rio Peñasco Valley, LA-2112 or Block Lookout in the Capitan Mountains); Pueblo (Gran Quivira, Pecos); Apache; southwestern, central, and northern Texas (Trans-Pecos Texas, central Texas [sites near Abilene, Waco, and Belton], Panhandle Aspect [Antelope Creek Phase]); northern Mexico (Casas Grandes); and Plains Caddoan (Arikara) (see Table 10 for populations and references). These samples are intended to represent a geographic range surrounding southeastern New Mexico, and were selected for the availability of actual metric data on individuals rather than summary statistics (with the exception of Pecos, Casas Grandes, and El-Najjar's figures from LA-2112), permitting the computation of a variety of commonly used facial indices for comparisons. These samples may include a considerable degree of temporal variability, however. It should be noted that in the following discussion no attempt is made to use statistical tests of metric differences, since the small sample sizes and variability within populations make almost all of these measurement differences statistically insignificant. What is intended is a preliminary description of the morphological and metrical similarities and differences among the various samples. All comparisons are based on the published descriptions, photographs, and measurements, not on direct examination of the material.

The dolichocranic and orthocranic Henderson male crania differ from the Pueblo norm, while the hyperbrachycranic and hypsicranic female crania are much more similar to Pueblos; deformation, however, distorts the female measurements towards the Pueblo values. The Henderson cranial shape indices are also in general comparable to the measurements of other southeast New Mexican skeletal samples, although female specimens in those samples are on average less extreme in their brachycrany than those of Henderson. The overall small size and relatively unprominent muscle attachments of the Henderson specimens are similar to Pueblo cranial norms. Mandibular breadth is slightly greater than in the Pecos sample, while symphyseal height is at or below the Pecos values.

A variety of contrasts may be noted between the Henderson specimens and the Pueblos. The broad zygoma, relatively broad orbits, and (in the case of males) broad nasal apertures are uncharacteristic of the typical Pueblo form and somewhat different from most of the other southeastern New Mexico specimens as well. One exception is the extreme breadth of the female from the site near the Rio Peñasco (Neumann 1940), which shifts the southeast New Mexico female zygomatic breadth mean higher than the male value and also higher than Henderson; Neumann attributes this breadth to the deformation of the Rio Peñasco cranium, however. The Henderson upper facial index of both sexes also reflects a broad face uncharacteristic of Pueblo groups. The other southeastern New Mexican samples are, with the exception of two males (Bartlett 1938, Campsite 1 and Campsite 2 males) more similar to Henderson in this respect (in fact, broader).

The glabellar prominence and slight degree of nasion depression of the Henderson males, are also not typically Pueblo.

Table 10
Selected cranial measurement and index means: Henderson Site and comparisons[1]

Measurements

Provenience (Sex)	GOL	XCB	BBH	TFH	NAH	ZYB	OBH	OBB	NLH	NLB
Henderson[2] (M)	18.47 (3) 1.050	13.40 (2) .424	13.40 (2) .283	11.62 (2) .255	6.95 (2) .262	14.33 (2) .601	3.37 (2) .170	4.14 (2) .219	5.17 (2) .007	2.77 (2) 0.
Henderson (F)	16.50 (3) .889	13.80 (2) .424	13.30 (2) .283	11.21 (3) .140	6.70 (3) .105	13.24 (2) .502	3.34 (3) .091	3.88 (3) .050	4.94 (3) .142	2.53 (3) .177
SE. New Mexico[3] (M)	18.02 (9) 1.168	13.62 (9) .620	13.25 (8) 1.276	10.76 (8) 1.390	6.75 (8) .424	13.04 (9) .766	3.38 (8) .173	3.81 (8) .173	5.00 (9) .384	2.43 (9) .184
SE. New Mexico (F)	17.57 (3) 1.286	13.97 (3) .907	12.63 (3) .961	11.03 (3) .551	6.50 (3) .624	13.70 (3) 1.054	3.51 (3) .115	3.75 (3) .050	5.05 (3) .132	2.60 (3) .200
LA-2112[4] (M)	17.43 --- ---	12.93 --- ---	12.95 --- ---	--- --- ---	6.50 --- ---	11.90 --- ---	3.75 --- ---	3.80 --- ---	4.60 --- ---	2.45 --- ---
LA-2112 (F)	17.03 --- ---	13.67 --- ---	13.15 --- ---	11.20 --- ---	6.90 --- ---	--- --- ---	3.55 --- ---	3.80 --- ---	4.70 --- ---	--- --- ---
Gran Quivira[5] (M)	17.48 (25)	13.89 (21)	13.78 (17)	12.47 (19)	7.45 (28)	13.93 (22)	3.45 (28)	3.88 (28)	5.20 (29)	2.57 (27)

Table 10 (cont.)

Provenience (Sex)	GOL	XCB	BBH	TFH	NAH	ZYB	OBH	OBB	NLH	NLB
	.952	.694	.422	.476	.408	.625	.224	.158	.269	.208
Gran Quivira (F)	16.72	13.55	13.25	11.32	6.84	12.99	3.44	3.74	4.84	2.51
	(28)	(26)	(20)	(31)	(35)	(31)	(35)	(35)	(35)	(35)
	.662	.515	.608	.575	.426	.426	.195	.172	.253	.136
Pecos[6] (M) (undeformed or combined)[7]	17.57	13.78	13.71	11.94	7.29	13.86	3.49	3.97	5.10	2.58
	(46)	(45)	(34)	(107)	(112)	(102)	(119)	(119)	(125)	(126)
	.815	.614	.649	.554	.395	.617	---	---	.274	.157
(deformed only)	16.43	14.54	14.07	---	---	---	---	---	---	---
	(95)	(91)	(80)	---	---	---	---	---	---	---
	.846	.613	.523	---	---	---	---	---	---	---
Pecos (F) (undeformed or combined)	16.37	13.80	13.39	11.33	6.90	12.99	3.44	3.83	4.82	2.53
	(26)	(25)	(21)	(71)	(75)	(68)	(80)	(80)	(86)	(86)
	.598	.614	.403	.587	.344	.336	---	---	.224	.183
(deformed only)	15.97	14.14	13.52	---	---	---	---	---	---	---
	(71)	(68)	(55)	---	---	---	---	---	---	---
	.831	.543	.400	---	---	---	---	---	---	---
Apache[8] (M)	17.46	14.77	12.93	11.53	7.17	14.07	3.54	3.89	5.20	2.61
	(17)	(17)	(17)	(8)	(14)	(14)	(17)	(17)	(17)	(17)
	.501	.384	.364	.492	.327	.436	.155	.156	.367	.195
Apache (F)	16.55	14.31	12.45	10.45	6.36	13.48	3.41	3.78	4.77	2.58

Table 10 (cont.)

Provenience (Sex)	GOL	XCB	BBH	TFH	NAH	ZYB	OBH	OBB	NLH	NLB
	(8) .735	(8) .368	(8) .450	(2) .495	(5) .270	(6) .508	(7) .184	(7) .177	(7) .304	(6) .183
SW. Texas[9] (M)	18.76 (11) .486	12.87 (11) .504	13.44 (10) .499	--- (0) ---	6.95 (8) .389	13.57 (11) .420	3.26 (11) .143	3.99 (11) .188	5.18 (11) .240	2.69 (11) .220
SW. Texas (F)	18.30 (10) .408	12.64 (10) .515	12.64 (10) .350	--- (0) ---	6.16 (7) .336	12.40 (9) .548	3.20 (10) .225	3.81 (10) .265	4.69 (10) .346	2.54 (10) .168
Cent. Texas[10] (M)	19.45 (2) .212	13.03 (17) .519	12.16 (17) .973	--- (0) ---	6.35 (15) .686	13.23 (17) .787	3.53 (2) .318	3.99 (2) .018	5.23 (2) .247	2.50 (14) .147
Cent. Texas (F)	--- (0) ---	13.00 (9) .527	11.28 (9) .869	--- (0) ---	6.28 (6) .382	12.48 (9) .694	--- (0) ---	--- (0) ---	--- (0) ---	2.23 (4) .263
Panhandle[11] (M)	18.06 (11) .982	14.07 (8) .464	13.65 (6) 1.067	12.04 (3) .249	7.03 (11) .336	13.05 (4) 1.434	3.58 (11) .266	4.30 (11) .256	5.34 (11) .303	2.65 (12) .204
Panhandle (F)	16.19 (6) .916	14.30 (2) .283	11.70 (1) ---	10.77 (3) .404	6.77 (4) .494	13.75 (1) ---	3.72 (5) .278	3.96 (4) .064	5.18 (4) .461	2.53 (6) .165
Casas Grandes[12] (M)	16.96 (25)	14.08 (27)	13.66 (8)	12.02 (4)	7.37 (6)	13.86 (5)	3.25 (9)	3.62 (7)	5.08 (9)	2.47 (10)

Table 10 (cont.)

Provenience (Sex)	GOL	XCB	BBH	TFH	NAH	ZYB	OBH	OBB	NLH	NLB
	1.221	.761	1.224	.332	.763	.472	---	---	.664	.221
Casas Grandes (F)	16.21 (30) .856	13.56 (32) .964	14.02 (13) .648	11.42 (4) .624	6.70 (9) 1.020	12.18 (5) 2.59	3.33 (9) ---	3.49 (7) ---	4.71 (8) .214	2.61 (8) .113
Arikara[13] (M)	18.24 (52) .546	14.29 (52) .454	13.47 (51) .468	12.21 (46) .594	7.60 (51) .348	14.15 (52) .447	3.64 (43) .199	3.99 (43) .115	5.56 (53) .213	2.62 (53) .179
Arikara (F)	17.36 (43) .488	13.66 (42) .474	12.81 (42) .359	11.47 (34) .588	7.16 (43) .406	13.05 (42) .429	3.56 (37) .164	3.84 (37) .100	5.18 (45) .262	2.53 (43) .160

Table 10 (cont.)

Indices

Provenience and Sex	Orbital Index	Nasal Index	Cranial Index	Length-Height Index	Cranial Module	Breadth-Height Index	Upper Facial Index
Henderson (M)	81.505	53.630	74.773	74.756	14.917	100.017	48.486
	(2)	(2)	(2)	(2)	(2)	(2)	(2)
	.217	.073	5.604	4.815	.024	1.056	.208
Henderson (F)	86.210	51.200	85.513	82.536	14.417	96.454	50.294
	(3)	(3)	(2)	(2)	(2)	(2)	(2)
	3.448	2.983	2.240	6.449	.354	5.015	2.549
SE. New Mexico (M)	88.761	48.811	75.997	73.950	14.954	97.223	51.639
	(8)	(9)	(9)	(8)	(8)	(8)	(8)
	4.628	4.452	7.530	6.344	.643	12.387	4.962
SE. New Mexico (F)	93.637	51.562	80.054	72.376	14.722	90.445	47.410
	(3)	(3)	(3)	(3)	(3)	(3)	(3)
	4.269	5.128	11.357	10.259	.340	3.471	1.800
Gran Quivira (M)	88.797	49.348	79.338	78.372	15.015	100.352	53.706
	(28)	(27)	(21)	(17)	(16)	(16)	(22)
	5.624	4.031	7.036	3.738	.347	4.406	2.907
Gran Quivira (F)	91.867	52.035	81.214	80.059	14.411	99.494	52.481
	(35)	(35)	(26)	(19)	(18)	(18)	(31)
	4.819	3.994	4.996	5.570	.316	4.058	3.030

Table 10 (cont.)

Provenience and Sex	Orbital Index	Nasal Index	Cranial Index	Length-Height Index	Cranial Module	Breadth-Height Index	Upper Facial Index
Pecos (M) (undeformed or combined)	87.80	50.44	78.30	78.11	15.05	99.33	52.09
	(120)	(124)	(43)	(34)	(33)	(33)	(90)
	4.57	4.27	4.81	3.95	.508	4.90	3.28
(deformed only)	---	---	88.93	85.78	14.80	96.94	---
	---	---	(91)	(80)	(80)	(78)	---
	---	---	6.30	5.10	.400	4.74	---
Pecos (F) (undeformed or combined)	89.87	52.60	84.32	82.00	14.49	97.67	53.00
	(83)	(86)	(25)	(21)	(18)	(21)	(61)
	4.81	4.13	5.96	3.36	.294	4.16	2.62
(deformed only)	---	---	88.90	85.14	14.52	95.28	---
	---	---	(68)	(55)	(54)	(53)	---
	---	---	6.53	4.36	.312	4.09	---
Apache (M)	91.098	50.390	84.654	74.119	15.053	87.592	51.169
	(17)	(17)	(17)	(17)	(17)	(17)	(12)
	4.517	3.945	2.869	3.083	.254	3.404	2.847
Apache (F)	90.112	54.210	86.595	75.295	14.437	86.986	48.368
	(7)	(6)	(8)	(8)	(8)	(8)	(4)
	2.713	1.661	3.560	2.858	.437	2.206	2.144
SW. Texas (M)	81.865	51.971	68.662	71.591	15.047	104.186	51.250
	(11)	(11)	(11)	(10)	(10)	(10)	(8)

Table 10 (cont.)

Provenience and Sex	Orbital Index	Nasal Index	Cranial Index	Length-Height Index	Cranial Module	Breadth-Height Index	Upper Facial Index
	4.447	4.049	3.598	2.709	.287	6.062	3.366
SW. Texas (F)	84.099	54.418	69.084	69.077	14.527	100.177	48.924
	(10)	(10)	(10)	(10)	(10)	(10)	(6)
	6.246	4.783	2.746	1.506	.291	5.476	3.318
Cent. Texas (M)	88.384	48.460	65.837	74.040	15.550	93.497	48.014
	(2)	(2)	(2)	(2)	(2)	(17)	(15)
	7.588	5.679	5.081	.808	.212	8.900	4.073
Cent. Texas (F)	---	---	---	---	---	86.752	50.173
	(0)	(0)	(0)	(0)	(0)	(9)	(6)
	---	---	---	---	---	5.755	5.264
Panhandle (M)	81.747	49.870	78.118	75.204	15.507	98.972	53.406
	(9)	(11)	(8)	(6)	(5)	(5)	(4)
	3.820	3.257	5.984	3.688	.440	5.364	4.089
Panhandle (F)	94.935	53.573	88.840	77.483	13.633	82.979	50.073
	(4)	(3)	(2)	(1)	(1)	(1)	(1)
	6.376	2.459	6.417	---	---	---	---
Casas Grandes (M)	94.0	51.7	84.1	80.0	14.76	---	52.1
	(9)	(8)	(20)	(5)	(5)	---	(4)
	9.57	10.96	9.37	6.87	.863	---	10.25
Casas Grandes (F)	95.2	55.4	80.2	87.3	13.98	---	54.7
	(8)	(6)	(25)	(10)	(10)	---	(4)

Table 10 (cont.)

Provenience and Sex	Orbital Index	Nasal Index	Cranial Index	Length-Height Index	Cranial Module	Breadth-Height Index	Upper Facial Index
	5.00	4.23	8.45	4.61	1.796	---	2.97
Arikara (M)	91.469 (43) 4.497	47.183 (53) 3.672	78.407 (52) 3.580	73.845 (51) 3.003	15.335 (51) .307	94.359 (51) 4.181	53.782 (50) 2.882
Arikara (F)	92.928 (37) 4.227	48.917 (43) 3.788	78.689 (42) 3.562	73.896 (42) 2.705	14.606 (41) .253	94.031 (41) 4.525	55.069 (41) 3.395

[1] See Appendix 4 for measurement abbreviations. Measurements (cm) given on top line of each entry, followed by sample size in parentheses, followed by standard deviation. Where raw data were published, all measurements, indices, and standard deviations were recalculated here. In a few cases, individuals with only a few measurable dimensions were dropped, so minor differences may exist between means listed here and means published in original sources. Except where noted, slight differences in measurement definitions (particularly dacryon versus lacrimale orbital breadth; or Howells' (1973:175) nasal height measurement to border of nasal aperture versus measurements on midline) are assumed negligible (Howells 1973:175; Hrdlička 1952:145, footnote 92; Stewart 1935:221). Where data were published, orbital measurements were averaged for right and left orbits.

[2] Henderson measurements based on data in Appendix 4, excluding those listed there as "affected by postmortem deformation".

[3] Includes measurements from three sources:

1) Unnamed site in Rio Peñasco Valley, 1 individual (Neumann 1940:17).
2) Miscellaneous sites in Guadalupe Mountains, 10 individuals (Bartlett 1938:62–63).
3) LA-2112 ("Block Lookout" or "Smokey Bear Ruin"), 1 individual (Reed 1984:284). Statistics and indices recalculated here.

[4]Based on summary statistics on unknown number of individuals per measurement from LA-2112 (El-Najjar 1976:91). Male statistics may include the individual included in southeastern New Mexico statistics (No. 2 above), although some measurements listed in Reed (1966) are listed as missing in El-Najjar (1976).

[5]Reed (1981:184–187). Statistics and indices recalculated here.

[6]Hooton (1930:33–78). Only summary statistics published.

[7]Where both deformed and undeformed value given, "undeformed or combined" value is actually undeformed subsample; where only one value given, "undeformed or combined" value is pooled deformed and undeformed sample.

[8]Hrdlička (1924:35–37). Statistics and indices recalculated here.

[9]Includes individuals from two sources, both in Trans-Pecos Texas. Statistics and indices recalculated here:

1) Miscellaneous sites in Val Verde, Culberson, and Brewster Co., 20 individuals (Stewart 1935:219–220).
2) Langtry Creek Burial Cave, 1 individual (Greer and Benfer 1963:242).

[10]Includes individuals from three sources in central Texas. Statistics and indices recalculated here:

1) Roberts and Alexander Mounds near Abilene, 1 individual each (Hrdlička 1938:170–172).
2) Aycock Site, near Belton, Bell Co., 16 individuals (Aynesworth 1936:34).
3) Unnamed multiple burial near Waco, 8 individuals (Watt and Meroney 1937:33).

Several measurements in latter two sources not comparable to measurements in other sources (i.e., cranial length measured from nasion, total facial height measured to mental tubercle, and nasal height is anomalously low in both cases [perhaps measured to rhinion?]). Thus, these 3 measurements, and indices derived from them, not considered here. Given apparent use of non-conventional anthropometric procedures by investigators of these two samples, other measurements may also be non-standard.

[11]Patterson (1974:120–182). Statistics and indices recalculated here. Patterson's use of maxillofrontale orbital breadth is incompatible with measurements from other sources used here, which use dacryon or lacrimale breadth. Thus, an approximation of dacryon breadth was derived from Patterson's value by subtracting 2.4 mm (constant based on average difference between dacryon and maxillofrontale orbital breadth values reported in Neumann [1950]).

[12]Based on "Medio II" period data (Benfer 1968:38–49). Only summary statistics published.

[13]Hrdlička (1927:60–67). Statistics and indices recalculated here.

The Henderson facial indices display some similarity to Apache (low upper facial index, high male nasal index, low female orbital index), central and particularly Trans-Pecos Texas populations (high male and intermediate female upper facial indices, low orbital index for both sexes, high male nasal index), as well as Panhandle Aspect specimens (low male orbital index) (Table 10). However, Henderson lacks the characteristic Apache low cranial height, flattened base (Neumann 1940:15, 1952:28), and (for males) short cranium. Similarly, a variety of contrasts may be seen between the measurements for Henderson and the Texas sample—for example the extreme dolichocrany of the southwest and central Texans.

Without a larger sample of material from Henderson, a larger range of comparable metric (and non-metric) observations, and a greater understanding of the genetic and developmental factors underlying cranial form, little may be said concerning the significance of these observations. However, as a preliminary basis for subsequent investigations, the following observations may be made:

1) Comparison with other southeastern New Mexico samples is inconclusive due to the extreme heterogeneity of that material (see Table 10, footnote 2 and 3 for list of material considered). The female from the Peñasco Valley, identified as Pueblo-like by Neumann (1940), has some similarities to the Henderson females in its broad zygoma, moderately retreating forehead, considerable post-orbital constriction, and trace median cresting. Cranial form varies greatly in the southeastern New Mexico comparative samples, ranging from dolichocranic to hyperbrachycranic and from chamaecranic to hypsicranic—probably in large part as a result of deformation. Orbital form varies also; the Goat Cave and Midden Circle males and Burial Cave 4 female (Bartlett 1938) most closely resemble Henderson in this variable. The males from Burial Caves 2 and 5 and from Midden Circle have nasal indices comparable to the breadth indicated at Henderson. Among females, the individual at Burial Cave 1 has an extreme chamaerrhine value far exceeding any at Henderson. The other two females are slightly narrower than Henderson. Male upper facial form in the comparative sample is extremely skewed; five of the specimens have upper facial indices comparable to Henderson, while three (Campsites 1 and 2 and Goat Cave) have much higher values (narrower faces). The three comparative female specimens' upper facial indices overlap with the two Henderson females, but have a lower average value (broader face).

2) Of the southeastern New Mexico comparative material, it is noteworthy that the metrics of both sexes from LA-2112 show little obvious similarity to the Henderson sample (exceptions are female cranial width, height, and total facial height). This is somewhat surprising given the geographical and chronological proximity and the material cultural similarity of this site to Henderson (Wiseman 1976). However, it is necessary to emphasize the small samples and limited measurements on which these conclusions are based.

3) The Henderson material is distinct from the eastern Pueblo groups represented by Gran Quivira and Pecos, most noticeably in aspects relating to facial breadth. These populations do exhibit similarities to the Henderson sample, however (see discussion above).

4) There is some similarity of the Henderson crania, particularly the males, to Apachean and Texas (particularly southwest Texas) groups. These are not close enough to warrant an identification of the Henderson population directly with either group. There is no basis to attribute an Athabascan identification to the

Henderson cranial form (assuming a correspondence between the Apache form and that of other Athabascan groups in the Southwest). Aside from the broad nose form at Casas Grandes, little similarity is evident between the Henderson and Casas Grandes metrics. Similarly, the Caddoan Arikara sample metrics show little resemblance to the Henderson Site values.

5) Thus, the Henderson material morphologically fits its intermediate geographical position—exhibiting a form distinct from, but with some similarities to, both the Pueblo and the Texas groups. Female crania tend more towards the Pueblo form than do the males (cf. Patterson 1974:275, 278, 289). Some of the similarities, particularly those relating to Pueblo head form, are probably exaggerated by culturally induced deformation. The similarities to some of the Texas samples are greater than to the Pueblo groups. At the present level of refinement, no statement can be made concerning the relative similarity of the Henderson sample to the Gran Quivira versus the Pecos Pueblo samples. Future studies of these relationships could help to clarify the fate of the Henderson population and other Pecos Valley horticulturalists following the abandonment of the villages in the area in the mid- to late fifteenth century.

6) The distinctiveness of the Henderson facial form from the Pueblo sample is perhaps significant in that it occurs despite apparent similarities in diet (described below), and hence despite similarities in developmental factors affecting facial form. Thus, it is possible to suggest, in part, a genetic basis for this difference. The Henderson population probably does not represent a simple movement of eastern Puebloans (Piro or Tompiro) onto the Plains. In this context it is also of interest to note the lack of close similarity between the Henderson sample and the metrics from the Capitan Mountain Lincoln Phase site of LA-2112 (see above), despite the many architectural and artifactual affinities between these two sites. We will return to the implications of these observations in the concluding discussion.

Skeletal Morphology, Summary, and Comparisons: Postcrania

Compared with other North American Indian groups, the Henderson postcrania exhibit considerable sexual dimorphism (although the two most fragmentary burials [Features 21 and 29] represent the largest female and the smallest [probable] male respectively, so that many of their measurements would probably decrease the inter-sex contrast). Table 11 presents several mean femoral and humeral measurements of the Henderson sample and selected comparative samples; the gross size and robusticity of many of the other postcranial elements follow similar trends to these bones. The Henderson measurements are considerably greater than comparative Pueblo material (this is true also of the mean of tibia length, with Feature 29 included in the calculation of the Henderson male mean). In absolute terms the Henderson male measurements are large, greater in all of the dimensions examined here than Hrdlička's mean North American Indian values. The femoral index of robusticity, a measure of shaft diameter relative to shaft length, is more moderate, and slightly lower than the North American mean; hence the Henderson shaft thickness is great but not proportionately as great as the shaft length. Robusticity does exceed the Pueblo (Pecos) values, however. The male measurements at Henderson do not differ greatly from some of the Texas comparative samples, although they are slightly larger than most.

Table 11
Femoral and humeral measurements from Henderson Site and selected comparative samples[1]

Measurement	Henderson[2]		Pecos[3]		G. Quivira[4]		SW. Texas[5]		Cent. Texas[6]		Panhandle[7]		N. American Mean[8]	
	M	F	M	F	M	F	M	F	M	F	M	F	M	F
Femur														
Bicondylar length	45.7	39.4	42.4	39.3	42.6	39.5	45.1	41.5	46.4	41.7	44.7	39.9	42.9*	40.7*
Max. head diam.	4.88	3.98	4.30	3.85	4.45	3.93	---	---	---	---	4.63	4.1	---	---
Mid-shaft a-p diam.	3.23	2.61	2.80	2.50	---	---	3.14	2.52	3.19	2.50	3.04	2.63	3.00	2.57
Mid-shaft m-l diam.	2.57	2.38	2.45	2.30	---	---	2.56	2.27	2.52	2.34	2.58	2.46	2.57	2.36
Robusticity index	12.81	12.30	12.38*	12.21*	---	---	12.64*	11.54*	12.27	11.76	12.63	12.50R	12.98	12.10
Humerus														
Max. length	32.8	28.3	30.9	28.7	---	---	31.6	29.1	32.7	---	31.1	28.7	---	---
Max. head diam.	4.70	3.80	4.38	3.85	4.47	3.82	---	---	---	---	4.26	3.80	---	---
Max. diam. mid-shaft	2.37	2.18	2.18	2.16	---	---	2.02	1.69	2.25	1.60L	2.27	2.18	2.21	---
Min. diam. mid-shaft	1.65	1.39	1.62	1.47	---	---	1.49	1.26	1.74	1.20L	---	---	1.62	---

[1]Measurements listed in table are pooled means of right and left sides.
R, right side only, based on single individual.
L, left side only, based on single individual.
*, calculated from means.
[2]From Appendix 5.
[3]Hooton (1930:134-137, 153-155).
[4]Reed (1981:191-195).
[5]Stewart (1935:224-225). Sites in Trans-Pecos Texas.
[6]Hrdlička (1938:175-176, 178-179, 181, 183-184). Sites in vicinity of Abilene, central Texas.
[7]Patterson (1974:129, 144-5, 189-192, 198-201, 206, 208-209). Panhandle Aspect sites. Note that several errors in published summary statistics were identified and corrected while using these statistics to calculate mean of left and right sides. One case (individual No. 28-112 [p. 145], right femur mid-shaft length and breadth) was deleted from calculation, as it represents an extreme outlier; perhaps length and breadth measurements were reversed in original source.
[8]Hrdlička (1938:176, 180, 184). Average of 17 unspecified North American Indian samples.

Stature estimates for the Henderson males yield mean values of 168.3 cm or 166.6 cm (Appendix 6; based on femoral and tibial length, respectively [the latter mean includes Feat. 29]; the estimates were calculated using Genovés' formulas, with 2.5 cm subtracted to approximate living stature [Steele and McKern 1969]). Both of these estimates exceed Hrdlička's (1935:226) early twentieth-century mean stature of 164.3 cm for living male Pueblo Indians.

The Henderson female postcrania are considerably smaller than those of the male, and in general resemble the Pueblo values (Table 11). These values are slightly lower than the female North American means and the means of most of the female Texas measurements (although where the means include Feat. 21, as in the mid-shaft and head measures, the difference is less, and in some cases is reversed). The Henderson female mean femoral robusticity index (which cannot be calculated for Feat. 21) is relatively great, exceeded only by the Panhandle Aspect value (which is represented by a single individual).

Female stature estimated on the basis of the femur is 151.7 cm (Appendix 6; calculated as described above), close to Hrdlička's (1935:226) value of 151.9 cm for recent Pueblo women. Mean stature estimated on the basis of the tibiae (which includes Feat. 21) is 154.1 cm, higher than the Pueblo value.

One additional observation of potential interest may be made concerning the Henderson postcrania. This relates to the observation of phalangeal fusion or reduction in the number of phalangeal segments previously noted in the individual burial descriptions (see Fig. 58 above). As indicated in Table 12, all individuals for which the fifth-digit distal phalanges of both feet were recovered exhibit fusion of the distal and middle phalanx on at least one side. Two of the adults from which the phalanges of only one side were recovered do not exhibit fusion.

Table 12
Fusion of toe elements:
Distal and middle phalanges of fifth digit (see Fig. 58)

Feature No.	Side		
	Left	Right	Unknown
1	a	p	a
3	a	a	a
8	F	p	a
9	p?	a	a
21	F	F	a
25	F	a	a
29	a	a	a
36	F	a	a
40	F	F	a
41	a	a	p

p, element present, not fused.
a, element not present.
F, fused distal and middle phalanges.

The mechanism responsible for such fusion has been shown to be heritable, resulting from the absence of secondary ossification centra and subsequent fusion of some adjoining phalanges (Garn et al. 1965). Given the high frequency of missing ossification centra noted in a sample of living Ohio white Americans (33% absence of the ossification centra between the middle and distal phalanges on the fifth toe [Garn et al. 1965:631]), and the lack of data on other populations, it is impossible to evaluate the observed frequency at Henderson (70% of recovered adult fifth toe distal-middle phalanges are fused). However, the high observed frequency and the presence of the trait both in the earliest burials at Henderson (Features 8, 21, 36, and 40) and in at least one of the small sample of later interments (Feat. 25) may reflect genetic continuity and close genetic relationship among the Henderson individuals. It must again be emphasized that further data on the frequency and distribution of this trait in Native American populations are needed before it can be adequately interpreted.

Health and Lifeways

The limited Henderson sample gives little indication of major health problems faced by the inhabitants of the site. The possible porotic hyperostosis on Feature 8 and mild periostitis on Feature 25 are the only evidence of systemic disease. In each case the evidence of the disease is mild. Faint horizontal (parallel to the occlusal surface) ripples and depressions are present on the labial surface of the anterior maxillary dentition of most of the individuals (particularly noticeable on Features 8, 25, and 41). This might represent trace enamel hypoplasia, but it is so faint that it probably does not constitute evidence of any particular morbidity-related developmental stress events, and would not be classified as hypoplasia in most classifications of the pathology.

The other major abnormalities noted involve peculiarities of fusion (fusion of the foot phalanges discussed above, fusion of two pairs of ribs on Feat. 41, and lack of fusion of the superior sacral element on Feat. 8) which have little relevance to the health of the population. The only information probably directly bearing on the cause of death of one of the individuals is the presence of the fetus associated with the adult female in Feature 40; presumably some complication associated with pregnancy resulted in death.

The generally large size of the Henderson individuals indicated by the stature estimates discussed above suggests a relatively healthy population. Similarly, the Henderson population exhibits considerable postcranial robusticity, which may reflect health as well as activities involving physical exertion (these observations may apply to both sexes if Feat. 21 measurements are included in the sample; they do not apply uniformly to female measurement means from which Feat. 21 must be omitted due to its fragmentary state). No fractures were evident on any of the individuals.

Dental health was, with a single exception, moderately good. Feature 25 had extreme, steeply sloped wear on all of its first molars, out of proportion with the wear on the rest of the dentition. The cause of this wear is not known, but it resulted in exposure of the pulp cavity, infection, and abscess formation. One apical abscess, not associated with caries, is also present (Feat. 1). Feature 1 also had one supernumerary tooth, a condition not associated with any condition affecting health. A dental anomaly of unknown origin, incisor roots of abnormally short length, occurs on one individual Feat. 8). There is no evidence of a dietary or disease origin for this condition.

A total of 216 intact teeth (excluding the Feat. 25 first molars, as well as teeth with fragmentary crowns) are present in the Henderson sample, 211 of which are in occlusion. Twelve of these are deciduous. Of these teeth, 6 to 11 (depending on the extent of damage required in identifying caries) are carious (see Appendix 2; interestingly, 67% to 80% of these caries occur in the teeth of males). Thus, out of a total of 211 teeth only 2.8% to 5.2% are carious. This level may be compared with a range of 0% to 5.3% (inter-population median 1%) for a sample of hunting-gathering populations, 0.4% to 10.3% (median 3.8%) for mixed agricultural/hunting-gathering populations, and 2.3% to 26.9% (median 8.1–9.6%) for agriculturalist populations (Turner 1979:625). Thus, the Henderson caries rate is most similar to that found in those populations with a mixed agricultural and hunting-gathering economy with a relatively high rate or those agricultural populations with a low one.

Aside from the caries rate, another aspect of the dentition sensitive to diet is the rate and form of dental wear. B. H. Smith examined dental attrition on the Henderson mandibular first molars using the criteria described in Smith (1984). Her measurements of wear-plane angle and corresponding wear stage are summarized in Table 13.

Table 13
Mandibular molar wear stage and wear-plane angle[1]

Feature No.	Wear Stage M_1	Wear-Plane Angle
1	4	+6.5
8	3	+2
25	6	+26[2]
36	3	+1
40	3	+9
41	4	(right) +3 (left) +8

[1]Positive angle indicates wear inclined buccally (see Smith 1984 for definition of wear stages and angle measurements).
[2]Measurement on these pathologically worn teeth only approximate, due to extreme steepness of plane.

Reliable conclusions concerning diet or food preparation based on this small sample are impossible. However, the Henderson material falls in and above the typical range of wear-plane angles of agriculturalists and far above the range typical of hunter-gatherers (Fig. 118). Smith also notes a relatively low rate of tooth wear in the Henderson sample (comparable to that seen at Gran Quivira), and a relatively heavy degree of calculus formation (see Appendix 2). All of these characteristics suggest that the Henderson Site inhabitants ate a diet of heavily processed soft foods characteristic of agriculturalists (B. H. Smith 1984, personal communication). It should be noted that the use of limestone metates at Henderson (and hence the introduction of less tough grit into the food than occurs with sandstone or other hard stone metates) might affect the observed wear.

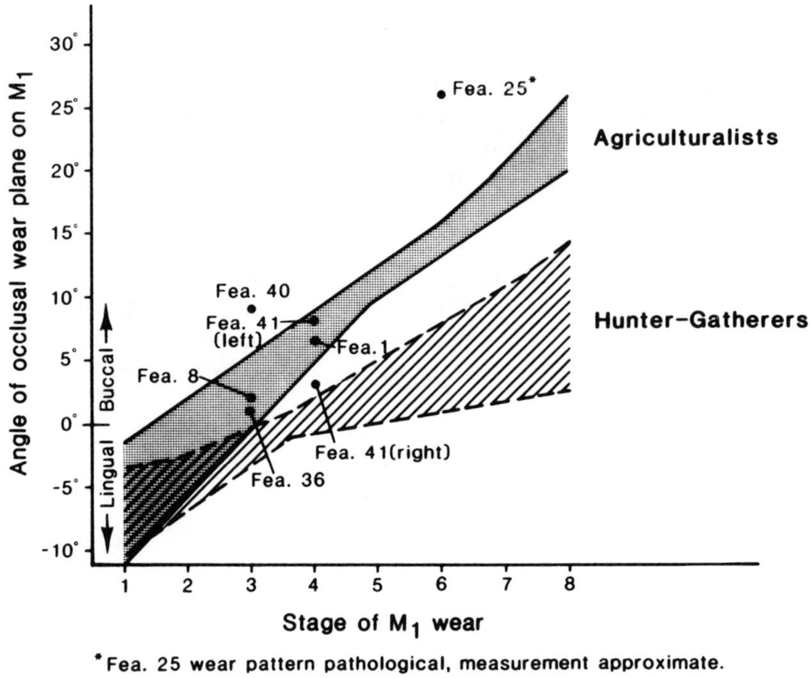

Fig. 118. Mandibular molar wear stage and wear-plane angle of Henderson sample, compared with range of hunter-gatherer and agriculturalist wear-plane regression lines. Measurements and observations made by B. H. Smith. This figure based on Figure 5 in Smith (1984:49), which differs in some details from regression data listed in Table 4 of same article; however, discrepancy does not affect position of Henderson data relative to agriculturalist and hunter-gatherer patterns.

Conclusions

As has been emphasized repeatedly above, little may be concluded with certainty on the basis of 11 individuals, two of which are infants. The indications discussed above may tentatively be said to suggest the following major points:

1) The Henderson diet was at least partially and probably heavily agricultural. This conforms to the archaeological evidence from the site of food-processing and cultivated plant remains (esp. corn), but is somewhat unexpected in light of the large quantity of bison bones that were recovered from the East Plaza. The dental data suggest that processed foods typical of an agriculturalist diet predominated at the Henderson Site, although the caries rate is at the lower end of the agriculturalist range. The evidence of the dental and faunal data combined point to a mixed economy, making extensive use of both agricultural resources and of buffalo.

2) The Henderson population was generally healthy, with an adequate diet. Little evidence of growth-arrest or disease-related stress is present.

3) Physically, the inhabitants of the Henderson Site have resemblances to both the Pueblo populations to their west and, more markedly, to the more scattered peoples of western Texas to their east and south. However, there is no evidence that the Henderson Site was settled by recent migrants from either area; instead, the data point to some degree of stability in the local population.

These conclusions are offered as a basis for further investigation of these and other issues concerning the prehistoric population of southeastern New Mexico. It is hoped that controlled excavation and analysis of additional material, as well as reanalysis of existing collections, will permit the development of a data base sufficient to place an assessment of the lifeways, health, social organization, and relationships of the peoples of this region upon a firmer foundation.

In closing, it is worth noting an issue of general theoretical interest that is raised by the Henderson burials. The relatively sudden appearance, in an area characterized by ephemeral hunter-gatherer sites, of a substantial horticulturally based community like Henderson, with its obvious architectural and artifactual similarities to horticultural communities in an adjacent region, most likely would be interpreted by Southwestern archaeologists as a case of migration or "site unit intrusion" (e.g., Beckes and Adovasio 1982). However, in the case of Henderson, the intermediate character of the population's physical form, as well as the intermediate nature of their economy which combines farming with a heavy reliance on buffalo hunting, does not comfortably fit a simple model of migration or "site unit intrusion" of Mogollon peoples from the west into the eastern Jornada periphery. Instead, these characteristics raise the possibility of a rapid *in situ* transformation of local hunting and gathering economies into horticulturally based systems, and the adoption by these local groups of many of the cultural trappings of their horticultural contemporaries to the west. Thus, the Henderson case may serve a more general lesson, to encourage archaeologists to take a new look at putative instances of migration elsewhere in North America that previously have been identified solely on the basis of apparent cultural similarities. Perhaps some of these assumed "migrations" will vanish upon closer examination of the skeletal remains of the supposed immigrants.

APPENDIX 1

STAGES OF FUSION OF OSSIFICATION CENTRA

Table A1
Stages of fusion of ossification centra[1]

Bone/Part	Feature No.	
	8	40
Spheno-occipital	2	2
Scapula		
acromion	3	3
vertebral border	0	0
lower angle	0	0
Clavicle		
sternal	0	0
Humerus		
head	2	2
distal	3	3
med. epicon.	3	3
Radius		
proximal	3	3
distal	2	2
Ulna		
proximal	3	3
distal	2	2
Sternum		
sect. 1–2	2	2
sect. 2–3	3	3
sect. 3–4	3	3
sect. 4-xiph.	0	0
Pelvis		
primary elem.	3	3
iliac crest	1	1
isch. tuberos.	2	2
Femur		
head	2	3
grtr. troch.	3	3
lssr. troch.	3	3
distal	2	3
Tibia		
proximal	2	2
distal	3	3
Fibula		
proximal	3	3
distal	2	3

[1]Stages: 0, unfused; 1, partially united; 2, fused but visible; 3, obliterated.

APPENDIX 2

DEGREE OF DENTAL ATTRITION

Table A2
Degree of dental attrition[1]

Feat. No.	Maxilla/ Mandible	Side	I1	I2	C	P3	P4	M1	M2	M3
			Deciduous Dentition							
3	Max.	R	2d	1d,pc	2d			+	1d	
		L	+	+	2d			2d	1d	
	Man.	R	+	+	1d			+	1d	
		L	2d	1d	+			+	1d	
			Permanent Dentition							
8	Max.	R	2	1	2	1	1	3	2	1*
		L	2	1	2	1	1	3	2	1*
	Man.	R	+	2	1	1	1	3	2c	1
		L	2	2	2	1	1	3	2c	1*
36	Max.	R	3	2	2	2	2	3	2	1c
		L	3	2	3	1	1	3	2	1
	Man.	R	3	2	2	2	2	3	2c	1
		L	3	2	3	1	2	3	2	1pc
40	Max.	R	2	2	2	2	1	3	3	–
		L	2	2	3	2	2	3	3	1*
	Man.	R	3	2	3	2	2	3	3	1
		L	3	2	3	2	2	3	3	1*
1	Max.	R	4a	3	3	2	3	4	3	2
		L	4	3	3	3	3	4	3	2
	Man.	R	4	3	3	1	2	4	3	2
		L	4	3	3	3	3	4	3	2
41	Max.	R	4	4	3	3	3	4	3pc	–
		L	4	4	3	3	3	4	3	2
	Man.	R	4	3	4	3	3	4	3	2pc
		L	4	3	4	3	3	4	3	2c
25	Max.	R	4	4	4	4	5	6$a	4	3
		L	4	4	4	5	5	6$a	4	3
	Man.	R	5	4	4	3	3	6$	4	3c
		L	5	4	4	4	4	6$a	4	3pc
21[2]	Max.	R	A/3	A/3	8	8	8	A	A	5
		L	A/3	8	8	–	A	A	A	A
	Man.	R	7	7	6	6	6	A/2	A/2	7
		L	–	+	6	6	6	7	A	6

[1]Dental attrition of burials in order of increasing wear stage (after Smith 1984). See Appendix 9 for data on isolated teeth.

Symbols and abbreviations:

- c, caries present on tooth.
- pc, possible caries.
- a, abscess associated with tooth.
- d, deciduous.
- +, broken crown, can not be scaled.
- *, not erupted to occlusal level.
- $, abnormal wear pattern.
- –, lost, post-mortem.
- A, lost, ante-mortem.
- A/3, represents one of three teeth, one of which was lost ante-mortem and two of which were lost post-mortem (i.e., one of the three teeth labeled this way was lost ante-mortem, but it is impossible to determine which one it was).
- A/2, same as A/3, except one of two teeth, one of which was lost ante-mortem and the other of which was lost post-mortem.

[2]Three additional unidentified incisors (or two incisors and one premolar) of Feature 21 are at stage 8; a molar (RM_1 or RM_2) is also at stage 8.

APPENDIX 3

DENTAL MEASUREMENTS

Table A3
Dental measurements[1]

side	l/w	Maxillary Dentition I	I	C	P	P	M	M	M	Mandibular Dentition I	I	C	P	P	M	M	M
Feature 1																	
R	l	8.6*	7.1	8.0	6.7	6.8	10.5	10.3	8.3	4.7	6.0	7.1	6.9	7.1	11.4*	10.8	9.8
	w	7.4	6.4	8.5	9.5	9.2	11.8	12.2e	10.1	5.7	6.1	7.1	7.7	8.3	10.4	10.6	9.9
L	l	8.7*	7.1	8.1	7.0	6.8	9.9	10.1	8.0	4.8	5.8	6.8	6.6	6.8	11.0*	11.1	10.7
	w	7.2	6.4	8.2	9.6	9.2	11.3	11.1	9.6	5.7	6.3	7.5	8.1	8.5	10.4	10.5	10.0
Feature 3 (deciduous teeth only)																	
R	l	7.5d	5.7d	8.0d	....	.....	8.1d	10.6d	.....	....	....	5.5d	....	....	.....	12.3d	.....
	w	5.2d	5.3d	6.5d	....	.....	9.9d	11.0d	.....	....	....	5.1d	....	....	.....	9.5d	.....
L	l	7.5d	....	7.6d	....	.....	.....	10.2d	.....	....	....	....	....	....	.....	11.8d	.....
	w	5.4d	....	6.7d	....	.....	.....	11.6d	.....	....	....	....	....	....	.....	9.7d	.....
Feature 8																	
R	l	9.1	8.0	8.2	7.4	7.8	11.1	10.7	.....	....	7.0	6.9	7.3	7.9	11.8	12.4	10.6r
	w	7.9	6.8	8.2	9.3	9.8	11.7	11.1	.....	....	6.3	7.7	7.2	8.3	10.7	10.6	10.1r
L	l	9.1	7.9	8.3	7.3	7.6	11.5	10.7	.....	5.8	6.6	7.0	7.2	7.6	11.9	11.8	.....
	w	7.6	6.6	8.1	9.2	9.7	11.6	11.1	.....	6.2	6.6	7.6	7.3	8.1	10.9	10.4	.....
Feature 25																	
R	l	8.9*	8.3*	8.6	8.0	7.3*	.....	9.6*	10.1*	4.8*	5.7*	7.5*	7.4*	7.4	.....	11.0*	10.5*
	w	7.6	7.0	9.1	10.4	9.8	.....	11.8	12.1	6.0	6.4	7.8	8.3	8.9	.....	10.9	11.1
L	l	9.7*	8.0*	8.6	7.7	7.3*	.....	10.2*	10.0*	4.6*	6.0*	7.5*	7.7*	7.3*	.....	11.1	10.1
	w	7.6	7.0	8.6	10.4	9.9	.....	11.8	11.2	5.8	6.5	8.1	8.5	8.9	.....	10.8	10.7
Feature 36																	
R	l	9.5	7.8	8.4	7.7	8.4	12.1	11.5	10.5	5.7	6.8	7.8	7.6	7.9	12.1	11.9	11.8
	w	8.2	6.5	9.0	10.0	10.2	12.7	12.5	11.5	6.3	6.8	8.7	8.2	8.3	11.5	11.1	10.7
L	l	9.6	8.0	8.3	7.8	8.0	11.8	11.1	10.2	5.9	6.6	7.5	7.3	7.9	12.3	11.8	11.3e
	w	8.0	6.5	9.3	10.3	9.8	12.6	12.5	11.1	....	6.7	....	8.0	8.5	11.5	11.1	11.5e

Table A3 (cont.)

side	l/w	Maxillary Dentition								Mandibular Dentition							
		I	I	C	P	P	M	M	M	I	I	C	P	P	M	M	M
Feature 40																	
R	l	9.6	7.6	7.9	7.7	7.5	11.0	10.3	.....	5.5	6.5	....	7.5	7.7	11.9	11.7	10.2
	w	....	....	8.3	9.6	9.9	11.6	11.1	.....	....	....	7.4	7.8	....	11.3	11.2	10.1
L	l	9.6	7.5	8.0	7.5	7.5	11.3	10.1	.....	5.5	6.4	6.9	7.7	8.0	12.0	11.9	.....
	w	7.6	6.7	8.2	9.7	9.9	11.6	10.9	.....	....	....	7.4	7.5	8.2	11.3	11.3	.....
Feature 41																	
R	l	9.4*	7.6	7.9	7.0	6.6	11.2*	10.0*	.....	5.3*	6.3*	7.4*	7.2	7.5	11.8*	11.5*	11.8
	w	7.7	6.3	9.0	9.8	9.3	12.0	11.2	.....	6.0	6.4	7.5	7.7	8.3	11.5	10.7	11.5
L	l	9.2*	7.4	8.2	7.2	6.6	11.1*	10.2*	8.8	5.3*	6.5*	7.4*	7.3	8.2	11.6*	.....	10.8r
	w	7.7	6.6	9.0	9.5	9.4	12.2	11.4	10.5	5.8	6.2	....	8.1	....	.....	10.4	10.3r

[1]Measurements are *maximum* diameters (mm), taken after Moorrees (1957:78-80). Since measurements are taken at point of maximum diameter, they often do not lie on tooth midline (see Moorrees). Axes of teeth defined as in Moorrees, with additional specification that "labial" surface for rotated teeth is defined as labial surface of the tooth when in its normal position rather than in its rotated position. Thus, mesio-distal length of rotated tooth may actually be measured in bucco-lingual orientation.

Symbols and abbreviations:

- R, right side.
- L, left side.
- l, length (mesio-distal).
- w, width (bucco-lingual).
- e, tooth has small extra cusp included in measurement.
- *, tooth displays degree of interproximal wear likely to have an effect on measurement greater than measurement error.
- d, deciduous tooth.
- r, rotated.

Feature 21 dentition not measured due to advanced wear. Feature 3 includes additional mandibular central incisor (side unknown) measuring 4.3 mm (length) by 4.1 mm (width). See Appendix 9 for data on isolated teeth.

APPENDIX 4

CRANIO-FACIAL AND MANDIBULAR MEASUREMENTS

Table A4
Cranio-facial and mandibular measurements[1]

	Feature No.						
Measure	1	8	21	25	36	40	41
Cranio-facial Measurements							
GOL	17.2d	15.5d	–	17.4d	19.5e	16.8d	18.5
NOL	17.1d	15.5d	–	17.1d	–	16.7	18.3
BNL	9.9d	9.9d	–	10.1d	–	10.5d	11.0
BBH	13.6cd	13.5d	–	13.6d	(13.0-13.5)e	13.1d	13.2
XCB	13.4cd	13.5d	–	13.7d	(13.5-14.5)e	14.1d	13.1
XFB	11.2cd	10.9d	–	11.2d	–	11.3d	11.3
STB	10.9d	10.2d	–	10.7d	–	10.4	10.6
ZYB	13.25cd	12.88d	–	14.75d	–	13.59d	13.90
WCB	6.95	6.55	–	7.41	–	7.07	7.25
ASB	10.67d	9.90d	–	10.76d	–	10.51d	11.12
BPL	10.1	9.94	–	9.9	–	10.80	9.86
NPH	6.55	6.45	–	6.83	–	6.44	6.53
UFH	6.80	6.71	–	7.13	–	6.59	6.76
NLH	5.11	4.86	–	5.17	–	4.87	5.16
OBH	3.31	3.45	–	3.49	–	3.28	3.25
OBB	3.89	3.83	–	4.29	–	3.93	3.98
NLB	2.65	2.33	–	2.77	–	2.62	2.77
MAB	6.47	6.35	–	7.02	–	6.23	6.64
MDH	2.71	2.16	2.62c	3.42	3.04c	2.37	3.32
ZMB	9.79	9.39	–	10.79	–	9.77	10.23
EKB	9.68	9.48	–	10.11	–	10.29	9.85
DKB	2.25	2.24	–	1.89	–	2.77	2.44
WNB	1.05	1.05	–	0.80	–	1.35	1.28
FRC	11.01cd	10.48d	–	11.38d	–	10.51d	10.99
IPL	4.66	4.42	–	4.48	–	4.76	4.42
MAL	5.3	5.34	–	5.4	–	5.60	5.3
TFH	11.37	11.17	–	11.80	–	11.10	11.44
Mandibular Measurements							
BCB	11.39c	12.41	14.08c	13.24	12.20ce	12.32e	12.37e
BGB	7.96c	9.40e	–	11.47	9.31ce	9.00e	9.04
SYH	3.22c	3.12	–	3.30	3.68e	3.23e	3.38
ARH	6.37	5.50	6.42	6.66	6.63	5.24	6.98
WRB	3.23	3.50	3.60	3.09	3.59	3.63	3.27

Table A4 (cont.)

[1]All values in cm, measured with spreading calipers (to nearest mm) or dial calipers (to nearest 0.1 mm). All measurements after Howells (1973) or Bass (1971). Measurements defined on left side taken on the right side when left is broken or missing; measurements defined as average of two sides are taken on one side only, when other side is broken or missing.

Symbols:

- c, significantly affected by post-mortem crushing.
- d, possibly affected by culturally induced deformation.
- e, estimate based on damaged bone.

Measurement abbreviations (after Howells 1973):

- GOL, glabello-occipital length.
- NOL, nasio-occipital length.
- BNL, basion-nasion length.
- BBH, basion-bregma height.
- XCB, maximum cranial breadth.
- XFB, maximum frontal breadth.
- STB, bistephanic breadth.
- ZYB, bizygomatic breadth.
- WCB, minimum cranial breadth.
- ASB, biasterionic breadth.
- BPL, basion-prosthion length.
- NPH, nasion-prosthion height.
- NLH, nasal height.
- OBH, orbit height, left.
- OBB, orbit breadth, left.
- NLB, nasal breadth.
- MAB, palate breadth, external.
- MDH, mastoid height.
- ZMB, bimaxillary breadth.
- EKB, biorbital breadth.
- DKB, interorbital breadth.
- WNB, simotic chord.
- FRC, nasion-bregma chord (frontal chord).

Measurement abbreviations (after Bass 1971):

- UFH, upper facial height (nasion-alveolare).
- IPL, palatal length, internal.
- MAL, maxillo-alveolar length, external.
- TFH, total facial height.
- BCB, bicondylar breadth.
- BGB, bigonial breadth.
- SYH, symphyseal height.
- ARH, height of ascending ramus.
- WRB, minimum breadth of ascending ramus.

APPENDIX 5

POSTCRANIAL MEASUREMENTS

Table A5
Postcranial measurements[1]

Element	Side	Feature No.							
		1	8	21	25	29	36	40	41
Clavicle									
max. length	R	14.0	13.3u	14.9r	15.9	-	16.2r	13.3*	15.2
	L	14.2r	13.5u	-*	15.9	-	16.1	13.1*	15.5
circumference at middle of	R	3.0	3.1	-*	4.0	-	3.2*	2.8	3.4
bone	L	2.9r	2.9	3.1	4.0	-	3.1	2.9	3.3
Scapula									
max. length	R	12.9	13.2	-*	15.0*	-	-*	12.5r	15.1
	L	13.0r	-*	-*	-*	-	-*	-*	-*
max. breadth	R	10.1	9.5u	-*	10.6	-	-*	9.5	-*
	L	10.1	-*	-*	-*	-	-*	-*	10.9
length of spine	R	12.8	12.6u	-*	14.2	-	-*	12.3r	14.4
	L	12.5r	-*	-*	-*	-	-*	-*	14.0
length of supra-spinous	R	4.1*	4.5*u	-*	4.9*	-	-*	4.0u	4.9
line	L	3.7	4.1u	-*	-*	-	-*	-*	-*
length of infra-spinous	R	9.9	10.5u	-*	11.3r	-	-*	9.6	11.5
line	L	10.3r	-*	-*	-*	-	-*	-*	12.0
Humerus									
max. length	R	28.7	28.9	-*	32.1	-	33.9r	27.8r	32.1
	L	27.9r	28.5	-*	32.5	-	34.4r	27.9	31.9
max. diam. mid-shaft	R	2.1	2.1	2.3e	2.7	-	2.4	2.0d	2.3
	L	2.2	-d	2.5e	2.4	-	2.3	2.0	2.1
min. diam. mid-shaft	R	1.3	1.4	1.5e	1.9	-	1.7	1.4d	1.6
	L	1.4	1.4	1.4e	1.7	-	1.5	1.3	1.5
max. diam. of head	R	3.9	-*	4.0	4.6r	-	4.9r	3.8	4.7
	L	3.7	3.7	-*	4.7	-	4.7	3.7	4.6
least circumference of	R	5.5	5.4	6.0	7.2	-	6.3r	5.1	6.2
shaft	L	5.7	5.4	6.0	6.5	-	5.9r	5.2	6.0
Ulna									
max. length	R	25.3	23.8	26.6a	28.1	-	27.8r	23.9	27.3
	L	25.1	23.5*	26.6	28.1*	-	-*	23.7	27.1
least circumference of	R	3.0	3.1	-*	3.8	-	3.4	3.2	3.2
shaft	L	3.0	3.1	3.4	3.6	-	3.2	3.0	3.0
Radius									

Table A5 (cont.)

Element	Side	Feature No. 1	8	21	25	29	36	40	41
max. length	R	23.4	21.6	25.1	-*	-	26.1r	21.9r	25.5
	L	23.0	21.4	25.3	26.3	-	-*	21.8*	25.4
Pelvis									
max. height	R	19.5*	18.8	21.2r	22.0r	-	22.3r	18.3	21.5
	L	-*	19.3	20.9r	21.8	-	22.5r	18.4	21.4
max. breadth	R	15.2r	13.4ru	15.5	16.7r	-	15.7*	14.0r	15.8
	L	15.1r	14.3	-*	16.0	-	16.8r	14.2	16.1
Femur									
max. length	R	41.2	40.2	-*	-*	-*	-*	39.2	45.2
	L	-*	40.8	-*	45.1r	-*	48.3*	39.3	-*
bicondylar length	R	40.0	39.5	-*	-*	-*	-*	38.7	45.1
	L	-*	40.1	-*	44.5r	-*	48.1*	38.5	-*
anterio-posterior diam. of mid-shaft	R	2.7	2.4	3.3	3.4e	3.1e	-*	2.5	3.1
	L	-*	2.4	-*	3.3	3.2e	3.3	2.6	3.2
medio-lateral diam. of mid-shaft	R	2.4	2.4	2.7	2.6e	2.4e	-*	2.1	2.7
	L	-*	2.6	-*	2.5	2.3e	2.7	2.1	2.8
max. diam. of head	R	3.9	3.9*	4.2	4.8*	-*	5.1*	3.9	4.8
	L	4.0	3.9	4.2	4.9	-*	5.0*	3.8	4.7
circumference of mid-shaft	R	7.9	7.4	8.5	9.5e	8.6e	-*	7.4	9.1
	L	-*	7.8	-*	9.2	8.9e	9.3	7.4	9.2
subtrochanteric anterior-posterior diam.	R	2.3	2.1	2.5	2.9	-*	-*	2.1	2.7
	L	2.5	2.1	-*	2.7	-*	2.7	2.1	2.6
subtrochanteric medio-lateral diam.	R	3.1	2.9	3.1	3.2	-*	-*	2.8	3.3
	L	3.0	2.9	-*	3.4	-*	3.2	-*	3.4
Tibia									
max. length	R	34.4	32.9	-*	37.7	37.0r	39.4r	32.3	39.8
	L	34.3	33.1	36.9	37.3	-*	39.5r	32.2	39.6
anterior-posterior diam. at nutrient foramen	R	3.4	3.3	4.2*	4.2	3.5	4.2	3.2	3.8
	L	3.3	3.3	-*	4.2	-	4.5	3.2d	3.8d
medio-lateral diam. at nutrient foramen	R	2.2	2.0	2.1*	2.5	2.2	2.6	1.8	2.3
	L	2.1	1.8	-*	2.3	2.2*	2.9	1.9d	2.2

Table A5 (cont.)

Element	Side	Feature No.							
		1	8	21	25	29	36	40	41
Fibula									
max. length	R	34.5	32.3	36.9r	37.9r	36.5	-*	-*	39.4
	L	34.0d	32.6*	37.1r	37.6d	-*	39.3	31.9	39.1

[1]After Bass (1971). Measurements in cm.
Symbols and abbreviations:
-, measurement not taken; element missing or judged too severely damaged.
r, damaged and reconstructed.
*, damaged (not fully reconstructable).
d, deformed.
u, unfused and epiphysis absent.
a, arthritis affects measurement.
e, mid-shaft location estimated.

APPENDIX 6

ESTIMATED STATURE OF HENDERSON POPULATION

Table A6
Estimated stature of Henderson population[1]

Feature No.	Sex	Femur Length[2] (cm)	Estimated Stature[3] [cm/(ft-in)]	Tibia Length[2] (cm)	Estimated Stature[3] [cm/(ft-in)]
1	F	41.2	154.0±3.8 (5' 0.5")	34.35	154.7±3.5 (5' 1.0")
8	F	40.5	152.1±3.8 (5' 0.0")	33.0	151.0±3.5 (4' 11.5")
21	F	---	---	36.9	161.7±3.5 (5' 3.5")
25	M	45.1	165.8±3.4 (5' 5.5")	37.5	164.8±2.8 (5' 5.0")
29	M?	---	---	37.0	163.8±2.8 (5' 5.0")
36	M	48.3	173.0±3.4 (5' 8.0")	39.45	168.6±2.8 (5' 6.0")
40	F	39.25	148.9±3.8 (4' 10.5")	32.25	149.0±3.5 (4' 10.5")
41	M	45.2	166.0±3.4 (5' 5.0")	39.7	169.1±2.8 (5' 6.5")

[1]After Steele and McKern (1969), based upon the Genovés' equations.
[2]Left and right measurements averaged where both available.
[3]2.5 cm subtracted from Genovés' formulas to approximate living stature (Steele and McKern 1969:224).

APPENDIX 7

SELECTED CRANIAL NON-METRIC TRAITS

Table A7
Selected cranial non-metric traits[1]

Observation[2]	Feature No.						
	1	8	21	25	36	40	41
1. Auditory torus	0?/2	0/2	0?/2	0/2	0?/2	0/2	0?/2
2. Palatine torus	0/1	0/1	0/1	0/1	---	0/1	0/1
3. Mandibular torus	0/2	0/2	0/2	0/2	0/2	0/2	0/2
4. Bregmatic ossicle	0/1[3]	0/1	---	0/1	0/1	0/1	0/1
5. Coronal ossicle	1/2	0/2	---	0/1	0?/2	0/2	0?/2
6. Ossicle at lambda	0/1	0/1[3]	1/1	0/1	0/1	0/1[3]	0/1
7. Lambdoidal ossicle	0/2	2/2	---	2/2	---	0/2	0/2
8. *Os Inca*	0/1	0/1	0/1	0/1	0/1	0/1	0/1
9. Riolan's ossicle	0/2	0/2	---	0?/2	0?/2	2/2	0/2
10. Asterionic ossicle	1/2	0/2	---	0?/2	0?/2	0/2	0/2
11. Parietal notch bone	0/2	0/2	0?/1	0/2	0/2	0/2	0/2
12. Temporo-squamous ossicles	0/2	0/2	---	0/2	0?/2	0/2	0/2
13. Epipteric bone	0/2	0/2	---	0/2	---	0/2	0/2
14. *Os Japonicum*	0?/2	0/2	0/1	0/2	0/2	0/2	0/2
15. Lacrimal foramen	0?/2	2/2	---	0?/2	---	2/2	1/2
16. Posterior ethmoid foramen	---	2/2	---	2/2	---	2/2	2?/2
17. Anterior ethmoid foramen extra-sutural	---	2/2	---	---	---	1/1	1/1
18. Accessory infra-orbital foramen	0/2	2/2	1?/1	2/2	1/1	2/2	0/2
19. Zygo-facial foramen	2/2	2/2	1?/1	2/2	---	2/2	2/2
20. Accessory zygo-facial foramina	1/1	2/2	---	2?/2	---	2/2	1?/2
21. Supra-orbital foramen	1?/2	2/2	0?/1	2?/2	1/2	2/2	1/2
22(24). Supra-orbital notch or frontal notch	1/2	1/2	1?/1	2/2	1/1	0/2	1/2
25. Frontal foramen	0/1	0?/2	0/1	1?/2[4]	1?/2	2/2[4]	1/2[4]
26. Parietal foramen	0/2	0/2[4]	1?/2	1?/2	0/1	1/1	1?/1
27. Mastoid foramen	2/2	2/2	2?/2	2/2	2/2	1/2	2?/2
28. Mastoid foramen extra-sutural	2/2[4]	2/2[4]	1?/1[4]	1?/2[4]	0/2	0/2[4]	2/2[4]
29. 'Zygo-root' foramen	1?/2	1?/2	1/1	2/2	---	1/1	1/2

Table A7 (cont.)

Observation[2]	Feature No.						
	1	8	21	25	36	40	41
30. Posterior condylar canal	2/2[4]	1/2	– – –	2/2	1/1	2/2	2/2
31. Hypoglossal canal double	0?/2	0/2	– – –	1/2	– – –	1?/2	0/2
32. Foramen of Huschke	0/2	0/2	0?/2	0/2	0/2	0/2	0/2
33. Foramen of Civinini[5]	0/2	0/2	– – –	1/2[4]	– – –	– – –	0/2
34. Foramen of Hyrtl	0/2	0/2	– – –	0/2	– – –	– – –	0/2
35. Foramen spinosum open	0/1	0/2	– – –	2/2[6]	– – –	1/2[6]	0/2
37. Foramen ovale incomplete	0/2	0/2	– – –	0/2	0?/1	0/2	0/2
39. Accessory lesser palatine foramen	0/1	0/2	– – –	1/2	– – –	1/2	0/2
42. Double (or multiple) mental foramen	0/2	0/2	0?/1	0/2	0?/2	0/2	0/2
44. Metopic suture	0/1	0/1	– – –	0/1	0/1	0/1	0/1
45. Fronto-temporal articulation	0/2	0/2	– – –	0/2	– – –	0/2	0/2
46. 'External frontal' sulcus	0/2	1/2	0?/2	0/2	0?/2	0/2	0?/2
47. Suture into the infra-orbital foramen	0/1	0/2	– – –	0/2	0/1	0/2	0/2
48. Petrosquamous suture	0/2	0/2	0/2	0?/2	0/2	0/2	0/2
49. Spine of Henle	0/2	0/2	1/2	2/2	2/2	2/2	2/2
50. Double condylar facet	0/2	0/2	0/2	0/2	0/2	0/2	0/2
51. Pre-condylar tubercle	0/2	0/2	0/1	0/2	0/1	0/2	0/2
52. Pharyngeal fossa	– – –	0/1	– – –	0/1	– – –	1/1[4]	0/1
53. Paramastoid process	0/2	0/2	0?/1	0/2	0/2	0/2	0/2
54. Mylohyoid bridge	0/2	0/2	– – –	1?/2	2/2	0/2	0/2

[1]Based upon trait definitions in Birkby (1973). Coding followed these definitions as closely as possible. It should be noted that the present investigator lacked previous experience with classification of non-metric traits. Where coding was ambiguous, an effort was made to code marginal traits as "present"; such marginal occurrences are indicated by footnote 4 below. Birkby's traits 23, 36, 38, 40, 41, and 43 were not coded here since they were judged too difficult to observe reliably on intact crania or to code consistently without prior experience. Birkby's traits 22 and 24 were combined here.

Symbols and abbreviations:

– – –, No observations possible (equivalent to 0/0 in coding system used here).

x/y, x out of y observable sites display the trait. For intact specimens, y=1 for traits on the midline; y=2 for lateral traits. Thus, for example, 1/2 indicates that out of 2 intact locations, one of them displayed the trait.

?, Observation partially obscured.

[2]Numbers refer to Birkby's (1973) trait list.

[3]Distinction between very small extra-sutural bones and extreme sutural complication unclear.

[4]Diminutive or marginal occurrence in one or both cases.

[5]Definition in Birkby (1973:39) does not quite match his illustration (p. 30), since the former indicates a bridge between a point on the lateral pterygoid plate to the spine of the sphenoid (located on the inferior surface of the greater wing of the sphenoid), while the illustration indicates a bridge between two points both located on the lateral pterygoid plate. The coding followed here uses the illustration as a guide; if the verbal description is followed then no occurrences should be coded for the Henderson sample.

[6]Partial opening.

APPENDIX 8

SELECTED DENTAL TRAITS

Table A8
Selected dental traits[1]

Observation	Feature No.					
	1	8	25	36	40	41
I^1 Palatal shoveling present	2/2	2/2	2/2	2/2	1/1	2/2
Labial shoveling present	0/2	0/2	0/2	2*/2	2*/2	0/2
U^2 Barrel shaped	0/2	0/2	0/2	0/2	0/1	1/2
M^1 Carabelli cusp, pit groove or ridge	0/2	0/2	---	0/2	2/2[2]	0/2
M^2 Cusp number '3+' or more	2*/2	2/2	2/2	2*/2	2/2	1*/2
M_1 Protostylid present	0/2	0/2	0/2	0/2	0/2	0/2
Groove pattern not '+'	0?/1	2/2[3]	---	0?/2	1?/2[3]	---
Cusp number ≥ 6	0?/2	0/2	---	0/2	0/2	0?/1
M_2 Groove pattern not '+'	2?/2[4]	2/2[3]	---	0/2	2/2[4]	0?/2
Cusp number ≥ 5	0?/2	1/2	0?/2	1?/2	2?/2	0?/1

[1]All definitions follow Sofaer et al. (1972:361).
Symbols and abbreviations:
---, No teeth observable (equivalent to 0/0 in coding system used here).
x/y, x out of y observable teeth exhibit trait.
?, Partially obscured by wear.
*, Trace or ambiguous case. Approximately 3+ cusps on at least one tooth; scoring was ambiguous.

[2]Trace bilateral Carabelli grooves.
[3]Y pattern.
[4]X pattern.

APPENDIX 9

ISOLATED HUMAN SKELETAL ELEMENTS

Table A9
Isolated human skeletal elements

Provenience					Description			
North	East	Top Elev.	Bot. Elev.	Item, Lot, Feat.	Side	Element	Age[1]	Comments[2]
512	534	100.58	100.48		?	distal hand phalanx	ad	
527	565	101.25	101.15		?	hand phalanx	in	Epiphysis unfused and missing. Distal articular surface missing.
525	562	100.97	100.97	Item 3	---	lumbar vertebra	ch	
510	532	101.06	101.06	Item 7	---	lumbar vertebral centrum	ad	Epiphyseal rings fused.
511-515	531-535	surf.	surf.		?	dI^1?	ch or in	Only lingual half of crown present. Slight shoveling present. Wear stage 3 or 4.
511-515	531-535	surf.	surf.		left	dI^2?	ch	Identification tentative; deciduous anterior dentition, not I_1 or I^1. Crown chipped. Wear stage 5. [— X 5.9 mm].
514	531	101.75	101.65		right	dM_2	in	Crown calcification nearly complete, no root formation; age just under one year. Deep buccal crease. Distal cusp chipped. [— X 8.8 mm].
523	564	101.45	101.35		right	dM_1	in	Root formation nearly complete; age just under 3 years. Wear stage 2. [11.7 X 9.2 mm].

Table A9 (cont.)

Provenience					Description			
North	East	Top Elev.	Bot. Elev.	Item, Lot, Feat.	Side	Element	Age[1]	Comments[2]
513	534	101.35	101.25		right	I^2	ad or ch	Root complete and apex closed. Shoveling present. Wear stage 2. Young adult or older child. [7.2 X 6.3 mm].
520	533	101.64	101.64	Item 1	?	sternal ossification centra	in or ch	2 sternal ossification centra. Bone associated with rib fragments (below) and with quartz crystal.
520	533	101.64	101.64	Item 1	?	rib fragments	in or ch	3 distal rib fragments. Bone associated with sternal ossification centra (above) and with quartz crystal.
527	565	100.62	100.25	Feat. 1?	– – –	mandibular fragment	in	Fragment of mandible at symphysis. Alveolus not present. No teeth present.
527	565	100.62	100.25	Feat. 1?	?	cranial fragment	in?	2 fragments. Thin and porous, probably infant. One of fragments has suture and texture that may be lacrimal, ethmoid, or sphenoid.
527	565	100.62	100.25	Feat. 1?	?	hand phalanx	in	Unfused.
528	564	101.25	101.15		?	unidentified tooth	ad	Anterior dentition, probably incisor. Wear stage 8; no enamel.

Table A9 (cont.)

Provenience					Description			
North	East	Top Elev.	Bot. Elev.	Item, Lot, Feat.	Side	Element	Age[1]	Comments[2]
525	566			Feat. 8	?	hand phalanx	in	From individual much younger than Feature 8 burial. Epiphysis unfused and missing.
Ctr-bar	Ctr-bar	surf.	surf.	Lot 1	?	hand phalanx	in	Unfused.
Ctr-bar	Ctr-bar	surf.	surf.	Lot 1	right?	radius	ch or in	Distal end missing. Proximal epiphysis unfused and missing.
Ctr-bar	Ctr-bar	surf.	surf.	Lot 1	left	M^1 or M^2	ch	Crown fragment. No wear.
Ctr-bar	Ctr-bar	surf.	surf.	Lot 1	?	metapodial	ch	Proximal end missing. Epiphysis unfused and missing.
Ctr-bar	Ctr-bar	surf.	surf.	Lot 1	right	maxillary molar	ad	Root broken off, crown badly chipped. Slight calculus deposit. Wear stage 6.
Ctr-bar	Ctr-bar	surf.	surf.	Lot 1	?	unidentified fragment	?	
Ctr-bar	Ctr-bar	surf.	surf.	Lot 1	?	hand phalanx	in	Unfused.
526	563	101.54	101.25	Lot 19	right	mandibular molar	ch or in	Crown complete, root formation has not begun. Crown chipped. No wear.
525	566	101.55	101.25	Lot 31	?	proximal 1st foot phalanx	ad	Fragmentary.
514	533	101.55	101.45	Lot 50	right	pisiform	ad	

Table A9 (cont.)

Provenience					Description			
North	East	Top Elev.	Bot. Elev.	Item, Lot, Feat.	Side	Element	Age[1]	Comments[2]
523	562	101.15	101.05	Lot 88	left	dM_2	in	Root formation about half complete. No visible wear. Age ca. 2–3 years. [11.1 X 8.9 mm].
523	562	101.15	101.05	Lot 88	?	hand phalanx	ad	
529	566	101.40	101.30	Lot 120	?	metapodial	in	Epiphysis unfused and missing.
517	533	101.89	101.60	Lot 123	right	thoracic vertebral neural arch	in or ch	Fragment. Not fused to centrum. Fusion to other half of arch can not be determined.
513	534	101.55	101.45	Lot 127	– – –	atlas	ch or in	Fragment, right articular facets.
524	569	101.30	101.20	Lot 128	left	hamate	ad	
514	534	101.45	101.35	Lot 129	?	metapodial?	in	Epiphysis unfused and missing.
514	534	101.45	101.35	Lot 129	?	metapodial?	in	Epiphysis unfused and missing.
524	565	101.15	101.05	Lot 133	left	sacral neural arch	in	Unfused. Posterior end broken and missing.
524	565	101.15	101.05	Lot 133	?	vertebral neural arch	in or ch	Fragmentary.
512	534	101.35	101.30	Lot 138	?	proximal foot phalanx	ad	
525	564	101.15	101.05	Lot 141	?	middle hand phalanx	ad	
520	533	102.08	101.65	Lot 148	– – –	cervical vertebra	ch	Missing posterior part of neural arch. Epiphyseal rings unfused and missing. Neural arch fused to centrum.
520	533	102.08	101.65	Lot 148	left?	humeral proximal epiphysis	ch	Identification tentative.

Table A9 (cont.)

Provenience					Description			
North	East	Top Elev.	Bot. Elev.	Item, Lot, Feat.	Side	Element	Age[1]	Comments[2]
520	533	102.08	101.65	Lot 148	– – –	lumbar vertebra	ch or in	Most of neural arch and centrum present, recent fusion evident. Epiphyseal rings unfused and missing.
520	533	102.08	101.65	Lot 148	– – –	vertebral or sacral centrum	in or ch	Unfused.
520	533	102.08	101.65	Lot 148	– – –	sacral segment	in or ch	Nearly complete. Wings fused to centrum, but segment not fused to another sacral segment.
520	533	102.08	101.65	Lot 148	– – –	vertebral centrum	in or ch	Thoracic?, unfused.
520	533	102.08	101.65	Lot 148	left	1st rib	in or ch	Distal end missing.
520	533	102.08	101.65	Lot 148	left	clavicle	in or ch	Distal fragment only.
515	535	102.04	101.60	Lot 160	– – –	vertebral centrum	in	Fragmentary. Unfused.
526	565	101.56	101.25	Lot 184	?	vertebral neural arch	in	Fragmentary.
516	534	101.20	101.00	Lot 188	?	foot phalanx	in	Epiphysis unfused and missing.
526	562	101.20	101.10	Lot 214	left	dM^1	in or ch	Root formation complete, possibly just beginning resorption. Wear stage 3. Age ca. 5–7 years. [7.7 X 9.4 mm].
525	569	101.30	101.20	Lot 237	left?	proximal 1st foot phalanx	ad	Fragmentary.
525	569	101.30	101.20	Lot 237	?	metapodial	in	Unfused.
524	569	101.19	101.10	Lot 244	?	unidentified vertebral? fragment	?	
526	567	101.15	101.06	Lot 245	right	dM^1	in	Crown about half calcified. No wear. Age ca. 0–1/2 years.

Table A9 (cont.)

Provenience					Description			
North	East	Top Elev.	Bot. Elev.	Item, Lot, Feat.	Side	Element	Age[1]	Comments[2]
527	566	101.45	101.35	Lot 252	right	ulna	ch or in	Distal end missing, proximal epiphysis unfused and missing.
520	533	101.65	101.45	Lot 270	?	hand phalanx	in	Epiphysis unfused and missing.
520	533	101.65	101.45	Lot 270	right	1st rib	ch	Distal half missing. Epiphyses unfused and missing.
520	533	101.65	101.45	Lot 270	– – –	sternal? ossification center	?	Unfused.
520	533	101.65	101.45	Lot 270	right	thoracic vertebral transverse process	ch	Epiphysis unfused and missing. Fragmentary.
519	533	101.65	101.40	Lot 287	?	proximal? hand phalanx	in or ch	Unfused.
519	533	101.65	101.40	Lot 287	?	proximal foot phalanx	in	Unfused.
519	533	101.65	101.40	Lot 297	– – –	sacral segment	in or ch	Nearly complete. Wings fused to centrum, but segment not fused to another segment.
529	566	101.30	101.20	Lot 325	– – –	vertebral centrum	in	Thoracic?, unfused.
527	567	101.30	101.25	Lot 326	right?	proximal foot phalanx	ad	
522-523	563-564	101.00	100.90	Lot 330	left	thoracic? vertebral neural arch	in	Fragmentary.
522-523	563-564	101.00	100.90	Lot 330	left	dM_2	in	Root broken off, at least one-third complete. No visible wear. Age ca. 3 years. [11.1 X 8.9 mm].
522-523	563-564	101.00	100.90	Lot 330	– – –	thoracic vertebral fragment	in or ch	Right neural arch and transverse process fragment. Unfused.
527	569	101.30	101.20	Lot 344	right	2nd cuneiform	ad	
523	564	101.08	100.90	Lot 380	– – –	sternal? ossification center	?	Unfused.

Table A9 (cont.)

Provenience					Description			
North	East	Top Elev.	Bot. Elev.	Item, Lot, Feat.	Side	Element	Age[1]	Comments[2]
527	549	100.50	100.40	Lot 537	left	4th metacarpal	ad	Distal articular surface missing.
530	565	101.30	101.20	Lot 540	?	hand phalanx	in	Unfused.
529	565	101.10	101.00	Lot 716	left	cervical neural arch	in	Unfused.
529	565	101.10	101.00	Lot 716	?	hand phalanx	in	Unfused.
529	565	101.10	101.00	Lot 716	?	metapodial	in	Unfused.
529	565	101.10	101.00	Lot 716	?	distal hand phalanx	in	Unfused.
529	565	101.10	101.00	Lot 716	?	metapodial	in	Unfused.
529	565	101.10	101.00	Lot 716	?	hand phalanx	in	Unfused.
523	568	101.10	101.00	Lot 717	left?	M^3	ad	Slight calculus deposit. Wear stage 3. [9.3 X 10.1 mm].
523	568	101.10	101.00	Lot 717	?	canine or lateral incisor	ad	Left mandibular or right maxillary. Crown chipped. Wear stage 5.
515	534			Feat. 41	?	hand distal 1st? phalanx	ad	
526	561	101.00	100.80	Lot 792	left	axis neural arch	in	Fragmentary.
518	533	101.65	101.40	Lot 828	?	proximal hand phalanx	ad	Proximal end missing.
515	534	102.04	101.60	Lot 835	?	unidentified tooth	ad?	Fragment of crown and root, premolar or molar. Wear stage at least 3 or 4.
525	567	101.55	101.25	Lot 836	---	vertebral or sacral centrum	in	Unfused.
515	535	101.30	101.20	Lot 838	left	3rd metatarsal	ad	
523	563	101.35	101.25	Lot 852	?	hand phalanx	in	Epiphysis unfused and missing, distal articular surface missing.
517	534	101.35	101.25	Lot 855	---	vertebral centrum	ch or in	Anterior fragment. Epiphyseal rings unfused and missing.

Table A9 (cont.)

Provenience					Description			
North	East	Top Elev.	Bot. Elev.	Item, Lot, Feat.	Side	Element	Age[1]	Comments[2]
517	534	101.35	101.25	Lot 855	?	unidentified ossification center	in	2 fragments.
517	534	101.35	101.25	Lot 855	?	unidentified ossification center	in?	
517	534	101.35	101.25	Lot 855	?	unidentified cranial fragment	ch or ad	
517	534	101.35	101.25	Lot 855	?	unidentified ossification center	in	Fragmentary.
514	534	101.10	101.00	Lot 858	right	pubis	in	Unfused.
516	535	101.60	101.40	Lot 872	– – –	sternal? ossification center	?	Unfused.
521	561	101.15	101.05	Lot 874	left?	dC[L]	in	Root formation complete or nearly complete. Age ca. 3 years. Wear stage 2. [6.9 X 5.6 mm].
523	565	101.45	101.35	Lot 882	left	lesser multangular (trapezoid)	ad	
522	565	101.15	101.05	Lot 900	left	calcaneus	ad	Superior surface damaged.
517	533	101.75	101.60	Lot 912	?	metapodial?	in	Proximal fragment.
529	566	101.05	101.00	Lot 1036	left	thoracic vertebral neural arch	in	Fragment. Not fused to centrum. Fusion to other half of arch can not be determined. Upper thoracic.
517	533	101.75	101.60	Lot 1072	?	1st? metacarpal?	in	Epiphysis unfused and missing. Distal? end has apparent 2nd epiphysis, partially fused.
517	533	101.75	101.60	Lot 1072	– – –	vertebral centrum	in or ch	Fragment, vertebral arch unfused.

Table A9 (cont.)

Provenience					Description			
North	East	Top Elev.	Bot. Elev.	Item, Lot, Feat.	Side	Element	Age[1]	Comments[2]
528	567	101.45	101.43	Lot 1083	right	mandibular fragment	in	Portion of right mandibular corpus from symphysis (includes small fragment of left half of mandible with visible line of fusion at symphysis) to distal end of deciduous second molar crypt. Only one tooth, dM_1 present. Calcification of crown slightly more than half complete. Early postnatal (<1/2 year). Most of alveolar border broken and missing.
528	565	101.25	101.15	Lot 1092	right	1st metatarsal	ad	Arthritis on distal articular surface. Fragmentary.
520	533	101.65	101.45	Lot 1135	left	ulna	ch or in	Distal end missing. Proximal epiphysis unfused and missing.
520	533	101.65	101.45	Lot 1135	---	sacral or vertebral centrum	in	Unfused.
520	533	101.65	101.45	Lot 1135	---	1st coccygeal element	ad	Not fused to sacrum or other coccygeal elements.
517	534	102.00	101.60	Lot 1144	---	vertebral centrum	ch	With broken ends of partially fused vertebral arch.
517	534	102.00	101.60	Lot 1144	---	vertebral centrum	ch	With broken ends of partially fused vertebral arch.

Table A9 (cont.)

Provenience					Description			
North	East	Top Elev.	Bot. Elev.	Item, Lot, Feat.	Side	Element	Age[1]	Comments[2]
529	560	101.20	101.10	Lot 1174	right	dI^2	in	Identification tentative. Tip of root broken off, but root is at least three-fourths complete. Wear stage 3. Age ca. 2–5 years. [5.3 X 4.0 mm].
528	565	101.68	101.25	Lot 1181	?	hand phalanx	in or ch	Epiphysis unfused and missing, distal articular surface missing.
516	534	101.40	101.20	Lot 1189	?	ossification center of sacral wing element	in	Unfused.
524	565	101.25	101.15	Lot 1190	right	4th metacarpal	ad	
517	534	101.60	101.35	Lot 1208	?	foot phalanx	in	Epiphysis unfused and missing.
526	565	101.56	101.25	Lot 1209	left?	I_2?	ch	Identification as I_2 rather than I_1 tentative. Root formation has begun but little is complete. No wear. Age ca. 5.5-6.0 years. [6.5 X 6.6 mm].
515	535	101.60	101.40	Lot 1219	?	hand phalanx	in	Epiphysis unfused and missing.
515	534	101.20	101.00	Lot 1244	left?	proximal 1st foot phalanx	ad	
515	534	101.20	101.00	Lot 1244	?	proximal 2nd? foot phalanx	ad	
515	534	101.85	101.80	Lot 1273	left	4th metatarsal	ad	
517	534	101.15	101.05	Lot 1283	– – –	2nd? coccygeal element	ad or ch	Not fused to other coccygeal elements.
513	534	100.95	100.85	Lot 1289	– – –	vertebral centrum	in	Unfused.
521	566	101.46	101.25	Lot 1320	?	distal foot phalanx	ad?	
522	566	101.46	101.25	Lot 1327	left	lumbar? vertebral neural arch	in	Fragmentary.
526	566	101.57	101.25	Lot 1331	?	metapodial	in	Epiphysis unfused and missing.

Table A9 (cont.)

Provenience					Description			
North	East	Top Elev.	Bot. Elev.	Item, Lot, Feat.	Side	Element	Age[1]	Comments[2]
522	562	101.15	101.05	Lot 1337	?	metapodial	in	Epiphysis unfused and missing, distal articular surface missing.
515	534	101.20	101.00	Lot 1341	right?	proximal 1st foot phalanx	ad	
528	564	101.66	101.25	Lot 1350	right	4th metacarpal	ad	Distal end missing.
516	535	101.30	101.20	Lot 1364	?	unidentified fragment	?	
521	565	101.25	101.15	Lot 1368	right	rib	ad	Head and neck only.
523	562	101.35	101.25	Lot 1383	right	dM^2	in	Early stage of root formation, no wear. Age ca. 1 year. [9.6 X 10.2 mm].
511	531	101.55	101.50	Lot 1394	left	lumbar? vertebral neural arch	in	Unfused.
518	533	102.10	101.75	Lot 1397	left	vertebral neural arch	ch or ad	Fragment, with both superior and inferior articular facets. Thoracic or lumbar.
518	533	102.10	101.75	Lot 1397	– – –	vertebral fragment	ch	Right neural arch and centrum fragment, partially fused.
523	565	101.15	101.05	Lot 1400	left?	proximal foot phalanx	ad	
524	565	101.35	101.25	Lot 1427	left?	distal 1st foot phalanx	ad?	
519	533	102.11	101.75	Lot 1443	– – –	vertebral centrum	in	Unfused.
519	533	102.11	101.75	Lot 1443	?	hand phalanx	in or ch	Epiphysis unfused and missing.
519	533	102.11	101.75	Lot 1443	?	proximal foot phalanx	ad	
511	549	100.00	99.90	Lot 1444	– – –	vertebral centrum	in or ch	Unfused.
508	550	99.90	99.80	Lot 1450	?	distal foot phalanx	?	Fragmentary.
517	534	101.60	101.35	Lot 1467	right?	thoracic? vertebral transverse process	in	Fragmentary. Epiphysis unfused and missing.
517	534	101.60	101.35	Lot 1467	– – –	thoracic vertebral fragment	in or ch	Fragment, right neural arch and transverse process.

Table A9 (cont.)

Provenience					Description			
North	East	Top Elev.	Bot. Elev.	Item, Lot, Feat.	Side	Element	Age[1]	Comments[2]
517	534	101.60	101.35	Lot 1467	?	unidentified ossification center	in or ch	Fragmentary.
517	534	101.60	101.35	Lot 1467	?	vertebral neural arch	in	Fragmentary.
522	535	100.45	100.40	Lot 1474	– – –	frontal? fragment	ch or ad	Portion of coronal suture present.
522	535	100.45	100.40	Lot 1474	?	hand phalanx	in or ch	Epiphysis unfused and missing.
523	565	101.25	101.15	Lot 1489	left	thoracic vertebral neural arch	in	Unfused.
523	565	101.25	101.15	Lot 1489	?	phalanx	ad?	Distal fragment.
523	565	101.25	101.15	Lot 1489	left	12th rib	in	Distal end missing. Epiphysis unfused and missing.
523	565	101.25	101.15	Lot 1489	right	lumbar? vertebral neural arch	in	Fragmentary. Unfused.
523	565	101.25	101.15	Lot 1489	– – –	lumbar vertebral neural arch	in	Fragmentary. Neural arch halves fused together.
514	534	101.00	100.90	Lot 1513	right	atlas neural arch	in	Unfused.
513	534	100.85	100.72	Lot 1523	right	lumbar? vertebral neural arch	in	Unfused.
513	534	100.85	100.72	Lot 1523	left	thoracic? vertebral neural arch	in	Unfused.
514	535	101.60	101.50	Lot 1537	left	ilium	in	Unfused.
522-523	563-564	101.10	101.00	Lot 1542	right?	head of unidentified rib	ad	
529	565	101.20	101.10	Lot 1543	?	proximal foot phalanx?	?	Fragmentary.
529	565	101.20	101.10	Lot 1543	?	metapodial	in	Epiphysis unfused and missing.
524	566	101.54	101.25	Lot 1553	right	rib fragment	in	Proximal end.
515	534	101.40	101.30	Lot 1572	left	1st metatarsal	ad	
515	534	101.40	101.30	Lot 1572	?	proximal hand phalanx	in	Epiphysis unfused and missing.
510	532	101.15	101.05	Lot 1581	left?	distal 1st foot phalanx	ad	
523	562	101.15	101.05	Lot 1589	– – –	vertebral centrum	in	Fragmentary. Unfused.

Table A9 (cont.)

Provenience					Description			
North	East	Top Elev.	Bot. Elev.	Item, Lot, Feat.	Side	Element	Age[1]	Comments[2]
528-529	562-563			Feat. 36	right	5th metatarsal	ad	Distal end missing.
508	551	99.60	99.50	Lot 1604	?	metapodial	in or ch	Unfused.
526	563	100.88	100.80	Lot 1634	left	humerus	ch or in	Distal half only, epiphysis unfused and missing.
522	566	101.15	101.05	Lot 1637	right	M_1 or M_2	ch	Root broken, at least half formed. Crown chipped. Deep buccal pit, possibly carious. Y-5 cusp pattern. Wear stage 1. [— X 11.4 mm].
514	535	100.70	100.60	Lot 1649	left?	proximal foot phalanx	ad	
514	535	100.70	100.60	Lot 1649	right	sacral neural arch	in	Unfused.
523	563	101.46	101.35	Lot 1659	?	middle hand phalanx	ad	Part of distal articular end missing.
514	531	101.75	101.65	Lot 1767	?	distal hand phalanx	ad	
514	535	101.25	101.10	Lot 1884	right	dC^R	in or ch	Identification tentative. Crown chipped. Root broken off, at least one-third complete. Wear stage 3.
514	535	101.25	101.10	Lot 1884	left	dM^2	in	Crown formation about one-half complete. Age ca. 1/2 year or slightly less. No wear.
Ctr-bar	Ctr-bar	surf.	surf.	Lot 1897	?	distal hand phalanx	ad	
522	566	101.15	101.05	Lot 1913	?	mandibular? premolar	ad	Crown chipped. Complete root present. Wear stage 6.

Table A9 (cont.)

Provenience					Description			
North	East	Top Elev.	Bot. Elev.	Item, Lot, Feat.	Side	Element	Age[1]	Comments[2]
520	533	102.08	101.65	Lot 1984	right?	mandibular canine or premolar?	ad	Crown chipped. Root broken off, but at least two-thirds complete. Wear stage 3. [— X 6.2 mm].
520	533	102.08	101.65	Lot 1984	left	dC^L	in or ch	Root formation complete. Wear stage 3. Age ca. 4–9 years. [7.2 X 6.5 mm].
515	534	101.60	101.40	Lot 2001	right?	I^2?	ch	Identification tentative. Crown chipped. Root about one-half formed. No wear. Age ca. 6–9 years. [— X 6.6 mm].
Ctr-bar	Ctr-bar	surf.	surf.	Lot 1	?	hand phalanx	ad	
Ctr-bar	Ctr-bar	surf.	surf.	Lot 1	left	2nd metacarpal	ad	
Ctr-bar	Ctr-bar	surf.	surf.	Lot 1	right	navicular (scaphoid)	ad	Distal lateral surface damaged.
Ctr-bar	Ctr-bar	surf.	surf.	Lot 1	– – –	vertebral centrum	in	Unfused.
Ctr-bar	Ctr-bar	surf.	surf.	Lot 1	right	triquetral	ad	
Ctr-bar	Ctr-bar	surf.	surf.	Lot 1	right	2nd metatarsal	ad	
Ctr-bar	Ctr-bar	surf.	surf.	Lot 1	right	triquetral	ad	

Table A9 (cont.)

Provenience					Description			
North	East	Top Elev.	Bot. Elev.	Item, Lot, Feat.	Side	Element	Age[1]	Comments[2]
Ctr-bar	Ctr-bar	surf.	surf.	Lot 1	?	middle hand phalanx	ad	
Ctr-bar	Ctr-bar	surf.	surf.	Lot 1	right?	5th? metatarsal	ad	Fragmentary.
Ctr-bar	Ctr-bar	surf.	surf.	Lot 1	right?	proximal foot phalanx	ad	
Ctr-bar	Ctr-bar	surf.	surf.	Lot 1	right	3rd metatarsal	ad	Small (6.3 cm max. length), but fully fused epiphysis, probably female.
Ctr-bar	Ctr-bar	surf.	surf.	Lot 1	---	sacral or vertebral centrum	in	Unfused.
Ctr-bar	Ctr-bar	surf.	surf.	Lot 1	right	3rd metatarsal	ad	Periostitis on shaft. Distal end missing.
Ctr-bar	Ctr-bar	surf.	surf.	Lot 1	?	hand phalanx	in or ch	Epiphysis unfused and missing.
Ctr-bar	Ctr-bar	surf.	surf.	Lot 1	?	middle hand phalanx	ad	
Ctr-bar	Ctr-bar	surf.	surf.	Lot 1	left?	proximal foot phalanx	ad	
Ctr-bar	Ctr-bar	surf.	surf.	Lot 1	?	unidentified epiphysis	in	
Ctr-bar	Ctr-bar	surf.	surf.	Lot 1	?	hand phalanx	in	Epiphysis unfused and missing.
Ctr-bar	Ctr-bar	surf.	surf.	Lot 1	?	middle? hand phalanx	ad	Fragmentary.

Table A9 (cont.)

Provenience					Description			
North	East	Top Elev.	Bot. Elev.	Item, Lot, Feat.	Side	Element	Age[1]	Comments[2]
Ctr-bar	Ctr-bar	surf.	surf.	Lot 1	right?	distal 1st foot phalanx	ad	
Ctr-bar	Ctr-bar	surf.	surf.	Lot 1	---	manubrium	in	
Ctr-bar	Ctr-bar	surf.	surf.	Lot 1	?	proximal hand phalanx	ad	
Ctr-bar	Ctr-bar	surf.	surf.	Lot 1	?	hand phalanx	in or ch	Epiphysis unfused and missing.
Ctr-bar	Ctr-bar	surf.	surf.	Lot 1	?	middle hand phalanx	ad	
Ctr-bar	Ctr-bar	surf.	surf.	Lot 1	?	distal hand phalanx	ad	
Ctr-bar	Ctr-bar	surf.	surf.	Lot 1	?	proximal hand phalanx	ad	
Ctr-bar	Ctr-bar	surf.	surf.	Lot 1	?	middle hand phalanx	ad	

[1] ad, adult; ch, child; in, infant or young child. These are rough indications of age: infant refers to very young individuals (ca. 4 years of age or younger), child refers to immature individuals (below ca. 16 years, older than ca. 4 years), and adult refers to any individual older than ca. 16 years. Where age identification is uncertain, two possible age classes are listed in the order of a subjective assessment of their probability. Age assessment is based on fusion, size, texture, and, for teeth, on stage of development and wear.

[2] Dental data include wear stage (as in Appendix 2) and mesio-distal length X bucco-lingual breadth (as in Appendix 3); measurements are in brackets. Elements with the comment "unfused" do not exhibit fusion on any of the epiphyses present.

APPENDIX 10

ARTIFACTS FROM FEATURE 3 BURIAL

Table A10a
Pottery bowl found with Feature 3 burial:
Metric attributes and description (see Figs. 27-32)[1]

Item No.	Type	Max. Diam. (cm)	Max. Height (cm)	Ave. Thick. (cm)	Exterior Treatment	Interior Treatment	Location and Comments
6a	Lincoln B/R	15.1	6.5	0.65±	Unslipped, unpolished, uneven surface; coils still visible near rim; bottom rounded; traces of smoothing and scraping; color ranges from brown near base to black clouding midway to rim to brick red near rim; coarse sand (quartzite?) temper particles visible, with some relatively large inclusions (2-3 mm).	Red-slipped and lightly polished; design in black mineral paint (see Figs. 30, 31).	Found between upper thighs of burial; on side with opening toward skull; Chupadero B/W jar (No. 6b; Figs. 33-35 and Table A10b-A10c) nested in bowl, also with mouth toward skull; radial form of design identical to example on large bowl, illustrated by Stewart (1983:53, his Fig. 3b), from the Sierra Blanca region west of Henderson.

[1]We are grateful to Carla Sinopoli of the Museum of Anthropology at the University of Michigan for her assistance in describing the ceramic vessels from Henderson.

Table A10b
Pottery jar found with Feature 3 burial:
Metric attributes (see Figs. 27–29, 33–35)

Item No.	Type	Max. Diam. (cm)	Max. Height (cm)	Ave. Thick. (cm)	Min. Neck Diam. (cm)	Max. Mouth Diam. (cm)	Height of Neck (cm)	Max. Breadth of Handle (cm)	Diam. of Base (cm)
6b	Chupadero B/W	13.8	11.7	0.55±	4.3	5.1	2.7	2.2	6.4

Table A10c
Pottery jar found with Feature 3 burial:[1]
Description (see Figs. 27–29, 33–35)

Item No.	Type	Exterior Treatment	Interior Treatment	Location and Comments
6b	Chupadero B/W	White-slipped, lightly burnished surface; base flat, unslipped, rough, with traces of scraping, but not footed; design in black mineral paint (see Figs. 33–35); black firing cloud on body of jar opposite handle; single outcurving strap handle from shoulder to just below rim; handle consists of 3 parallel strips or coils of clay (bonding between strips prominent); rim outflaring, slightly thinned or tapering; minor rim damage in excavation; heavy prehistoric rim damage.	Mouth area smoothed, but unslipped; interior unsmoothed and unslipped; temper fine-grained (sand?).	Found on abdomen and between upper thighs of burial; on side with opening toward skull; nested in Lincoln B/R bowl (No. 6a; Figs. 30–32 and Table A10a), also with mouth toward skull; jar contained 2 *Olivella* shell beads (Nos. 5–6; Fig. 38e-f and Table A10f), 2 tubular bone beads (Nos. 2–3; Fig. 37e-f and Table A10h), 2 tiny turquoise discs (Nos. 4-5; Fig. 39d-e and Table A10i), 1 purple fluorite crystal (No. 4; Fig. 40d and Table A10j), and 1 unfused human ossification centrum; these items probably displaced into jar from right wrist of burial.

[1]We are grateful to Carla Sinopoli of the Museum of Anthropology at the University of Michigan for her assistance in describing the ceramic vessels from Henderson.

Table A10d
Prayer-stick found with Feature 3 burial (see Fig. 27–29, 36)

Item No.	Max. Length (cm)	Max. Breadth (cm)	Max. Thick. (cm)	Material[1]	Location and Comments
1	5.30	1.70	0.25	Wood probably *Populus*	On right chest of burial (see Figs. 27–29); preservation due to partial mineralization; may represent stylized corn plant or feather; proximal end (end farthest from skull) rough and slightly irregular, as though broken from larger item prior to burial; associated with 3 or 4 *Olivella* shell beads (Nos. 1–4; Fig. 38a-d and Table A10f) and 1 tubular bone bead made from bird forewing (ulna; No. 1; Fig. 37d and Table A10h); possibly also associated with 1 small green fluorite pebble (No. 3; Fig. 40c and Table A10j).

[1]We are grateful to Richard I. Ford of the Laboratory of Ethnobotany at the University of Michigan for identifying this and other ethnobotanical specimens from Henderson.

Table A10e
Disc-shell beads found with Feature 3 burial

Total No.	Ave. No. Beads per cm (N)	Total Strand(s) Length (cm)	Diameter Ave. $\pm 1\sigma$ (N) (cm)	Location and Comments
58	6.2 (20)	9.4	0.398±0.024 (50)	Found in Feat. 7, a small post hole within Feat. 3; probably displaced by rodent activity from left wrist of burial; associated with 2 turquoise beads (Nos. 1–2; Fig. 39a-b and Table A10i), 1 miniature obsidian point (No. 1; Fig. 37a and Table A10k-A10l), 1 small brachiopod fossil (No. 2; Fig. 40b and Table A10j), and 1 clear quartz crystal (No. 1; Fig. 40a and Table A10j).
86	6.6 (20)	13.1	0.416±0.024 (75)	Found near right wrist; associated with 1 turquoise bead (No. 3; Fig. 39c and Table A10i) and 2 large disc-shaped bone beads (Nos. 1–2; Fig. 37b-c and Table A10g); and possibly associated with 2 or 3 *Olivella* beads (Nos. 4?, 5–6; Fig. 38d-f and Table A10f), 2 tubular bone beads (Nos. 2–3; Fig. 37e-f and Table A10h), 2 tiny turquoise discs (Nos. 4-5; Fig. 39d-e and Table A10i), which probably had been inset in lateral perforations in either the *Olivella* or the tubular bone beads, and 1 or 2 fluorite crystals (1 purple, 1 green; Nos. 3–4; Fig. 40c-d and Table A10j).

Table A10f
Olivella shell beads found with Feature 3 burial (see Fig. 38a-f)[1]

Item No.	Max. Length (cm)	Max. Breadth (cm)	Species[2]	Location and Comments
1	1.57	0.74	*O. dama* (Wood,1828)	On right side of chest near proximal end of prayer-stick (end farthest from skull); originally either worn around neck or attached to end of prayer-stick; associated with 2 or 3 other *Olivella* shell beads (Nos. 2, 3, and 4?), 1 tubular bone bead (No. 1; Fig. 37d and Table A10h), and perhaps 1 green fluorite pebble (No. 3; Fig. 40c and Table A10j).
2	1.48	0.76	"	On right side of chest near proximal end of prayer-stick (end farthest from skull); originally either worn around neck or attached to end of prayer-stick; associated with 2 or perhaps 3 other *Olivella* shell beads (Nos. 1, 3, and 4?), 1 tubular bone bead (No. 1; Fig. 37d and Table A10h), and perhaps 1 green fluorite pebble (No. 3; Fig. 40c and Table A10j).
3	1.55	0.77	"	On right side of chest near proximal end of prayer-stick (end farthest from skull); originally either worn around neck or attached to end of prayer-stick; associated with 2 or perhaps 3 other *Olivella* shell beads (Nos. 1–2, and 4?), 1 tubular bone bead (No. 1; Fig. 37d and Table A10h), and perhaps 1 green fluorite pebble (No. 3; Fig. 40c and Table A10j).
4	1.47	0.70	"	On right side of chest adjacent to right humerus; may have been displaced by slumping or rodent activity from original association with 3 other *Olivella* beads (Nos. 1–3), 1 tubular bone bead (No. 1; Fig. 37d and Table A10h), and 1 green fluorite pebble (No. 3; Fig. 40c and Table A10j); originally either worn around neck, attached to prayer-stick, or worn around right wrist.

Table A10f (cont.)

Item No.	Max. Length (cm)	Max. Breadth (cm)	Species[2]	Location and Comments
5	1.93	0.90	*O. dama*(?)	One of 2 large *Olivella* beads (Nos. 5-6) inside Chupadero B/W jar (No. 6b; Figs. 33–35 and Tables A10b-A10c) on lower abdomen of burial; 0.35 cm hole drilled through lateral surface of shell at midpoint on longitudinal axis; 1 of 2 small turquoise discs (Nos. 4-5; Fig. 39d-e and Table A10i) originally may have been placed in hole with mastic (see Table A10i, item 4); when excavated both discs were loose in jar fill; discs instead may have been placed with mastic in lateral holes of 2 associated tubular bone beads (Nos. 2–3; Fig. 37e-f and Table A10h); bead, along with other items, probably slumped into jar from right wrist.
6	1.92	0.87	*O. dama*(?)	One of 2 large *Olivella* beads (Nos. 5-6) inside Chupadero B/W jar (No. 6b; Figs. 33–35 and Tables A10b-A10c); 0.36 cm hole drilled through lateral surface, possibly for placement of small turquoise disc (see description for No. 5 above); bead, along with other items, probably slumped into jar from right wrist.

[1]Numbers in parentheses are values, measured on slightly damaged specimens, which closely approximate true values; numbers in brackets are minimum values measured on broken specimens.
[2]We are grateful to James H. McLean, Curator of Malacology, Los Angeles County Museum of Natural History, for species identifications.

Table A10g
Disc-shaped bone beads found with Feature 3 burial (see Fig. 37b-c)

Item No.	Diameter (cm)	Thickness (cm)	Location and Comments
1	0.80	0.33	Near right wrist; associated with another large disc-shaped bone bead (No. 2 below), 86 small disc-shell beads (Table A10e), and 1 turquoise bead (No. 3; Fig. 39c and Table A10i); probably also originally associated with items displaced from right wrist by slumping or rodent activity into Chupadero B/W jar (No. 6b; Fig. 33–35 and Tables A10b-A10c); these include 2 laterally perforated tubular bone beads (Nos. 2–3; Fig. 37e-f and Table A10h), 2 laterally perforated *Olivella* beads (Nos. 5–6; Fig. 38e-f and Table A10f); 2 tiny turquoise discs (Nos. 4–5; Fig. 39d-e and Table A10i), and 1 purple fluorite pebble (No. 4; Fig. 40d and Table A10j).
2	0.74	0.19	Near right wrist; for associations, see discussion of disc-shaped bone bead (No. 1) above.

Table A10h
Tubular bone beads found with Feature 3 burial (see Fig. 37d-f)

Item No.	Max. Length (cm)	Max. Breadth (cm)	Species	Element	Location and Comments
1	3.68	0.60	Bird	Ulna	Thin-walled, hollow bone tube, with slight curvature longitudinally, cut from ulna midshaft; circular cross section; ends cut perpendicular to longitudinal axis and polished; several cutmarks around perimeter near one end of tube, almost forming pair of decorative grooves; found near prayer-stick; either attached to stick or possibly worn around neck; associated with 3 or 4 *Olivella* shell beads (Nos. 1–3, and 4?; Fig. 38a-d and Table A10f) and perhaps 1 small green fluorite pebble (No. 3; Fig. 40c and Table A10j).

Table A10h (cont.)

Item No.	Max. Length (cm)	Max. Breadth (cm)	Species	Element	Location and Comments
2	2.49	1.44	Bird(?)	?	Thin-walled, hollow bone tube; irregular cross section, with one side broader and flatter, the other narrower and more rounded; ends cut perpendicular to longitudinal axis and polished; 2 short cutmarks, perpendicular to long axis, near one end of tube (too short to form decorative grooves); single lateral perforation (0.45 cm in diameter) at midpoint of long axis on broader, flatter side; deep, v-shaped indentation cut into each end parallel to long axis on side opposite lateral perforation; found inside Chupadero B/W jar (No. 6b; Figs. 33–35 and Tables A10b-A10c) in association with another slightly narrower, laterally perforated bone tube (No. 3 below), 2 *Olivella* shell beads, each with lateral perforation (Nos. 5–6; Fig. 38e-f and Table A10f), 2 tiny turquoise discs (Nos. 4-5; probable inserts in lateral perforations of *Olivella* beads or tubular bone beads; Fig. 39d-e and Table A10i), and 1 small purple fluorite crystal (No. 4; Fig. 40d and Table A10j); all of these items probably slumped into jar from right hand or wrist of burial.

Table A10h (cont.)

Item No.	Max. Length (cm)	Max. Breadth (cm)	Species	Element	Location and Comments
3	2.64	1.21	Bird(?)	?	Thin-walled (thicker than No. 2 above), hollow bone tube; elliptical cross section, with 2 broader, flatter surfaces and 2 narrower, more curved surfaces; ends cut perpendicular to long axis and polished; single lateral perforation (0.44 cm in diameter) at midpoint of long axis on 1 of broader surfaces; deep, v-shaped indentation cut into each end parallel to long axis on side opposite lateral perforation; contained peculiar wooden (species?) insert in place within tube directly beneath lateral perforation; insert cylindrical, 0.70 cm in length by 0.56 cm in diameter (these dimensions do not reflect probable shrinkage); function of insert unknown, and its presence in tube may be fortuitous; found inside Chupadero B/W jar associated with tubular bone bead No. 2 and other items (see discussion of above).

Table A10i
Turquoise found with Feature 3 burial (see Fig. 39a-e)

Item No.	Type	Max. Length (cm)	Max. Width (cm)	Max. Thick. (cm)	Weight (g)	Description	Location and Comments
1	Bead	0.55	0.52	0.19	0.09	Irregular, with one edge semi-circular and other edge quasi-rectangular; tiny biconical(?) hole at center.	In Feat. 7, a small post hole within Feat. 3; probably displaced by rodent activity from left hand or wrist of Feat. 3 burial; found with turquoise bead or small pendant (No. 2), 58 small disc-shell beads (Table A10e), a miniature obsidian point (No. 1; Fig. 37a and Tables A10k-A10l), 1 tiny brachiopod fossil (No. 2; Fig. 40b and Table A10j), and 1 clear quartz crystal (No. 1; Fig. 40a and Table A10j).
2	Bead or Pendant	0.60	0.67	0.24	0.15	Trapezoidal, with moderately to strongly outcurving sides and slightly rounded corners; small biconical hole at smaller end.	In Feat. 7, a small post hole within Feat. 3; probably displaced by rodent activity from left hand or wrist of Feat. 3 burial; found with turquoise bead (No. 1) and other items (see discussion of No. 1 above).

Table A10i (cont.)

Item No.	Type	Max. Length (cm)	Max. Width (cm)	Max. Thick. (cm)	Weight (g)	Description	Location and Comments
3	Bead or Pendant	0.73	0.72	0.19	0.17	Slightly irregular, with one edge semi-circular and other edge nearly rectangular; corners strongly rounded; approaching trapezoidal form; small, uniconical? hole at smaller end.	Close to right wrist; associated with 86 small disc-shell beads (Table A10e), 2 large disc-shaped bone beads (Nos. 1–2; Fig. 37b-c and Table A10g); perhaps also associated with 2 or 3 *Olivella* shell beads (Nos. 4, 5–6; Fig. 38d-f and Table A10f), 2 tubular bone beads (Nos. 2–3; Fig. 37e-f and Table A10h), 2 tiny turquoise discs (Nos. 4–5; see below), and 1 or 2 fluorite pebbles (1 purple, 1 green; Nos. 3–4; Fig. 40c-d and Table A10j).

Table A10i (cont.)

Item No.	Type	Max. Length (cm)	Max. Width (cm)	Max. Thick. (cm)	Weight (g)	Description	Location and Comments
4	Disc	0.50	0.44	0.12	0.05	Unperforated tiny ovoid disc	One of 2 discs in fill of Chupadero B/W jar (No. 6b; Figs. 33–35 and Tables A10b-A10c) on lower abdomen and between upper thighs of burial; jar also contained 2 laterally perforated *Olivella* beads (Nos. 5–6; Fig. 38e-f and Table A10f) and 2 laterally perforated tubular bone beads (Nos. 2–3; Fig. 37e-f and Table A10h); discs possibly set with mastic in lateral holes in shell or bone beads; dark stains around edge of discs may have been mastic, but no traces of mastic in holes of beads; other items in jar fill include 1 purple fluorite pebble (No. 4; Fig. 40d and Table A10j), and 1 small unfused ossification centrum (probable human); materials perhaps placed in jar at time of burial or more likely displaced after burial from right hand or wrist.
5	Disc	0.42	0.38	0.13	0.03	Unperforated, tiny ovoid disc	One of 2 discs in fill of Chupadero B/W jar on lower abdomen and between upper thighs of Feat. 3 burial (see discussion of No. 4 above).

Table A10j
Minerals and fossil found with Feature 3 burial (see Fig. 40a-d)

Item No.	Item	Max. Length (cm)	Max. Breadth (cm)	Max. Thick. (cm)	Weight (g)	Location and Comments
1	Quartz crystal, clear, single termination	0.95	0.40	0.40	0.19	In Feat. 7, a small post hole within Feat. 3; unperforated; associated with 1 tiny obsidian point (No. 1; Fig. 37a and Tables A10k-A10l), 1 small brachiopod fossil (No. 2 below), 58 small disc-shell beads (Table A10e), and 2 turquoise beads (No. 1–2; Fig. 39a-b and Table A10i); probably displaced by rodent activity from left hand or wrist of Feat. 3 burial.
2	Brachiopod fossil *Wellerella* cf. *delicatula*[1] (Dunbar & Conrad, 1932); Lower Permian; known from Southwestern U.S., Texas, and mid-continent region.	0.70	0.61	0.36	0.17	In Feat. 7, a small post hole within Feat. 3; unperforated; for associations, see discussion of quartz crystal (No. 1) above.

Table A10j (cont.)

Item No.	Item	Max. Length (cm)	Max. Breadth (cm)	Max. Thick. (cm)	Weight (g)	Location and Comments
3	Fluorite pebble (probable), bright apple green; tiny, ovoid, smooth, waterworn.	0.65	0.48	0.41	0.11	Unperforated; near right wrist; either worn around wrist, or more likely attached to prayer-stick and displaced by rodent activity or slumping; if worn around wrist, associated with 86 disc-shell beads (Table A10e), 1 turquoise bead (No. 3; Fig. 39c and Table A10i), and 2 disc-shaped bone beads (Nos. 1–2; Fig. 37b-c and Table A10g), plus items in fill of Chupadero B/W jar (No. 6b; Figs. 33–35 and Tables A10b-A10c) which probably slumped from right wrist; these include 2 laterally perforated tubular bone beads (Nos. 2–3; Fig. 37e-f and Table A10h), 2 laterally perforated *Olivella* beads (Nos. 5–6; Fig. 38e-f and Table A10f), 2 turquoise discs (Nos. 4–5; Fig. 39d-e and Table A10i), and 1 purple fluorite pebble (No. 4; Fig. 40d and Table A10j); if No. 3 attached to prayer-stick, it may have been associated with 3–4 *Olivella* beads (Nos. 1–4; Fig. 38a-d and Table A10f) and 1 tubular bone bead (No. 1; Fig. 37d and Table A10h); these items instead may have been worn around neck.

Table A10j (cont.)

Item No.	Item	Max. Length (cm)	Max. Breadth (cm)	Max. Thick. (cm)	Weight (g)	Location and Comments
4	Fluorite pebble, purple; subangular with light abrasion; may be slightly waterworn.	0.87	0.83	0.58	0.58	Unperforated; in fill of Chupadero B/W jar (No. 6b; Figs. 33–35 and Tables A10b-A10c); for associations, see discussion of green fluorite pebble (No. 3) above.

[1] We are grateful to Sandy Carlson of the Museum of Paleontology at the University of Michigan for identifying the brachiopod.

Table A10k
Projectile point found with Feature 3 burial:
Metric attributes (see Fig. 37a)

Item No.	Max. Length[1] (cm)	Max. Width[2] (cm)	Max. Thick.[3] (cm)	Weight (g)	Min. Neck Width[4] (cm)	Max. Base/Stem Width[5] (cm)	Max. Length of Haft-Element[6] (cm)
1	0.81	0.66	0.12	0.04	0.35	0.66	0.32

[1] Maximum length from tip to most proximal part of base, measured parallel to longitudinal axis.
[2] Maximum width on base, measured perpendicular to longitudinal axis.
[3] Maximum thickness, regardless of location on specimen.
[4] Minimum distance between notches.
[5] Maximum width of haft-element.
[6] Maximum length from most distal edge of notches to most proximal part of base, measured parallel to longitudinal axis.

Table A10l
Projectile point found with Feature 3 burial:
Description of point and material (see Fig. 37a)

Item No.	Haft Type	Material Type and Description	Location and Comments
1	Tiny, u- to v-shaped side notches; broadly indented, concave base (approaching basal notch).	Obsidian, black, nearly opaque except along thinnest margins.	Crudely flaked spall; both dorsal and ventral surfaces unretouched except for minimal trimming (nibbling) along margins to shape outline; found in Feat. 7 post hole with 58 disc-shell beads (Table A10e), 2 turquoise beads (Nos. 1–2; Fig. 39a-b and Table A10i), 1 small brachiopod fossil (No. 2; Fig. 40b and Table A10j), and 1 clear quartz crystal (No. 1; Fig. 40a and Table A10j); point and other items probably displaced by rodent activity from left hand or wrist.

APPENDIX 11

ARTIFACTS FROM FEATURE 8 BURIAL

Table A11a
Disc-shell beads found with Feature 8 burial

Total No.	Ave. No. Beads per cm (N)	Total Strand(s) Length (cm)	Diameter Ave. $\pm 1\sigma$ (N) (cm)	Location and Comments
3570	9.6 (304)	370.3	0.364±0.036 (100)	Five, and more likely 6 strands, probably extending entirely around neck to point of closure; total length of beads would provide 5 complete strands, each 74.1 cm (29.2 in) in length; or 6 complete strands, each 61.7 cm (24.3 in) in length; number of strands indicated by stacked strand segments still in situ on chest of individual (estimated total strand length is compatible with this figure).

Table A11b
Olivella shell beads found with Feature 8 burial (see Fig. 38g-i)

Item No.	Max. Length (cm)	Max. Breadth (cm)	Species[1]	Location and Comments
1	1.46	0.69	*O. dama* (Wood, 1828)	In chest area, probably part of multiple-strand disc-shell bead necklace (Table A11a).
2	1.62	0.84	"	Location same as No. 1 above
3	1.32	0.67	"	Location same as No. 1 above

[1]We are grateful to James H. McLean, Curator of Malacology, Los Angeles County Museum of Natural History, for species identifications.

Table A11c
Tubular shell beads found with Feature 8 burial (see Fig. 51)

Item No.	Max. Length (cm)	Max. Breadth (cm)	Species[1]	Location and Comments
1	3.16	1.08	*Tripsycha tripsycha* (Pilsbry & Lowe, 1932)	Uncoiled tip of vermetid gastropod; located adjacent to midshaft of left humerus (strung together with Nos. 2-3).
2	4.10	0.86	*Tripsycha tripsycha* (Pilsbry & Lowe, 1932)	Uncoiled tip of vermetid gastropod; located adjacent to midshaft of left humerus (strung together with Nos. 1, 3).
3	4.20	1.47	Unidentified large bivalve	Located adjacent to midshaft of left humerus (strung together with Nos. 1–2); two pairs of parallel grooves incised around perimeter of bead, one pair at each end; spacing between grooves within each pair approx. 0.15 to 0.20 cm; spacing between pairs of grooves approx. 3.36 cm (inner groove to inner groove).

[1]We are grateful to James H. McLean, Curator of Malacology, Los Angeles County Museum of Natural History, for species identifications.

Table A11d

Glycymeris shell bracelets found with Feature 8 burial (see Figs. 45–50)

Item No.	Max. Diam. of Hinge Axis (cm)	Max. Diam. Perp. to Hinge Axis (cm)	Max. Height at Hinge (cm)	Max. Height Opp. Hinge (cm)	Max. Thick. at Hinge (cm)	Species[1]	Location and Comments
1	8.93	8.57	2.50	1.00	1.29	*Glycymeris gigantea* (Reeve, 1843)	Around distal right humerus near elbow; hinge area has 3 small holes drilled into exterior surface forming stylized face (2 eyes and mouth); right eye drilled through, left eye part way, mouth drilled through; at least 7 (probably 9 or 10) short grooves or ticks cut into underside at narrowest point opposite hinge area; ticks ca. 0.34 cm long and evenly spaced ca. 0.49 cm apart; ticks start flush with edge most distant from hinge.

Table A11d (cont.)

Item No.	Max. Diam. of Hinge Axis (cm)	Max. Diam. Perp. to Hinge Axis (cm)	Max. Height at Hinge (cm)	Max. Height Opp. Hinge (cm)	Max. Thick. at Hinge (cm)	Species[1]	Location and Comments
2	8.87	8.80	2.15	0.87	1.21	*Glycymeris gigantea* (Reeve, 1843)	Around left humerus near elbow; 3 holes drilled into hinge area forming stylized face (2 eyes and mouth); both eyes drilled part way, mouth drilled through; bracelet broken in 2 pieces and repaired with biconical holes adjacent to breaks (1 on each side of each break); isolated hole near left eye but just off hinge area (repair hole?; probably not part of face); exterior surface opposite hinge painted with parallel, obliquely oriented bands; bands instead could be stains from former wrapping (less likely due to absence of stains on interior); bands ca. 0.18 cm wide, ca. 0.15 cm apart, and brownish-black (original color unknown); pattern visible for at least 4 cm; no ticks on undersurface opposite hinge.

[1]We are grateful to James H. McLean, Curator of Malacology, Los Angeles County Museum of Natural History, for species identifications.

Table A11e
Turquoise found with Feature 8 burial (see Fig. 39f-h)

Item No.	Type	Max. Length (cm)	Max. Width (cm)	Max. Thick. (cm)	Weight (g)	Description	Location and Comments
1	Earring (?)	2.12	1.43	0.30	1.51	Slightly trapezoidal, with moderately outcurving sides and rounded corners; biconical hole at smaller end.	Just below gonial region of right side of mandible, as though originally suspended from right ear (instead may have been attached to extreme right side of multiple-strand disc-shell bead necklace (Table A11a) found on upper chest of burial); matching specimen (No. 2) found just below gonial region of left side of mandible.
2	Earring (?)	2.11	1.39	0.34	1.58	Trapezoidal, with strongly outcurving sides and rounded corners; biconical hole at smaller end.	Just below gonial region of left side of mandible, as though originally suspended from left ear (instead may have been attached to extreme left side of multiple-strand disc-shell bead necklace (Table A11a) found on upper chest of burial); matching specimen (No. 1) found just below gonial region of right side of mandible.
3	Bead	0.72	0.60	0.18	0.10	Rectangular (irregular, grading toward ovoid), with outcurving sides and rounded corners; biconical(?) hole off center, near one of long edges.	Under 3rd left rib; probably part of multiple-strand disc-shell bead necklace (Table A11a) found on chest of burial.

APPENDIX 12

ARTIFACTS FROM FEATURE 25 BURIAL

Table A12a
Prayer-stick found with Feature 25 burial (see Figs. 72–74)

Item No.	Max. Length (cm)	Max. Breadth (cm)	Max. Thick. (cm)	Material[1]	Location and Comments
1	23.0	2.0–3.5	1.5	*Juglans* sp. (Walnut)	Made from 2-year old sprout or new limb; bark removed, stick trimmed and squared off; on pit floor in front (west) of chest, just north of right hand; originally placed on chest (same as Feat. 3 prayer-stick), or held in right hand (less likely); 14–15 *Olivella* beads (Nos. 1–2, 3a-3b, 4–5, 10–11, 12a-12b, 13-16, 18?; Fig. 38j-w and Table A12c) attached in spiral around distal (north) end of stick; 1 clear quartz crystal (No. 6; Fig. 40e and Table A12e), 2 unperforated turquoise pieces (Nos. 7a-7b; Fig. 39i-j and Table A12d), 1 purple fluorite pebble (No. 8; Fig. 40f and Table A12e), and perhaps a pea-sized organic item (No. 9, not identified, decayed; see entry No. 33 in Table A16a) attached to proximal end of stick, probably with mastic; 3 disc-shell beads (Table A12b), found near stick, probably originally attached; no trace of mastic or color on stick.

[1]We are grateful to Richard I. Ford of the Laboratory of Ethnobotany at the University of Michigan for identifying this and other ethnobotanical specimens.

Table A12b
Disc-shell beads found with Feature 25 burial

Total No.	Ave. No. Beads per cm (N)	Total Strand(s) Length (cm)	Diameter Ave. ± 1σ (N) (cm)	Location and Comments
3	10.2 (3)	0.29	0.386±0.032 (3)	Three beads (Nos. 13, 17, 18) found by fine-screening fill directly beneath and near proximal end of prayer-stick (closest to hand); probably originally attached to stick.

Table A12c
Olivella shell beads found with Feature 25 burial (see Fig. 38j-w and Table A12a)[1]

Item No.	Max. Length (cm)	Max. Breadth (cm)	Species[2]	Location and Comments
1	1.54	0.71	*O. dama* (Wood, 1828)	Part of cluster of *Olivella* beads associated with (and probably attached to) prayer-stick (Fig. 38j; see Fig. 74 for arrangement of beads and other materials on stick).
2	1.69	0.78	"	Part of cluster of *Olivella* beads associated with (and probably attached to) prayer-stick (Fig. 38k; see Fig. 74 for arrangement of beads and other materials on stick); 0.21 cm hole drilled(?) through one side of shell near midpoint on longitudinal axis.
3a	(1.40)	0.66	"	Part of cluster of *Olivella* beads associated with (and probably attached to) prayer-stick (Fig. 38l; see Fig. 74 for arrangement of beads and other materials on stick).
3b	1.28	0.65	"	Part of cluster of *Olivella* beads associated with (and probably attached to) prayer-stick (Fig. 38m; see Fig. 74 for arrangement of beads and other materials on stick).
4	(1.47)	0.77	"	Part of cluster of *Olivella* beads associated with (and probably attached to) prayer-stick (Fig. 38n; see Fig. 74 for arrangement of beads and other materials on stick).
5	1.48	0.70	"	Part of cluster of *Olivella* beads associated with (and probably attached to) prayer-stick (Fig. 38o; see Fig. 74 for arrangement of beads and other materials on stick).
10	1.67	0.82	"	Part of cluster of *Olivella* beads associated with (and probably attached to) prayer-stick (Fig. 38p; see Fig. 74 for arrangement of beads and other materials on stick).

Table A12c (cont.)

Item No.	Max. Length (cm)	Max. Breadth (cm)	Species[2]	Location and Comments
11	1.63	0.80	"	Part of cluster of *Olivella* beads associated with (and probably attached to) prayer-stick (Fig. 38q; see Fig. 74 for arrangement of beads and other materials on stick).
12a	1.41	0.73	"	Part of cluster of *Olivella* beads associated with (and probably attached to) prayer-stick (Fig. 38r; see Fig. 74 for arrangement of beads and other materials on stick).
12b	1.49	0.78	"	Part of cluster of *Olivella* beads associated with (and probably attached to) prayer-stick (Fig. 38s; see Fig. 74 for arrangement of beads and other materials on stick).
13	--	--	" (?)	Part of cluster of *Olivella* beads associated with (and probably attached to) prayer-stick (see Fig. 74 for arrangement of beads and other materials on stick); No. 13 badly decomposed; disintegrated during excavation.
14	1.08	0.56	"	Part of cluster of *Olivella* beads associated with (and probably attached to) prayer-stick (Fig. 38t; see Fig. 74 for arrangement of beads and other materials on stick).
15	1.47	0.74	"	Part of cluster of *Olivella* beads associated with (and probably attached to) prayer-stick (Fig. 38u; see Fig. 74 for arrangement of beads and other materials on stick).
16	1.36	0.71	"	Part of cluster of *Olivella* beads associated with (and probably attached to) prayer-stick; found adjacent to prayer-stick; precise position uncertain (Fig. 38v; see Fig. 74).

Table A12c (cont.)

Item No.	Max. Length (cm)	Max. Breadth (cm)	Species[2]	Location and Comments
18	1.48	0.74	"	Probably part of cluster of *Olivella* beads associated with (and probably attached to) prayer-stick; found during excavation in general vicinity of prayer-stick; precise position uncertain (Fig. 38w; see Fig. 74).

[1]Numbers in parentheses are values, measured on slightly damaged specimens, which closely approximate true values.
[2]We are grateful to James H. McLean, Curator of Malacology, Los Angeles County Museum of Natural History, for species identifications.

Table A12d

Turquoise found with Feature 25 burial (see Fig. 39i-j)[1]

Item No.	Type	Max. Length (cm)	Max. Width (cm)	Max. Thick. (cm)	Weight (g)	Description	Location and Comments
7a	Piece	1.11	(0.77)	0.33	0.52	Unperforated, nearly rectangular piece, with moderately outcurving sides and slightly rounded corners (Fig. 39i); 1 of long edges broken (no evidence for incomplete perforation in break); 1 face and edge with break display yellowish hue or stain, perhaps from heat or residue of mastic; hue not present directly in break, suggesting fracture resulted from heat; fragment from break not recovered.	On proximal end of prayer-stick (end closest to right hand); lack of perforation suggests piece attached by binding or mastic (no traces of either recovered); also attached to same part of prayer-stick were 1 clear quartz crystal (No. 6; Fig. 40e and Table A12e) with termination toward distal (north) end of stick, 1 tiny unperforated piece of turquoise (No. 7b), 1 small pebble of purple fluorite (No. 8; Fig. 40f and Table A12e), and possibly a pea-sized organic item (decayed, not identified).
7b	Piece	0.40	0.39	0.15	0.03	Unperforated, tiny, quasi-trapezoidal piece, with outcurving sides and rounded corners (Fig. 39j); base of trapezoid rough, as though piece were broken from larger specimen; not fragment from No. 7a above.	Adjacent to turquoise piece No. 7a; too large and elongated to have been inset in lateral perforation of *Olivella* bead No. 2 (Fig. 38k and Table A12c), and unlikely to have been displaced from bead's position near distal (north) end of stick; probably attached (with mastic?) to proximal end of stick with other items enumerated above (see No. 7a above).

[1]Number in parentheses is value, measured on slightly damaged specimen, which closely approximates true value.

Table A12e
Minerals found with Feature 25 burial (see Fig. 40e-f)

Item No.	Type	Max. Length (cm)	Max. Breadth (cm)	Max. Thick. (cm)	Weight (g)	Location and Comments
6	Quartz crystal	2.40	0.63	0.51	1.15	Clear, with single termination; on proximal (south) end of prayer-stick (No. 1; Fig. 73-74 and Table A12a); unperforated; probably attached with mastic; termination toward skull (north); adjacent to 2 turquoise pieces (Nos. 7a-7b; Fig. 39i-j and Table A12d), 1 purple fluorite pebble (No. 8), and perhaps a pea-sized organic item (decayed, not identified); 14–15 *Olivella* beads (Nos. 1–2, 3a-3b, 4–5, 10–11, 12a-12b, 13–16, 18?; Fig. 38j-w and Table A12c) attached in spiral around distal end of stick; 3 disc-shell beads (Nos. 13, 17, 18; Table A12b), found near stick, probably also originally attached.
8	Fluorite pebble	1.16	0.80	0.60	0.78	Purple; subangular to subrounded, abraded, waterworn; on proximal (south) end of prayer-stick (No. 1; Figs. 73–74 and Table A12a); unperforated; probably attached with mastic; see discussion of No. 6 above.

APPENDIX 13

ARTIFACTS FROM FEATURE 29 BURIAL

Table A13a
Mussel shell ornaments found with Feature 29 burial (see Fig. 37g-h)[1]

Item No.	Type	Max. Length (cm)	Max. Breadth (cm)	Max. Thick. (cm)	Species[2]	Description	Location and Comments
14a	Pendant (?)	[1.88]	[4.00]	0.18	*Cyrtonaias tampicoensis*(?) (Lea, 1838)	Semi-circular or "butterfly" shape, with hole drilled near midpoint of (and close to) straight side (Fig. 37g); damaged both prehistorically and in excavation; trace of previous drill hole near one end of straight edge, suggesting pendant reworked from larger piece.	In cluster of lithics (Figs. 85, 86 and Table A13g) and turtle shell "gaming pieces" (Fig. 84 and Tables A13b-A13c) adjacent to left femur (see also Figs. 81–83).
46	Pendant blank (?)	[2.47]	[1.97]	0.16	*Cyrtonaias tampicoensis*(?) (Lea, 1838)	Quasi-triangular, with one rounded angle and slightly outcurving sides (Fig. 37h); no perforation.	In cluster of lithics (Figs. 85, 86 and Table A13g) and turtle shell "gaming pieces" (Fig. 84 and Tables A13b-A13c) adjacent to left femur (see also Figs. 81–83).

[1] Numbers in brackets are minimum values measured on broken specimens.
[2] These ornaments were too small to be positively identified. However, numerous identifiable freshwater mussel shells were recovered from room fill and East Plaza trash, many with cuts from which ornaments had been removed. All of these were *C. tampicoensis*. We are grateful to John B. Burch, Curator of Mollusks, Museum of Zoology, University of Michigan, for species identification.

Table A13b
Bone artifacts found with Feature 29 burial:
Metric attributes (see Figs. 84, 87)[1]

Item No.	Artifact	Fig. No.	Max. Length (cm)	Max. Breadth (cm)	Max. Thick. (cm)
13a(17)	Scapula knife(?)	87h	[8.70]	[5.15]	[0.90][2]
13b	"Gaming piece"	84a	3.01	1.14	0.38
15	"Gaming piece"	84b	2.90	1.08	0.37
16	"Gaming piece"	84c	3.01	1.10	0.40
22	"Gaming piece"	84d	2.28	1.27	0.27
23	"Gaming piece"	84e	3.00	1.16	0.34
24	"Gaming piece"	84f	1.21	1.21	0.40
25	"Gaming piece"	84g	2.67	1.05	0.40
26	"Gaming piece"	84h	[2.27]	(1.10)	0.37
27	"Gaming piece"	84i	2.90	1.10	0.32
28	"Gaming piece"	84j	1.18	1.18	0.34
39	"Awl" or "hairpin" medial fragment	87a	[4.55]	[0.79]	[0.66]
40	"Awl" or "hairpin" distal fragment	87b	[3.74]	[0.64]	[0.60]
41	"Awl" or "hairpin" distal fragment	87c	[5.10]	[0.89]	[0.50]
42–43	"Awl" or "hairpin" distal fragment	87d	[7.00]	[0.57]	[0.54]
44	"Awl" or "hairpin"(?) medial fragment	87e	[4.98]	[0.86]	[0.38]
47	"Awl" or "hairpin" distal fragment	87f	[8.24]	[1.18]	[0.44]
49	"Awl" or "hairpin" nearly complete	87g	14.73	[1.20]	[0.45]

[1]Numbers in parentheses are values, measured on slightly damaged specimens, which closely approximate true values; numbers in brackets are minimum values measured on broken specimens.
[2]Height of broken spine near proximal end of blade.

Table A13c
Bone artifacts found with Feature 29 burial:
Description and materials (see Figs. 84, 87)

Item No.	Artifact	Description	Location and Comments
13a(17)	Scapula knife(?) fragment	Proximal blade, left; probable antelope (*Antilocapra*); distal end and spine broken off or removed prehistorically; weathered; damaged in excavation; anterior lateral blade edge unaltered; posterior lateral edge removed parallel to spine and approx. 2.0–2.5 cm from spine midline; this edge is thin (ca. 0.10 cm), polished, with small nicks at regular intervals as though used as knife or scraper/shredder; 2 large, deep use-nicks in edge; patch of red ocher on undersurface of blade (surface opposite spine); found horizontal, spine down, 1 edge on top of, and in contact with, left femur.	Overlying cluster of lithics (Figs. 85, 86 and Table A13g) and turtle shell "gaming pieces" (Fig. 84 and Table A13b-A13c) adjacent to left femur (see also Figs. 81–83).
13b	"Gaming piece"	Turtle shell; quasi-rectangular, with rounded corners and slightly outcurving lateral edges; concavo-convex in longitudinal section; convex surface naturally pitted; no perforation.	In cluster of lithics (Figs. 85, 86 and Table A13g) adjacent to left femur (see also Figs. 81–83).
15	"Gaming piece"	Turtle shell; quasi-rectangular, with rounded corners and slightly outcurving lateral edges; concavo-convex in longitudinal section; convex surface naturally pitted; no perforation.	In cluster of lithics (Figs. 85, 86 and Table A13g) adjacent to left femur (see also Fig. 81–83).
16	"Gaming piece"	Turtle shell; quasi-rectangular, with rounded corners and slightly outcurving lateral edges; concavo-convex in longitudinal section; convex surface naturally pitted; no perforation.	In cluster of lithics (Figs. 85, 86 and Table A13g) adjacent to left femur (see also Figs. 81–83).

Table A13c (cont.)

Item No.	Artifact	Description	Location and Comments
22	"Gaming piece"	Turtle shell; quasi-rectangular, almost ovoid; concavo-convex in longitudinal section; convex surface naturally pitted; no perforation.	In cluster of lithics (Figs. 85, 86 and Table A13g) adjacent to left femur (see also Figs. 81–83).
23	"Gaming piece"	Turtle shell; quasi-rectangular, with rounded corners and slightly outcurving lateral edges; damaged during excavation, but largely restorable; concavo-convex in longitudinal section; convex surface is naturally pitted; no perforation.	In cluster of lithics (Figs. 85, 86 and Table A13g) adjacent to left femur (see also Figs. 81–83).
24	"Gaming piece"	Bone (or turtle shell?); circular; plano-concave in section, thick; 2 mutually perpendicular sets of cutmarks or incisions on concave surface; less distinct, unidirectional cutmarks on flat surface; no natural pitting; single perforation, ca. 0.20 cm in diameter, penetrating half-way through piece in center of flat surface.	In cluster of lithics (Figs. 85, 86 and Table A13g) adjacent to left femur (see also Figs. 81–83).
25	"Gaming piece"	Turtle shell; quasi-rectangular, with rounded corners and slightly outcurving lateral edges; concavo-convex in longitudinal section; convex surface naturally pitted; no perforation.	In cluster of lithics (Figs. 85, 86 and Table A13g) adjacent to left femur (see also Figs. 81–83).
26	"Gaming piece"	Turtle shell; quasi-rectangular, with rounded corners and slightly outcurving lateral edges; damaged during excavation and only partially restorable; concavo-convex in longitudinal section; convex surface naturally pitted; no perforation.	In cluster of lithics (Figs. 85, 86 and Table A13g) adjacent to left femur (see also Figs. 81–83).

Table A13c (cont.)

Item No.	Artifact	Description	Location and Comments
27	"Gaming piece"	Turtle shell; quasi-rectangular, with rounded corners and slightly outcurving lateral edges; concavo-convex in longitudinal section; convex surface naturally pitted; no perforation.	In cluster of lithics (Figs. 85, 86 and Table A13g) adjacent to left femur (see also Figs. 81–83).
28	"Gaming piece"	Turtle shell; circular; slightly concavo-convex in section; convex surface naturally pitted; single perforation, ca. 0.21 cm in diameter, penetrating half-way through piece in center of concave (non-pitted) surface.	In cluster of lithics (Figs. 85, 86 and Table A13g) adjacent to left femur (see also Figs. 81–83).
39	"Awl" or "hairpin" medial fragment	Deer- or antelope-sized, long-bone shaft fragment (split metapodial?); working end and butt missing; may be part of same awl as point fragment No. 42–43 below, but pieces do not conjoin; butt end may have eroded off when upper body of burial was destroyed; lateral edges smoothed.	In cluster of at least 5 pointed bone objects near left knee (see Figs. 81–83).
40	"Awl" or "hairpin" distal fragment	Probable deer- or antelope-sized, long-bone shaft fragment (split metapodial?); working end tapers to sharp, awl-like point; mid-section and butt end missing (probably eroded off when upper body of burial was destroyed); point smoothed and slightly polished; lateral edges smoothed.	In cluster of at least 5 pointed bone objects near left knee (see Figs. 81–83).
41	"Awl" or "hairpin" distal fragment	Deer- or antelope-sized, long-bone shaft fragment (split metapodial?); working end tapers toward point, but tip missing rendering form of point unknown; butt end missing (probably eroded off when upper body of burial was destroyed); lateral edges smoothed.	In cluster of at least 5 pointed bone objects near left knee (see Figs. 81–83).

Table A13c (cont.)

Item No.	Artifact	Description	Location and Comments
42–43	"Awl" or "hairpin" distal fragment	Probable deer- or antelope-sized, long-bone shaft fragment (split metapodial?); 2 adjacent restorable fragments; working end tapers to sharp, awl-like point; butt end missing; may be part of same awl as medial section No. 39 above, but pieces do not conjoin; butt end missing (probably eroded off when upper body of burial was destroyed); point polished; lateral edges smoothed.	In cluster of at least 5 pointed bone objects near left knee (see Figs. 81–83).
44	"Awl" or "hairpin"(?) medial section	Probable deer- or antelope-sized, long-bone shaft fragment (split metapodial?); working end and butt missing; originally may have conjoined with "awl" tip No. 40, 41, 42–43, or 47, or instead may be fragment of another specimen which was eroded off when upper body of burial was destroyed; one lateral edge shows trace of polish.	In cluster of at least 5 pointed bone objects near left knee (see Figs. 81–83).
47	"Awl" or "hairpin" distal fragment	Deer- or antelope-sized, long-bone shaft fragment (split metapodial?); working end tapers to smooth, flattened point; point not ideally suited to piercing; butt end missing (damaged by rodents and probably eroded off when upper body of burial was destroyed); lateral edges smoothed.	In cluster of at least 5 pointed bone objects near left knee (see Figs. 81–83).
49	"Awl" or "hairpin" nearly complete	Deer- or antelope-sized, long-bone shaft fragment (split metapodial?); working end tapers to smooth, flattened point; point not ideally suited to piercing; broader butt end trimmed and rough edges smoothed; lateral edges smoothed; severe lateral damage from rodent gnawing toward butt end.	In cluster of at least 5 pointed bone objects near left knee (see Figs. 81–83).

Table A13d
Minerals found with Feature 29 burial (see Fig. 40g-h)

Item No.	Type	Max. Length (cm)	Max. Breadth (cm)	Max. Thick. (cm)	Weight (g)	Location and Comments
51b	Red ocher fragment	0.90	0.75	0.45	0.25	No signs of use or abrasion; beneath left femur near cluster of lithics (Figs. 85, 86 and Table A13g) and turtle shell "gaming pieces" (Fig. 84 and Tables A13b-A13c; see also Figs. 81–83).
61	Quartz crystal	1.77	1.19	0.94	3.00	Clear; blocky fragment broken from much larger crystal; no trace of termination and only part of 1 lateral face; found near northern edge of burial pit in contact with bedrock walls and well above level of other grave offerings; may have been displaced (ca. 45 cm) from other artifacts near left femur, or may be isolated offering or spurious item in pit fill.

Table A13e
Projectile point or knife found with Feature 29 burial:
Metric attributes (see Fig. 86g)

Item No.	Max. Length[1] (cm)	Max. Width[2] (cm)	Max. Thick.[3] (cm)	Weight (g)	Min. Neck Width[4] (cm)	Max. Base/Stem Width[5] (cm)	Max. Length of Haft-Element[6] (cm)
45	[4.92]	2.68	0.75	10.08	0.66	0.72	0.76

[1] Maximum length from tip to most proximal part of base, measured parallel to longitudinal axis; number in brackets is minimum value measured on broken specimen.
[2] Maximum width on blade, measured perpendicular to longitudinal axis.
[3] Maximum thickness, regardless of location on specimen.
[4] Minimum distance between notches.
[5] Maximum width of haft-element.
[6] Maximum length from most distal edge of notches to most proximal part of base, measured parallel to longitudinal axis.

Table A13f
Projectile point or knife found with Feature 29 burial:
Description of point and material (see Fig. 86g)

Item No.	Haft Type	Material Type and Description	Location and Comments
45	Haft-element resembles small version of eastern Late Archaic "turkey tail"; shallow, open, semicircular side notches, close to base; rounded base.	Alibates; dark maroon (dominant) and light bluish gray, banded, wavy; moderate luster.	Proximal two-thirds of bifacial hafted knife; in cluster of lithics (Figs. 85, 86 and Table A13g) and turtle shell "gaming pieces" (Fig. 84 and Tables A13b-A13c) adjacent to left femur (see also Figs. 81–83).

Table A13g
Lithics found with Feature 29 burial (see Figs. 85, 86)

Item No.	Fig. No.	Max. Length[1] (cm)	Max. Breadth[2] (cm)	Max. Thick.[3] (cm)	Material	Description	Location and Comments
18	85a	3.57	2.69	0.46	Light bluish-gray to tan chert; moderate luster slightly mottled; streaks and patches of yellowish-brown; chalky tan to white cortex over most of dorsal surface.	Large unretouched flake fragment, split longitudinally through bulb.	In cluster of lithics and turtle shell "gaming pieces" (Figs. 84-86 and Tables A13b-A13c) adjacent to left femur (see also Figs. 81-83); trace of red ocher.
19	85b	3.61	3.25	0.65	Bluish-gray chert, with numerous tiny black specks; dull luster; tan to yellowish-brown cortex on platform and 1 lateral edge.	Large unretouched flake	In cluster of lithics and turtle shell "gaming pieces" (Figs. 84-86 and Tables A13b-A13c) adjacent to left femur (see also Figs. 81-83); trace of red ocher.
20	85h	4.83	3.59	1.62	Bluish-gray to gray chert, with occasional small dark gray mottles; moderate luster; chalky tan to white cortex on exterior.	Core, minimally used, made from split chert nodule; several small flakes removed bifacially from 1 edge; single elongate, parallel-sided removal from ventral surface.	In cluster of lithics and turtle shell "gaming pieces" (Figs. 84-86 and Tables A13b-A13c) adjacent to left femur (see also Figs. 81-83).
21	86a	3.46	2.38	0.82	Gray chert with light bluish-gray banding; moderate luster; trace of chalky tan to white matrix on 1 surface	Flake with bulbar area intentionally removed, or small fragment from split nodule; several removals from both surfaces, forming crude biface; heavy, irregular (denticulate) unifacial (ventral) use damage along 1 edge.	In cluster of lithics and turtle shell "gaming pieces" (Figs. 84-86 and Tables A13b-A13c) adjacent to left femur (see also Figs. 81-83).

Table A13g (cont.)

Item No.	Fig. No.	Max. Length[1] (cm)	Max. Breadth[2] (cm)	Max. Thick.[3] (cm)	Material	Description	Location and Comments
29	85c	4.01	4.50	0.98	Light gray chert; dull luster; trace of chalky tan cortex at distal end.	Large, unretouched, "side-struck" flake.	In cluster of lithics and turtle shell "gaming pieces" (Figs. 84-86 and Tables A13b-A13c) adjacent to left femur (see also Figs. 81-83).
30	85i	3.71	1.98	1.14	Light to dark gray chert; moderate luster; traces of chalky tan to brown cortex on 2 edges.	Crude chunk or fragment of small, irregular split pebble; possible fragment of core.	In cluster of lithics and turtle shell "gaming pieces" (Figs. 84-86 and Tables A13b-A13c) adjacent to left femur (see also Figs. 81-83).
31	86d	4.22	2.47	1.02	Light gray to gray chert, banded, with patches of tan to grayish white; moderate luster; grayish-white cortex on 1 surface.	Ovoid biface with 1 end moderately pointed.	In cluster of lithics and turtle shell "gaming pieces" (Figs. 84-86 and Tables A13b-A13c) adjacent to left femur (see also Figs. 81-83).
32	85d	3.68	3.28	0.73	Light gray chert, with single prominent, narrow, dark gray band; dull to moderate luster; grayish-white cortex on platform and distal edge.	Large, unretouched flake from rounded (water-worn?) cobble.	In cluster of lithics and turtle shell "gaming pieces" (Figs. 84-86 and Tables A13b-A13c) adjacent to left femur (see also Figs. 81-83).
33	85e	3.36	1.89	0.99	Gray chert, with small dark gray mottles; moderate luster; somewhat chalky, grayish-white cortex along 1 lateral edge; trace of smooth, grayish-white nodule exterior(?) on platform.	Elongate, thick, unretouched flake.	In cluster of lithics and turtle shell "gaming pieces" (Figs. 84-86 and Tables A13b-A13c) adjacent to left femur (see also Figs. 81-83).

Table A13g (cont.)

Item No.	Fig. No.	Max. Length[1] (cm)	Max. Breadth[2] (cm)	Max. Thick.[3] (cm)	Material	Description	Location and Comments
34	85f	3.76	3.59	1.34	Light gray to gray to yellowish-brown chert, mottled; moderate luster; thin, irregular, yellowish-brown cortex over much of dorsal surface.	Thick, crude, unretouched flake from weathered nodule or cobble.	In cluster of lithics and turtle shell "gaming pieces" (Figs. 84-86 and Tables A13b-A13c) adjacent to left femur (see also Figs. 81-83).
35	85g	4.64	3.70	1.39	Gray chert, with many tiny black specks; prominent band of dark gray to black chert near 1 margin; dull luster; yellowish-brown cortex along 1 lateral edge.	Large, thick, blocky, unretouched flake, removed from large, tabular core.	In cluster of lithics and turtle shell "gaming pieces" (Figs. 84-86 and Tables A13b-A13c) adjacent to left femur (see also Figs. 81-83).
36	86e	4.33	4.71	0.86	Light gray chert, with small dark gray mottles; moderate luster; tan to grayish-white cortex on exterior surface.	Distal end of very large, thin, ovoid, bifacial knife; flaking not invasive, leaving most of dorsal and ventral surfaces unretouched.	In cluster of lithics and turtle shell "gaming pieces" (Figs. 84-86 and Tables A13b-A13c) adjacent to left femur (see also Figs. 81-83).
48a	85j	4.55	3.52	1.12	Light gray to gray chert, lightly banded; dull to moderate luster; small area of chalky tan cortex at proximal end; thin, yellowish-brown patina or weathering on exterior (dorsal) surface.	Large, thick platform-trimming flake from tabular core (portion of original platform along 1 lateral edge); fine bifacial use damage along lateral edge opposite platform remnant (i.e., tool used as "backed knife").	In cluster of lithics and turtle shell "gaming pieces" (Figs. 84-86 and Tables A13b-A13c) adjacent to left femur (see also Figs. 81-83).
48b	86b	3.67	1.92	0.44	Light gray chert, slightly banded; dull to moderate luster; trace of tan cortex on platform.	Elongate, blade-like flake, with moderately heavy, bifacially alternating use damage on both lateral edges.	In cluster of lithics and turtle shell "gaming pieces" (Figs. 84-86 and Tables A13b-A13c) adjacent to left femur (see also Figs. 81-83).

Table A13g (cont.)

Item No.	Fig. No.	Max. Length[1] (cm)	Max. Breadth[2] (cm)	Max. Thick.[3] (cm)	Material	Description	Location and Comments
48c	86f	2.00	2.60	0.88	Light gray to gray chert, banded; dull to moderate luster; lightly abraded and patinated exterior surface of original pebble or cobble (waterworn?) preserved on platform.	Proximal fragment of crude (perhaps ovate) biface, worked bifacially along at least 1 lateral edge (opposite edge and distal end broken off).	In cluster of lithics and turtle shell "gaming pieces" (Figs. 84-86 and Tables A13b-A13c) adjacent to left femur (see also Figs. 81-83).
51a	86c	1.88	2.62	0.68	Pale maroon, with faint mottling or banding of light bluish gray; Alibates-like; moderate luster; platform and exterior surface entirely covered with abraded, pitted, and patinated cortex of small waterworn river cobble.	Lightly utilized(?), nearly circular, "side-struck" flake; trace of use on rounded edge opposite platform.	Found under left femur, near cluster of lithics and turtle shell "gaming pieces" (Figs. 84-86 and Tables A13b-A13c; see also Figs. 81-83.

[1]For flakes with platforms or on which percussion axis can be determined unambiguously, maximum length is measured perpendicular to platform or parallel to percussion axis; for chunks, core fragments, and other specimens in which the platform or percussion axis cannot be identified, maximum length is the maximum dimension of the specimen, regardless of orientation.

[2]Maximum breadth, measured perpendicular to maximum length.

[3]Maximum thickness, regardless of location on specimen.

APPENDIX 14

ARTIFACTS FROM FEATURE 36 BURIAL

Table A14a
Disc-shell beads found with Feature 36 burial

Total No.	Ave. No. Beads per cm (N)	Total Strand(s) Length (cm)	Diameter Ave. $\pm 1\sigma$ (N) (cm)	Location and Comments
169	7.2 (20)	22.9	0.424±0.024 (100)	Clustered near right wrist; either worn around wrist or in some manner associated with or attached to projectile point Cluster 1 (Figs. 91, 93 and Tables A14d, A14f); associated with 7 or 8 *Olivella* shell beads (Nos. 52–58, and possibly No. 26; Fig. 38ff-ll, y[?] and Table A14b).

Table A14b
Olivella and *Agaronia* shell beads found with Feature 36 burial (see Fig. 38x-nn)[1]

Item No.	Max. Length (cm)	Max. Breadth (cm)	Species[2]	Location and Comments
1	2.36	1.10	*Agaronia testacea* (Lamarck, 1811)	Fig. 38x; under chin, associated with 5 turquoise pendants (Nos. 1-5; Fig. 39k-o and Table A14c); probably worn around neck.
26	1.76	0.76	*O. dama* (Wood, 1828)	Fig. 38y; against midshaft region of left radius; probably originally part of concentration of beads (Nos. 52–58) near right wrist, either worn on wrist, or associated with point Cluster 1 (Fig. 93 and Tables A14d, A14f).
31	1.59	0.78	"	Fig. 38z; on left femur near midshaft; probably originally associated with point Cluster 2 (Fig. 94 and Tables A14e, A14g).
36	1.38	0.71	"	Fig. 38aa; against 2nd lumbar vertebra, directly within point Cluster 2 (Fig. 94 and Tables A14e, A14g).
49	1.39	0.70	"	Fig. 38bb; near base of feature pit, approx. 8 cm south of point Cluster 2 (Fig. 94 and Tables A14e, A14g; near bead No. 59); probably originally associated with points.
50a	1.39	0.65	"	Fig. 38cc; under proximal end of left femur; probably originally associated with point Cluster 2 (Fig. 94 and Tables A14e, A14g).
50b	1.45	0.72	"	Fig. 38dd; location same as No. 50a above.

Table A14b (cont.)

Item No.	Max. Length (cm)	Max. Breadth (cm)	Species[2]	Location and Comments
51	1.35	0.68	"	Fig. 38ee; near base of feature pit, approx. 10 cm south of point Cluster 2 (Fig. 94 and Tables A14e, A14g); probably originally associated with points.
52	1.66	0.77	"	Fig. 38ff; near right wrist, associated with bead Nos. 53-58; either worn on wrist, or originally associated with point Cluster 1 (Fig. 93 and Tables A14d, A14f).
53	1.48	0.76	"	Fig. 38gg; near right wrist, associated with bead Nos. 52, 54–58; either worn on wrist, or originally associated with point Cluster 1 (Fig. 93 and Tables A14d, A14f).
54	1.28	0.63	"	Fig. 38hh; near right wrist, associated with bead Nos. 52-53, 55–58; either worn on wrist, or originally associated with point Cluster 1 (Fig. 93 and Tables A14d, A14f).
55	(1.24)	0.66	"	Fig. 38ii; near right wrist, associated with bead Nos. 52-54, 56–58; either worn on wrist, or originally associated with point Cluster 1 (Fig. 93 and Tables A14d, A14f).
56	1.75	0.83	"	Fig. 38jj; near right wrist, associated with bead Nos. 52-55, 57–58; either worn on wrist, or originally associated with point Cluster 1 (Fig. 93 and Tables A14d, A14f).

Table A14b (cont.)

Item No.	Max. Length (cm)	Max. Breadth (cm)	Species[2]	Location and Comments
57	1.34	0.72	"	Fig. 38kk; near right wrist, associated with bead Nos. 52-56, 58; either worn on wrist, or originally associated with point Cluster 1 (Fig. 93 and Tables A14d, A14f).
58	1.25	0.63	"	Fig. 38ll; near right wrist, associated with bead Nos. 52-57; either worn on wrist, or originally associated with point Cluster 1 (Fig. 93 and Tables A14d, A14f).
59	[1.18]	0.72	"	Fig. 38mm; near base of feature pit, approx. 8 cm south of point Cluster 2 (Fig. 94 and Tables A14e, A14g); probably originally associated with points.
60	1.41	0.71	"	Fig. 38nn; near 2nd lumbar vertebra, directly associated with point Cluster 2 (Fig. 94 and Tables A14e, A14g).

[1]Numbers in parentheses are values, measured on slightly damaged specimens, which closely approximate true values; numbers in brackets are minimum values measured on broken specimens.
[2]We are grateful to James H. McLean, Curator of Malacology, Los Angeles County Museum of Natural History, for species identifications.

Table A14c
Turquoise found with Feature 36 burial (see Fig. 39k-o)

Item No.	Type	Max. Length (cm)	Max. Width (cm)	Max. Thick. (cm)	Weight (g)	Description	Location and Comments
1	Pendant	1.20	1.26	0.32	0.84	Trapezoidal, with lightly outcurving sides and rounded corners (Fig. 39k); biconical hole at smaller end (earlier hole on edge indicates pendant broken in use and redrilled).	Under chin; associated with 4 other turquoise pendants (Nos. 2–5) and large *Agaronia testacea* shell bead (No. 1; Fig. 38x and Table A14b); probably worn around neck.
2	Pendant	1.42	1.27	0.31	1.03	Trapezoidal, with lightly outcurving sides and rounded corners (Fig. 39l); biconical hole at smaller end.	Under chin; associated with 4 other turquoise pendants (Nos. 1, 3–5) and large *Agaronia testacea* shell bead (No. 1; Fig. 38x and Table A14b); probably worn around neck.
3	Pendant	1.57	1.19	0.28	0.86	Trapezoidal (elongated), with lightly outcurving sides and rounded corners; shortest edge of trapezoid strongly outcurving (Fig. 39m); biconical hole at smaller end.	Under chin; associated with 4 other turquoise pendants (Nos. 1–2, 4–5) and large *Agaronia testacea* shell bead (No. 1; Fig. 38x and Table A14b); probably worn around neck.
4	Pendant	1.68	1.50	0.45	1.82	Trapezoidal, with lightly outcurving sides and rounded corners (Fig. 39n); biconical hole at smaller end (earlier hole on edge indicates pendant broken in use and redrilled).	Under chin; associated with 4 other turquoise pendants (Nos. 1–3, 5) and large *Agaronia testacea* shell bead (No. 1; Fig. 38x and Table A14b); probably worn around neck.

Table A14c (cont.)

Item No.	Type	Max. Length (cm)	Max. Width (cm)	Max. Thick. (cm)	Weight (g)	Description	Location and Comments
5	Pendant	1.91	1.52	0.38	1.81	Trapezoidal, with strongly out-curving sides and rounded corners (Fig. 39o); biconical hole at smaller end.	Under chin; associated with 4 other turquoise pendants (Nos. 1–4) and large *Agaronia testacea* shell bead (No. 1; Fig. 38x and Table A14b); probably worn around neck.

Table A14d
Projectile points and knives found with Feature 36 burial (Cluster 1):[1]
Metric attributes (see Figs. 95–97)

Item No.[2]	Max. Length[3] (cm)	Max. Width[4] (cm)	Max. Thick.[5] (cm)	Weight (g)	Min. Neck Width[6] (cm)	Max. Base/Stem Width[7] (cm)	Max. Length of Haft-Element[8] (cm)
1	3.54	1.83	0.41	1.58	0.43	0.66	0.79
2	3.99	(2.78)[9]	0.51	4.00	1.31	1.46	0.83
3	6.20	(3.77)[9]	0.52	8.84	2.31	(2.83)[10]	1.18
5	5.12	[3.11][11]	0.44	5.45	1.56	2.45	1.29
6	5.07	3.85	0.58	8.10	1.75	2.01	1.00
7	7.34	2.72	0.78	14.18	1.38	1.91	1.38
8	7.04	4.51	0.81	18.87	1.80	2.28	1.21
9	5.09	(3.45)[9]	0.60	8.59	1.80	1.97	0.92
10	4.08	2.98	0.54	4.61	1.40	1.40	1.12
11	3.83	2.13	0.51	3.57	1.18	1.32	0.85
12	3.17	1.79	0.40	1.69	0.75	1.22	0,83
13	(3.51)[12]	2.14	0.67	4.37	1.47	1.73	1.23
14	1.09	0.79	0.17	0.10	0.30	0.79	0.47
15	3.63	2.33	0.41	2.40	0.67	(0.68)[10]	(0.50)[13]
16	4.29	2.39	0.48	4.19	1.22	2.22	0.80
17	3.78	2.31	0.58	4.24	1.54	2.34	1.16
19	2.08	1.26	0.33	0.58	0.63	0.76	0.39
20	3.67	(1.99)[14]	0.53	3.28	1.29	1.67	1.12
22	4.50	1.90	0.69	6.52	1.65(?)[15]	1.74	(1.16)[15]
23	4.56	2.05	0.63	5.94	1.06	0.84	1.18
24	4.27	2.09	0.63	5.11	1.38	1.86	1.04
27	5.00	2.47	0.99	9.74	1.46	1.96	1.27
28	3.94	2.51	0.67	5.73	1.43	1.77	1.01
29	(5.34)[12]	(2.95)[9]	0.56	6.68	1.37	(2.01)[16]	1.22
30	4.60	(2.85)[9]	0.51	5.35	1.31	1.76	1.20

Table A14d (cont.)

Item No.[2]	Max. Length[3] (cm)	Max. Width[4] (cm)	Max. Thick.[5] (cm)	Weight (g)	Min. Neck Width[6] (cm)	Max. Base/Stem Width[7] (cm)	Max. Length of Haft-Element[8] (cm)
46	4.31	(2.79)[9]	0.49	5.02	1.34	1.51	1.44
47	6.27	3.25	0.62	12.51	2.65	3.25	1.42
48	1.67	1.15	0.30	0.40	n.a.	1.15	n.a.

[1] Numbers in parentheses are values, measured on slightly damaged specimens, which closely approximate true values; numbers in brackets are minimum values measured on broken specimens; n.a., not applicable.

[2] Sequential field numbers; missing numbers are items other than points (e.g., beads).

[3] Maximum length from tip to most proximal part of base parallel to long axis.

[4] Maximum width on blade or base, perpendicular to long axis.

[5] Maximum thickness.

[6] Minimum distance between notches; in contracting stem varieties, width at distal end of stem (i.e., at shoulder or point where stem joins blade).

[7] Maximum width of haft-element; in contracting stem varieties, maximum width at proximal end of stem (i.e., at base of stem).

[8] In notched varieties, maximum length from most distal edge of notches to most proximal part of base, parallel to long axis; in contracting stem varieties, maximum length from distal end of stem (i.e., at shoulder or point where stem joins blade) to most proximal part of stem, parallel to long axis.

[9] One or both tangs damaged.

[10] Base damaged

[11] One or both tangs broken.

[12] Tip damaged.

[13] Stem damaged.

[14] One or both tangs may be reworked.

[15] Notches indistinct and asymmetrically placed.

[16] One or both edges damaged.

[17] Base reworked and possibly damaged.

Table A14e
Projectile points and knives found with Feature 36 burial (Cluster 2): Metric attributes (see Figs. 98, 99)[1]

Item No.[2]	Max. Length[3] (cm)	Max. Width[4] (cm)	Max. Thick.[5] (cm)	Weight (g)	Min. Neck Width[6] (cm)	Max. Base/Stem Width[7] (cm)	Max. Length of Haft-Element[8] (cm)
18	4.76	3.56	0.66	8.25	1.70	1.97	1.05
25	3.94	2.11	0.62	4.54	1.44	1.81	1.01
32	3.07	2.21	0.52	3.14	1.37	1.65	0.70
33	3.09	1.49	0.36	1.43	0.63	0.97	0.60
34	5.06	(2.89)[9]	0.51	6.46	1.37	(1.67)[10]	1.30
35	7.94	3.28	0.76	21.53	2.25	(2.41)[17]	1.59
37	5.98	2.90	0.62	9.15	1.58	1.42	1.20
38	6.11	3.33	0.61	9.29	2.25	3.33	1.75
39	3.63	(2.19)[9]	0.56	4.05	1.40	(1.68)[10]	0.98
40	8.82	4.33	0.94	30.85	3.47	4.33	1.98
41	12.65	4.90	1.09	58.22	1.94	2.12	1.93
42	8.56	3.65	0.71	23.74	2.71	3.64	1.75
43	4.10	(2.62)[9]	0.51	3.88	1.34	1.50	0.70
44	3.80	(2.15)[9]	0.46	3.01	1.00	1.38	0.83
45	3.44	(1.94)[9]	0.43	2.59	1.02	1.09	0.61

[1] Numbers in parentheses are values, measured on slightly damaged specimens, which closely approximate true values; numbers in brackets are minimum values measured on broken specimens; n.a., not applicable.
[2] Sequential field numbers; missing numbers are items other than points (e.g., beads).
[3] Maximum length from tip to most proximal part of base, parallel to long axis.
[4] Maximum width on blade or base, perpendicular to long axis.
[5] Maximum thickness.
[6] Minimum distance between notches; in contracting stem varieties, width at distal end of stem (i.e., at shoulder or point where stem joins blade).

[7] Maximum width of haft-element; in contracting stem varieties, maximum width at proximal end of stem (i.e., at base of stem).

[8] In notched varieties, maximum length from most distal edge of notches to most proximal part of base, parallel to long axis; in contracting stem varieties, maximum length from distal end of stem (i.e., at shoulder or point where stem joins blade) to most proximal part of stem, parallel to long axis.

[9] One or both tangs damaged.

[10] Base damaged

[11] One or both tangs broken.

[12] Tip damaged.

[13] Stem damaged.

[14] One or both tangs may be reworked.

[15] Notches indistinct and asymmetrically placed.

[16] One or both edges damaged.

[17] Base reworked and possibly damaged.

Table A14f
Projectile points and knives found with Feature 36 burial (Cluster 1): Description of points and materials (see Figs. 95–97)

Item No.[1]	Red Ocher[2]	Haft Type	Material Type and Description[3]	Location and Comments[4]
1	+	Narrow, irregular, slightly expanding stem; sharply tanged; broad corner notches; straight base.	Petrified wood; banded dark brown, with lines of tiny white specks (wood grain); opaque; dull luster.	Fig. 95a
2	+	Broad, slightly expanding stem; broadly tanged; broad corner notches; straight base.	Chert; heavily weathered; patinated areas light brown; unpatinated areas light brownish gray; opaque; dull luster.	Fig. 95b; both sides of blade (distal half) reworked after heavy patina had formed.
3	+	Broad expanding stem; sharply tanged; narrow, moderately deep corner notches; straight base.	Edwards Plateau chert; light gray; opaque, except along margins; dull luster.	Fig. 95c
5	+	Broad expanding stem; sharply tanged; narrow, deep corner notches; slightly convex base.	Possible Edwards Plateau chert; faintly banded light whitish gray; opaque; moderate luster; prominent white band (opaque, waxy) on distal end of blade.	Fig. 95d
6	+	Broad, slightly expanding stem; sharply tanged; narrow, deep basal notches; straight base.	Edwards Plateau chert; light brownish gray, with single white patch; opaque; moderate luster.	Fig. 95e; possible light grinding or abrasion on lateral edge of one tang.

Table A14f (cont.)

Item No.[1]	Red Ocher[2]	Haft Type	Material Type and Description[3]	Location and Comments[4]
7	–	Broad expanding stem; barely tanged; irregular, shallow corner notches (1 narrow, 1 open); convex base.	Alibates; banded maroon (dominant), rust-colored, and light bluish gray, with single brownish black patch; opaque; dull luster.	Fig. 95f; portion of original tabular block preserved on base.
8	+	Broad expanding stem; sharply tanged; narrow, deep basal notches; straight base.	Edwards Plateau chert; light brownish gray, with many small light brown mottles; opaque; dull luster.	Fig. 95g; possible light abrasion or grinding on one lateral tang and blade edge; slight polish on one face of blade at tip.
9	+	Broad, slightly expanding stem; sharply tanged; narrow, deep basal to corner notches; straight base.	Edwards Plateau chert; one side of blade heavily patinated; patina light brownish gray; unpatinated areas medium brownish gray; opaque; dull luster.	Fig. 95h; one side of blade and base reworked after heavy patina had formed; possible light abrasion or grinding on lateral edge of one tang.
10	+	Broad straight stem; one side sharply tanged; straight base.	Igneous? chert; probably weathered and patinated; pale brown to brownish gray; pinkish hue on both faces (heat treated?); opaque; dull luster; grayish white patch (opaque, waxy) on blade margin distal to stem.	Fig. 95i; black surface stain on both faces (manganese?) from long surface exposure; one or both blade edges may have been slightly reworked before patina or manganese stain had been formed.

Table A14f (cont.)

Item No.[1]	Red Ocher[2]	Haft Type	Material Type and Description[3]	Location and Comments[4]
11	+	Moderate-sized, slightly expanding stem; not tanged; broad, shallow corner notches; straight base.	Chert; light brownish gray; opaque; dull luster.	Fig. 95j; made on minimally retouched flake; base formed by unretouched terminal hinge fracture of original flake.
12	+	Narrow expanding stem; slightly tanged; narrow, moderately deep corner notches; slightly convex base.	Chert; faintly banded light grayish white to whitish gray; opaque; dull luster.	Fig. 96a; surface of blade tip visibly polished from use in piercing or gouging.
13	+	Broad, slightly expanding stem; not tanged; broad, shallow corner notches (approaching side notches); convex base.	Chert; pale brown (dominant), with thin rust-colored bands; both faces have pinkish hue and incipient potlid fractures (heat treated); opaque; dull to moderate luster.	Fig. 96b
14	–	Tiny v-shaped side notches; broadly indented, concave base (approaching basal notch).	Probable Alibates; lightly banded reddish pink (dominant) and maroon; opaque; moderate luster.	Fig. 96c
15	+	Narrow, asymmetrical, straight to slightly expanding stem (broken off?); sharply tanged; irregular shallow, basal notches (1 narrow, 1 open); base missing.	Alibates; banded maroon (dominant), light bluish gray, and grayish white; linear, tiny maroon speckles; opaque; dull luster.	Fig. 96d

Table A14f (cont.)

Item No.[1]	Red Ocher[2]	Haft Type	Material Type and Description[3]	Location and Comments[4]
16	–	Slightly tanged; narrow, moderately deep side notches (close to base); slightly convex base.	Jasper or chalcedony (possible Tecovas); dark red; opaque; moderate luster, with white chalcedony patch (translucent, waxy) at base.	Fig. 96e
17	–	Broad expanding stem; slightly tanged; broad, shallow corner notches; straight base.	Igneous(?) chert; faintly banded light pinkish brown; opaque; dull, slightly grainy luster; many small oval white (opaque, waxy) mottles.	Fig. 96f
19	–	Narrow expanding stem; slightly tanged; small, shallow corner notches; straight to slightly convex base.	Chalcedony; white, with two small rust-colored bands; translucent; waxy luster.	Fig. 96g
20	–	Broad expanding stem; slightly tanged on one side; broad, shallow corner notches; straight to slightly convex base.	Chert; pale brown (dominant) to light yellowish brown; opaque; moderate to waxy luster.	Fig. 96h; small trace of cortex on one face; both blade edges slightly irregular, perhaps due to reworking.
22	–	Broad, very slightly expanding stem; not tanged; very shallow, asymmetrically placed side notches; straight base.	Jasper; dark yellowish brown, with small yellowish patches and small light gray to clear vuggy mottles; opaque; dull to moderate, slightly grainy luster.	Fig. 96i

Table A14f (cont.)

Item No.[1]	Red Ocher[2]	Haft Type	Material Type and Description[3]	Location and Comments[4]
23	–	Narrow, irregular, tapering stem; not tanged; no true notches; irregular base.	Chert; mottled to swirled black and light gray, with small patches of white; opaque; dull luster.	Fig. 96j; made on strongly curved flake; most retouch confined to convex face; tip retouched bifacially into drill.
24	+	Not tanged; small, shallow, semi-circular side notches; slightly concave base.	Possible Edwards Plateau chert; light brownish gray; small patch of grayish white at tip; opaque; dull luster.	Fig. 97a; abrasion or grinding on lateral edges of base, on blade edges just distal to notches, and both edges at tip.
27	+	Broad expanding stem; one side slightly tanged; shallow corner notches (1 narrow, 1 open); convex base.	Possible Edwards Plateau chert; highly weathered and patinated; faintly banded pale brown; opaque; dull luster; small patch of gray (opaque, waxy) on blade.	Fig. 97b; heavy abrasion or grinding on lateral edge of tang.
28	+	Broad, slightly expanding stem; one side slightly tanged; shallow corner notches (1 narrow, 1 open); straight to slightly convex base.	Chert; dark gray to dark brown (base) and medium brown (tip); opaque; moderate to waxy luster; patch of light brown cortex (dull, grainy) on blade.	Fig. 97c; heavy abrasion on lateral edges distal to notches; tip heavily ground and rounded from use as drill.
29	–	Broad expanding stem; sharply tanged; narrow, deep corner notches; straight base.	Chert; dark brown; opaque; dull luster.	Fig. 97d; heavy abrasion or grinding on both edges of blade and at least one tang; slight burin-like damage at tip.

Table A14f (cont.)

Item No.[1]	Red Ocher[2]	Haft Type	Material Type and Description[3]	Location and Comments[4]
30	+	Broad, slightly expanding stem; sharply tanged; narrow, deep basal (or corner?) notches; slightly convex base.	Possible Edwards Plateau chert; light brownish gray, with small light brownish gray mottles; pinkish to lavender hue (heat treated); opaque; moderate luster.	Fig. 97e; no crazing or potlid fractures.
46	+	Broad, nearly straight stem; slightly tanged; broad, open corner notches; slightly convex base.	Possible Edwards Plateau chert; heavily weathered and patinated; unpatinated reworked areas light brownish gray; patinated areas (dominant) pale brown; opaque; dull luster.	Fig. 97f; one side of blade reworked after heavy patina had formed; moderate abrasion or grinding on lateral edge of one tang.
47	+	Not tanged; shallow, moderately open side notches; straight base.	Edwards Plateau chert; medium to dark gray; semi-translucent; moderate luster.	Fig. 97g; both faces of blade lightly patinated; light abrasion or grinding on one or both lateral edges of base below notches; base slightly reworked after patina had formed.
48	–	No stem or notches; corners slightly tanged; slightly indented, straight base (original point probably stemmed, slightly tanged, and corner notched; stem probably broken in use and base reworked into triangular point).	Edwards Plateau chert; banded light to dark gray; opaque; moderate luster.	Fig. 97h

[1]Sequential field numbers; missing numbers are items other than points (e.g., beads).
[2]Presence (+), absence (−); determined by visual inspection only.
[3]Materials identified by visual inspection only; assistance in identifications provided by Dee Ann Story, Curtis Tunnell, David S. Dibble, Larry D. Banks, Harry J. Shafer, Michael Collins, and Robert H. Leslie.
[4]Abrasion identified by visual inspection only.

Table A14g
Projectile points and knives found with Feature 36 burial (Cluster 2):
Description of points and materials (see Figs. 98, 99)

Item No.[1]	Red Ocher[2]	Haft Type	Material Type and Description[3]	Location and Comments[4]
18	+	Broad expanding stem; sharply tanged; narrow, deep basal notches; slightly convex base.	Edwards Plateau chert; light brownish gray; opaque; moderate luster.	Fig. 98a; possible tiny impact fracture on one face originating at tip.
25	+	Broad expanding stem; one side slightly tanged; shallow, small corner notches; convex base.	"Fingerprint" chert (probably from Sacramento Mountain region; resembles Kay County, Okla. chert, but lacks visible fusilinid fossils); finely banded light brown and medium brown; slightly pinkish hue (heat treated?); opaque; moderate to waxy luster.	Fig. 98b
32	+	Broad, slightly expanding stem; one side sharply tanged; small, shallow corner notches; slightly concave base.	Probable Alibates dark purple with tiny mottles of light bluish gray; large reddish zone along one edge; opaque; dull luster.	Fig. 98c; matting or coiled basketry adhering to one face.
33	+	Small, narrow expanding stem; slightly tanged; small, narrow corner notches; slightly concave base.	Possible Edwards Plateau chert; light brownish gray to light yellowish brown; opaque; dull to moderate luster.	Fig. 98d

Table A14g (cont.)

Item No.[1]	Red Ocher[2]	Haft Type	Material Type and Description[3]	Location and Comments[4]
34	+	Broad, slightly expanding stem; sharply tanged; narrow, deep corner notches; straight base.	Possible Edwards Plateau chert; heavily weathered and patinated; pale brown (dominant) to brownish gray; slight pinkish hue on one face of blade (heat treated?); opaque; dull luster.	Fig. 98e; no crazing or potlid fractures; curvilinear black surface stain (manganese?) on one side of blade from long surface exposure; both edges slightly reworked after patina had formed.
35	+	Broad expanding stem; not tanged; shallow side notches; concave base (reworked or damaged).	Edwards Plateau chert; dark gray, with small light gray mottles; opaque; waxy luster.	Fig. 98f; beveled knife; probably broken in use near original midpoint and reworked at break to create side-notched haft-element.
37	+	Broad, slightly contracting, straight stem; one side slightly tanged; straight to slightly concave base.	Possible Edwards Plateau chert; light brownish gray to light yellowish brown; opaque; dull to moderate luster.	Fig. 98g; no visible abrasion or grinding on stem.
38	–	Not tanged; shallow, relatively narrow side notches; slightly convex base.	Edwards Plateau chert; light brownish gray; opaque, except along margins; moderate luster.	Fig. 98h; possible light abrasion or grinding on lateral edge of one tang; tip slightly polished and rounded.

Table A14g (cont.)

Item No.[1]	Red Ocher[2]	Haft Type	Material Type and Description[3]	Location and Comments[4]
39	+	Broad, slightly expanding stem; not tanged (tangs may have been reworked); irregular, shallow, open corner notches; straight to slightly concave base.	Possible Alibates; lightly banded grayish white (dominant), with traces of light brownish gray and light reddish brown; opaque; moderate luster.	Fig. 98i; each notch made by removing single large percussion flake (possibly reworked to remove tangs?); tip tapers as though for use as drill; no visible abrasion or grinding.
40	+	Not tanged; shallow, relatively narrow side notches; concave base.	Edwards Plateau chert; light brownish gray blade, with light gray patch near base; opaque; moderate luster.	Fig. 99a; possible light abrasion or grinding on lateral edges of base below notches.
41	+	Haft-element resembles eastern Late Archaic "Turkey Tail"; shallow, open, semicircular side notches; rounded base.	Chert; wavy banded dark (chocolate) brown and medium brown; resembles longitudinal section of pine wood grain, but material does not appear to be petrified wood; material may be unusual variant of Alibates, though resemblance is remote; see discussion, chapter 2; opaque; moderate luster.	Fig. 99b

Table A14g (cont.)

Item No.[1]	Red Ocher[2]	Haft Type	Material Type and Description[3]	Location and Comments[4]
42	+	Not tanged; shallow, moderately open side notches; straight base.	Probable Alibates; broadly banded light bluish gray (dominant) and light brownish gray to light brown; small traces of white to grayish white; opaque; moderate luster.	Fig. 99c; beveled blade; may be broken beveled knife with new haft-element reworked along original break; no evidence of former break detectable; portions of original tabular block preserved on one face of blade; opposite face of blade polished (from use?) on elevated ridges between flake scars.
43	+	Broad, slightly expanding stem; sharply tanged; small, narrow basal notches (close to corners); straight base.	Alibates; banded dark maroon (dominant), light maroon to purple, and light bluish gray; opaque; dull luster.	Fig. 99d; one edge of blade partly reworked.
44	+	moderate-sized expanding stem; sharply tanged; narrow, deep corner notches; straight to slightly concave base.	Chert; banded light gray to light brownish gray; opaque; dull to moderate luster.	Fig. 99e

Table A14g (cont.)

Item No.[1]	Red Ocher[2]	Haft Type	Material Type and Description[3]	Location and Comments[4]
45	+	Moderate-sized, slightly expanding stem; small, shallow, irregular corner notches; slightly convex base.	Possible Edwards Plateau chert; heavily weathered and patinated; pale brown to brownish gray; pinkish hue (heat treated?); opaque; dull luster.	Fig. 99f; heavy abrasion or grinding on base, proximal end of one blade edge, and distal end of other blade edge; most heavily abraded blade edge also partly reworked; one face of blade and stem has black stain (manganese?) from long surface exposure.

[1] Sequential field numbers; missing numbers are items other than points (e.g., beads).
[2] Presence (+), absence (−); determined by visual inspection only.
[3] Materials identified by visual inspection only; assistance in identifications provided by Dee Ann Story, Curtis Tunnell, David S. Dibble, Larry D. Banks, Harry J. Shafer, Michael Collins, and Robert H. Leslie.
[4] Abrasion identified by visual inspection only.

APPENDIX 15

ARTIFACTS FROM FEATURE 40 BURIAL

Table A15a
Pottery bowl found with Feature 40 burial:
Metric attributes and description (see Figs. 105-109)[1]

Item No.	Type	Max. Diam. (cm)	Max. Height (cm)	Ave. Thick. (cm)	Exterior Treatment	Interior Treatment	Location and Comments
1	Heshotauthla Polychrome	29.7	12.2	0.65±	Orange-red slip (bright); polished, crackled surface; dark black, friable core, filled (40-50%) with fine to medium grayish-white grit temper (crushed volcanic rock?); 3 stylized butterflies (bats or water insects?) in black glaze paint (Figs. 106-109); 2 butterflies in black only (max. wingspans 9.0 cm and 7.5 cm); 1 butterfly with white dots in wings (max. wingspan 9.0 cm; Fig. 106); small brown firing clouds on sides of vessel; bottom of bowl rounded, smooth.	Orange-red slip (bright); polished, crackled surface; black glaze paint, heavy, uniform, very few bubbles, no drips; lines uneven, poorly executed; geometric design of parallel lines, zigzags, and other elements; design field divided in thirds.	Found inverted over head and face of burial (see Figs. 103, 104); vessel complete, but broken in place subsequent to burial (not "killed").

[1]We are grateful to Carla Sinopoli, David H. Snow, Barbara Mills, T. J. Ferguson, and Stephanie Whittlesey for their assistance in identifying and describing this vessel.

Table A15b
Turquoise found with Feature 40 burial (see Fig. 39p)

Item No.	Type	Max. Length (cm)	Max. Width (cm)	Max. Thick. (cm)	Weight (g)	Description	Location and Comments
1	Pendant	2.01	1.27	0.31	1.05	Rectangular, with moderately outcurving sides and rounded corners (Fig. 39p); small, biconical hole at one end; pale, almost grayish-white in color.	On upper right ribs, overlying right scapula; probably worn around neck.

APPENDIX 16

PERISHABLE VEGETAL ARTIFACTS FROM HENDERSON

Table A16a
Identification of organic materials found with Henderson burials[1]

Identification	Material	Description	Feat. No.	Location
1. Twined mat	Clay impression	See Table A16b and Fig. 22	1	L. humerus
2. Twined mat	Clay impression	See Table A16b and Fig. 23	1	Skull (left side)
3. Twined mat	Clay impression	3 pieces; same type as No. 2 above	1	Skull (left side)
4. Bark	Coniferous?	Decayed frags.	1	R. ilium
5. Bark	Dicot. root	Small frags.	1	L. orbit
6. Warp	Grass	Small frags.	1	Skull
7. Twined mat	Grass	1 weft and 2 warp frags.	1	Neck (behind)
8. Cordage	Vegetal fiber	z-twist, 2-strand, 16.5 mm long	3	L. foot
9. Cordage	Vegetal fiber	z-twist, 2-strand, 10 pieces	3	L. foot
10. Cordage	Vegetal fiber	z-twist, 2-strand, 8 pieces	3	L. foot
11. Twined mat	Grass	Warp and weft frags.	3	L. foot
12. Plug?	Dicot.? wood	0.70 cm long by 0.56 cm diam. (distorted by shrinkage?)	3	Inside tubular bone bead No. 3 (see Table A10h)
13. Prayer-stick	Dicot. wood	*Populus*? (see Fig. 36)	3	On chest

Table A16a (cont.)

Identification	Material	Description	Feat. No.	Location
14. Post	Dicot. wood	*Populus*?; small decayed frags.	7	Post pit within Feat. 3
15. Coiled basket	Clay impression	Coil 3.9 mm diam.	8	R. knee
16. Coiled basket	Clay impression	Coil 2.9 mm diam. (see Fig. 52)	8	On chest (between skull and r. knee)
17. Coiled basket	Clay impression	Coil 3.3 mm diam.	8	R. ribs
18. Red color	Clay impression	No obvious structure	8	Skull (behind)
19. Coiled basket	Clay impression	Coil 2.3 mm diam.	8	R. scapula
20. Root	Dicot.	Recent intrusive growth	8	R. femur (under)
21. Rootlets	Dicot.	Recent intrusive growth[2]	8	Skull (right side)
22. Rootlets	Dicot.	Recent intrusive growth[2]	8	Chest
23. Rootlets	Dicot.	Recent intrusive growth[2]	8	Skull (inside)
24. Plaited mat or basket	Yucca	1 frag. (see Fig. 53)	8	Skull (behind)
25. Coiled basket	Clay impression	Coil 2.9 mm diam.	8	L. knee
26. Twined mat	Grass	12 frags. (see Table A16b and Fig. 66)	21	L. foot

Table A16a (cont.)

Identification	Material	Description	Feat. No.	Location
27. Twined mat	Grass	Warp frags.	21	L. temporal
28. Cordage	Vegetal fiber	z-twist, 2-strand, 11 pieces	21	L. foot
29. Prayer-stick	Dicot. wood	*Juglans* (walnut); see Figs. 73–74	25	Slumped from chest
30. Twined mat	Clay impression	See Table A16b	25	West margin of burial pit
31. Twined mat	Grass	See Table A16b	25	Pit base near chest
32. Twined mat	Grass	Warp frags.	25	Pit base near chest
33. Unknown	Organic	Possibly bark	25	Proximal end of prayer-stick (Item No. 9; see Table A12a)
34. Coiled basket	Wood and yucca	1 rod (frag.), coil 7.5 mm diam.	36	Lumbar region
35. Coiled basket	Wood	1 rod, coil 7.5 mm diam.	36	Lumbar region
36. Basket rods	Wood	Coiled basket frags.	36	Lumbar region
37. Basket rods	Wood	Coiled basket frags.	36	Lumbar region
38. Sticks (basket rods?)	Wood	15 frags.	36	R. wrist

[1] We are extremely grateful to Richard I. Ford for examining the matting, basketry, prayer-sticks, and other organic materials found with the Henderson burials.

[2] These specimens in the field were thought to be string or cordage.

Table A16b
Attributes of twined matting found with Henderson burials[1]

No.[2]	Material	Twining Type	Stitch Slant	Warp Width	No. of Warps/cm	Weft Row Gap	Feat. No.	Location
1	Impression	Open	---	6.4	2.0	17.7	1	L. humerus
2	Impression	Open	---	7.4	1.7	20.2	1	Skull (left side)
26	Grass	Open	S	5.1	2.0	18.7	21	L. foot
30	Impression	Open	---	4.7	2.5	---	25	West margin of burial pit
31	Grass	Open	S	5.2	2.0	11.5	25	Pit base near chest

[1]We are extremely grateful to Richard I. Ford for examining the matting, basketry, prayer-sticks, and other organic materials found with the Henderson burials.
[2]See Table A16a.

APPENDIX 17

LOT NUMBER SYSTEM

At the beginning of the first field season in 1980, we labeled every artifact (bone, lithic, ceramic, etc.) with complete provenience information. This information included the Museum of New Mexico site number (LA-1549); grid square (followed by a sequential field item number and quadrant within the 1 m square, when appropriate; e.g., 515N533E/1/W); and stratigraphic level (usually an upper and lower value in meters above or below Datum A=100.00 m). Where a single, precise elevation for an item was shot in with a transit, a 1 cm range is coded in this appendix (e.g., 100.91–100.90 m).

It quickly became apparent that this labeling procedure was too cumbersome and time-consuming. We therefore initiated an alternative system in which a single, unique, sequential lot number was assigned to each discrete provenience, usually a bag of material from a single excavation level in a single 1 m square. Lot numbers were written directly on every item, on the bags themselves (which have been saved as a backup record until publication of the system), and in a master notebook. Lot numbers were assigned in the order that bags were received; as a consequence, they do not correspond in any straightforward manner to provenience or level. Thus, a permanent, published record of the lot numbers and their associated provenience information is vital to assure that archaeologists in the future can reanalyze the Henderson material with full access to all essential data.

The following information is recorded in this appendix:

Column **Information**

2–5 *Sequential Lot Number* (note that there are small gaps in the sequence because a few lot numbers were never assigned).

9999=no lot number assigned (indicates that complete provenience information was recorded directly on the material)

7–9 *Grid North* (in meters)

11–13 *Grid East* (in meters)

15–16 *Field Item Number* (sequential by grid square; usually assigned to significant items for which an exact elevation was determined).

99=no item number assigned

18 *Quadrant* (within 1-m grid square; especially important when square spanned a wall; quadrant indicates on which side of wall item was found).

1=N
2=E
3=S
4=W
5=NE
6=SE
7=SW
8=NW
9=no quadrant recorded

20–25 *Upper Level* (in meters above or below Datum A=100.00 m).

999.99=no level determined

27–32 *Lower Level* (in meters above or below Datum A = 100.00 m).

999.99 = no level determined

34–35 *Feature Number* (i.e., burials, pits, hearths, post holes, etc.).

99 = non-feature

37–38 *Comments*

01 = all items on Center Bar surface disturbed by pothunting
02 = item in contact with room floor
03 = items from multiple squares during surface shovel stripping
04 = material recovered in fill of pedestals
05 = item associated with another numbered item
06 = material from cleaning profile
07 = material from Level C
08 = material from Lens 1
99 = all other materials

Table A17a
Lot number system used at Henderson Site

Lot No.	Grid North	Grid East	Item No.	Quad	Upper Level	Lower Level	Feat. No.	Comm.
0001	522	534	99	9	102.25	102.24	99	01
0002	526	565	99	9	101.15	101.05	99	99
0003	521	562	99	9	101.15	101.05	99	99
0004	513	534	99	9	101.15	101.05	99	99
0005	525	561	99	1	100.90	100.85	99	99
0006	525	561	04	1	100.94	100.93	99	99
0007	523	567	99	9	101.25	101.15	99	04
0008	522	566	99	9	101.25	101.15	99	04
0009	526	564	99	9	101.54	101.25	99	99
0010	526	565	99	9	101.25	101.15	99	99
0011	515	533	99	9	101.80	101.70	99	99
0012	511	535	99	9	101.15	101.05	99	99
0013	513	535	99	9	101.45	101.35	99	04
0014	510	534	99	9	101.15	101.05	99	99
0015	513	530	99	9	101.70	101.65	99	04
0016	527	563	99	9	100.95	100.85	99	99
0017	526	563	99	9	101.05	100.88	99	99
0018	527	563	99	9	101.05	100.95	99	99
0019	525	563	99	9	101.54	101.25	99	99
0020	526	566	99	9	101.15	101.05	99	99
0021	522	564	99	9	101.46	101.25	99	99
0022	528	564	99	2	101.15	101.05	99	99
0023	528	565	99	9	101.05	100.95	99	99
0024	512	535	99	9	101.10	101.05	99	99
0025	524	562	99	9	101.06	101.05	99	99
0026	512	531	99	9	101.45	101.40	99	99
0027	515	534	99	9	100.70	100.65	99	99
0028	513	534	99	9	101.15	101.05	99	99
0029	515	533	99	9	101.40	101.30	99	99
0030	523	535	99	9	100.72	100.54	99	02
0031	525	566	99	9	101.55	101.25	99	99
0032	512	532	99	9	101.78	101.77	99	03
0033	514	530	99	9	101.65	101.55	99	99
0034	508	533	99	9	101.00	100.99	99	03
0035	508	528	99	9	101.00	100.99	99	03
0036	516	533	99	2	100.75	100.70	99	99
0037	521	565	99	9	101.15	101.05	99	99
0038	521	563	99	9	101.39	101.25	99	99
0039	524	562	99	9	101.25	101.15	99	99
0040	512	533	99	9	101.30	101.25	99	99
0041	513	535	99	9	101.50	101.45	99	99
0042	515	533	99	9	101.70	101.60	99	99
0043	513	533	99	9	101.89	101.80	99	99
0044	525	564	99	9	101.30	101.25	99	99
0045	515	533	99	9	101.60	101.50	99	99

Table A17a (cont.)

Lot No.	Grid North	Grid East	Item No.	Quad	Upper Level	Lower Level	Feat. No.	Comm.
0046	510	534	99	9	101.28	101.15	99	99
0047	521	563	99	9	101.25	101.15	99	04
0048	513	533	99	9	101.65	101.60	99	99
0049	524	561	99	9	101.36	101.25	99	99
0050	514	533	99	9	101.55	101.45	99	99
0051	522	561	99	9	101.34	101.25	99	99
0052	525	562	99	1	100.90	100.85	99	99
0053	515	535	07	9	101.07	101.06	99	99
0054	514	535	99	1	101.00	100.90	99	99
0055	514	535	99	9	101.45	101.35	99	99
0056	525	566	99	9	101.55	101.25	99	99
0057	523	562	99	9	101.25	101.15	99	99
0058	514	535	99	9	101.50	101.45	99	04
0059	516	533	99	9	101.55	101.45	99	99
0060	514	532	99	9	101.70	101.60	99	99
0061	522	563	99	9	101.25	101.15	99	04
0062	526	564	99	4	100.90	100.80	99	99
0063	525	562	04	1	100.93	100.92	99	99
0064	522	563	99	9	101.25	101.15	99	99
0065	516	533	99	9	101.75	101.65	99	99
0066	513	534	99	9	101.40	101.30	99	04
0067	512	532	99	9	101.55	101.50	99	99
0068	511	530	99	9	101.30	101.20	99	04
0069	525	565	99	9	101.15	101.05	99	99
0070	514	534	99	1	100.37	100.36	09	99
0071	512	530	99	9	101.50	101.40	99	04
0072	523	564	99	9	101.25	101.15	99	99
0073	513	533	99	9	101.55	101.50	99	99
0074	514	531	99	9	102.04	101.95	99	99
0075	525	565	99	9	101.54	101.53	99	03
0076	512	535	99	9	101.30	101.25	99	99
0077	514	534	99	9	101.35	101.25	99	99
0078	514	530	99	9	101.90	101.85	99	99
0079	514	535	99	9	101.35	101.25	99	99
0080	510	532	99	9	101.20	101.15	99	99
0081	522	561	99	9	101.15	101.05	99	99
0082	511	532	99	9	101.15	101.10	99	99
0083	512	530	99	9	101.70	101.60	99	04
0084	515	535	99	9	101.20	101.10	99	99
0085	512	530	99	9	101.60	101.50	99	04
0086	523	561	99	9	101.25	101.15	99	99
0087	523	561	99	9	101.15	101.05	99	99
0088	523	562	99	9	101.15	101.05	99	99
0089	510	533	99	9	101.20	101.15	99	99
0090	513	530	99	9	101.55	101.45	99	99
0091	516	533	99	9	102.09	101.75	99	99
0092	515	535	99	9	101.20	101.10	99	99

Table A17a (cont.)

Lot No.	Grid North	Grid East	Item No.	Quad	Upper Level	Lower Level	Feat. No.	Comm.
0093	513	534	99	9	101.35	101.25	99	99
0094	515	534	99	9	100.70	100.65	99	99
0095	523	562	99	9	101.25	101.15	99	99
0096	525	564	99	9	101.25	101.15	99	99
0097	512	535	99	9	101.16	101.05	99	99
0098	512	530	99	9	101.45	101.40	99	99
0099	514	535	99	9	101.70	101.60	99	04
0100	513	530	99	9	101.70	101.65	99	99
0101	512	530	99	9	101.40	101.35	99	04
0102	512	532	99	9	101.50	101.45	99	99
0103	512	533	99	9	101.25	101.20	99	99
0104	512	533	01	9	101.25	101.20	99	99
0105	512	533	02	9	101.23	101.22	99	99
0106	512	531	99	9	101.40	101.35	99	99
0107	514	534	99	9	101.55	101.45	99	99
0108	526	564	99	9	101.25	101.15	99	99
0109	525	566	99	9	101.25	101.15	99	99
0110	526	562	07	9	100.94	100.93	99	99
0111	526	562	08	9	100.90	100.89	99	99
0112	529	566	99	9	101.73	101.60	99	04
0113	526	562	06	9	100.92	100.91	99	99
0114	527	562	99	9	101.10	101.00	99	99
0115	513	535	99	9	101.45	101.35	99	99
0116	545	602	99	9	098.82	098.81	99	99
0117	556	537	99	9	100.26	100.25	99	03
0118	514	535	99	9	101.75	101.65	99	99
0119	542	594	99	9	099.27	099.26	99	99
0120	529	566	99	9	101.40	101.30	99	99
0121	510	530	99	9	101.10	101.00	99	99
0122	510	533	04	9	101.02	101.01	99	99
0123	517	533	99	9	101.89	101.60	99	99
0124	522	565	99	9	101.35	101.25	99	99
0125	522	565	99	9	101.25	101.15	99	99
0126	523	565	99	9	101.15	101.05	99	99
0127	513	534	99	9	101.55	101.45	99	99
0128	524	569	99	9	101.30	101.20	99	99
0129	514	534	99	9	101.45	101.35	99	99
0130	514	530	99	9	101.50	101.40	99	04
0131	512	530	99	9	101.55	101.50	99	99
0132	515	534	99	9	100.65	100.60	99	02
0133	524	565	99	9	101.15	101.05	99	99
0134	512	532	99	9	101.35	101.30	99	99
0135	525	562	99	9	101.30	101.25	99	99
0136	525	563	99	9	100.95	100.90	99	99
0137	522	561	99	1	101.07	101.06	99	99
0138	512	534	99	9	101.35	101.30	99	99
0139	513	534	99	9	101.45	101.35	99	99

Table A17a (cont.)

Lot No.	Grid North	Grid East	Item No.	Quad	Upper Level	Lower Level	Feat. No.	Comm.
0140	512	513	99	9	101.50	101.45	99	99
0141	525	564	99	9	101.15	101.05	99	99
0142	512	532	99	9	101.60	101.55	99	99
0143	524	535	99	3	100.82	100.57	99	02
0144	514	532	99	9	101.95	101.90	99	99
0145	529	566	99	9	101.60	101.50	99	04
0146	512	532	99	9	101.25	101.15	99	99
0147	517	534	99	9	101.25	101.05	99	04
0148	520	533	99	9	102.08	101.65	99	99
0149	511	533	99	9	101.30	101.25	99	99
0150	517	534	99	9	100.64	100.60	99	99
0151	513	533	99	9	101.89	101.88	99	03
0152	524	567	99	9	101.51	101.25	99	99
0153	511	533	99	9	101.25	101.20	99	99
0154	515	535	99	9	101.20	101.10	99	99
0155	511	533	99	9	101.20	101.15	99	99
0156	523	561	99	9	101.15	101.05	99	99
0157	526	566	99	9	101.25	101.15	99	99
0158	521	566	99	9	101.15	101.05	99	99
0159	512	533	99	9	101.35	101.30	99	99
0160	515	535	99	9	102.04	101.60	99	99
0161	512	535	99	9	101.41	101.35	99	99
0162	516	534	99	9	100.70	100.65	99	99
0163	529	565	99	9	101.30	101.20	99	99
0164	516	535	99	9	101.40	101.30	99	99
0165	517	533	99	2	100.95	100.85	99	99
0166	526	567	99	9	101.25	101.15	99	99
0167	513	535	99	9	100.95	100.85	99	99
0168	515	535	99	9	101.20	101.10	99	99
0169	523	566	05	9	101.09	101.08	99	99
0170	517	534	99	9	100.75	100.65	99	99
0171	521	567	99	9	101.25	101.15	99	99
0172	526	566	99	9	101.57	101.25	99	99
0173	526	569	99	9	101.30	101.20	99	99
0174	526	562	99	9	101.30	101.20	99	99
0175	528	567	99	9	101.35	101.25	99	99
0176	525	568	99	9	101.30	101.20	99	99
0177	529	566	99	9	101.50	101.40	99	99
0178	522	563	99	9	101.44	101.25	99	99
0179	526	562	05	9	100.91	100.90	99	99
0180	508	528	99	9	100.76	100.75	99	03
0181	526	562	09	9	100.82	100.81	99	99
0182	514	533	99	9	102.08	101.85	99	99
0183	512	534	99	9	101.30	101.25	99	99
0184	526	565	99	9	101.56	101.25	99	99
0185	522	561	99	9	101.10	101.05	99	99
0186	526	568	99	9	101.55	101.25	99	99

Table A17a (cont.)

Lot No.	Grid North	Grid East	Item No.	Quad	Upper Level	Lower Level	Feat. No.	Comm.
0187	527	566	99	9	101.27	101.15	99	99
0188	516	534	99	9	101.10	101.00	99	99
0189	528	567	99	9	101.43	101.35	99	99
0190	521	563	99	9	101.15	101.05	99	04
0191	514	535	99	9	101.55	101.45	99	99
0192	523	567	99	9	101.47	101.25	99	99
0193	526	562	99	9	101.30	101.20	99	99
0194	526	562	01	9	101.29	101.28	99	99
0195	523	563	99	9	101.25	101.15	99	04
0196	513	534	99	9	101.55	101.45	99	99
0197	528	564	99	2	101.05	100.95	99	99
0198	522	563	99	9	101.15	101.05	99	04
0199	514	530	99	9	101.95	101.85	99	04
0200	528	563	99	9	101.35	101.25	99	99
0201	510	530	99	9	101.40	101.30	99	04
0202	516	534	99	9	100.64	100.63	99	02
0203	525	562	99	1	100.85	100.81	99	99
0204	525	564	99	8	101.05	100.95	99	99
0205	514	530	99	9	101.85	101.75	99	99
0206	527	563	99	9	100.95	100.85	99	99
0207	526	563	99	9	101.25	101.15	99	99
0208	526	564	99	9	101.15	101.05	99	99
0209	513	535	99	9	100.69	100.45	06	99
0210	521	567	99	9	101.15	101.05	99	04
0211	515	534	06	9	100.70	100.60	99	04
0212	516	533	99	9	100.90	100.85	99	99
0213	516	534	99	9	100.64	100.63	99	02
0214	526	562	99	9	101.20	101.10	99	99
0215	528	567	01	9	101.57	101.56	99	99
0216	527	566	05	9	101.38	101.37	99	99
0217	510	531	99	9	101.20	101.10	99	99
0218	526	562	04	9	100.93	100.92	99	99
0219	526	562	02	9	100.95	100.94	99	99
0220	513	534	99	9	101.50	101.45	99	99
0221	525	562	99	1	101.05	100.90	99	99
0222	525	563	99	1	101.05	100.95	99	99
0223	514	535	99	1	100.70	100.63	99	02
0224	522	564	99	9	101.25	101.15	99	99
0225	524	562	99	9	101.35	101.25	99	99
0226	513	530	99	9	101.65	101.55	99	04
0227	528	567	99	9	101.35	101.25	99	99
0228	526	567	99	9	100.90	100.84	99	99
0229	527	566	99	9	101.65	101.55	99	99
0230	528	567	99	9	101.45	101.35	99	99
0231	528	566	99	9	101.05	100.95	99	99
0232	514	534	99	1	100.47	100.38	09	03
0233	513	528	99	9	101.51	101.50	99	03

Table A17a (cont.)

Lot No.	Grid North	Grid East	Item No.	Quad	Upper Level	Lower Level	Feat. No.	Comm.
0234	525	568	99	9	101.40	101.30	99	99
0235	528	567	99	9	101.25	101.15	99	99
0236	529	566	99	9	101.30	101.10	99	06
0237	525	567	99	9	101.30	101.20	99	99
0238	527	566	04	9	101.38	101.37	99	99
0239	537	500	99	9	100.76	100.75	99	99
0240	528	567	02	9	101.45	101.35	99	99
0241	526	562	99	9	101.40	101.30	99	99
0242	527	566	99	9	101.20	101.10	16	99
0243	523	566	99	9	101.25	101.15	99	99
0244	524	569	99	9	101.19	101.10	99	99
0245	526	567	99	9	101.15	101.06	99	99
0246	512	533	99	9	101.70	101.60	99	99
0247	526	563	01	9	101.95	101.94	99	99
0248	524	568	99	9	101.20	101.10	99	99
0249	527	561	99	9	101.30	101.10	99	99
0250	527	561	99	9	101.10	100.90	99	99
0251	526	562	99	9	101.00	100.90	99	99
0252	527	566	99	9	101.45	101.35	99	99
0253	528	564	99	9	101.15	101.10	99	99
0254	515	533	99	9	102.10	102.00	99	99
0255	527	561	99	9	101.49	101.20	99	99
0256	527	566	99	9	101.25	101.17	16	99
0257	527	566	99	9	101.35	101.25	99	99
0258	528	567	99	9	101.02	100.90	17	99
0259	512	535	99	9	101.35	101.30	99	99
0260	527	561	01	9	101.37	101.36	99	99
0261	527	567	99	9	101.40	101.30	99	99
0262	527	567	06	9	101.29	101.28	99	99
0263	522	566	99	9	101.15	101.05	99	04
0264	516	534	99	9	100.90	100.85	99	99
0265	522	567	99	9	101.42	101.25	99	99
0266	521	566	99	9	101.46	101.25	99	99
0267	527	569	01	9	101.30	101.29	99	99
0268	515	535	99	9	100.70	100.65	99	02
0269	516	534	99	9	101.60	101.40	99	99
0270	520	533	99	9	101.65	101.45	99	99
0271	512	532	99	9	101.65	101.60	99	99
0272	528	566	99	9	101.68	101.25	99	99
0273	517	534	99	9	100.85	100.75	99	99
0274	515	534	99	9	100.00	100.90	99	99
0275	521	567	99	9	101.37	101.25	99	99
0276	523	566	99	9	101.15	101.05	99	99
0277	522	567	99	9	101.25	101.15	99	99
0278	527	567	08	9	101.20	101.19	99	99
0279	526	567	99	9	101.58	101.25	99	99
0280	529	566	99	9	101.10	101.00	99	99

Table A17a (cont.)

Lot No.	Grid North	Grid East	Item No.	Quad	Upper Level	Lower Level	Feat. No.	Comm.
0281	526	562	99	9	100.84	100.80	99	99
0282	527	566	06	9	101.23	101.22	99	05
0283	522	566	99	9	101.25	101.15	99	99
0284	523	567	99	9	101.47	101.25	99	99
0285	515	533	99	9	101.30	101.20	99	99
0286	516	534	99	9	101.20	101.00	99	99
0287	519	533	99	9	101.65	101.40	99	99
0288	526	568	99	2	101.25	101.15	99	99
0289	527	564	99	9	101.58	101.25	99	99
0290	525	562	01	1	100.99	100.98	99	99
0291	519	533	99	9	100.60	100.40	99	99
0292	516	534	99	9	101.20	101.00	99	99
0293	512	533	99	9	101.60	101.55	99	99
0294	512	533	99	9	101.40	101.30	99	04
0295	516	534	99	9	101.60	101.40	99	99
0296	511	532	99	9	101.25	101.20	99	99
0297	519	533	99	9	101.65	101.40	99	99
0298	527	563	99	9	101.57	101.25	99	99
0299	519	533	99	9	101.65	101.40	99	99
0300	527	563	01	9	101.92	101.91	99	99
0301	526	562	10	9	100.61	100.60	99	99
0302	524	562	99	9	101.15	101.05	99	99
0303	527	567	99	9	101.20	101.15	53	99
0304	528	562	03	9	100.82	100.81	99	99
0305	525	561	05	9	100.91	100.90	99	99
0306	528	562	02	9	100.92	100.91	99	99
0307	528	562	01	9	100.96	100.95	99	99
0308	527	567	99	9	101.15	101.11	53	99
0309	527	567	01	9	101.51	101.50	99	99
0310	527	567	99	9	101.64	101.50	99	99
0311	527	567	02	9	101.51	101.50	99	99
0312	527	567	03	9	101.64	101.50	99	99
0313	528	564	99	9	101.45	101.35	99	99
0314	528	564	99	9	101.10	101.00	99	99
0315	527	566	03	9	101.36	101.35	99	99
0316	527	566	01	9	101.42	101.41	99	99
0317	527	566	02	9	101.35	101.34	99	99
0318	528	567	02	9	101.35	101.25	99	04
0319	529	565	99	9	101.40	101.30	99	99
0320	524	569	99	9	101.40	101.30	99	99
0321	527	562	07	9	100.78	100.77	99	99
0322	527	562	05	9	100.79	100.78	99	99
0323	527	562	06	9	100.79	100.78	99	99
0324	529	566	99	9	101.50	101.40	99	04
0325	529	566	99	9	101.30	101.20	99	99
0326	527	567	99	9	101.31	101.30	99	02
0327	527	562	99	9	101.00	100.90	99	99

Table A17a (cont.)

Lot No.	Grid North	Grid East	Item No.	Quad	Upper Level	Lower Level	Feat. No.	Comm.
0328	522	563	99	9	100.90	100.80	20	03
0329	527	566	99	9	101.20	101.10	99	99
0330	522	563	99	9	101.00	100.90	20	03
0331	530	565	99	9	101.75	101.50	99	99
0332	527	562	02	9	100.86	100.85	99	99
0333	528	563	03	9	100.87	100.86	99	99
0334	526	561	04	9	101.00	100.80	99	99
0335	526	561	03	9	100.90	100.89	99	99
0336	528	563	05	9	100.83	100.82	99	99
0337	528	563	04	9	100.83	100.82	99	99
0338	527	569	99	9	101.60	101.56	99	99
0339	526	561	01	9	100.95	100.94	99	99
0340	524	569	01	9	100.91	100.90	99	99
0341	528	563	07	9	100.79	100.78	99	99
0342	526	561	02	9	100.97	100.96	99	99
0343	527	562	03	9	100.84	100.83	99	99
0344	527	569	99	9	101.30	101.20	99	99
0345	528	563	99	9	100.90	100.80	99	99
0346	528	563	99	9	101.25	101.15	99	99
0347	524	569	99	9	101.30	101.20	99	99
0348	528	563	99	9	101.35	101.25	99	99
0349	529	566	99	9	101.10	101.00	99	99
0350	527	562	99	9	100.70	100.60	99	99
0351	528	567	99	9	101.16	101.02	17	99
0352	527	567	03	9	101.50	101.49	99	99
0353	527	567	04	9	101.46	101.45	99	99
0354	527	566	05	9	101.43	101.42	99	99
0355	527	562	99	9	100.91	100.90	99	99
0356	527	566	99	9	101.35	101.25	99	02
0357	527	566	99	9	101.25	101.20	16	99
0358	527	567	99	9	101.50	101.40	99	99
0359	526	562	99	9	101.10	100.00	99	99
0360	529	565	99	9	101.50	101.40	99	99
0361	526	561	99	9	101.20	101.00	99	99
0362	526	561	99	9	101.38	101.20	99	99
0363	527	563	99	9	100.80	100.70	99	99
0364	530	565	99	9	101.50	101.30	99	99
0365	528	563	99	9	101.05	100.95	99	99
0366	525	561	99	1	100.70	100.61	99	99
0367	526	562	99	9	100.80	100.70	99	99
0368	527	563	99	9	101.24	100.84	99	99
0369	527	563	99	9	101.24	101.00	99	99
0370	527	565	99	9	101.15	101.08	99	99
0371	526	564	99	9	101.60	101.50	99	99
0372	527	564	99	9	100.80	100.50	25	06
0373	528	563	06	9	100.81	100.80	99	99
0374	527	565	99	9	101.17	101.10	99	99

Table A17a (cont.)

Lot No.	Grid North	Grid East	Item No.	Quad	Upper Level	Lower Level	Feat. No.	Comm.
0375	527	565	11	9	101.01	101.00	99	99
0376	527	564	03	2	101.00	100.99	99	99
0377	523	528	03	9	101.14	101.13	99	99
0378	523	568	02	9	101.21	101.20	99	99
0379	529	563	01	1	101.30	101.29	99	99
0380	523	564	99	9	101.08	100.90	99	99
0381	527	565	99	9	101.08	100.99	99	02
0382	528	567	99	9	101.15	101.05	99	99
0383	530	565	99	9	101.75	101.50	99	99
0384	524	569	99	9	101.00	100.90	99	99
0385	523	569	99	9	101.36	101.10	99	99
0386	526	547	99	9	100.74	100.60	99	99
0387	526	562	99	9	100.70	100.60	99	99
0388	528	563	99	9	100.95	100.10	99	99
0389	528	563	08	9	100.71	100.70	99	06
0390	572	561	04	9	100.78	100.77	99	99
0391	523	565	99	2	101.18	101.17	99	99
0392	527	561	99	9	101.76	101.75	28	99
0393	527	549	99	1	100.77	100.60	99	99
0394	526	548	99	9	100.60	100.50	99	99
0395	527	561	99	9	100.80	100.70	99	99
0396	526	566	99	9	100.96	100.90	99	99
0397	526	547	02	9	100.34	100.33	99	99
0398	527	550	04	9	100.44	100.43	99	99
0399	527	549	03	9	100.36	100.35	99	99
0400	523	564	01	9	101.04	101.03	99	99
0401	526	547	03	9	100.31	100.30	99	99
0402	526	566	05	9	101.02	101.01	99	99
0403	526	550	99	9	100.51	100.40	99	99
0404	526	565	99	9	101.57	101.56	99	03
0405	527	549	99	9	100.60	100.50	99	99
0406	527	548	99	9	100.78	100.50	99	99
0407	526	548	99	9	100.74	100.60	99	99
0408	526	564	99	9	101.29	100.76	99	06
0409	525	563	99	1	100.85	100.70	99	99
0410	526	549	99	9	100.40	100.30	99	99
0411	528	561	99	6	101.80	101.76	99	99
0412	528	561	05	9	100.58	100.57	99	02
0413	527	564	02	4	101.25	101.24	99	99
0414	528	561	06	9	100.58	100.57	99	02
0415	523	568	04	9	101.15	101.14	99	09
0416	526	566	99	9	100.90	100.80	26	99
0417	528	561	08	9	100.58	100.57	99	02
0418	527	569	02	9	101.26	101.25	99	99
0419	526	562	99	9	100.60	100.37	22	99
0420	526	562	12	9	100.81	100.80	99	99
0421	528	561	12	9	100.58	100.57	99	02

Table A17a (cont.)

Lot No.	Grid North	Grid East	Item No.	Quad	Upper Level	Lower Level	Feat. No.	Comm.
0422	527	564	99	9	100.80	100.50	25	99
0423	526	564	02	4	100.91	100.90	99	99
0424	529	560	01	9	101.50	101.49	99	99
0425	528	561	13	9	100.58	100.57	99	02
0426	528	561	04	9	100.58	100.57	99	02
0427	528	561	15	9	100.58	100.57	99	02
0428	528	561	09	9	100.58	100.57	99	02
0429	528	561	16	9	100.58	100.57	99	02
0430	528	561	10	9	100.58	100.57	99	02
0431	528	561	11	9	100.58	100.57	99	02
0432	528	561	12	9	100.58	100.57	99	02
0433	528	561	12	9	100.58	100.57	99	02
0434	528	561	12	9	100.58	100.57	99	02
0435	500	555	99	9	100.26	100.25	99	03
0436	529	563	04	9	101.31	101.30	99	99
0437	523	564	01	9	101.25	101.24	99	99
0438	502	552	99	9	100.31	100.30	99	03
0439	527	562	99	9	101.40	101.30	99	99
0440	501	598	99	9	099.91	099.90	99	03
0441	527	550	03	9	100.51	100.50	99	99
0442	526	550	02	9	100.41	100.40	99	99
0443	527	561	06	9	100.76	100.75	28	99
0444	572	561	03	9	100.78	100.77	99	99
0445	526	547	01	9	100.41	100.40	99	99
0446	528	561	07	9	100.58	100.57	99	02
0447	522	563	99	9	101.01	101.00	99	01
0448	527	562	04	9	100.81	100.80	99	99
0449	526	549	03	9	100.35	100.34	99	99
0450	528	561	01	9	100.90	100.89	99	99
0451	572	561	05	9	100.78	100.77	99	99
0452	528	565	08	9	101.06	101.05	99	99
0453	527	567	10	9	101.07	101.06	99	99
0454	527	549	01	9	100.54	100.53	99	99
0455	527	549	02	9	100.50	100.49	99	99
0456	528	567	99	9	101.07	100.77	18	99
0457	526	549	02	9	100.29	100.28	99	99
0458	526	549	01	9	100.42	100.41	99	99
0459	528	565	07	9	101.05	101.04	99	99
0460	528	565	09	9	100.99	100.98	99	99
0461	528	565	06	9	101.03	101.02	99	99
0462	527	565	10	9	100.99	100.98	99	99
0463	527	567	09	9	100.08	100.07	55	99
0464	527	563	02	9	100.84	100.83	99	99
0465	529	565	01	9	101.44	101.43	99	99
0466	527	563	03	9	100.78	100.77	99	99
0467	528	561	04	9	100.75	100.74	99	99
0468	523	563	99	9	101.10	101.00	99	04

Table A17a (cont.)

Lot No.	Grid North	Grid East	Item No.	Quad	Upper Level	Lower Level	Feat. No.	Comm.
0469	526	550	99	9	100.30	100.28	99	99
0470	526	550	04	9	100.26	100.25	99	99
0471	528	561	03	9	100.77	100.76	99	99
0472	527	550	08	9	100.37	100.36	99	99
0473	527	566	06	9	101.23	101.22	99	99
0474	510	558	99	9	100.51	100.50	99	03
0475	526	550	99	9	100.70	100.28	99	99
0476	526	561	06	9	100.75	100.74	99	99
0477	527	564	01	1	101.19	101.18	99	99
0478	527	550	07	9	100.35	100.34	99	99
0479	527	563	04	9	100.70	100.60	99	99
0480	527	550	05	9	100.35	100.34	99	99
0481	526	561	05	9	100.79	100.78	99	99
0482	526	548	01	9	100.29	100.28	99	99
0483	528	562	04	9	100.78	100.77	99	99
0484	527	561	02	9	100.82	100.81	99	99
0485	526	550	01	9	100.54	100.53	99	99
0486	528	563	99	9	100.80	100.60	99	99
0487	528	563	99	9	101.55	101.45	99	99
0488	528	563	02	9	101.48	101.47	99	99
0489	526	547	99	9	100.50	100.40	99	99
0490	526	549	99	9	100.50	100.40	99	99
0491	526	549	99	9	100.74	100.61	99	99
0492	528	563	99	9	100.80	100.70	99	99
0493	527	567	99	9	101.20	101.09	50	99
0494	527	564	99	1	101.14	101.13	99	99
0495	529	565	99	9	101.60	101.50	99	99
0496	527	565	99	9	101.08	101.05	99	99
0497	528	562	99	9	100.60	100.55	99	02
0498	526	561	99	9	100.70	100.60	99	99
0499	528	563	99	9	101.67	101.55	99	99
0500	528	563	01	9	101.57	101.56	99	99
0501	526	548	99	9	100.40	100.30	99	99
0502	523	568	99	9	101.42	101.20	99	99
0503	526	547	99	9	101.60	101.30	99	99
0504	527	550	99	9	100.77	100.60	99	99
0505	526	569	99	9	101.40	101.29	99	99
0506	526	548	99	9	100.40	100.30	99	99
0507	527	564	99	1	101.15	101.05	99	99
0508	528	563	99	9	100.70	100.60	99	99
0509	527	550	99	9	100.71	100.70	99	99
0510	528	562	99	9	100.70	100.60	99	99
0511	526	527	99	9	101.00	100.88	23	99
0512	527	562	99	9	100.70	100.60	99	99
0513	525	568	99	9	101.51	101.40	99	99
0514	529	566	99	9	101.60	101.50	99	99
0515	528	567	99	9	101.67	101.55	99	99

Table A17a (cont.)

Lot No.	Grid North	Grid East	Item No.	Quad	Upper Level	Lower Level	Feat. No.	Comm.
0516	527	548	99	9	100.40	100.30	99	99
0517	526	549	99	9	100.60	100.50	99	99
0518	508	550	99	9	100.30	100.10	99	99
0519	528	563	99	9	101.15	101.05	99	99
0520	524	568	99	9	101.30	101.20	99	99
0521	527	550	99	9	100.40	100.30	99	99
0522	526	567	99	9	101.06	101.05	99	99
0523	507	550	99	9	100.28	100.20	99	99
0524	529	565	99	9	101.72	101.60	99	99
0525	509	550	99	9	100.53	100.30	99	99
0526	527	568	99	9	101.60	101.40	99	99
0527	507	550	99	9	100.48	100.30	99	99
0528	523	563	99	9	101.05	100.90	99	99
0529	526	550	99	9	101.41	101.30	99	99
0530	527	564	99	9	100.98	100.88	25	99
0531	526	546	99	9	101.79	101.60	99	99
0532	527	550	99	9	100.60	100.50	99	99
0533	527	563	99	9	100.70	100.60	99	99
0534	526	567	99	9	100.69	100.59	23	99
0535	526	550	99	9	100.28	100.20	99	99
0536	509	550	99	9	100.30	100.10	99	99
0537	527	549	99	9	100.50	100.40	99	99
0538	527	550	99	9	100.77	100.60	99	99
0539	526	547	99	9	100.40	100.30	99	99
0540	530	565	99	3	101.30	101.20	99	99
0541	527	563	99	9	100.90	100.80	99	99
0542	527	566	99	9	101.10	101.00	99	99
0543	526	563	99	9	100.80	100.70	99	99
0544	529	566	99	9	101.73	101.60	99	99
0545	527	566	99	9	101.55	101.45	99	99
0546	524	568	99	9	101.48	101.30	99	99
0547	526	548	99	9	100.50	100.40	99	99
0548	528	561	99	9	101.30	101.00	99	99
0549	529	561	99	9	101.66	101.30	99	99
0550	527	562	99	9	101.53	101.40	99	99
0551	527	548	99	9	100.50	100.40	99	99
0552	526	563	99	9	100.88	100.80	99	99
0553	512	549	99	9	100.00	099.90	99	99
0554	509	550	99	9	100.10	099.90	99	99
0555	508	548	99	9	099.61	099.60	99	99
0556	508	549	99	9	099.61	099.60	99	99
0557	512	549	99	9	100.00	099.90	99	99
0558	510	549	99	9	100.10	100.00	99	99
0559	511	550	99	9	100.00	099.90	99	99
0560	512	549	99	9	100.10	100.00	99	99
0561	511	550	99	9	100.00	099.90	99	99
0562	509	549	99	9	099.90	099.80	99	99

Table A17a (cont.)

Lot No.	Grid North	Grid East	Item No.	Quad	Upper Level	Lower Level	Feat. No.	Comm.
0563	510	549	99	9	099.90	099.80	99	99
0564	510	549	99	9	099.90	099.80	99	99
0565	508	550	99	9	100.12	099.98	99	99
0566	509	549	99	9	099.70	099.60	99	99
0567	509	550	99	9	099.68	099.67	99	99
0568	508	550	99	9	099.80	099.68	99	99
0569	509	549	99	9	099.70	099.60	99	99
0570	509	549	99	9	099.64	099.63	99	99
0571	510	549	99	9	099.90	099.80	99	99
0572	511	550	99	9	099.79	099.78	99	99
0573	509	550	99	9	099.75	099.74	99	99
0574	509	549	99	9	099.80	099.70	99	99
0575	509	550	99	9	099.73	099.72	99	99
0576	509	549	99	9	099.59	099.58	99	99
0577	511	550	99	9	099.90	099.80	99	99
0578	511	550	99	9	100.00	099.90	99	99
0579	508	549	99	9	099.64	099.63	99	99
0580	510	549	99	9	100.00	099.90	99	99
0581	507	550	99	9	099.90	099.80	99	99
0582	512	549	99	9	099.90	099.80	99	99
0583	511	550	99	9	100.10	100.00	99	99
0584	509	549	99	9	100.00	099.90	99	99
0585	510	550	99	9	100.10	100.00	99	99
0586	510	550	99	9	100.30	100.10	99	99
0587	511	550	99	9	100.10	100.00	99	99
0588	508	549	99	9	100.10	100.00	99	99
0589	509	550	99	9	100.10	100.00	99	99
0590	529	564	99	9	101.73	101.40	99	99
0591	529	564	01	9	101.44	101.43	99	99
0592	525	569	99	9	101.47	101.40	99	99
0593	511	550	99	9	100.10	100.00	99	99
0594	509	549	99	9	100.10	100.00	99	99
0595	509	549	99	9	100.30	100.10	99	99
0596	526	550	05	9	100.28	100.27	99	99
0597	509	550	99	9	100.10	099.90	99	99
0598	509	548	99	9	100.30	100.10	99	99
0599	509	550	99	9	099.90	099.60	99	99
0600	509	549	99	9	100.00	099.90	99	99
0601	509	550	99	9	099.64	099.60	99	99
0602	509	549	99	9	099.60	099.50	99	99
0603	510	549	99	9	099.70	099.60	99	99
0604	510	549	99	9	099.70	099.60	99	99
0605	509	550	99	9	099.70	099.60	99	99
0606	510	549	99	9	099.70	099.69	99	99
0607	510	549	99	9	099.80	099.70	99	99
0608	510	549	99	9	099.80	099.70	99	99
0609	512	549	99	9	099.90	099.80	99	99

Table A17a (cont.)

Lot No.	Grid North	Grid East	Item No.	Quad	Upper Level	Lower Level	Feat. No.	Comm.
0610	508	550	99	9	099.70	099.60	99	99
0611	510	549	99	8	099.70	099.60	99	99
0612	512	549	99	9	099.90	099.80	99	99
0613	509	548	99	9	099.90	099.80	99	99
0614	509	548	99	9	100.10	100.00	99	99
0615	509	549	99	9	099.58	099.57	99	99
0616	512	549	99	9	099.90	099.80	99	99
0617	512	549	99	9	099.90	099.80	99	99
0618	512	549	99	9	099.90	099.80	99	99
0619	512	549	99	9	099.90	099.80	99	99
0620	509	549	99	9	099.60	099.50	99	99
0621	508	551	99	9	099.90	099.80	99	99
0622	508	551	99	9	099.76	099.75	99	99
0623	512	549	99	9	099.83	099.82	99	99
0624	512	549	99	9	099.90	099.80	99	99
0625	509	548	99	9	100.10	100.00	99	99
0626	512	549	99	9	099.90	099.80	99	99
0627	512	549	99	9	099.90	099.80	99	99
0628	510	549	99	9	099.70	099.60	99	99
0629	510	549	99	9	099.80	099.70	99	99
0630	510	549	99	9	099.95	099.94	99	99
0631	510	549	99	9	099.80	099.70	99	99
0632	510	549	99	9	099.80	099.70	99	99
0633	510	549	99	9	099.80	099.70	99	99
0634	509	549	99	9	100.52	100.51	99	03
0635	529	563	99	9	101.73	101.40	99	99
0636	528	550	99	9	100.50	100.40	99	99
0637	523	568	99	9	101.20	101.10	99	99
0638	527	549	99	9	100.40	100.30	99	99
0639	562	564	04	9	100.76	100.63	99	99
0640	508	552	99	9	100.02	099.95	99	99
0641	512	549	99	9	099.90	099.80	99	99
0642	510	549	99	9	099.90	099.80	99	99
0643	510	549	99	9	099.80	099.70	99	99
0644	510	549	99	9	099.80	099.70	99	99
0645	509	550	99	9	099.80	099.70	99	99
0646	508	552	99	9	100.17	100.16	99	99
0647	512	549	99	9	099.90	099.80	99	99
0648	510	550	99	9	100.01	100.00	99	99
0649	510	549	99	9	099.80	099.70	99	99
0650	511	550	99	9	100.00	099.90	99	99
0651	526	549	99	9	100.40	100.30	99	99
0652	527	567	99	9	101.21	101.20	99	99
0653	510	549	99	9	099.80	099.70	99	99
0654	510	550	99	9	100.01	100.00	99	99
0655	511	550	99	9	100.10	100.00	99	99
0656	511	550	99	9	100.00	099.90	99	99

Table A17a (cont.)

Lot No.	Grid North	Grid East	Item No.	Quad	Upper Level	Lower Level	Feat. No.	Comm.
0657	512	549	99	9	099.80	099.78	99	99
0658	527	562	99	9	101.40	101.30	99	99
0659	527	567	07	9	101.25	101.24	99	99
0670	529	561	99	9	101.30	101.10	99	99
0671	510	541	99	9	100.76	100.75	99	03
0672	507	550	99	9	100.28	100.10	99	99
0673	507	550	99	9	099.80	099.70	99	99
0674	509	548	99	9	099.70	099.60	99	99
0675	511	549	99	9	099.90	099.80	99	99
0676	509	550	99	9	099.60	099.50	99	99
0677	509	550	99	9	099.50	099.40	99	99
0678	510	550	99	9	099.90	099.80	99	99
0679	510	550	99	9	100.00	099.90	99	99
0680	510	549	99	9	099.70	099.60	99	99
0681	510	550	99	9	100.00	099.90	99	99
0682	510	549	99	9	099.60	099.56	99	99
0683	508	552	99	9	100.02	099.88	99	99
0684	512	550	99	9	100.09	100.00	99	99
0685	512	550	99	9	100.00	099.90	99	99
0686	512	549	99	9	099.80	099.70	99	99
0687	512	550	99	9	100.00	099.90	99	99
0688	509	549	99	9	099.60	099.50	99	99
0689	508	549	99	9	099.64	099.60	99	99
0690	508	549	99	9	099.60	099.50	99	99
0691	510	549	99	9	099.70	099.60	99	99
0692	510	549	99	9	099.70	099.60	99	99
0693	509	549	99	9	099.50	099.40	99	99
0694	508	550	99	9	099.60	099.50	99	99
0695	510	549	99	9	099.63	099.62	99	99
0696	511	549	99	9	099.90	099.80	99	99
0697	508	549	99	9	099.64	099.63	99	99
0698	509	548	99	9	099.80	099.70	99	99
0699	507	550	99	9	099.80	099.70	99	99
0700	510	550	99	9	099.80	099.70	99	99
0701	507	550	99	9	099.70	099.60	99	99
0702	509	547	99	9	099.90	099.80	99	99
0703	512	550	99	9	100.00	099.90	99	99
0704	509	549	99	9	099.60	099.50	99	99
0705	512	550	99	9	099.90	099.80	99	99
0706	509	547	99	9	100.00	099.90	99	99
0707	510	550	99	9	099.67	099.66	99	99
0708	508	550	99	9	099.70	099.60	99	99
0709	509	548	99	9	099.60	099.50	99	99
0710	510	550	99	9	099.90	099.80	99	99
0711	508	556	99	9	100.35	100.34	99	99
0712	508	556	99	9	100.37	100.36	99	99
0713	510	550	99	9	099.90	099.80	99	99

Table A17a (cont.)

Lot No.	Grid North	Grid East	Item No.	Quad	Upper Level	Lower Level	Feat. No.	Comm.
0714	511	549	99	9	099.90	099.80	99	99
0715	509	548	99	9	099.90	099.80	99	99
0716	529	565	99	9	101.10	101.00	99	99
0717	529	565	99	9	101.10	101.00	99	99
0718	523	568	99	9	101.10	101.00	99	99
0719	508	551	99	9	099.90	099.80	99	99
0720	509	548	99	9	099.90	099.80	99	99
0721	510	549	99	9	099.74	099.73	99	99
0722	510	549	99	9	099.60	099.56	99	99
0723	510	549	99	9	099.50	099.44	99	99
0724	510	549	99	9	099.60	099.56	99	99
0725	508	551	99	9	099.80	099.70	99	99
0726	508	551	99	9	099.91	099.70	99	99
0727	508	551	99	9	099.70	099.60	99	99
0728	508	553	99	9	100.30	100.20	99	99
0729	508	554	99	9	100.47	100.30	99	99
0730	510	548	99	9	100.48	100.30	99	99
0731	526	547	99	9	100.30	100.24	99	99
0732	509	550	99	9	099.70	099.60	99	99
0733	511	549	99	9	100.51	100.30	99	99
0734	507	550	99	9	099.70	099.60	99	99
0735	507	550	99	9	099.70	099.60	99	99
0736	509	548	99	9	099.70	099.60	99	99
0737	526	550	03	9	100.36	100.35	99	99
0738	527	550	99	9	100.30	100.20	99	99
0739	527	567	99	9	100.79	100.70	40	99
0740	509	549	99	9	100.10	100.00	99	99
0741	490	523	99	9	099.10	099.00	99	99
0742	528	561	99	9	100.64	100.54	99	99
0743	509	550	99	9	100.10	099.90	99	99
0744	509	550	99	9	099.60	099.50	99	99
0745	511	549	99	9	100.00	099.90	99	99
0746	511	549	99	9	100.00	099.90	99	99
0747	510	548	99	9	100.30	100.10	99	99
0748	527	564	99	9	101.58	101.25	99	99
0749	509	549	99	9	100.00	099.90	99	99
0750	526	546	99	9	101.60	101.50	99	99
0751	508	549	99	9	099.90	099.80	99	99
0752	527	561	99	9	100.70	100.60	99	99
0753	510	546	99	9	100.30	100.10	99	99
0754	509	548	99	9	099.90	099.80	99	99
0755	509	549	99	9	100.10	100.00	99	99
0756	509	548	99	9	099.90	099.80	99	99
0757	526	567	99	9	100.70	100.60	40	99
0758	528	561	99	9	100.74	100.64	99	99
0759	508	553	99	9	100.47	100.30	99	99
0760	526	550	99	9	100.61	100.50	99	99

Table A17a (cont.)

Lot No.	Grid North	Grid East	Item No.	Quad	Upper Level	Lower Level	Feat. No.	Comm.
0761	510	548	99	9	100.48	100.30	99	99
0762	508	554	99	9	100.30	100.20	99	99
0763	528	562	99	9	101.00	100.90	99	99
0764	510	550	99	9	099.80	099.70	99	99
0765	527	567	99	9	101.00	100.88	40	99
0766	512	549	99	9	099.80	099.70	99	99
0767	512	549	99	9	099.90	099.80	99	99
0768	509	549	99	9	100.10	100.00	99	99
0769	526	563	99	9	100.70	100.60	99	99
0770	512	550	99	9	100.00	099.90	99	99
0771	510	532	99	9	101.15	101.05	99	99
0772	512	550	99	9	100.10	100.00	99	99
0773	512	532	99	9	101.45	101.40	99	99
0774	510	549	99	9	100.20	100.10	99	99
0775	509	550	99	9	099.70	099.60	99	99
0776	511	550	99	9	100.10	100.00	99	99
0777	508	551	99	9	099.80	099.70	99	99
0778	515	534	99	9	100.60	099.90	41	99
0779	509	557	99	9	100.58	100.40	99	99
0780	509	547	99	9	100.10	100.00	99	99
0781	509	547	99	9	100.30	100.10	99	99
0782	529	567	03	2	101.21	101.20	99	99
0783	508	551	99	9	099.90	099.80	99	99
0784	509	548	99	9	099.80	099.70	99	99
0785	508	551	99	9	099.90	099.80	99	99
0786	509	550	99	9	099.61	099.60	99	99
0787	510	550	99	9	100.10	100.00	99	99
0789	508	549	99	9	100.00	099.90	99	99
0790	508	549	99	9	100.00	099.90	99	99
0791	510	546	99	9	100.30	100.10	99	99
0792	526	561	99	9	101.00	100.80	99	99
0793	510	546	99	9	100.54	100.30	99	99
0794	510	550	99	9	100.10	100.00	99	99
0795	511	550	99	9	100.10	100.00	99	99
0796	528	562	99	9	101.60	101.30	99	99
0797	511	550	99	9	100.50	100.30	99	99
0798	527	568	99	9	101.60	101.40	99	99
0799	527	568	99	9	101.40	101.30	99	99
0800	526	567	99	9	100.79	100.69	23	99
0801	508	549	99	9	099.90	099.80	99	99
0802	508	556	99	9	100.40	100.30	99	99
0803	526	561	99	9	100.80	100.70	99	99
0804	523	569	99	9	101.36	101.14	99	03
0805	527	569	99	9	101.40	101.30	99	99
0806	528	561	99	9	100.57	100.15	32	99
0807	508	551	99	9	099.80	099.70	99	99
0808	509	547	99	9	100.10	100.00	99	99

Table A17a (cont.)

Lot No.	Grid North	Grid East	Item No.	Quad	Upper Level	Lower Level	Feat. No.	Comm.
0809	509	548	99	9	099.60	099.55	99	99
0810	511	549	99	9	099.90	099.80	99	99
0811	510	550	99	9	099.80	099.70	99	99
0812	509	551	99	9	099.90	099.80	99	99
0813	510	548	99	3	099.60	099.55	99	99
0814	511	550	99	9	100.00	099.90	99	99
0815	509	549	99	9	099.60	099.50	99	99
0816	510	530	99	9	100.05	101.00	99	99
0817	512	533	99	9	101.30	101.20	99	99
0818	527	563	99	9	101.27	101.15	99	99
0819	517	534	99	9	100.85	100.65	99	04
0820	515	535	99	9	101.30	101.20	99	99
0821	514	535	99	1	100.80	100.70	99	99
0822	514	535	99	9	100.90	100.80	99	99
0823	516	534	99	9	100.85	100.80	99	99
0824	527	563	99	9	101.57	101.25	99	99
0825	516	535	99	9	101.20	101.00	99	99
0826	510	531	99	9	101.25	101.20	99	99
0827	516	534	99	9	100.80	100.75	99	99
0828	518	533	99	9	101.65	101.40	99	99
0829	516	535	99	9	101.20	100.00	99	99
0830	517	534	99	9	101.05	100.95	99	99
0831	524	566	99	9	101.54	101.25	99	99
0832	510	532	99	9	101.15	101.05	99	99
0833	516	535	99	9	102.02	101.60	99	99
0834	508	528	99	9	100.76	100.75	99	03
0835	515	534	99	9	102.04	101.60	99	99
0836	525	567	99	9	101.55	101.25	99	99
0837	524	564	99	9	101.52	101.45	99	99
0838	515	535	99	9	101.30	101.20	99	99
0839	517	534	99	9	100.95	100.85	99	99
0840	528	565	99	9	101.15	101.05	99	99
0841	517	533	99	2	101.15	101.05	99	99
0842	517	534	99	9	101.25	101.15	99	99
0843	509	548	99	9	100.51	100.50	99	03
0844	513	528	99	9	101.51	101.50	99	03
0845	511	532	99	9	101.35	101.30	99	99
0846	510	530	99	9	101.10	101.05	99	99
0847	526	564	99	2	101.06	101.05	99	02
0848	525	566	99	9	101.15	101.05	99	99
0849	524	563	99	9	101.15	101.05	99	99
0850	515	535	99	9	101.10	100.90	99	99
0851	516	535	99	9	101.00	100.80	99	99
0852	523	563	99	9	101.35	101.25	99	99
0853	511	530	99	9	101.30	101.25	99	99
0854	520	533	99	9	102.08	101.65	99	99
0855	517	534	99	9	101.35	101.25	99	99

Table A17a (cont.)

Lot No.	Grid North	Grid East	Item No.	Quad	Upper Level	Lower Level	Feat. No.	Comm.
0856	525	561	99	1	101.05	100.90	99	99
0857	511	532	99	9	101.25	101.15	99	99
0858	514	534	99	1	101.10	101.00	99	99
0859	511	532	99	9	101.35	101.25	99	99
0860	514	534	03	9	101.08	101.07	99	99
0861	512	530	99	9	101.70	101.65	99	99
0862	515	534	99	9	101.00	100.90	99	99
0863	510	531	99	9	101.36	101.35	99	03
0864	517	533	99	2	101.05	100.85	99	99
0865	525	567	99	3	101.25	101.15	99	99
0866	508	533	99	9	101.10	101.09	99	03
0867	516	535	99	9	100.63	100.62	99	99
0868	526	568	99	9	101.55	101.25	99	99
0869	512	534	99	9	101.50	101.45	99	99
0870	511	535	03	9	101.15	101.14	99	99
0871	523	562	99	9	101.42	101.35	99	99
0872	516	535	99	9	101.60	101.40	99	99
0873	522	561	99	9	101.15	101.05	99	99
0874	521	561	99	9	101.15	101.05	99	99
0875	516	535	99	9	101.20	101.00	99	99
0876	524	563	99	9	101.25	101.15	99	99
0877	521	564	99	9	101.25	101.15	99	99
0878	515	535	99	9	102.04	101.60	99	99
0879	526	563	99	9	100.95	100.90	99	99
0880	510	532	99	9	101.30	101.25	99	99
0881	524	564	99	9	101.15	101.05	99	99
0882	523	565	99	9	101.45	101.35	99	99
0883	523	565	01	9	101.36	101.35	99	99
0884	511	535	99	9	101.25	101.15	99	99
0885	509	548	99	9	100.10	100.00	99	99
0886	539	551	99	9	101.40	101.20	99	99
0887	511	549	99	9	100.20	100.10	99	99
0888	522	535	99	9	100.72	100.54	99	99
0889	512	549	99	9	099.90	099.80	99	99
0890	510	548	99	9	100.10	100.00	99	99
0891	509	550	99	9	099.80	099.70	99	99
0892	510	550	99	9	099.90	099.80	99	99
0893	526	544	99	9	100.40	100.30	99	99
0894	523	562	99	9	101.05	101.04	99	99
0895	511	535	99	9	101.32	101.25	99	99
0896	521	562	99	9	101.37	101.25	99	99
0897	514	534	99	9	101.35	101.25	99	99
0898	509	546	99	9	100.30	100.10	99	99
0899	507	550	99	9	100.28	100.10	99	99
0900	522	565	99	9	101.15	101.05	99	99
0901	513	534	99	3	100.99	100.85	99	99
0902	509	548	99	9	099.70	099.60	99	99

Table A17a (cont.)

Lot No.	Grid North	Grid East	Item No.	Quad	Upper Level	Lower Level	Feat. No.	Comm.
0903	512	549	99	9	100.00	099.90	99	99
0904	508	550	99	9	100.10	100.06	99	99
0905	509	549	99	9	099.90	099.80	99	99
0906	510	550	99	9	099.90	099.80	99	99
0907	508	550	99	9	099.80	099.70	99	99
0908	515	535	99	9	101.90	101.70	99	99
0909	508	549	99	9	099.40	099.33	99	99
0910	512	533	99	9	101.40	101.35	99	99
0911	512	549	99	9	099.90	099.80	99	99
0912	517	533	99	9	101.75	101.60	99	99
0913	510	530	99	9	101.15	101.10	99	99
0914	511	531	99	2	101.25	101.15	99	99
0915	517	533	99	2	101.30	101.15	99	99
0916	526	565	99	9	100.75	100.70	99	99
0917	512	534	99	9	101.45	101.40	99	99
0918	510	531	99	9	101.35	101.30	99	99
0919	509	548	99	9	100.51	100.50	99	03
0920	510	549	99	9	100.00	099.90	99	99
0921	522	564	99	0	101.46	101.25	99	99
0922	524	564	99	9	101.25	101.15	99	99
0923	523	564	99	9	101.15	101.05	99	02
0924	513	534	99	9	100.95	100.85	99	99
0925	513	531	99	9	102.03	101.90	99	99
0926	513	534	99	9	101.55	101.50	99	99
0927	524	563	99	9	101.35	101.25	99	99
0928	510	549	99	9	099.70	099.60	99	99
0929	511	549	99	9	099.90	099.80	99	99
0930	526	562	99	9	101.49	101.40	99	99
0931	508	552	99	9	101.02	100.95	99	99
0932	509	549	99	9	099.70	099.60	99	99
0933	511	549	99	9	099.90	099.80	99	99
0934	509	549	99	9	099.70	099.60	99	99
0935	510	549	99	9	099.90	099.80	99	99
0936	512	549	99	9	099.90	099.80	99	99
0937	512	549	99	9	099.90	099.80	99	99
0938	511	547	99	9	100.20	100.10	99	99
0939	509	548	99	9	099.70	099.60	99	99
0940	509	550	99	9	099.80	099.70	99	99
0941	511	550	99	9	100.00	099.90	99	99
0942	510	549	99	9	099.56	099.50	99	99
0943	508	552	99	9	100.15	100.14	99	99
0944	512	549	99	9	099.80	099.70	99	04
0945	507	550	99	9	100.20	100.10	99	99
0946	529	562	99	1	101.40	101.20	99	99
0947	512	549	99	9	099.90	099.80	99	99
0948	508	548	99	9	100.30	100.10	99	99
0949	509	547	99	9	100.50	100.30	99	99

Table A17a (cont.)

Lot No.	Grid North	Grid East	Item No.	Quad	Upper Level	Lower Level	Feat. No.	Comm.
0950	509	550	99	9	099.90	099.80	99	99
0951	508	533	99	9	101.06	101.05	99	03
0952	508	549	99	9	099.80	099.70	99	99
0953	509	548	99	9	100.51	100.50	99	03
0954	509	557	99	9	100.58	100.40	99	99
0955	509	547	99	9	100.10	100.00	99	99
0956	513	535	99	9	101.35	101.25	99	99
0957	508	552	99	9	100.20	100.10	99	99
0958	523	569	99	9	101.10	101.00	99	99
0959	508	549	99	9	099.60	099.50	99	99
0960	511	550	99	9	100.10	100.00	99	99
0961	514	534	99	2	100.63	100.50	09	99
0962	527	563	99	9	101.15	101.05	99	99
0963	508	551	99	9	099.90	099.80	99	99
0964	510	550	99	9	100.30	100.10	99	99
0965	517	553	99	2	100.85	100.75	99	99
0966	524	561	99	9	101.25	101.15	99	99
0967	521	567	99	9	101.15	101.05	99	99
0968	513	530	99	9	101.85	101.80	99	99
0969	517	534	99	9	101.25	101.15	99	99
0970	524	562	99	9	101.15	101.05	99	99
0971	515	534	99	9	101.60	101.40	99	99
0972	527	562	99	9	101.20	101.10	99	99
0973	522	562	99	9	101.25	101.15	99	99
0974	513	533	99	9	101.50	101.40	99	99
0975	525	566	99	9	101.25	101.15	99	99
0976	512	535	99	9	101.30	101.25	99	99
0977	508	550	99	9	100.53	100.30	99	99
0978	529	562	99	9	101.73	100.43	99	99
0979	512	532	99	9	101.45	101.40	99	99
0980	523	567	99	9	101.25	101.15	99	99
0981	522	565	99	9	101.25	101.15	99	99
0982	512	533	99	9	101.55	101.50	99	99
0983	508	552	99	9	100.02	099.80	99	99
0984	512	550	99	9	100.09	100.00	99	99
0985	512	532	99	9	101.60	101.55	99	99
0986	526	563	99	9	100.64	100.63	30	99
0987	510	566	99	9	100.54	100.30	99	99
0988	521	566	99	9	101.21	101.15	99	99
0989	508	551	99	9	099.80	099.70	99	99
0990	512	550	99	9	100.54	100.30	99	99
0991	509	547	99	9	100.30	100.10	99	99
0992	509	548	99	9	099.70	099.60	99	99
0993	511	532	99	9	101.60	101.55	99	99
0994	521	515	99	9	100.20	100.10	99	99
0995	508	549	99	9	099.50	099.40	99	99
0996	510	550	99	9	100.10	100.00	99	99

Table A17a (cont.)

Lot No.	Grid North	Grid East	Item No.	Quad	Upper Level	Lower Level	Feat. No.	Comm.
0997	510	550	99	9	100.00	099.90	99	99
0998	509	548	99	9	099.80	099.70	99	99
0999	524	563	99	9	101.25	101.15	99	99
1000	522	534	99	9	102.25	102.24	99	01
1001	526	550	99	9	100.76	100.60	99	99
1002	524	566	99	9	101.15	101.05	99	99
1003	522	534	99	9	101.49	101.48	99	99
1004	514	532	99	9	101.80	101.70	99	99
1005	524	569	99	9	101.10	101.00	99	99
1006	525	566	99	9	101.50	101.50	99	03
1007	522	534	99	9	102.25	102.24	99	01
1008	509	547	99	9	100.00	099.90	99	99
1009	507	550	99	9	099.80	099.70	99	99
1010	513	535	99	9	101.05	100.95	99	99
1011	507	550	99	9	099.80	099.70	99	99
1012	510	550	99	9	100.50	100.30	99	99
1013	508	549	99	9	100.20	100.10	99	99
1014	510	549	99	9	099.90	099.80	99	99
1015	507	550	99	9	099.80	099.70	99	99
1016	510	550	99	9	100.00	090.00	99	99
1017	509	548	99	9	099.70	099.60	99	99
1018	512	532	99	9	101.79	101.78	99	03
1019	522	565	99	9	101.46	101.35	99	99
1020	509	548	99	9	100.48	100.30	99	99
1021	508	550	99	9	099.40	099.35	99	99
1022	522	561	99	9	101.20	101.10	99	99
1023	524	567	99	9	101.51	101.25	99	99
1024	508	550	99	9	099.50	099.40	99	99
1025	510	550	99	9	099.90	099.80	99	99
1026	522	515	99	9	100.30	100.20	99	99
1027	526	546	99	9	101.50	101.40	99	99
1028	515	534	99	9	101.60	101.40	99	99
1029	508	550	99	9	099.70	099.60	99	99
1030	507	550	99	9	099.80	099.70	99	99
1031	512	550	99	9	100.30	100.10	99	99
1032	510	549	99	9	100.00	099.90	99	99
1033	507	550	99	9	099.90	099.80	99	99
1034	509	549	99	9	099.80	099.70	99	99
1035	510	549	99	9	099.90	099.80	99	99
1036	529	560	99	9	101.05	101.00	50	99
1037	505	550	99	9	099.80	099.70	99	99
1038	509	548	99	9	099.60	099.50	99	99
1039	560	540	99	9	100.35	099.92	37	99
1040	510	550	99	9	099.80	099.70	99	99
1041	508	549	99	9	099.80	099.70	99	99
1042	511	550	99	9	100.30	100.10	99	99
1043	513	534	99	9	101.50	101.45	99	99

Table A17a (cont.)

Lot No.	Grid North	Grid East	Item No.	Quad	Upper Level	Lower Level	Feat. No.	Comm.
1044	525	564	99	8	100.95	100.90	99	99
1045	510	530	99	9	101.39	101.30	99	99
1046	512	534	99	9	101.30	101.20	99	99
1047	511	550	99	9	100.30	100.10	99	99
1048	525	561	99	9	101.05	100.90	99	99
1049	511	530	99	9	101.45	101.40	99	99
1050	513	533	99	9	101.80	101.75	99	99
1051	521	563	99	9	101.15	101.05	99	99
1052	507	550	99	9	099.70	099.60	99	99
1053	528	563	99	9	100.56	100.24	36	99
1054	526	561	99	9	100.61	100.60	99	02
1055	511	550	99	9	100.00	099.90	99	99
1056	510	549	99	9	099.60	099.51	99	99
1057	508	549	99	9	100.41	100.20	99	99
1058	508	550	99	9	100.30	100.10	99	99
1059	511	534	99	9	101.35	101.30	99	99
1060	509	550	99	9	099.50	099.40	99	99
1061	509	547	99	9	100.00	099.90	99	99
1062	508	551	99	9	099.70	099.60	99	99
1063	510	549	99	9	099.50	099.44	99	99
1064	511	547	99	9	100.20	100.10	99	99
1065	510	549	99	9	099.50	099.44	99	99
1066	512	549	99	9	100.00	099.90	99	99
1067	525	561	99	1	100.81	100.70	99	99
1068	522	534	99	9	102.25	102.24	99	01
1069	509	556	99	9	100.40	100.30	99	99
1070	510	548	99	9	100.12	100.00	99	99
1071	509	550	99	9	099.60	099.50	99	99
1072	517	533	99	9	101.75	101.60	99	99
1073	509	548	99	9	100.51	100.50	99	03
1074	511	549	99	9	100.00	099.90	99	99
1075	527	564	99	2	101.25	101.15	99	99
1076	526	564	99	9	101.25	101.15	99	99
1077	523	563	99	9	101.15	101.05	99	99
1078	516	535	99	9	100.80	100.70	99	99
1079	510	548	99	9	100.00	099.90	99	99
1080	508	549	99	9	099.60	099.50	99	99
1081	525	562	99	1	101.05	100.95	99	99
1082	517	534	99	9	101.05	100.85	99	99
1083	528	567	99	9	101.45	101.43	99	99
1084	512	532	99	9	101.70	101.65	99	99
1085	522	515	99	9	100.42	100.30	99	99
1086	510	530	99	9	101.30	101.20	99	99
1087	526	550	99	9	100.18	100.10	99	99
1088	527	565	99	9	101.15	101.08	99	99
1089	513	530	99	9	101.80	101.75	99	99
1090	508	549	99	9	099.50	099.40	99	99

Table A17a (cont.)

Lot No.	Grid North	Grid East	Item No.	Quad	Upper Level	Lower Level	Feat. No.	Comm.
1091	524	567	99	9	101.51	101.25	99	99
1092	528	565	99	9	101.25	101.15	99	99
1093	514	531	99	9	101.85	101.75	99	99
1094	510	532	99	9	101.25	101.20	99	99
1095	511	531	99	9	101.60	101.55	99	99
1096	508	556	99	9	100.34	100.23	99	04
1097	528	562	99	9	100.90	100.80	99	99
1098	528	565	99	9	100.99	100.98	99	02
1099	526	563	99	9	100.63	100.37	30	99
1100	510	532	99	9	101.06	101.05	04	02
1101	527	561	99	9	100.80	100.77	99	99
1102	508	556	99	9	100.51	100.40	99	99
1103	508	552	99	9	100.20	100.14	99	99
1104	508	550	99	9	099.60	099.50	99	99
1105	508	557	99	9	100.53	100.40	99	99
1106	516	535	99	9	102.06	101.60	99	99
1107	509	549	99	9	099.60	099.50	99	99
1108	512	550	99	9	100.09	100.00	99	99
1109	509	549	99	9	100.00	099.90	99	99
1110	516	535	99	9	101.20	101.00	00	99
1111	511	549	99	9	100.51	100.30	99	99
1112	511	550	99	9	100.00	099.90	99	99
1113	511	550	99	9	100.00	099.90	99	99
1114	522	514	99	9	100.40	100.30	99	99
1115	523	564	99	9	101.25	101.15	99	99
1116	512	534	99	9	101.30	101.25	99	99
1117	522	567	99	9	101.25	101.15	99	99
1118	525	564	99	9	101.15	101.05	99	99
1119	515	534	01	9	101.42	101.41	99	99
1120	509	556	99	9	100.56	100.40	99	99
1121	512	532	99	9	101.30	101.25	99	99
1122	521	565	99	9	101.25	101.15	99	99
1123	527	563	99	2	101.30	101.20	99	99
1124	522	566	99	9	101.15	101.05	99	99
1125	517	533	99	9	101.60	101.50	99	99
1126	513	535	99	9	100.85	100.75	99	99
1127	510	550	99	9	100.00	099.90	99	99
1128	509	550	99	9	100.10	099.90	99	99
1129	510	549	99	9	099.90	099.80	99	99
1130	511	534	99	9	101.25	101.15	99	99
1131	511	549	99	9	100.30	100.20	99	99
1132	512	535	99	9	101.15	101.05	99	04
1133	509	546	99	9	100.10	100.00	99	99
1134	511	533	99	9	101.45	101.40	99	04
1135	520	533	99	9	101.65	101.45	99	99
1136	514	535	99	9	101.65	101.55	99	99
1137	522	565	99	9	101.15	101.05	99	99

Table A17a (cont.)

Lot No.	Grid North	Grid East	Item No.	Quad	Upper Level	Lower Level	Feat. No.	Comm.
1138	510	548	99	9	100.10	100.00	99	99
1139	511	533	99	9	101.50	101.45	99	99
1140	509	548	99	9	099.90	099.80	99	99
1141	517	534	99	9	100.69	100.68	99	99
1142	514	535	99	1	101.10	101.00	99	99
1143	516	534	99	9	102.09	101.60	99	99
1144	517	534	99	9	102.00	101.60	99	99
1145	517	534	99	9	100.95	100.85	99	99
1146	527	548	99	9	100.50	100.40	99	99
1147	508	552	99	9	100.45	100.30	99	99
1148	522	567	99	9	101.15	101.05	99	99
1149	527	561	99	9	100.80	100.60	99	99
1150	513	530	99	9	101.15	101.05	99	99
1151	508	551	99	9	099.70	099.60	99	99
1152	522	515	99	9	100.20	100.10	99	99
1153	522	534	99	9	102.25	102.24	99	01
1154	511	547	99	9	100.54	100.30	99	99
1155	526	563	99	9	101.54	101.25	99	99
1156	524	564	99	9	101.45	101.35	99	99
1157	514	533	99	9	101.75	101.65	99	99
1158	508	550	99	9	099.60	099.50	99	99
1159	526	563	99	9	101.05	100.88	99	99
1160	521	565	99	9	101.15	101.05	99	99
1161	510	533	99	9	101.09	101.08	99	99
1162	523	565	99	9	101.35	101.25	99	99
1163	528	562	99	9	101.30	101.00	99	99
1164	514	534	99	1	100.90	100.80	99	99
1165	515	534	99	9	101.30	101.20	99	99
1166	516	535	99	9	101.40	101.30	99	99
1167	521	561	99	9	101.28	101.15	99	99
1168	509	546	99	9	100.10	100.00	99	99
1169	528	567	99	9	100.55	100.45	99	99
1170	516	535	99	9	101.20	101.00	99	99
1171	508	551	99	9	100.49	100.30	99	99
1172	511	530	99	9	101.35	101.30	99	99
1173	517	533	99	2	101.05	100.95	99	99
1174	529	566	99	9	101.20	101.10	99	99
1175	521	567	99	9	101.15	101.05	99	99
1176	515	534	99	9	100.75	100.70	99	99
1177	507	550	99	9	100.10	100.00	99	99
1178	509	548	99	9	099.80	099.70	99	99
1179	509	547	99	9	100.00	099.90	99	99
1180	514	534	99	9	101.75	101.65	99	99
1181	528	515	99	9	101.68	101.25	99	99
1182	508	551	99	9	100.10	100.00	99	99
1183	528	562	99	9	100.80	100.70	99	99
1184	527	565	99	9	101.62	101.25	99	99

Table A17a (cont.)

Lot No.	Grid North	Grid East	Item No.	Quad	Upper Level	Lower Level	Feat. No.	Comm.
1185	510	549	99	9	100.30	100.20	99	99
1186	508	553	99	9	100.20	100.10	99	99
1189	516	534	99	9	101.40	101.20	99	99
1190	524	565	99	9	101.25	101.15	99	99
1191	509	550	99	9	100.10	099.90	99	99
1192	510	549	99	9	100.20	100.10	99	99
1193	516	535	99	9	100.80	100.70	99	99
1194	515	535	99	9	100.90	100.70	99	99
1195	512	530	99	9	101.65	101.60	99	99
1196	510	549	99	9	100.51	100.30	99	99
1197	521	561	99	9	101.15	101.05	99	99
1198	508	549	99	9	099.70	099.60	99	99
1199	515	535	99	9	101.10	100.90	99	99
1200	516	535	99	9	101.40	101.30	99	99
1201	523	563	99	9	101.25	101.15	99	99
1202	517	533	99	2	101.30	101.15	99	99
1203	508	550	99	9	099.90	099.80	99	99
1204	507	550	99	8	100.10	099.79	99	99
1205	510	533	99	9	101.25	101.20	99	99
1206	517	533	00	9	101.50	101.40	99	99
1207	516	535	99	9	101.20	101.00	99	99
1208	517	534	99	9	101.60	101.35	99	99
1209	526	565	99	9	101.56	101.25	99	99
1210	507	550	99	9	099.80	099.70	99	99
1211	523	566	99	9	101.51	101.25	99	99
1212	510	550	99	9	100.10	100.00	99	99
1213	509	550	99	9	099.90	099.80	99	99
1214	514	534	99	1	100.63	100.45	09	99
1215	514	534	06	1	100.60	100.59	09	99
1216	523	535	99	9	100.72	100.54	99	99
1217	527	565	99	9	101.25	101.15	99	99
1218	508	551	99	9	100.30	100.20	99	99
1219	515	535	99	9	101.60	101.40	99	99
1220	509	548	99	9	099.70	099.60	99	99
1221	512	549	99	9	100.10	100.00	99	99
1222	510	547	99	9	100.52	100.30	99	99
1223	511	550	99	9	100.00	099.90	99	99
1224	509	548	99	9	099.80	099.70	99	99
1225	511	549	99	9	100.10	100.00	99	99
1226	510	548	99	9	099.90	099.80	99	99
1227	509	550	99	9	099.90	099.80	99	99
1228	509	549	99	9	100.30	100.10	99	99
1229	529	563	99	9	101.00	100.80	99	99
1230	509	549	99	9	099.61	099.50	99	99
1231	507	550	99	9	100.00	099.90	99	99
1232	512	550	99	9	100.30	100.10	99	99
1233	523	569	99	9	101.20	101.00	99	99

Table A17a (cont.)

Lot No.	Grid North	Grid East	Item No.	Quad	Upper Level	Lower Level	Feat. No.	Comm.
1234	512	534	99	9	101.58	101.50	99	99
1235	509	548	99	9	099.70	099.60	99	99
1236	511	550	99	9	099.90	099.80	99	99
1237	508	550	99	9	099.70	099.60	99	99
1238	521	565	99	9	101.44	101.25	99	99
1239	522	563	99	9	101.15	101.05	99	99
1240	508	550	99	9	100.00	099.90	99	99
1241	528	562	99	9	100.79	100.65	99	04
1242	510	549	99	9	100.00	099.90	99	99
1243	510	535	99	9	101.16	101.05	99	99
1244	515	534	99	9	101.20	101.00	99	99
1245	510	548	99	9	100.00	099.90	99	99
1246	509	550	99	9	099.70	099.60	99	99
1247	511	531	99	9	101.35	101.30	99	99
1248	509	549	99	9	099.80	099.70	99	99
1249	526	569	99	9	101.53	101.40	99	99
1250	514	533	99	9	102.04	101.85	99	99
1251	525	563	99	9	101.15	101.05	99	99
1252	509	549	99	9	101.51	100.30	99	99
1253	511	549	99	9	100.20	100.10	99	99
1254	508	551	99	9	100.49	100.30	99	99
1255	510	534	99	9	101.15	101.05	99	99
1256	512	549	99	9	100.54	100.30	99	99
1257	517	534	99	9	101.15	101.05	99	99
1258	525	561	99	9	101.25	101.15	99	99
1259	512	549	99	9	100.10	100.00	99	99
1260	525	562	99	1	100.70	100.67	99	04
1261	527	567	99	9	101.20	101.10	99	99
1262	511	549	99	9	100.20	100.10	99	99
1263	508	549	99	9	099.80	099.70	99	99
1264	521	564	99	9	101.42	101.25	99	99
1265	509	548	99	9	100.00	099.90	99	99
1266	525	561	99	1	100.85	100.80	99	99
1267	529	564	99	9	101.40	101.20	99	99
1268	510	548	99	9	100.00	099.90	99	99
1269	510	547	99	9	100.20	100.10	99	99
1270	509	549	99	9	099.80	099.70	99	99
1271	529	563	99	9	101.00	100.80	99	99
1272	510	533	99	9	101.15	101.10	99	99
1273	515	534	99	9	101.85	101.80	99	99
1274	521	535	99	9	100.73	100.52	99	99
1275	512	550	99	9	100.00	099.90	99	99
1276	509	549	99	9	099.60	099.50	99	99
1277	522	562	99	9	101.38	101.25	99	99
1278	510	548	99	9	100.00	099.90	99	99
1279	527	562	99	9	100.80	100.70	99	99
1280	528	564	99	9	101.25	100.98	99	99

Table A17a (cont.)

Lot No.	Grid North	Grid East	Item No.	Quad	Upper Level	Lower Level	Feat. No.	Comm.
1281	527	562	99	9	100.60	100.55	99	99
1282	508	550	99	9	100.00	099.90	99	99
1283	517	534	99	9	101.15	101.05	99	99
1284	511	549	99	9	100.10	100.00	99	99
1285	527	563	99	9	100.60	100.50	99	99
1286	524	564	99	9	101.35	101.25	99	99
1287	528	565	99	9	101.68	101.15	99	04
1288	509	548	99	9	099.50	099.40	99	99
1289	513	534	99	9	100.95	100.85	99	99
1290	524	565	99	9	101.45	101.35	99	99
1291	515	535	99	9	100.75	100.70	99	99
1292	517	534	99	9	101.15	101.05	99	99
1293	514	534	99	1	101.25	101.10	99	99
1294	523	563	99	9	101.15	101.05	99	99
1295	513	534	99	9	101.05	100.95	99	99
1296	518	533	99	9	101.65	101.40	99	99
1297	513	535	99	9	100.75	100.65	99	99
1298	526	566	99	9	101.02	100.35	99	99
1299	514	535	99	1	101.10	101.00	99	99
1300	512	533	99	9	101.30	101.20	99	99
1301	515	535	99	9	100.90	100.70	99	99
1302	528	565	99	9	101.25	101.15	99	99
1303	523	561	99	9	101.25	101.15	99	99
1304	523	563	99	9	101.25	101.15	99	99
1305	516	534	99	9	101.60	101.40	99	99
1306	508	551	99	9	100.49	099.91	99	99
1307	516	534	99	9	101.60	101.40	99	99
1308	527	565	99	9	101.62	101.25	99	99
1309	524	563	99	9	101.40	101.35	99	99
1310	510	532	99	9	101.15	101.05	99	99
1311	514	535	99	1	101.10	101.00	99	99
1312	522	562	99	9	101.25	101.15	99	99
1313	517	534	99	9	101.05	100.95	99	99
1314	529	563	99	9	101.20	101.00	99	99
1315	511	530	99	9	101.51	101.50	99	03
1316	513	530	99	9	101.25	101.15	99	99
1317	527	566	99	9	101.01	101.00	99	02
1318	513	533	99	9	101.76	101.75	99	03
1319	513	533	99	9	101.50	101.40	99	99
1320	521	566	99	9	101.46	101.25	99	99
1321	525	564	99	9	101.40	101.35	99	99
1322	530	565	99	9	101.21	101.20	99	99
1323	511	550	99	9	100.20	100.10	99	99
1324	521	562	99	9	101.25	101.15	99	99
1325	515	534	99	9	101.40	101.30	99	99
1326	511	549	99	9	100.10	100.00	99	99
1327	522	566	99	9	101.46	101.25	99	99

Table A17a (cont.)

Lot No.	Grid North	Grid East	Item No.	Quad	Upper Level	Lower Level	Feat. No.	Comm.
1328	527	564	99	2	101.05	100.99	99	02
1329	528	561	99	9	101.00	100.80	99	99
1330	516	534	99	9	101.00	100.90	99	99
1331	526	566	99	9	101.27	101.25	99	99
1332	510	548	99	9	099.90	099.80	99	99
1333	511	549	99	9	100.30	100.20	99	99
1334	509	549	99	9	099.70	099.60	99	99
1335	512	549	99	9	100.00	099.90	99	99
1336	508	549	99	9	099.60	099.50	99	99
1337	522	562	99	9	101.15	101.05	99	99
1338	509	546	99	9	100.30	100.10	99	99
1339	513	534	99	9	101.05	100.95	99	99
1340	515	533	99	9	102.00	101.80	99	99
1341	515	534	99	9	101.20	101.00	99	99
1342	511	546	99	9	100.30	100.20	99	99
1343	522	570	99	1	101.04	100.90	99	99
1344	512	549	99	9	100.30	100.20	99	99
1345	509	512	99	9	099.80	099.70	99	99
1346	528	564	99	9	101.62	101.25	99	99
1347	525	563	99	1	100.90	100.85	99	99
1348	511	547	99	9	100.30	100.20	99	99
1349	508	549	99	9	099.80	099.70	99	99
1350	526	564	99	9	101.66	101.25	99	99
1351	508	561	99	9	100.20	100.10	99	99
1352	509	547	99	9	099.90	099.80	99	99
1353	508	551	99	9	100.49	099.91	99	04
1354	525	563	99	1	100.70	100.65	99	99
1355	507	550	99	9	100.00	099.90	99	99
1356	513	534	99	9	101.25	101.15	99	99
1357	508	551	99	9	100.10	100.00	99	99
1358	529	564	99	9	101.20	101.00	99	99
1359	521	515	99	9	100.62	100.30	99	99
1360	527	562	99	9	100.90	100.80	99	99
1361	509	548	99	9	099.70	099.60	99	99
1362	513	530	99	9	101.65	101.60	99	99
1363	510	549	99	9	100.10	100.00	99	99
1364	516	535	99	9	101.30	101.20	99	99
1365	507	550	99	9	099.80	099.70	99	99
1366	523	564	99	9	101.45	101.35	99	99
1367	527	561	99	9	100.76	100.75	99	99
1368	521	565	99	9	101.25	101.15	99	99
1369	528	565	01	9	101.25	101.24	99	99
1370	522	564	99	9	101.46	101.25	99	99
1371	528	566	99	9	101.25	101.15	99	99
1372	508	549	99	9	099.60	099.50	99	99
1373	510	550	99	9	100.30	100.10	99	99
1374	525	529	99	9	101.35	101.30	99	99

Table A17a (cont.)

Lot No.	Grid North	Grid East	Item No.	Quad	Upper Level	Lower Level	Feat. No.	Comm.
1375	509	548	99	9	100.51	100.50	99	03
1376	539	551	99	9	101.20	101.00	99	99
1377	509	550	99	9	099.80	099.70	99	99
1378	510	549	99	9	099.80	099.70	99	99
1379	510	550	99	9	100.10	100.00	99	99
1380	509	548	99	9	099.90	099.80	99	99
1381	560	540	99	9	100.35	099.92	37	99
1382	512	549	99	9	100.20	100.10	99	99
1383	523	562	99	9	101.35	101.25	99	99
1384	510	549	99	9	100.20	100.10	99	99
1385	511	549	99	9	100.00	099.90	99	99
1386	528	566	99	9	101.15	101.05	99	99
1387	526	568	99	2	101.15	101.05	99	99
1388	508	552	99	9	100.30	100.20	99	99
1389	511	550	99	9	100.00	099.90	99	99
1390	507	550	99	9	099.70	099.60	99	99
1391	511	547	99	9	100.54	100.30	99	99
1392	510	547	99	9	100.30	100.20	99	99
1393	509	550	99	9	099.80	099.70	99	99
1394	511	531	99	9	101.55	101.50	99	99
1395	509	549	99	9	099.60	099.50	99	99
1396	515	534	99	9	101.40	101.30	99	99
1397	518	533	99	9	102.10	101.75	99	99
1398	507	550	99	9	100.10	100.00	99	99
1399	510	550	99	9	100.10	100.00	99	99
1400	523	565	99	9	101.15	101.05	99	99
1401	524	562	99	9	101.35	101.25	99	99
1402	510	549	99	9	099.90	099.80	99	99
1403	516	535	99	9	100.70	100.65	99	02
1404	517	533	99	2	101.05	100.95	99	99
1405	514	535	99	9	101.55	101.45	99	99
1406	510	549	99	9	100.30	100.20	99	99
1407	512	550	99	9	100.00	099.90	99	99
1408	508	556	99	9	100.30	100.32	99	99
1409	528	567	99	9	101.25	101.15	99	99
1410	523	566	99	9	101.15	101.05	99	99
1411	515	535	99	9	100.70	100.65	99	99
1412	509	556	99	9	100.40	100.30	99	99
1413	523	565	99	9	101.25	101.15	99	99
1414	508	550	99	9	099.80	099.70	99	99
1415	511	550	99	9	099.90	099.80	99	99
1416	509	550	99	9	099.70	099.60	99	99
1417	510	549	99	9	100.00	099.90	99	99
1418	509	549	99	9	099.70	099.60	99	99
1419	509	549	99	9	099.60	099.50	99	99
1420	511	546	99	9	100.51	100.30	99	99
1421	509	549	99	9	099.90	099.80	99	99

Table A17a (cont.)

Lot No.	Grid North	Grid East	Item No.	Quad	Upper Level	Lower Level	Feat. No.	Comm.
1422	516	535	99	9	101.20	101.00	99	99
1423	510	550	99	9	099.90	099.80	99	99
1424	512	549	99	9	100.10	100.00	99	99
1425	509	550	99	9	100.10	099.90	99	99
1426	508	550	99	9	099.90	099.80	99	99
1427	524	565	99	9	101.35	101.25	99	99
1428	517	533	99	2	100.75	100.65	99	99
1429	513	534	99	9	101.35	101.25	99	99
1430	525	563	99	1	100.45	100.35	99	99
1431	526	549	99	9	100.74	100.60	99	99
1432	515	534	99	9	100.64	100.63	99	02
1433	511	549	99	9	100.01	100.00	99	99
1434	510	549	99	9	100.00	099.90	99	99
1435	512	535	99	9	101.15	101.10	99	99
1436	510	549	99	9	099.70	099.60	99	99
1437	522	570	99	1	101.14	101.04	99	99
1438	510	548	99	9	099.90	099.80	99	99
1439	511	550	99	9	100.00	099.90	99	99
1440	525	566	99	9	100.35	100.25	99	99
1441	513	535	99	9	100.27	100.23	06	99
1442	514	533	99	9	101.45	101.35	99	99
1443	519	533	99	9	102.11	101.75	99	99
1444	511	549	99	9	100.00	099.90	99	99
1445	509	548	99	9	099.90	099.80	99	99
1446	508	550	99	9	100.12	100.00	99	99
1447	508	549	99	9	100.20	100.10	99	99
1448	508	528	99	9	100.76	100.75	99	03
1449	526	564	99	9	101.54	101.25	99	99
1450	508	550	99	9	099.90	099.80	99	99
1451	523	565	99	9	101.45	101.35	99	99
1452	517	534	99	9	101.05	100.95	99	99
1453	512	549	99	9	100.54	100.30	99	99
1454	510	549	99	9	100.20	100.10	99	99
1455	511	549	99	9	099.90	099.80	99	99
1456	512	535	99	9	101.25	101.20	99	99
1457	526	563	99	9	101.15	101.05	99	99
1458	515	533	01	9	101.58	101.57	99	99
1459	512	531	99	9	101.50	101.40	99	04
1460	510	546	99	9	100.30	100.10	99	99
1461	507	550	99	9	099.90	099.80	99	99
1462	508	551	99	9	100.10	100.00	99	99
1463	524	562	99	9	101.20	101.15	99	99
1464	516	534	99	9	100.65	100.63	99	02
1465	525	562	99	9	101.15	101.05	99	99
1466	560	540	99	9	100.35	099.92	37	99
1467	517	534	99	9	101.60	101.35	99	99
1468	527	561	99	9	100.80	100.60	99	02

Table A17a (cont.)

Lot No.	Grid North	Grid East	Item No.	Quad	Upper Level	Lower Level	Feat. No.	Comm.
1469	539	551	99	9	100.00	099.80	99	99
1470	527	561	99	9	100.77	100.60	99	02
1471	515	535	99	9	100.75	100.70	99	99
1472	516	533	99	2	101.35	101.10	99	99
1473	509	547	99	9	100.00	099.90	99	99
1474	522	535	99	9	100.54	100.53	99	02
1475	509	557	99	9	100.40	100.30	99	99
1476	511	535	99	9	101.15	101.10	99	99
1477	515	533	99	9	102.00	101.80	99	99
1478	517	534	99	9	101.35	101.20	99	99
1479	514	534	99	1	101.70	101.60	99	99
1480	526	565	99	9	100.80	100.70	01	99
1481	514	535	99	1	100.90	100.80	99	99
1482	521	515	99	9	100.14	100.00	99	99
1483	514	534	99	1	101.00	100.90	99	99
1484	513	532	99	9	101.50	101.40	99	99
1485	526	566	99	9	101.02	100.95	99	99
1486	511	532	99	9	101.30	101.25	99	99
1487	509	548	99	9	100.10	100.00	99	99
1488	512	549	99	9	099.90	099.80	99	99
1489	523	565	99	9	101.25	101.15	99	99
1490	560	540	99	9	100.35	099.92	37	99
1491	525	564	99	9	100.90	100.80	99	99
1492	518	533	99	9	101.65	101.40	99	99
1493	510	549	99	9	100.51	100.30	99	99
1494	522	565	99	9	101.35	101.25	99	99
1495	528	562	99	9	100.56	099.87	36	99
1496	524	561	99	9	101.30	101.10	99	99
1497	507	550	99	9	099.80	099.70	99	99
1498	522	534	99	9	100.58	100.57	99	02
1499	523	569	99	9	100.97	100.96	34	99
1500	508	550	99	9	099.70	099.60	99	99
1501	522	565	99	9	101.35	101.25	99	99
1502	516	533	99	9	102.09	101.80	99	99
1503	525	563	99	1	100.55	100.45	99	99
1504	511	546	99	9	100.51	100.30	99	99
1505	522	564	99	9	101.42	101.25	99	99
1506	508	549	99	9	100.00	099.90	99	99
1507	523	563	99	9	101.15	101.05	99	99
1508	523	568	99	9	101.42	101.20	99	04
1509	539	551	99	9	101.20	101.00	99	99
1510	527	565	99	9	101.62	101.25	99	99
1511	513	535	99	9	101.05	100.95	99	99
1512	539	551	99	9	100.20	100.00	99	99
1513	514	534	99	1	101.00	100.90	99	99
1514	523	569	99	9	101.00	100.90	99	99
1515	512	530	99	9	101.40	101.35	99	99

Table A17a (cont.)

Lot No.	Grid North	Grid East	Item No.	Quad	Upper Level	Lower Level	Feat. No.	Comm.
1516	516	533	99	2	101.00	100.90	99	99
1517	490	523	99	9	099.10	098.90	38	99
1518	514	530	99	9	102.06	102.00	99	99
1519	528	561	99	9	101.59	101.30	99	99
1520	522	562	99	9	101.15	101.05	99	99
1521	526	567	99	9	101.15	101.05	99	02
1522	523	562	99	9	101.15	101.05	99	04
1523	513	534	99	1	100.85	100.72	99	02
1524	523	563	99	9	100.80	100.70	99	99
1525	509	547	99	4	099.95	099.90	99	99
1526	525	562	99	1	100.82	100.70	99	99
1527	516	534	99	9	101.40	101.30	99	99
1528	514	531	99	9	101.95	101.90	99	99
1529	518	533	99	9	101.75	101.65	99	99
1530	522	514	99	9	100.30	100.20	99	99
1531	514	534	99	9	101.65	101.55	99	99
1532	521	515	99	9	100.31	100.20	99	99
1533	521	563	99	9	101.25	101.15	99	99
1534	512	533	99	9	101.45	101.40	99	99
1535	508	551	99	9	099.91	099.70	99	99
1536	525	562	99	1	100.67	100.60	99	99
1537	514	535	99	9	101.60	101.50	99	04
1538	539	551	99	9	101.40	101.20	99	99
1539	511	533	99	9	101.20	101.19	99	02
1540	508	552	99	8	100.00	099.71	99	99
1541	516	533	99	9	102.09	100.70	99	06
1542	522	563	99	9	101.10	101.00	20	04
1543	529	565	99	9	101.20	101.10	99	99
1544	510	548	99	9	099.90	099.80	99	99
1545	513	535	99	9	100.75	100.65	99	99
1546	516	534	99	9	102.09	101.60	99	99
1547	510	550	99	9	099.90	099.80	99	99
1548	516	535	99	9	101.00	100.80	99	99
1549	511	549	99	9	099.90	099.80	99	99
1550	513	535	99	9	101.25	101.15	99	99
1551	513	535	99	9	101.35	101.25	99	99
1552	509	547	99	2	099.95	099.90	99	99
1553	524	566	99	9	101.54	101.25	99	99
1554	515	534	99	9	100.55	099.86	41	99
1555	529	563	99	3	101.40	101.20	99	99
1556	512	550	99	9	099.90	099.80	99	99
1557	512	531	99	9	101.70	101.65	99	99
1558	513	535	99	2	101.69	100.65	99	06
1559	527	561	99	9	100.75	100.74	28	99
1560	522	561	99	9	101.25	101.15	99	99
1561	523	563	99	9	100.90	100.80	99	99
1562	517	533	99	2	101.40	101.30	99	99

Table A17a (cont.)

Lot No.	Grid North	Grid East	Item No.	Quad	Upper Level	Lower Level	Feat. No.	Comm.
1563	516	533	99	9	101.75	101.65	99	99
1564	515	535	99	9	101.60	101.40	99	99
1565	526	564	99	9	101.15	101.05	99	99
1566	511	550	99	9	099.90	099.80	99	99
1567	525	563	99	1	100.90	100.85	99	99
1568	515	535	99	9	101.40	101.30	99	99
1569	529	564	99	9	101.20	101.00	99	99
1570	512	531	99	9	101.50	101.45	99	99
1571	524	564	99	9	101.06	101.05	99	99
1572	515	534	99	9	101.40	101.20	99	04
1573	511	532	99	9	101.15	101.05	99	99
1574	523	561	99	9	101.34	101.25	99	99
1575	522	567	99	9	101.15	101.05	99	99
1576	513	534	99	9	101.65	101.60	99	99
1577	508	533	99	9	101.06	101.05	99	03
1578	513	532	99	9	101.70	101.60	99	99
1579	514	534	99	9	101.55	101.45	99	99
1580	525	561	99	9	101.15	101.05	99	99
1581	510	532	99	9	101.15	101.05	99	02
1582	513	532	99	9	101.60	101.50	99	99
1583	508	550	99	9	099.70	099.60	99	99
1584	529	563	99	3	100.80	100.60	99	99
1585	524	563	99	9	101.40	101.35	99	99
1586	513	534	99	9	101.45	101.35	99	99
1587	515	534	99	9	100.75	100.70	99	99
1588	516	533	99	2	101.10	101.00	99	99
1589	523	562	99	9	101.15	101.05	99	99
1590	513	531	99	9	101.60	101.50	99	99
1591	513	535	99	9	101.45	101.40	99	99
1592	515	534	99	9	100.80	100.75	99	99
1593	527	567	99	9	101.10	101.00	99	02
1594	527	550	99	5	100.20	100.00	99	99
1595	512	531	99	9	101.82	101.70	99	03
1596	528	562	99	9	100.56	099.87	36	99
1597	527	567	99	9	101.01	100.32	40	99
1598	522	515	99	9	100.10	100.00	99	99
1599	523	564	99	9	101.50	101.45	99	03
1600	512	549	99	9	100.30	100.20	99	99
1601	526	566	99	9	100.96	100.95	99	02
1602	526	565	99	9	101.05	100.95	01	99
1603	513	535	99	9	100.45	100.27	06	07
1604	508	551	99	4	099.60	099.50	99	99
1605	523	564	99	9	100.90	100.80	99	99
1606	524	567	99	9	101.25	101.15	99	99
1607	515	534	99	9	100.90	100.85	99	99
1608	513	534	99	9	101.70	101.65	99	99
1609	508	550	99	9	099.70	099.60	99	99

Table A17a (cont.)

Lot No.	Grid North	Grid East	Item No.	Quad	Upper Level	Lower Level	Feat. No.	Comm.
1610	517	533	99	9	101.50	101.40	99	99
1611	523	565	99	9	101.52	101.45	99	99
1612	514	533	99	9	101.35	101.25	99	99
1613	512	535	99	9	101.20	101.15	99	99
1614	525	567	99	9	101.15	101.05	99	99
1615	511	546	99	9	100.20	100.10	99	99
1616	508	557	99	9	100.40	100.30	99	99
1617	512	530	99	9	101.82	101.70	99	99
1618	523	564	99	9	101.35	101.25	99	99
1619	524	565	99	9	101.54	101.45	99	99
1620	560	540	99	9	100.35	099.92	37	99
1621	510	548	99	9	099.80	099.60	99	99
1622	526	566	99	9	100.79	100.78	26	99
1623	510	549	99	9	099.80	099.70	99	99
1624	560	540	99	9	100.35	099.92	37	99
1625	512	533	99	9	101.60	101.55	99	99
1626	513	531	99	9	101.70	101.60	99	04
1627	513	530	99	9	102.03	101.90	99	99
1628	525	564	99	9	101.15	101.05	99	99
1629	515	534	99	9	101.20	101.00	99	99
1630	510	530	99	9	101.20	101.15	99	99
1631	516	534	99	9	102.09	101.60	99	99
1632	528	567	99	9	101.68	101.25	99	99
1633	508	553	99	9	100.20	100.10	99	99
1634	526	563	99	9	100.88	100.80	99	99
1635	510	530	99	9	101.20	101.10	99	04
1636	522	561	99	9	101.25	101.15	99	99
1637	522	566	99	9	101.15	101.05	99	99
1638	515	534	99	9	100.90	100.85	99	99
1639	513	531	99	9	101.50	101.40	99	99
1640	514	533	99	9	101.65	101.55	99	99
1641	513	535	99	9	100.95	100.85	99	99
1642	514	532	99	9	102.01	102.00	99	03
1643	511	532	99	9	101.45	101.40	99	99
1644	513	535	99	9	100.85	100.75	99	99
1645	510	530	99	9	101.30	101.25	99	99
1646	509	548	99	9	100.51	100.50	99	03
1647	527	562	99	9	101.40	101.30	99	99
1648	527	562	99	9	100.53	100.52	99	02
1649	514	535	99	9	100.70	100.60	99	99
1650	522	565	99	9	101.46	101.35	99	99
1651	511	531	99	9	101.35	101.25	99	99
1652	515	533	99	9	102.10	102.00	99	99
1653	515	535	99	9	102.04	101.40	99	99
1654	513	535	99	9	101.15	101.05	99	99
1655	512	531	99	9	101.40	101.35	99	99
1656	527	565	99	9	100.90	100.80	01	99

Table A17a (cont.)

Lot No.	Grid North	Grid East	Item No.	Quad	Upper Level	Lower Level	Feat. No.	Comm.
1657	516	534	99	9	100.75	100.70	99	99
1658	525	564	99	9	101.45	101.40	99	99
1659	523	563	99	9	101.46	101.35	99	99
1660	527	565	99	9	100.95	100.90	01	99
1661	517	533	99	9	100.85	100.65	99	04
1662	527	561	99	9	100.58	100.53	35	08
1663	526	568	99	2	101.25	101.15	99	99
1664	513	534	03	9	101.24	101.23	99	99
1665	513	535	99	9	100.66	100.42	05	99
1666	523	536	99	4	100.92	100.58	99	99
1667	523	561	99	9	101.25	101.15	99	99
1668	525	567	99	1	101.25	101.15	99	99
1669	514	531	99	9	101.45	101.35	99	99
1670	517	534	99	9	100.60	100.30	99	99
1671	522	562	99	9	101.05	101.02	99	99
1672	514	533	99	9	101.85	101.75	99	99
1673	524	565	99	9	101.25	101.15	99	99
1674	515	530	99	9	101.40	101.30	99	99
1675	526	550	99	3	100.28	100.27	99	99
1676	517	533	99	2	100.65	100.64	99	02
1677	527	567	99	9	101.10	101.00	99	02
1678	525	566	99	9	100.70	100.65	08	99
1679	513	530	99	9	101.85	101.80	99	04
1680	527	565	99	9	101.05	100.95	01	99
1681	512	550	99	9	100.13	100.04	31	99
1682	560	540	99	9	100.35	099.92	37	99
1683	514	534	99	1	100.80	100.70	99	99
1684	527	561	99	9	100.80	100.70	99	99
1685	523	566	99	9	101.25	101.15	99	99
1686	516	533	99	1	100.90	100.85	99	99
1687	526	565	99	9	101.25	101.15	99	99
1688	527	567	99	9	101.10	101.06	55	99
1689	514	534	99	1	100.38	100.37	09	99
1690	515	550	99	9	100.61	100.60	99	03
1691	523	568	99	9	101.20	101.10	99	04
1692	525	566	99	9	100.75	100.70	08	99
1693	509	510	99	9	099.80	099.70	99	99
1694	514	535	99	9	101.75	101.65	99	99
1695	507	550	99	9	099.90	099.80	99	99
1696	511	534	99	9	101.35	101.30	99	99
1697	511	531	99	2	101.25	101.15	99	99
1698	517	533	99	2	100.85	100.75	99	99
1699	510	550	99	9	100.10	100.00	99	99
1700	511	531	99	2	101.35	101.25	99	99
1701	526	567	99	9	101.01	100.32	40	99
1702	514	532	99	9	101.90	101.85	99	99
1703	511	533	99	9	101.53	101.50	99	99

Table A17a (cont.)

Lot No.	Grid North	Grid East	Item No.	Quad	Upper Level	Lower Level	Feat. No.	Comm.
1704	522	534	99	9	102.25	102.24	99	01
1705	524	562	99	9	101.41	101.35	99	99
1706	525	566	99	9	101.15	101.05	99	99
1707	524	564	19	9	101.01	101.00	99	99
1708	511	535	02	9	101.07	101.06	99	99
1709	526	563	99	9	101.15	101.05	99	99
1710	516	533	99	2	100.85	100.80	99	99
1711	514	534	99	9	101.85	101.75	99	04
1712	516	533	99	2	100.80	100.75	99	99
1713	525	567	99	1	101.15	101.10	99	99
1714	523	534	99	9	100.63	100.55	99	02
1715	528	561	99	9	100.80	100.74	99	99
1716	526	568	99	4	101.15	101.10	99	99
1717	526	567	99	9	100.88	100.79	23	99
1718	522	534	99	9	102.25	102.24	99	01
1719	509	547	99	4	100.00	099.90	99	99
1720	528	565	99	9	100.98	100.80	19	99
1721	508	551	99	9	100.00	099.90	99	99
1722	521	566	99	9	101.25	101.15	99	99
1723	525	562	99	9	101.15	101.05	99	99
1724	514	533	99	9	101.55	101.45	99	99
1725	526	565	99	9	101.05	101.00	99	99
1726	514	534	99	1	100.65	100.64	99	02
1727	513	533	99	9	101.90	101.80	99	04
1728	515	535	99	9	101.21	101.20	99	99
1729	529	564	99	9	100.96	100.66	39	99
1730	513	531	99	9	101.90	101.80	99	04
1731	527	567	99	9	100.88	100.79	40	99
1732	517	534	99	9	100.95	100.85	99	06
1733	512	531	99	9	101.65	101.60	99	99
1734	527	561	99	9	100.90	100.80	99	99
1735	516	535	99	9	100.80	100.70	99	99
1736	511	531	99	9	101.40	101.35	99	99
1737	508	528	99	9	100.76	100.75	99	03
1738	525	566	99	9	100.90	100.88	08	02
1739	516	534	05	9	100.25	100.24	99	99
1740	509	549	99	9	099.40	099.30	99	99
1741	527	567	99	9	101.10	101.06	55	99
1742	513	535	99	9	100.69	100.68	99	02
1743	527	564	99	4	101.24	100.94	99	06
1744	528	561	99	9	101.00	100.80	99	06
1745	526	565	99	9	100.95	100.90	01	99
1746	512	535	02	9	101.08	101.07	99	99
1747	526	564	99	9	100.95	100.90	99	99
1748	523	566	03	9	101.11	101.10	99	99
1749	516	534	99	9	101.60	101.40	99	99
1750	525	566	99	9	100.88	100.80	08	99

Table A17a (cont.)

Lot No.	Grid North	Grid East	Item No.	Quad	Upper Level	Lower Level	Feat. No.	Comm.
1751	526	566	99	9	100.95	100.94	99	02
1752	525	562	02	1	100.91	100.90	99	99
1753	514	534	99	1	100.38	100.37	09	99
1754	526	566	99	9	101.02	100.95	99	99
1755	516	535	99	9	100.64	100.63	99	02
1756	526	561	99	9	100.60	100.37	33	99
1757	516	533	99	9	101.55	101.45	99	99
1758	522	534	99	9	102.25	102.24	99	01
1759	525	561	99	1	101.10	101.05	99	06
1760	527	567	99	9	101.01	100.32	40	99
1761	513	534	99	9	101.65	101.60	99	99
1762	514	530	99	9	101.60	101.55	99	99
1763	528	564	99	2	101.05	100.95	99	99
1764	511	532	99	9	101.50	101.45	99	99
1765	513	530	99	9	101.80	101.75	99	99
1766	513	534	99	9	101.05	100.95	99	99
1767	514	531	99	9	101.75	101.65	99	99
1768	511	533	99	9	101.40	101.35	99	99
1769	511	530	99	9	101.25	101.20	99	99
1770	524	561	99	9	101.25	101.15	99	99
1771	511	532	99	9	101.55	101.50	99	99
1772	525	563	99	9	101.15	101.05	99	99
1773	514	531	99	9	101.90	101.85	99	99
1774	511	533	99	9	101.45	101.40	99	99
1775	525	565	99	9	101.30	101.25	99	99
1776	513	530	99	9	101.45	101.35	99	99
1777	514	530	99	9	101.95	101.90	99	99
1778	512	531	99	9	101.65	101.60	99	99
1779	522	534	99	9	102.25	102.24	99	01
1780	513	530	99	9	101.35	101.25	99	99
1781	523	562	99	9	101.15	101.05	99	99
1782	512	532	99	9	101.40	101.35	99	99
1783	514	531	99	9	101.85	101.75	99	99
1784	514	534	99	9	101.90	101.75	99	99
1785	516	534	99	9	101.20	101.00	99	99
1786	525	565	99	9	101.25	101.15	99	99
1787	515	534	99	9	101.30	101.20	99	99
1788	511	530	99	9	101.35	101.30	99	99
1789	512	530	99	9	101.60	101.55	99	99
1790	526	563	07	9	100.93	100.92	99	99
1791	523	564	99	9	101.25	101.15	99	99
1792	512	532	99	9	101.55	101.50	99	99
1793	525	565	99	9	101.15	101.05	99	99
1794	512	532	99	9	101.55	101.50	99	99
1795	511	531	99	9	101.30	101.20	99	99
1796	513	533	99	9	101.76	101.75	99	03
1797	513	530	99	9	101.60	101.55	99	99

Table A17a (cont.)

Lot No.	Grid North	Grid East	Item No.	Quad	Upper Level	Lower Level	Feat. No.	Comm.
1798	515	533	99	9	101.50	101.40	99	99
1799	515	533	99	9	101.80	101.70	99	99
1800	511	531	99	9	101.50	101.45	99	99
1801	512	534	99	9	101.50	101.45	99	99
1802	512	534	99	9	101.35	101.30	99	99
1803	514	530	99	9	101.75	101.65	99	99
1804	522	565	99	9	101.46	101.35	99	99
1805	524	561	99	9	101.25	101.15	99	99
1806	525	564	99	9	101.15	101.05	99	99
1807	516	534	99	9	101.40	101.30	99	99
1808	512	534	99	9	101.40	101.35	99	99
1809	512	535	99	9	101.30	101.25	99	99
1810	514	531	99	9	101.90	101.85	99	99
1811	512	532	99	9	101.40	101.35	99	99
1812	513	534	99	9	101.05	100.95	99	99
1813	526	563	03	9	100.93	100.92	99	99
1814	513	533	99	9	101.76	101.75	99	03
1815	515	534	99	9	100.70	100.65	99	99
1816	516	535	99	9	101.30	101.20	99	99
1817	516	535	99	9	101.60	101.40	99	99
1818	524	565	99	9	101.45	101.35	99	99
1819	515	534	99	9	101.60	101.40	99	99
1820	515	534	99	9	101.20	101.00	99	99
1821	513	532	99	9	101.90	101.80	99	99
1822	521	566	99	9	101.46	101.25	99	99
1823	514	534	99	1	100.80	100.70	99	99
1824	513	531	99	9	101.70	101.60	99	99
1825	521	566	99	9	101.46	101.25	99	99
1826	516	534	99	9	101.20	101.00	99	99
1827	522	534	99	9	102.25	102.24	99	01
1828	515	535	99	9	101.20	101.10	99	99
1829	524	563	99	9	101.25	101.15	99	99
1830	523	563	99	9	101.46	101.35	99	99
1831	516	535	99	9	101.40	101.30	99	99
1832	513	535	99	9	100.95	100.85	99	99
1833	516	535	99	9	101.30	101.20	99	99
1834	512	531	99	9	101.55	101.50	99	99
1835	513	528	99	9	101.51	101.50	99	03
1836	512	535	99	9	101.30	101.25	99	99
1837	513	535	99	9	100.95	100.85	99	99
1838	521	535	99	9	100.73	100.52	99	99
1839	522	534	99	9	102.25	102.24	99	01
1840	527	562	99	9	100.70	100.60	99	99
1841	508	528	99	9	100.76	100.75	99	03
1842	508	556	99	9	100.35	100.34	99	99
1843	525	562	99	9	101.25	101.15	99	99
1844	513	528	99	9	101.51	101.50	99	03

Table A17a (cont.)

Lot No.	Grid North	Grid East	Item No.	Quad	Upper Level	Lower Level	Feat. No.	Comm.
1845	523	566	99	9	101.51	101.25	99	99
1846	515	534	99	9	101.00	100.90	99	99
1847	516	535	99	9	100.53	100.48	99	99
1848	513	533	99	9	101.80	101.75	99	99
1849	525	565	99	9	101.45	101.40	99	99
1850	521	564	99	9	101.15	101.05	99	99
1851	522	534	99	9	102.25	102.24	99	01
1852	512	534	99	9	101.30	101.25	99	99
1853	526	568	99	4	101.15	101.10	99	99
1854	522	534	99	9	102.25	102.24	99	01
1855	515	534	99	9	101.40	101.30	99	99
1856	522	534	99	9	102.25	102.24	99	01
1857	512	534	99	9	101.45	101.40	99	99
1858	514	534	99	1	101.25	101.10	99	99
1859	512	534	99	9	100.58	100.48	99	99
1860	522	563	99	9	101.15	101.05	99	99
1861	514	531	99	9	101.85	101.75	99	99
1862	521	563	99	9	101.40	101.35	99	99
1863	514	535	99	0	101.50	101.45	99	99
1864	525	561	99	9	101.25	101.15	99	99
1865	513	535	99	9	101.45	101.40	99	99
1866	524	566	99	9	101.54	101.25	99	99
1867	510	533	99	9	101.35	101.30	99	99
1868	513	532	99	9	101.80	101.70	99	99
1869	512	532	99	9	101.55	101.50	99	99
1870	516	534	99	9	100.75	100.70	99	99
1871	513	532	99	9	101.40	101.35	99	99
1872	526	566	99	9	101.15	101.05	99	99
1873	513	533	99	9	101.89	101.70	99	99
1874	516	533	99	9	102.10	101.35	99	99
1875	514	531	99	9	102.04	101.95	99	99
1876	513	533	99	9	101.80	101.65	99	99
1877	517	533	99	9	101.89	101.75	99	99
1878	524	563	99	9	101.35	101.25	99	99
1879	512	534	99	9	101.40	101.35	99	99
1880	526	564	99	9	101.25	101.15	99	99
1881	525	563	99	9	101.25	101.20	99	99
1882	513	535	99	9	101.45	101.40	99	99
1883	512	533	99	9	101.50	101.45	99	99
1884	514	535	99	1	101.25	101.10	99	99
1885	524	567	99	9	101.25	101.15	99	99
1886	525	563	99	9	101.25	101.20	99	99
1887	523	566	99	9	101.25	101.15	99	99
1888	522	534	99	9	102.25	102.24	99	01
1889	524	563	99	9	101.35	101.25	99	99
1890	512	533	99	9	101.78	101.70	99	99
1891	513	532	99	9	101.50	101.40	99	99

Table A17a (cont.)

Lot No.	Grid North	Grid East	Item No.	Quad	Upper Level	Lower Level	Feat. No.	Comm.
1892	517	534	07	9	101.04	101.03	99	99
1893	511	533	99	9	101.45	101.40	99	99
1894	512	532	99	9	101.82	101.70	99	99
1895	511	530	99	9	101.40	101.35	99	99
1896	514	534	99	1	101.25	101.10	99	99
1897	522	534	99	9	102.25	102.24	99	01
1898	512	531	99	9	101.60	101.55	99	99
1899	521	563	99	9	101.15	101.05	99	99
1900	514	531	99	9	101.35	101.25	99	99
1901	516	533	99	9	101.65	101.55	99	99
1902	512	532	99	9	101.60	101.55	99	99
1903	512	534	99	9	101.30	101.20	99	99
1904	514	535	99	1	101.25	101.10	99	99
1905	526	566	99	9	101.15	101.05	99	99
1906	516	533	99	9	101.45	101.35	99	99
1907	522	562	99	9	101.15	101.05	99	99
1908	518	533	01	2	101.43	101.42	99	99
1909	514	535	99	9	101.35	101.25	99	99
1910	513	534	99	9	101.05	100.95	99	99
1911	521	562	99	9	101.25	101.15	99	99
1912	522	562	99	9	101.38	101.25	99	99
1913	522	566	99	9	101.15	101.05	99	99
1914	516	535	99	9	102.06	101.60	99	99
1915	522	562	99	9	101.15	101.05	99	99
1916	513	535	99	9	101.25	101.15	99	99
1917	521	566	99	9	101.25	101.15	99	99
1918	520	533	99	9	102.08	101.65	99	99
1919	510	532	99	9	101.20	101.15	99	99
1920	525	563	99	9	101.20	101.15	99	99
1921	523	564	99	9	101.15	101.05	99	99
1922	515	535	99	9	101.90	101.30	99	99
1923	514	531	99	9	101.75	101.65	99	99
1924	524	564	99	9	101.06	101.05	99	02
1925	522	567	99	9	101.42	101.25	99	99
1926	518	533	99	9	101.75	101.65	99	99
1927	527	565	99	9	101.25	101.15	99	99
1928	518	533	99	9	101.65	101.40	99	99
1929	523	561	99	9	101.25	101.15	99	99
1930	515	534	99	9	101.00	100.90	99	99
1931	522	534	99	9	102.25	102.24	99	01
1932	523	566	99	9	101.15	101.05	99	99
1933	521	567	99	9	101.15	101.05	99	99
1934	516	534	99	9	100.70	100.65	99	99
1935	528	564	99	9	101.66	101.25	99	99
1936	520	533	99	9	101.65	101.45	99	99
1937	522	567	99	9	101.42	101.25	99	99
1938	522	561	99	9	101.25	101.15	99	99

Table A17a (cont.)

Lot No.	Grid North	Grid East	Item No.	Quad	Upper Level	Lower Level	Feat. No.	Comm.
1939	522	534	99	9	102.25	102.24	99	01
1940	524	563	99	9	101.35	101.25	99	99
1941	528	565	99	9	101.68	101.25	99	99
1942	513	535	99	9	101.15	101.05	99	99
1943	512	532	99	9	101.82	101.70	99	99
1944	514	535	99	1	101.00	100.90	99	99
1945	510	532	99	9	101.20	101.15	99	99
1946	513	533	99	9	101.50	101.40	99	99
1947	512	535	99	9	101.15	101.05	99	99
1948	513	532	99	9	101.50	101.40	99	99
1949	524	565	99	9	101.45	101.35	99	99
1950	513	532	99	9	101.40	101.35	99	99
1951	522	564	99	9	101.46	101.25	99	99
1952	516	534	99	9	101.60	101.40	99	99
1953	515	535	99	9	101.90	101.30	99	99
1954	514	534	99	1	100.90	100.80	99	99
1955	510	532	99	9	101.25	101.20	99	99
1956	528	565	99	9	101.68	101.25	99	99
1957	525	567	99	9	101.15	101.05	99	99
1958	517	534	99	9	100.85	100.75	99	99
1959	514	532	99	9	101.80	101.70	99	99
1960	513	535	99	9	100.95	100.85	99	99
1961	516	535	99	9	102.06	101.60	99	99
1962	514	534	99	1	101.10	101.00	99	99
1963	513	532	99	9	102.00	101.90	99	99
1964	512	531	99	9	101.55	101.50	99	99
1965	523	561	99	9	101.25	101.15	99	99
1966	516	535	99	9	102.06	101.60	99	99
1967	517	533	99	2	101.40	101.30	99	99
1968	515	535	99	9	100.90	100.70	99	99
1969	515	534	99	9	101.40	101.30	99	99
1970	514	531	99	9	101.45	101.35	99	99
1971	511	532	99	9	101.40	101.35	99	99
1972	513	533	99	9	101.76	101.75	99	03
1973	525	565	99	9	101.40	101.35	99	99
1974	515	534	99	9	100.75	100.70	99	99
1975	513	533	99	9	101.75	101.70	99	99
1976	516	535	99	9	102.06	101.60	99	99
1977	523	567	99	9	101.25	101.15	99	99
1978	515	535	99	9	101.30	101.20	99	99
1979	524	564	99	9	101.25	101.15	99	99
1980	516	534	99	9	102.09	101.60	99	99
1981	514	534	99	1	101.25	101.10	99	99
1982	524	565	99	9	101.45	101.35	99	99
1983	513	534	99	9	101.60	101.55	99	99
1984	520	533	99	9	102.08	101.65	99	99
1985	513	531	99	9	101.80	101.75	99	99

Table A17a (cont.)

Lot No.	Grid North	Grid East	Item No.	Quad	Upper Level	Lower Level	Feat. No.	Comm.
1986	513	530	99	9	101.45	101.35	99	99
1987	514	532	99	9	101.50	101.40	99	99
1988	527	565	99	9	101.13	101.10	99	99
1989	516	534	99	9	100.65	100.60	99	99
1990	514	532	99	9	101.60	101.50	99	99
1991	525	564	99	9	101.35	101.30	99	99
1992	513	533	99	9	101.70	101.65	99	99
1993	511	531	99	9	101.45	101.40	99	99
1994	514	533	99	2	100.70	100.62	99	99
1995	527	565	99	9	101.25	101.15	99	99
1996	521	536	99	4	100.80	100.56	99	99
1997	525	565	99	9	101.35	101.30	99	99
1998	513	533	99	9	101.76	101.75	99	03
1999	511	534	99	9	101.30	101.25	99	99
2000	516	535	99	9	102.06	101.60	99	99
2001	515	534	99	9	101.60	101.40	99	99
2002	513	533	99	9	101.60	101.55	99	99
2003	513	530	99	9	101.90	101.85	99	99
2004	513	535	99	9	100.95	100.85	99	99
2005	515	535	99	9	101.10	100.90	99	99
2006	513	530	99	9	101.45	101.35	99	99
2007	513	531	99	9	101.75	101.70	99	99
2008	511	533	99	9	101.35	101.30	99	99
2009	512	531	99	9	101.40	101.35	99	99
2010	513	534	99	9	101.05	100.95	99	99
2011	527	565	99	9	101.15	101.05	99	99
2012	518	533	99	9	101.65	101.40	99	99
2013	513	530	99	9	101.75	101.70	99	99
2014	525	564	11	9	101.10	101.09	99	99
2015	516	534	99	9	100.65	100.60	99	99
2016	513	530	99	9	101.35	101.25	99	99
2017	511	531	99	9	101.45	101.40	99	99
2018	517	534	99	9	102.00	101.60	99	99
2019	514	531	99	9	101.65	101.55	99	99
2020	514	530	99	9	101.85	101.80	99	99
2021	514	531	99	9	101.55	101.45	99	99
2022	525	564	99	9	101.30	101.25	99	99
2023	514	530	99	9	102.00	101.95	99	99
2024	525	563	99	9	101.30	101.25	99	99
2025	513	535	99	9	101.15	101.05	99	99
2026	513	533	99	9	101.76	101.75	99	03
2027	513	535	99	9	101.09	100.95	99	99

REFERENCES CITED

Aynesworth, K. H.
1936 Biographic Studies of Twenty-One Skulls of Central Texas Indians. *Central Texas Archeological Society* 2:30–34.

Bartlett, Katherine
1938 Skeletal Material. In Reconnaissance and Excavation in Southeastern New Mexico, by H. P. Mera, pp. 61–67. *American Anthropological Association Memoir* 51.

Basehart, Harry W.
1974 Mescalero Apache Subsistence Patterns and Socio-Political Organization. In *Apache Indians XII*, compiled and edited by David A. Horr, pp. 1–153. New York: Garland Publishing.

Bass, William M.
1971 *Human Osteology: A Laboratory and Field Manual of the Human Skeleton.* Special Publication. Columbia, Missouri: Missouri Archaeological Society.

Beckes, M. R., and J. M. Adovasio
1982 Perspectives on the Origins and Affinities of Mogollon on the Eastern Periphery. In *Mogollon Archaeology: Proceedings of the 1980 Mogollon Conference.* Edited by Patrick H. Beckett and Kira Silverbird, pp. 201–209. Ramona, California: Acoma Books.

Bell, Robert H.
1958 *Guide to the Identification of Certain American Indian Projectile Points.* Special Bulletin No. 1. Oklahoma City: Oklahoma Anthropological Society.

1960 *Guide to the Identification of Certain American Indian Projectile Points.* Special Bulletin No. 2. Oklahoma City: Oklahoma Anthropological Society.

Benfer, Robert Alfred B., Jr.
1968 *An Analysis of a Prehistoric Skeletal Population, Casas Grandes, Chihuahua, Mexico.* Unpublished Ph.D. Dissertation. Austin: University of Texas.

Birkby, Walter Hudson
1973 *Discontinuous Morphological Traits of the Skull as Population Markers in the Prehistoric Southwest.* Unpublished Ph.D. Dissertation. Tucson: University of Arizona.

Bolton, Herbert Eugene (editor)
1946 *Spanish Exploration in the Southwest, 1542–1706.* New York: Barnes and Noble.

Brothwell, D. R.
1972 *Digging up Bones, The Excavation, Treatment and Study of Human Skeletal Remains.* Ithaca: Cornell University Press.

Damon, P. E., C. W. Ferguson, A. Long, and E. I. Wallick
1974 Dendrochronologic Calibration of the Radiocarbon Time Scale. *American Antiquity* 39(2):350–366.

Eighmy, Jeffrey L.
1980 *Archeomagnetism: A Handbook for the Archeologist.* Cultural Resource Management Series, Heritage Conservation and Recreation Service Publication No. 58. Washington: U.S. Department of the Interior, Heritage Conservation and Recreation Service.

El-Najjar, Mahmoud Y., and J. Simon Bruder
1976 Human Skeletal Remains from the Smokey Bear Ruin (LA-2112). In *Multi-Disciplinary Investigations at the Smokey Bear Ruin, (LA-2112), Lincoln County, New Mexico*, by Regge N. Wiseman, pp. 43–47. Monograph No. 4. Las Cruces: COAS Publishing and Research.

Garn, S. M., C. G. Rohmann, and F. N. Silverman
1965 Missing Secondary Ossification Centra of the Foot. Inheritance and Developmental Meaning. *Annales de Radiologie* 8:624–644.

Gilbert, B. Miles, and Thomas W. McKern
1973 A Method for Aging the Female Os Pubis. *American Journal of Physical Anthropology* 38:31–38.

Greer, John W., and Robert A. Benfer
1963 Langtry Creek Burial Cave, Val Verde County, Texas. *Bulletin of the Texas Archeological Society* 33:229–251.

Hammond, George P., and Agapito Rey
1966 *The Rediscovery of New Mexico, 1580–1594.* Albuquerque: University of New Mexico Press.

Hooton, Earnest Albert
1930 *The Indians of Pecos Pueblo, A Study of their Skeletal Remains.* Papers of the Phillips Academy Southwestern Expedition. New Haven: Yale University Press.

Howells, W. W.
1973 *Cranial Variation in Man, A Study by Multivariate Analysis of Patterns of Difference Among Recent Human Populations.* Papers of the Peabody Museum of Archaeology and Ethnology Vol. 67. Cambridge: Harvard University.

Hrdlička, Aleš
1924 Catalogue of Human Crania in the United States National Museum Collections. *Proceedings of the U.S. National Museum* Vol. 63(2480), Art. 12.

1927 Catalogue of Human Crania in the United States National Museum Collections. *Proceedings of the U.S. National Museum* Vol. 69(2631), Art. 5.

1935 The Pueblos. With Comparative Data on the Bulk of the Tribes of the Southwest and Northern Mexico. *American Journal of Physical Anthropology* 20(o.s.):235–290.

1938 Skeletal Remains from Northern Texas. *Bulletin of the Texas Archeological and Paleontological Society* 10:169–192.

1952 *Hrdlička's Practical Anthropometry*. Fourth edition, edited by T. D. Stewart. Philadelphia: Wistar Institute of Anatomy and Biology.

Irving, E.
1964 *Paleomagnetism*. New York: John Wiley and Sons.

İşcan, M. Yaşar, and Patricia Miller-Shaivitz
1984 Discriminant Function Sexing of the Tibia. *Journal of Forensic Sciences* 29:1087–1093.

Kelley, Jane Holden
1984 *The Archaeology of the Sierra Blanca Region of Southeastern New Mexico*. Anthropological Paper 74. Ann Arbor: University of Michigan Museum of Anthropology.

Klasner, Lily
1972 *My Girlhood Among Outlaws*, edited by Eve Ball. Tucson: University of Arizona Press.

Klein, J., J. C. Lerman, P. E. Damon, and E. K. Ralph
1982 Calibration of Radiocarbon Dates: Tables Based on the Consensus Data of the Workshop on Calibrating the Radiocarbon Time Scale. *Radiocarbon* 24(2):103–150.

Koritzer, R. T.
1977 An Anthropological Approach to the Study of Dental Pathology. In *Orofacial Growth and Development*, edited by A. A. Dahlberg and T. M. Graber, pp. 283–299. The Hague: Mouton.

Krogman, Milton Marion
1973 *The Human Skeleton in Forensic Medicine*. Springfield: Charles C. Thomas.

Lang, Richard W., and Arthur H. Harris
1984 *The Faunal Remains from Arroyo Hondo Pueblo, New Mexico: A Study in Short-Term Subsistence Change*. Arroyo Hondo Archaeological Series 5. Santa Fe: School of American Research Press.

McKern, Thomas W., and T. D. Stewart
1957 *Skeletal Age Changes in Young American Males*. Headquarters Quartermaster Research & Development Command, Technical Report EP-45. Natich, Mass.: Quartermaster Research & Development Center, Environmental Protection Research Division.

Metcalf, Artie L.
1982 Fossil Unionacean Bivalves from Three Tributaries of the Rio Grande. In *Proceedings of the Symposium on Recent Benthological Investigations in Texas and Adjacent States*, edited by J. R. Davis, pp. 43–58. Austin: Texas Academy of Science, Aquatic Sciences Section.

Moorrees, Coenraad F. A.
1957 *The Aleut Dentition*. Cambridge: Harvard University Press.

Neumann, Georg

1940 Analysis of the Skeletal Material. In A Variation of Southwestern Pueblo Culture, by Jesse D. Jennings, pp. 13–20. *Laboratory of Anthropology, Technical Series, Bulletin* No. 10. Santa Fe: Archaeological Survey, Laboratory of Anthropology.

1950 *Racial Differentiation in the American Indian.* Unpublished Ph.D. Dissertation. Chicago: University of Chicago.

1952 Archeology and Race in the American Indian. In *Archeology of Eastern United States*, edited by James B. Griffin, pp. 13–34. Chicago: University of Chicago Press.

Parry, William J., and John D. Speth

1984 *The Garnsey Spring Campsite: Late Prehistoric Occupation in Southeastern New Mexico.* Technical Report 15. Ann Arbor: University of Michigan Museum of Anthropology.

Patterson, David K.

1974 *An Analysis of the Human Skeletal Material from the Antelope Creek Focus of Northern Texas.* Unpublished M.A. Thesis. Portales: Eastern New Mexico University.

Phenice, T. W.

1969 A Newly Developed Visual Method of Sexing the Os Pubis. *American Journal of Physical Anthropology* 30:297–302.

Ralph, E. K., H. N. Michael, and M. C. Han

1973 Radiocarbon Dates and Reality. *MASCA Newsletter* 9(1):1–20.

Reed, Erik K.

1967 Variations of the Spine in Human Skeletal Material from Southwestern Archaeological Collections. In *Miscellaneous Papers in Paleopathology: I*, edited by William D. Wade, pp. 30–39. Technical Series No. 7. Flagstaff: Museum of Northern Arizona.

1981 Human Skeletal Material from the Gran Quivira District. In Contributions to Gran Quivira Archeology, edited by Alden C. Hayes, pp. 75–118. *Publications in Archeology* 17. Washington: National Park Service.

1984 Skeletal Analysis of the Adult Burial in Room 1. In *The Archaeology of the Sierra Blanca Region of Southeastern New Mexico*, edited by Jane Holden Kelley, pp. 284–285. Anthropological Paper 74. Ann Arbor: University of Michigan Museum of Anthropology.

Rose, Martin R., Jeffrey S. Dean, and William J. Robinson

1981 *The Past Climate of Arroyo Hondo, New Mexico, Reconstructed from Tree Rings.* Arroyo Hondo Archaeological Series 4. Santa Fe: School of American Research Press.

Shinkle, James D.

1966 *Reminiscences of Roswell Pioneers.* Roswell, N.M.: Hall-Poorbaugh Press.

Smiley, Francis E.

1985 *The Chronometrics of Early Agricultural Sites in Northeastern Arizona: Approaches to the Interpretation of Radiocarbon Dates.* Unpublished Ph.D. Dissertation. Ann Arbor: University of Michigan.

Smith, B. Holly

1984 Patterns of Molar Wear in Hunter-Gatherers and Agriculturalists. *American Journal of Physical Anthropology* 63:39–56.

Sofaer, J. A., J. D. Niswander, and C. J. MacLean

1972 Population Studies on Southwestern Indian Tribes. *American Journal of Physical Anthropology* 37:357–366.

Speth, John D.

1983 *Bison Kills and Bone Counts: Decision Making by Ancient Hunters.* Chicago: University of Chicago Press.

Steele, D. Gentry, and Thomas W. McKern

1969 A Method for Assessment of Maximum Long Bone Length and Living Stature from Fragmentary Long Bones. *American Journal of Physical Anthropology* 31:215–228.

Steen, E.

1850 Report to Lt. L. McLaws, Dona Ana, New Mexico, January 13, 1850. The National Archives, Record Group No. 98.

Stewart, Joe D.

1983 Structural Analysis of Three Rivers Redware Designs. *Kiva* 49(1–2):39–65.

Stewart, T. D.

1935 Skeletal Remains from Southwestern Texas. *American Journal of Physical Anthropology* 20(o.s.):213–231.

1954 Metamorphosis of the Joints of the Sternum in Relation to Age Changes in Other Bones. *American Journal of Physical Anthropology* 12:519–535.

Stuiver, Minze

1982 A High-Precision Calibration of the AD Radiocarbon Time Scale. *Radiocarbon* 24(1):1–26.

Suchey, Judy M., Dean V. Wiseley, Richard F. Green, and Thomas T. Noguchi

1979 Analysis of Dorsal Pitting of the Os Pubis in an Extensive Sample of Modern American Females. *American Journal of Physical Anthropology* 51:517–539.

Suhm, Dee Ann, and Edward B. Jelks (editors)

1962 *Handbook of Texas Archeology: Type Descriptions.* Special Publication No. 1. Austin: Texas Archaeological Society.

Tarling, D. H.

1971 *Principles and Applications of Paleomagnetism.* London: Chapman and Hall.

Thomas, Alfred B.

1932 *Forgotten Frontiers.* Norman: University of Oklahoma Press.

Turner, Christy G., II
1979 Dental Anthropological Indications of Agriculture Among the Jomon People of Central Japan. *American Journal of Physical Anthropology* 51:619–639.

Todd, T. Wingate, and D. W. Lyon
1924 Endocranial Suture Closure; Its Progress and Age Relationship, I. Adult Males of White Stock. *American Journal of Physical Anthropology* 7:325–384.

Ubelaker, Douglas
1978 Human Skeletal Remains, Excavation, Analysis, Interpretation. *Manual on Archaeology* 2. Washington, D.C.: Taraxacum.

Watt, Frank H., and W. P. Meroney
1937 Supplementary Report on Mass Burial Near Waco. *Central Texas Archeologist* 3:25–33.

Whitlock, V. H.
1970 *Cowboy Life on the Llano Estacado*. Norman: University of Oklahoma Press.

Wiseman, Regge N.
1976 *Multi-Disciplinary Investigations at the Smokey Bear Ruin, (LA-2112), Lincoln County, New Mexico.* Monograph No. 4. Las Cruces: COAS Publishing and Research.

1985 Bison, Fish and Sedentary Occupations: Startling Data from Rocky Arroyo (LA 25277), Chaves County, New Mexico. In *Views of the Jornada Mogollon*, edited by Colleen M. Beck, pp. 30–32. Contributions in Anthropology 12. Portales: Eastern New Mexico University.